Tl

Serit

M000229015

John Stott (NT)
Derek Tidball (Bible Themes)

The Message of
Kings

The Message of Kings

God is present

John W. Olley

Research Associate
Vose Seminary, Perth

Inter-Varsity Press

InterVarsity Press
P.O. Box 1400, Downers Grove, IL 60515-1426
Internet: www.ivpress.com
E-mail: email@ivpress.com

© *John W. Olley 2011*

Published in the United States of America by InterVarsity Press, Downers Grove, Illinois, with permission from Inter-Varsity Press, England.

InterVarsity Press® is the book-publishing division of InterVarsity Christian Fellowship/USA®, a movement of students and faculty active on campus at hundreds of universities, colleges and schools of nursing in the United States of America, and a member movement of the International Fellowship of Evangelical Students. For information about local and regional activities, write Public Relations Dept., InterVarsity Christian Fellowship/USA, 6400 Schroeder Rd., P.O. Box 7895, Madison, WI 53707-7895, or visit the IVCF website at <www.intervarsity.org>.

All Scripture quotations, unless otherwise indicated, are taken from the THE HOLY BIBLE, NEW INTERNATIONAL VERSION®, NIV® *Copyright © 1973, 1978, 1984, 2011 by Biblica, Inc.™ Used by permission. All rights reserved worldwide.*

ISBN 978-0-8308-2435-9

Printed in the United States of America ∞

 InterVarsity Press is committed to protecting the environment and to the responsible use of natural resources. As a member of Green Press Initiative we use recycled paper whenever possible. To learn more about the Green Press Initiative, visit <www.greenpressinitiative.org>.

Library of Congress Cataloging-in-Publication Data

Olley, John W. (John William), 1938-
The message of Kings: God is present / John W. Olley.
*   p. cm.*
Includes bibliographical references.
ISBN 978-0-8308-2435-9 (pbk.: alk. paper)
1. Bible. O.T. Kings—Commentaries. I. Title.
BS1335.53.O45 2011
222'.507—dc23

                                                                            2011032891

| **P** | 17 | 16 | 15 | 14 | 13 | 12 | 11 | 10 | 9 | 8 | 7 | 6 | 5 | 4 | 3 | 2 |
| **Y** | 26 | 25 | 24 | 23 | 22 | 21 | 20 | 19 | 18 | 17 | 16 | 15 | 14 | 13 | 12 |

Contents

E. To the end of Israel (2 Kings 14 – 17)

F. From trust to exile – to the end of Judah (2 Kings 18 – 25)

BST The Bible Speaks Today

GENERAL PREFACE

THE BIBLE SPEAKS TODAY describes three series of expositions, based on the books of the Old and New Testaments, and on Bible themes that run through the whole of Scripture. Each series is characterized by a threefold ideal:

- to expound the biblical text with accuracy
- to relate it to contemporary life, and
- to be readable.

These books are, therefore, not 'commentaries', for the commentary seeks rather to elucidate the text than to apply it, and tends to be a work rather of reference than of literature. Nor, on the other hand, do they contain the kinds of 'sermons' that attempt to be contemporary and readable without taking Scripture seriously enough. The contributors to *The Bible Speaks Today* series are all united in their convictions that God still speaks through what he has spoken, and that nothing is more necessary for the life, health and growth of Christians than that they should hear what the Spirit is saying to them through his ancient – yet ever modern – Word.

ALEC MOTYER
JOHN STOTT
DEREK TIDBALL
Series editors

Author's preface

How long does it take to prepare a sermon? 'All of my life up till now' fits my reading of 1 and 2 Kings. I am grateful to parents and church leaders who started me early on Scripture Union readings covering the whole Bible regularly, including Kings. The first Sunday School class I taught made a model of Solomon's temple and while a university student my participation in Beach Missions included dramatising Josiah's discovery of the Book of the Law. Stories of Elijah on Mount Carmel and Naaman's healing had their place in sermons I heard and preached. These were however generally treated as isolated stories, not part of an extended narrative. Studies for pastoral ministry at Morling College, Sydney, helped me to look carefully at the biblical text itself and I saw how much the Old Testament related to everyday life, especially when taken in large blocks. That did not sit easily with readings in church services and 'sermon texts' being much shorter. Teaching in Hong Kong for a decade brought fresh challenges – I began to see how my own cultural background influenced my reading of Scripture.

In the 1980s I began to look at the historical books in new light. Several works were appearing on features of biblical narrative. There was narrative artistry as biblical writers told not simply to inform, or to record the past, but to communicate and bring about change amongst the hearers. The questions were not only what did words mean and what did we learn about the past, but what was being said to hearers in a writer's present – and hence to subsequent readers such as ourselves. As I looked at aspects such as selection and arrangement of material, style and language, and links with other parts of Scripture, the message came alive, often with a fresh directness and surprising depth of relevance. Narrative with its various characters and plot is able to describe and illuminate the complexities of life – life as we experience it. It engages us as people, not just as minds.

In classes at Vose Seminary, Perth, I began to explore these areas, including relevance for today, with students from varied cultural backgrounds. Other opportunities came with an invitation to teach on 1 and 2 Kings at the Singapore Baptist Theological Seminary and later during some study leave at Spurgeon's College, London. The relevance of the book of Kings to many issues became evident that were rarely handled in sermons, due to time constraints or styles of sermon. I saw that people needed help in how to read biblical narrative. My experience is that, after crossing the initial barrier of foreignness and habits of short readings, many soon find Kings closer to the world we know today than perhaps any other book in Scripture! We read of material prosperity, political manoeuvering, buildings for worship, power plays and wars between nations, changing national fortunes and alliances, compromised worship, bloody *coup d'états* (one in the name of God), fight for survival in famine, mixed religious affiliations, injustice, violence and oppression, international trade, state-led religious reforms, and compassionate care for people on the fringe. Throughout is the presence of God and repeated calls to follow his ways. Here is a book which throws light on following God in all areas of life, not only within the walls of church or family.

One outcome of my teaching and preaching was a series of studies, *First and Second Kings Then and Now: 'In the midst of change, God'.*[1] I am grateful to David Firth, then at Morling College, for encouraging me in the publication and to Ross Clifford, Principal, for permission to include material from that work in the present exposition. The invitation to write on the book of Kings for The Bible Speaks Today series has been a humbling and rewarding opportunity to interact more intensively with the text, including passages not included in the earlier work. The encouragement and feedback from Alec Motyer (General Editor) and Philip Duce (Senior Commissioning Editor) has been greatly valued. The journey over many years has been shared with my wife, Elaine (this is the fiftieth year of our marriage). Together we have learned to listen to what God is saying in his Word. She has continually helped me in grappling with the 'today' of God's message and in communicating to others. Our children, David, Linda and Catherine and their families have ensured lively family discussions, a reminder that faith is to be lived across generations – also a feature of the Kings narrative.

As I complete the writing (but not the end of seeking to hear God speak through Kings), I affirm the value of reading the Bible in 'books', and how God's Spirit uses narrative to shine light into many facets of our lives in the world today. In a variety of ways images of success still current today are critiqued and diverse situations faced

---

[1] Eastwood, NSW: Morling Press, 2001.

as we seek to know and walk in God's ways. I have seen how God in his grace uses imperfect people. Alongside ways in which syncretism 'aroused the Lord's anger' there are amazing reminders of God's compassion and grace. New Testament parallels and developments came readily to mind – not least regarding Davidic kingship, the temple, idolatry, the prophetic word and living an obedient faith in the complexities of communities and nations. Kings is indeed a light along the path of following Christ today.

This work is naturally a result of my own journey with the text and before God. I have sought to make clear in the text features which have informed my understanding of what the text is communicating, aided by many others – my journey has been in company with many, as footnotes will demonstrate. The exposition discusses ways in which I have heard the text speaking to life and witness today. I invite you to journey with me – or rather with the God whose Spirit inspired the writer of Kings. Solomon's prayer expresses the goal: 'so that all the peoples of the earth may know that the LORD is God and that there is no other'.[2]

JOHN OLLEY

---

[2] 1 Kgs 8:60.

Commentaries and other works

Commentaries

With 1 and 2 Kings being forty-seven chapters covering more than four hundred years of turbulent history, commentators have a diversity of interests. Likewise users of commentaries come with a multiplicity of backgrounds and questions seeking answers. Thus commentaries vary widely, both in approach and detail. Works listed here are later referred to by the author's surnames.

Brueggemann, W., *1 and 2 Kings*, Smyth & Helwys Bible Commentary (Macon: Smyth & Helwys, 2000).

Cogan, M., *I Kings: A New Translation with Introduction and Commentary*, Anchor Bible, 10 (Garden City, New York: Doubleday, 2001).

Cogan, M. and H. Tadmor, *II Kings: A New Translation with Introduction and Commentary*, Anchor Bible, 11 (Garden City, New York: Doubleday, 1988).

Cohn, Robert L., *2 Kings*, Berit Olam (Collegeville, Minnesota: Liturgical Press, 2000).

Conti, M., ed., *1 – 2 Kings, 1 – 2 Chronicles, Ezra, Nehemiah, Esther*, Ancient Christian Commentary on Scripture (Downers Grove: InterVarsity Press, 2008).

DeVries, S. J., *1 Kings*, Word Biblical Commentary, 12 (Nashville: Thomas Nelson, rev. edn, 2003).

Gotom, M., '1 and 2 Kings', in *Africa Bible Commentary*, edited by T. Adeyomo (Nairobi: WordAlive; Grand Rapids: Zondervan, 2006), pp. 409–466.

Gray, J., *I & II Kings: A Commentary*, Old Testament Library (London: SCM, 3rd edn, 1977).

Hobbs, T. R., *2 Kings*, Word Biblical Commentary, 13 (Waco: Word Books, 1985).

House, P. R., *1, 2 Kings*, New American Commentary (Nashville: Broadman and Holman, 1995).

Jones, G. H., *1 and 2 Kings*, 2 volumes, New Century Bible (London: Marshall, Morgan & Scott; Grand Rapids: Eerdmans, 1984).

Konkel, A. H., *1 & 2 Kings*, NIV Application Commentary (Grand Rapids: Zondervan, 2006).

Leithart, P. J., *1 & 2 Kings*, Brazos Theological Commentary on the Bible (Grand Rapids: Brazos, 2006).

Monson, J., '1 Kings' in *Zondervan Illustrated Bible Backgrounds Commentary*, edited by J. H. Walton, vol. 3 (Grand Rapids: Zondervan, 2009), pp. 2–109.

Nelson, R. D., *First and Second Kings*, Interpretation (Atlanta: John Knox, 1987).

Provan, I. W., *1 and 2 Kings*, New International Biblical Commentary (Carlisle: Paternoster; Peabody: Hendrickson, 1995).

Provan, I. W., '2 Kings' in *Zondervan Illustrated Bible Backgrounds Commentary*, edited by J. H. Walton, vol. 3 (Grand Rapids: Zondervan, 2009), pp. 110–219 (cited as Provan, *ZIBBC*).

Rice, G., *Nations under God. A Commentary on the Book of 1 Kings*, International Theological Commentary (Edinburgh: Handsel; Grand Rapids: Eerdmans, 1990).

Seow, C.-L., 'The First and Second Books of Kings: Introduction, Commentary, and Reflections', in *The New Interpreter's Bible*, vol. 3 (Nashville: Abingdon, 1999), pp. 1–296.

Sweeney, M.A., *I & II Kings: A Commentary*, Old Testament Library (Louisville and London: Westminster John Knox, 2007).

Walsh, J. T., *1 Kings*, Berit Olam (Collegeville, Minnesota; Liturgical Press, 1996).

Walton, J. H., V. H. Matthews and M. W. Chavalas, *The IVP Bible Background Commentary: Old Testament* (Downers Grove: InterVarsity Press, 2000), pp. 355–412.

Wiseman, D. J., *1 and 2 Kings*, Tyndale Old Testament Commentary (Leicester: Inter-Varsity Press, 1993).

Other Resources

Two volumes of collected articles are cited using the editors' names:

Knoppers, G. N. and J. G. McConville, eds, *Reconsidering Israel and Judah: Recent Studies on the Deuteronomistic History*, Sources for Biblical and Theological Study, 8 (Winona Lake, Indiana: Eisenbrauns, 2000).

Lemaire, A. and B. Halpern, eds, *The Books of Kings: Sources, Composition, Historiography and Reception*, Supplements to Vetus Testamentum, 129 (Leiden and Boston: Brill, 2010).

Referred to by abbreviation:

ABD
: *The Anchor Bible Dictionary*, edited by D. N. Freedman, 6 volumes (New York: Doubleday, 1992; also on CD-ROM).

ANET
: *Ancient Near Eastern Texts Relating to the Old Testament*, edited by J. B. Pritchard, 3rd edition with supplement (Princeton: Princeton University Press, 1969).

COS
: *The Context of Scripture*, edited by W. W. Hallo and K. L. Younger, Jr., 3 vols (Leiden and Boston: Brill, 1997–2002). Citations include vol. no. and text no. as well as pages.

DCH
: *The Dictionary of Classical Hebrew*, 8 vols, edited by D. J. A. Clines (Sheffield: Sheffield Phoenix Press, 1993–).

DJG
: *Dictionary of Jesus and the Gospels*, edited by J. B. Green, S. McKnight and I. H. Marshall (Leicester: Inter-Varsity Press; Downers Grove: InterVarsity Press, 1992).

DNTB
: *Dictionary of New Testament Background*, edited by C. A. Evans and S. E. Porter (Leicester: Inter-Varsity Press; Downers Grove: InterVarsity Press, 2000).

DOTHB
: *Dictionary of the Old Testament: Historical Books*, edited by B. T. Arnold and H. G. M. Williamson (Leicester: Inter-Varsity Press; Downers Grove: InterVarsity Press, 2005).

DOTP
: *Dictionary of the Old Testament: Pentateuch*, edited by T. D. Alexander and D. W. Baker (Leicester: Inter-Varsity Press; Downers Grove: InterVarsity Press, 2003).

DOTWPW
: *Dictionary of the Old Testament: Wisdom, Poetry and Writings*, edited by T. Longman, III and P. Enns (Leicester: Inter-Varsity Press; Downers Grove: InterVarsity Press, 2008).

HALOT
: L. Koehler and W. Baumgartner, *The Hebrew and Aramaic Lexicon of the Old Testament*, revised by W. Baumgartner and J. J. Stamm (Leiden: Brill, 2001).

NBD
: *New Bible Dictionary*, 3rd edn, edited by J. D. Douglas *et al.* (Leicester: Inter-Varsity Press, 1996).

NIDB
: *The New Interpreter's Dictionary of the Bible*, 5 vols, edited by K. D. Sakenfeld *et al.* (Nashville: Abingdon, 2006–9).

NIDOTTE	*New International Dictionary of Old Testament Theology and Exegesis*, edited by W. VanGemeren (Grand Rapids: Zondervan, 1997; CD-ROM, 2001).
TDOT	*Theological Dictionary of the Old Testament*, 15 vols to date, edited by G. J. Botterweck and H. Ringgren, translated by J. T. Willis, G. W. Bromiley, D. E. Green and D. W. Stott (Grand Rapids: Eerdmans, 1974–).

Texts and Versions

AV/KJV	Authorized Version/King James Version (1611)
EVV	English Versions
MT	Masoretic Text (traditional Hebrew text of the OT)
LXX	Septuagint (early Greek translation of the OT)
NETS	*A New English Translation of the Septuagint and the Other Greek Translations Traditionally Included under That Title*, edited by A. Pietersma and B. G. Wright (New York and Oxford: Oxford University Press, 2007)
NIV	New International Version (2011)
NJPSV	*Tanakh: The Holy Scriptures: The New JPS Translation according to the Traditional Hebrew Text* (Philadelphia: Jewish Publication Society, second edn, 1999)
NLT	New Living Translation (2004)
NRSV	New Revised Standard Version (1989)
NT	New Testament
OT	Old Testament
REB	Revised English Bible (1989)
RSV	Revised Standard Version (1952; 2nd edn 1971)

Within the exposition of passages in 1 Kings, references to 1 Kings will cite only chapter and verse, unless there is ambiguity, and similarly for the 2 Kings section.

Introducing 1 and 2 Kings

1. Setting the scene

Success stories are popular. Whether of individuals, organizations, churches, businesses, armies or nations, examples abound of movement from small beginnings to prominence, from poverty to prosperity, of victory despite difficulties, of renewal after devastation. The stories encourage and inspire, with books written on 'how to succeed' based on these experiences. What then is the value of the narrative of Kings[1] which goes in the opposite direction?

At the end of 1 and 2 Samuel the Israelites were at a peak of blessing. In terms of the promises to the ancestors, Abraham,[2] Isaac and Jacob,[3] at the exodus and on entry into the land of Canaan,[4] they could see how much God had fulfilled his word. Now they were as numerous 'as the sand on the seashore'.[5] After the turbulence of the period of judges and even some internal dissension during David's reign there was peace and unity. David had defeated or made peace with the surrounding nations, resulting in Davidic hegemony from the River Euphrates to the Wadi of Egypt.[6] Further, David had centralized worship in Jerusalem, bringing there the ark, the sacred box that focused the covenant made between Yahweh[7] and Israel at Sinai, and plans were in hand to build a temple. The centuries-old

---

[1] The simple 'Kings' will be used to refer to the combined '1 and 2 Kings'.
[2] Gen. 12:1–3; 15:5–7; 22:15–18.
[3] Gen. 26:2–5, 24; 28:13–14.
[4] Exod. 3:7–10; Deut. 11:1–25; Josh. 24:2–13.
[5] Gen. 22:17; 1 Kgs 4:20.
[6] 2 Sam. 8:1–14 (cf. 1 Kgs 8:65); promised in Deut. 11:24.
[7] Yahweh is the likely pronunciation of the consonants, YHWH, God's personal name (Exod. 3:13–15). Later Jewish tradition refrained from speaking the name, using instead the title *Adonai*, 'Lord'. Similarly the earliest Greek translation (275 BC) used *kyrios*, 'Lord', later in the NT to be a common title for Jesus. English versions generally have 'LORD' (using small capitals). Use of Yahweh is a reminder of the personal relationship between God and his people.

promises to Abraham and the covenant at Sinai had been joined with promises to David that his throne would be established for ever.[8] The concluding chapter (2 Sam. 24) was a reminder of the danger of human pride, but that seemed to have been resolved. It must have looked as if life could only get better. Indeed, at the beginning of Kings, Solomon's reign brought peace and security and dynamic international trade.[9]

In contrast, at the end of Kings the people faced complete reversal:

- For more than 600 years they had lived in the land God had given them – now they were exiles 500 miles (800 km) away.
- For 400 years a continuous Davidic dynasty was centred in Jerusalem as God had promised – now the king was in exile, subject to the goodwill of the Babylonian emperor.[10]
- For 400 years Jerusalem had been the centre of religious and political life, attacked but never destroyed, protected by the presence of God in their midst[11] – now the city lay in ruins.
- For more than 350 years the temple, built by Solomon, had been not only the place to which they came to offer sacrifices, but the very 'house of God', the place from which Yahweh ruled over all nations, the centre of the earth; his 'throne' may be in heaven but Jerusalem was the 'footstool'.[12] Now it had been razed.
- Further, the place of exile was the very region from which Abraham had been called to 'go',[13] and the centre of the nation that ruled over them was the magnificent and powerful large walled city of Babylon, the early centre of human arrogance that God judged.[14]

It seems that all is lost. Everything gained since Abraham's trusting obedience appears to have been stripped away. What possible future can there be? The goal of Abraham's call was that 'all peoples on earth be blessed through you',[15] but now

[8] 2 Sam. 6 – 7.
[9] 1 Kgs 4:25; 9:26–28; 10:4, 22, 28–29.
[10] 2 Kgs 25: 27–30.
[11] Pss 46, 48, 87.
[12] Ps. 99:1–5; 132:7; Isa. 6:1.
[13] Gen. 11:27 – 12:1; 15:7; Neh. 9:7.
[14] Gen. 11:9. 'Babel' is the Hebrew name used throughout the OT. 'Babylon', seen in EVV everywhere except Gen. 11:9, follows the Greek form.
[15] Gen. 12:3; 18:18. The word translated 'peoples' is rendered 'clans' in Gen. 10:5, 18, 20, 31, 32 (and 'kinds' of creatures in Gen. 8:19). The promise is universal in its spread.

Where does such an outcome leave the mission once given to Abraham? If Israel was to be the bearer of the message of God's creative purposes to the world, how is that message to be borne in the absence of a visible Israel?[16]

How can a story of reversal, told by the very people who suffered that defeat, an account which is a predominantly damning recital of the reigns of successive kings, be of value today? How can this part of the God-breathed Scriptures equip us 'for every good work'?[17]

As 'children of Abraham' by faith,[18] 'grafted into' the olive tree of Israel,[19] this story belongs to all Christians. It is not something that happened to 'others' but is the story of 'our ancestors' and hence 'our' story as well! It has been said of houses 'that whatever happens in the world – whatever is discovered or created or bitterly fought over – eventually ends up, in one way or another in your house. Wars, famines, the Industrial Revolution, the Enlightenment – they are all there.'[20] In richer and often surprising ways the narrative of God's dealings with his people in the period of Kings is part of the history that has shaped and is to continue to shape the faith and life of the church and of individual believers.[21]

The destruction of Jerusalem with forced exile of thousands has parallels with many situations in world history. Deeper than physical destruction and geographical dislocation is social and psychological disorientation, with crises of identity. We continue to see the impact amongst many refugees and dispossessed indigenous peoples.

This catastrophe brought into question everything that had hitherto given the people their identity: land, temple, city and king were all tied together by the promises of Yahweh, their God, endorsed by centuries of experience! Was there any way forward, any hope?

The OT shows wide-ranging responses to destruction and exile: apostasy,[22] despair and anguished questioning,[23] or blaming God for being unfair, punishing them for the sins of previous generations.[24] Others, especially between the first major exile of 597 BC and the

---

[16] J. G. McConville, *God and Earthly Power: An Old Testament Political Theology, Genesis–Kings* (London: T.&T. Clark, 2006), p. 151.

[17] 2 Tim. 3:16–17.

[18] Gal. 3:7; Jas 2:21.

[19] Rom. 11:17–24.

[20] B. Bryson, *At Home: A Short History of Private Life* (London: Doubleday, 2010), p. 5.

[21] 1 Cor. 10:1–13; Heb. 4:11. For use of Kings by the church fathers see Conti.

[22] Ezek. 8:12 in Jerusalem; Jer. 44:15–19, amongst exiles in Egypt.

[23] Ps. 89; Lamentations; Ezek. 37:11.

[24] Ezek. 18:2; compare 2 Kgs 23:25–27.

final destruction of 587 BC, believed that everything would soon return to normal.[25] Some wondered whether Marduk, the chief god of Babylon, was more powerful than Yahweh.[26]

Into the confusion God's Word came in two complementary ways. One is seen in the books of the prophets: Jeremiah and Ezekiel address audiences in the decades around the destruction, while Isaiah 40 – 66 speaks to people near the end of the exile. Another way was through the retelling of the past. Such is Kings, which ends with an event in 561 BC, the middle of the exile. While certainly incorporating earlier material and covering a period of four hundred years in generally chronological order, Kings is more than a compilation of past records. It is different from 'books of the annals of the kings of Israel/Judah' to which the writer often refers.[27] The writer of the current form of Kings has of necessity been selective in his use of earlier material.[28] He himself is experiencing the disaster to which past actions of kings, prophets and people have led and writes not 'for the sake of the record' or nostalgia, but as 'preached history'.[29] As we move through the book we will seek to be sensitive to how the various passages address the exilic situation. That in turn helps as we ask how the book addresses readers today. In the telling of the narrative of Kings the God who spoke of the past to the present of exiles continues by his Spirit to speak to our present.

Kings can be read simply as an account of the sinfulness of kings and people that led initially to the fall of Samaria and end of the northern kingdom of Israel, and ultimately to the destruction of Jerusalem and exile. It is a story of wilful and persistent idolatry and associated injustice that resulted inevitably in the fulfilment of the curses that had been part of the covenant warnings given by God.[30] Such a message of deserved judgment can lead to despair and hope-lessness, a feeling that there is no future.

There is more however than God saying, 'I told you so.' While any way forward requires owning the consequences of deep-seated

[25] Jer. 28:1–4; 29:1–23.

[26] Isa. 46; Bel (v. 1) is another name for Marduk and Nebo is his son. Much in Isa. 40 – 48 proclaims the incomparability of Yahweh and the 'no-thing-ness' of other gods.

[27] 1 Kgs 14:19, 29, etc. They are a kind of court diary recording events as they occur.

[28] For brief overviews of 'authorship' and 'text', see J. G. McConville, 'Kings, Books of', *DOTHB*, pp. 623–624, and A. Walters, 'Text and Textual Criticism', *DOTHB*, pp. 954–958.

[29] To use the phrase coined by Nelson, p. 2. A later retelling is 1 and 2 Chronicles, written after 400 BC following the return of groups of exiles, rebuilding of the temple and the work of Ezra and Nehemiah.

[30] E.g., Deut. 28:15–68. Such a negative purpose was argued in the influential work of M. Noth, *The Deuteronomistic History* (Sheffield: JSOT, 1981; German orig., second edn 1957 [first edn, 1943]).

persistent rebellion, of personal and corporate sin, the book points beyond human failure and God's judgment. Throughout are pointers of hope, of God's continuing purposes and of the people's response in the present. Kings tells the story of the past so that, in light of Yahweh's purposes and promises, people will change their lifestyles in the present.

Times of turmoil can be occasions for re-assessment of values and changes in life direction. Periods of economic turmoil, such as the Great Depression of the 1930s in Western countries and the Global Financial Crisis from 2008, have led many to question their dependence on financial security and the selfish quest for material prosperity as a symbol of personal or group worth and status. Intermingled have been wars and disasters, together with changing cultural patterns and clashes around the globe. Individual or family experiences of health crises, or the sudden death of someone near, cause many to realize the importance of neglected relationships and raise questions of the meaning of life. Widespread disasters such as earthquake, flood and fire can result in a greater awareness of the importance of community, with its cooperation rather than competition, its sharing of resources rather than self-centred acquisition. Experiences of upheaval, with the loss of what seemed so secure, often bring questioning of beliefs about God. 'Why?' 'How, if at all, is God involved?' 'How can you say God loves us when this happens?' 'What is the way forward?' Into such turmoil Kings can come with unexpected relevance. It was people who were 'harassed and helpless' on whom Christ looked with 'compassion'[31] and to whom he sent out his disciples.

Kings tells of material prosperity, political manoeuvering, power plays between nations, changing national fortunes and alliances, compromised worship, *coup d'états*, droughts and wars, mixed religious affiliations, international trade, injustice, violence and oppression, children dying – all situations familiar in the world today. With these topics often dominating news, Kings is a major book within the Bible to remind us that God is present in all aspects of life, fulfilling his mission. Further, everyday life is the arena in which we are called as God's people to live our worship, trust and obedience and it is on dimensions of this life that the reading of Kings can throw light.

The story of reversal has potential also to assist Christians experiencing either growth or decrease in church life. Church history is replete with examples of rise and decline, whether at the level of countries or towns. Who could have predicted a century ago the rise of the church in Asia and Africa and the declining influence in

[31] Matt. 9:36.

Europe? Some readers may be in settings of decline: for them the pointers of hope and way forward in Kings can encourage. Others may be enjoying growth: here can be found clues for evaluating growth that is God-honouring, bringing blessing to others.

2. Reading Kings today

a. As history

The narrative is straightforward for the first eleven chapters, with Israel and Judah united under Solomon. 1 Kings 12 begins the parallel and intertwining story of two kingdoms: in the north Israel, the larger, with its capital successively at Shechem, Tirzah and Samaria, and Judah in the south, with its capital, Jerusalem.[32] It is not easy to tell parallel, sometimes interlocking, stories, each covering two hundred years! For the period of the two kingdoms (1 Kgs 12:20 – 2 Kgs 17:6) the writer follows a simple method. He tells the story of Israel in the north for the reign of its first king, Jeroboam, and then turns to the south, relating the reigns of the kings of Judah which started during Jeroboam's reign, namely, Rehoboam, Abijah and Asa (see chart of kings, pp. 36–37). Then it is back to Israel and the kings commencing during Asa's reign, Nadab, Baasha, Elah, Zimri, Omri, Ahab (Elijah comes in here), followed by Jehoshaphat's reign in Judah which started during Ahab's reign, and so on. In this way Kings 'makes a claim about the interrelated stories and fates of the two kingdoms. Though ruled by different dynasties, they are yet "two nations under God".'[33]

Geography and history are intertwined. Then as now, location, terrain and climate influenced the economy, social interaction through trade and migration, political and military pressures, both internal and external, and religion. The region of Israel and Judah is not large, only 150 miles (240 km) north to south, from Dan to Beersheba. To the east is desert and to the west, sea. Its location on the narrow land bridge between Africa, Asia and Europe meant being the meat in the sandwich between the much larger nations of Egypt to the south, and Aram (Syria), Assyria and Babylon (and later, Persia, Greece and Rome) who approached from the north. Israel was more open and exposed than Judah: the major trade routes – and routes for armies – were either to the east of the Jordan, or through Galilee and the coastal plain.

[32] In Kings 'Israel' generally refers to the northern kingdom, not the whole 'people of God'. In the books of the prophets the northern kingdom is sometimes called 'Ephraim', the dominant tribe.
[33] R. L. Cohn, 'The Literary Structure of Kings', in Lemaire and Halpern, p. 113.

Much is hilly: the north-south mountains, with Jerusalem relatively remote at 2600 feet (800 m) above sea level, run parallel to the Jordan valley which is entirely below sea level, the Dead Sea being 1300 ft (400 m) below. The climate is Mediterranean, with dry summers and wet winters, livelihood depending on rains and springs rather than rivers. New life comes in autumn with the early rains after the death of summer.

Kings tells of events involving all these interactions and influences. The chart on pages 36–37 includes the dominant surrounding powers. For the past two hundred years the interest of scholars (and others) has been to go to and behind the text to find out 'what happened'. Information from archaeology has been used to fill in the gaps. In this approach the biblical text has been used mainly as a *window* through which to recreate the world of the monarchic period.

Like any historian the writer of Kings used sources. Court records are mentioned with other sources being evident through differing styles. The uniform pattern of words at the beginning and end of each king's reign is evidence of an editorial framework linking the whole (see further on p. 28). Of necessity, as in all history writing, the writer was highly selective. He continually reminds his readers that more details are in 'the book of the annals of the kings of Israel/ Judah',[34] a pointer that what he has included has a purpose. Further, there is a distinction between 'the book of the annals of Solomon' (1 Kgs 11:41) and the other 'annals', and while 'the books of the annals' separate the two kingdoms, the narrative intertwines them. These features point to the importance of the reign of Solomon, which we will note ends with signs of decline subsequently worked out in both kingdoms, and to the intermingling of the practices of the two kingdoms despite political distinction.[35]

b. As story

When we tell something of our journey with Christ, or the history of our church, we usually have some aim related to the situation of the audience. That affects both what we include and how we tell the story.[36] The writer responsible for the present form of Kings is like a movie or documentary producer who carefully selects not only the events but also the angle of view and pace of the narrative. Kings

[34] 1 Kgs 14:19, 29, etc., not to be confused with the later biblical books (as may happen with AV/KJV and RSV's 'book of the chronicles . . . ').

[35] G. Goswell, 'Titles Without Texts: What the Lost Books of the Bible Tell Us About the Books We Have', *Colloquium* 4 (2009), pp. 73–93, especially pp. 84–85.

[36] The term 'story' does not imply fiction but rather highlights that a speaker/writer is telling some continuous narrative using accepted cultural conventions.

relates events of the past, with features of story-telling, including plot and characterization. The purpose is not so much to provide a window through to the past as a *picture* to help us see and reflect on the past: the aim is not to take us to the past but to bring the past into our present. Using the word 'reflect' suggests that the narrative becomes also a *mirror* helping us see better our present (Jas 1:22–25), the revelation of God shining into our life today. The narrative is about the past, told in a way that addresses the hearer and reader in the present. It aims not simply to inform but to bring understanding and change.

> A few years ago, a story about computers was making the rounds ... Someone asked a computer expert whether computers could think. 'Computers will show they can think', said the expert, 'when, after you have asked the computer a question, the answer comes, "That reminds me of a story."'
>
> Indeed, few words are so irresistible as 'Let me tell you a story' ... Storytelling intertwines entertainment and the transmission of wisdom.[37]

Our age has an insatiable appetite for stories: movies are watched in cinemas, on TV and computer screens around the globe, musical theatre is played to packed houses, and sales of novels continue to grow. Some stories are watched or read purely for entertainment or escape or to fill in time, yet there are always those that are 'good' or 'stirring' or 'disturbing'. In some way they involve us. They make us think, causing us to see ourselves or our world differently. Sometimes they bring about change in attitudes and actions. While never exactly the same as our lives or our society, in some way we identify with them. Often it is the very difference or strangeness that has the impact. The difference shows more starkly some feature of life that we have overlooked, or at least helps us see that feature in a new way. A mirror can confront us by being a straight reflection (which we may like or dislike!), by reflecting light onto something that has been in the shadows or outside our normal direct vision or, in the case of a concave mirror, focusing light on an object. Significantly the majority of Scripture is in the form of narrative through which God shines his light, that, 'sharper than any double-edged sword, it penetrates even to dividing soul and spirit, joints and marrow; it judges the thoughts and attitudes of the heart'.[38]

---

[37] W. L. Holladay, *Long Ago God Spoke* (Minneapolis: Fortress, 1995), p. 88.
[38] Heb. 4:12.

Stories are different from lectures, or 'how to' manuals, or works of systematic theology in three significant ways:

- Through multiple characters they more readily deal with complex issues – and life as we experience it *is* complex. In human relationships and actions decisions often involve multiple factors, motives can be mixed and consequences of actions unforeseen.
- They involve the hearer, reader or viewer who is caught up in the story. At times a surface reading of Kings seems to encourage a positive response towards a person or action, and yet literary clues point to some criticism, relativizing or even negating the commendation. For example, how is one to interpret Solomon's 'glory' and 'wisdom', or Jehu's purge, or Elijah's boldness, or Josiah's death?[39] Diverse responses are given by commentators and preachers. At times the writer may be deliberately ambiguous, helping the reader to see beneath the surface.[40]
- Finally, they are often open-ended. They move our thoughts in certain directions but do not provide a tidy 1–2–3 summary or answer to all our questions. They address not only our minds but also our emotions and will. The parables of Jesus are an excellent example. The story of the Good Samaritan (Luke 10:25–37) impacts in different ways from a treatise on the meaning of 'love' and 'neighbour'.

Kings can have that impact. The names and situations are foreign and the contexts of readers today around the world have countless differences, yet Kings can help us see in fresh ways aspects of our own lives, both personal and corporate. There may be parallels between the original hearers, the people of God in exile, and ourselves. There may be times when we identify with a character (or with what that person is doing or thinking or experiencing) or when another repels us. The narrative can point to reasons then for failure and success that provide light for our now.

c. Both story and history

What is the relationship of 'what is being told' to 'what happened'? Some recent writers see that question as irrelevant: a story can have

---

[39] See discussion of relevant passages.

[40] D. G. Firth's 'Ambiguity', in *Words and the Word*, edited by D. G. Firth and J. A. Grant (Nottingham: Inter-Varsity Press, 2008), pp. 151–184, discusses different forms and purposes.

an impact and be true even though it never happened. To date there is little archaeological evidence that can be said to prove that many of the biblical events happened, particularly those of the reigns of David and Solomon, and so some scholars are sceptical about historical reliability. What has been found is material providing political and cultural background and describing contemporary historical events, along with seals and inscriptions mentioning names.[41]

At the same time it must be affirmed that the biblical writers themselves purport to be giving a reliable account of the past, shown not least by their footnoting and attention to detail. The lessons of history can hardly be lessons if there is no history! Yet, as we have said, their concern is not simply to relate the past. They are seeking changes in the present. They present a narrative, told according to the conventions of their day.[42]

Which is more 'true', a painting or a photograph? Paintings often give a better picture of what is important (to the painter), of true character. Interestingly, we speak of 'getting the picture' when we refer beyond facts to understanding. A painting of a person is not the person: it represents (or re-presents) aspects of the reality of the person, following conventions understood in a community. Even good photographs are themselves posed, with lighting used to effect: we often say of a photograph, 'That's captured her personality' or 'He's not really like that'. Ancient Egyptian drawings always had people's faces looking sideways and medieval European artists drew biblical characters with halos, while artists today use a variety of styles. Each seeks to present a true picture in its own time and culture. Stories too are representations. Through plot, characterization, dialogue and other literary conventions they seek to highlight truth and to arouse a response.

It is helpful to remember that until the advent of the printing press in the fifteenth century and an increase in literacy, the great majority of people *heard*, rather than read, the Bible. That is still so in many cultures. When our local congregation listened to recordings of the Scriptures, we were surprised how we 'saw' familiar

[41] Several details are given in Wiseman, in his introduction (pp. 35–40) and throughout the commentary. See articles in *NBD* and *DOTHB*, and in more detail, I. Provan, V. P. Long and T. Longman, III, *A Biblical History of Israel* (Louisville: Westminster John Knox, 2003). W. G. Dever, 'Archaeology and the Question of Sources in Kings' in Lemaire and Halpern, pp. 517–538, has useful charts showing correlations between Kings and archaeological data.

[42] See S. L. McKenzie, 'Historiography, Old Testament', *DOTHB*, pp. 418–425; Y. Amit, 'Narrative Art of Israel's Historians', *DOTHB*, pp. 708–715; and Provan, pp. 1–22 ('Introduction'). More detailed is V. P. Long, *The Art of Biblical History* (Grand Rapids: Zondervan; Leicester: Apollos, 1994).

passages in a new light. To *listen* to the text is to remember that it was designed initially for ears, not eyes. A number of characteristics are evident in biblical narrative, with similarities to stage plays or movies:

- Much content and plot development is conveyed through conversations, commonly involving only two people. Dialogue has immediacy, drawing in the hearer more directly.
- Characters are of different types: some are portrayed in depth, with many characteristics (like us), while others are single type, e.g., good, bad, wise, foolish; sometimes one character is a foil to another while others have only a walk-on part; and yet all have a role in building up the total picture.
- The telling of a story has pace: some items are dealt with very quickly (one or two phrases or sentences); others are drawn out, sometimes through repetition of words or phrases. When we *read, we* choose what to spend time thinking about and what to gloss over. When we *listen*, the *narrator* determines the focus.

As we explore Kings these features will be noted as they help us see more clearly the writer's emphases and concerns.

d. God participates

A striking feature of biblical narrative is the part played by God. He is a participant and often one of the pair in a dialogue. Immediately that raises problems for many modern (and postmodern) people. It is not common to regard God as a participant in everyday life and politics. In writing 'history' (in the technical sense used by historians), or writing an article for a newspaper on politics or economics, it is not usual to include God in any description of events. One looks for patterns of sociopolitical processes, in ways similar to scientists investigating physical and biological processes. Of course, it is faith in God as creator that makes it possible to look for these patterns and processes: God works in and through processes he has brought into being. But have we lost something by bracketing out God from conversation and narrative, by simply talking about processes and keeping silent about God's involvement? Kings can help us reflect on this question.

Kings has God as subject in various ways. The most explicit is through his speaking to prophets who announce his word, with fulfilment generally through 'normal' processes. Much of the narrative is about human decisions and actions, to which God responds through his prophets. There is interplay between human actions and God's purposes.[43]

What is clear is that the narrator's interest is not so much with the story of political Israel and Judah as with the relationship between God and his people in the midst of the challenges and vicissitudes of national life.

Despite the extent of common material, Kings remains unique among ancient near eastern historical writing. The mixture of military, political, legal and social affairs in an overtly religious narrative, including accounts of the activities of prophets, is unrivalled.[44]

That becomes relevant to all Christians, since the New Testament reminds us that in Christ, by grace, we have been grafted in to the true vine (Rom. 11:13–24); we too are 'children of Abraham' (Gal. 3:7). When we read about God and people in Kings, we can reflect on God and the church today. I have found myself much more interested in several events in world history of recent centuries as family history research has uncovered ancestors who participated in and were shaped by those events: the history has become 'mine', throwing new light on my present. In a far greater and richer manner, in Christ the history of Israel and Judah is our history. As this history is of a continuing relationship with God who is fulfilling his purposes for his creation, the issue for our future is more than what is going to happen to us: it is what God is saying through Kings to us in our present contexts as we look to the future.

History, story, God: the three come together in the Book of Kings.

Our writer . . . is an author who is burdened by a multiple responsibility. He is responsible to the facts he reports not to distort them; he is responsible to his readers to offer them a coherent and meaningful narrative; he is also responsible to the future Israel that they may read and learn from the past. Above all, he is responsible to God, whose hand he has seen in past events and whose word he now delivers.[45]

---

[43] A stimulating work is J. Ellul, *The Politics of God and the Politics of Man* (Grand Rapids: Eerdmans, 1972), looking at seven narratives in 2 Kings.

[44] A. R. Millard, 'Kings and External Textual Sources: Assyrian, Babylonian and North-West Semitic', in Lemaire and Halpern, p. 201.

[45] Hobbs, p. xxxiii.

3. Major Themes

a. Kings and prophets

Two repetitive literary patterns are evident in Kings, one involving the succession of kings, the other the fulfilment of the word of God through prophets. The first stands out and appears to be the determining and relentless line of history – as in school where I learnt about kings and queens of England – but the other undercuts, highlighting the action of God and his prophets.

(i) Kings and the promises to David

Standard formulae are used in structuring Kings, commencing from the death of Solomon (1 Kgs 11:41–43):

JUDAH	ISRAEL
'In the . . . year of (name), king of Israel, N^1 became king of Judah.'	'In the . . . year of (name), king of Judah, N^3 became king of Israel.'
Age, duration of reign, and name of queen mother.	Duration of reign and place of capital.
Evaluation of standing in comparison with 'David his father'.	Censure: 'He did evil in the eyes of Yahweh, because he walked in the ways of Jeroboam (son of Nebat), who caused Israel to sin. . . . (or similar, referring always to Jeroboam)
Narrative 'As for the other events of N^1's reign . . . are they not written in the book of the annals of the kings of Judah?'	Narrative 'As for the other events of N^3's reign . . . are they not written in the book of the annals of the kings of Israel?'
Concluding statement that he 'rested with his ancestors and was buried with them in the city of David his father. And N^2 his son succeeded him.'	Concluding statement that he 'rested with his ancestors and N^4 succeeded him as king'

By evaluating each king before the narrative, the writer provides a lens through which to read what follows. Before reading of political or military successes or failures, or of economic prosperity or decline, we are reminded of the priority of faith commitment expressed in worship. That is what counts in the long run: relationship with Yahweh is the core of all areas of national life.

All kings of the northern kingdom 'fail', the evidence being the continuation of Jeroboam's religious policies that were politically inspired, resulting from lack of trust in the promises of God (see on 1 Kgs 12: 25–33, pp. 135–139). The evaluation of the kings of Judah is mixed: only two are exemplary,[46] six are praised with the qualification that 'the high places were not removed',[47] while the rest are condemned.[48] In each case we read specifically of aspects of worship: was their commitment to worship of Yahweh alone? The variation, even oscillation, is of ongoing relevance as a 'good' king is not necessarily followed by a 'good' son, nor a 'bad' king by a 'bad' son. There is influence from the past, but each generation is responsible for its own actions (cf. 2 Kgs 14:6; Ezek. 18).

The question of Yahweh's commitment to his promises to David is a key theme, evident more widely than in the formulaic comparison. The promises are mentioned occasionally as a reason for God's continuing blessing despite a king's failure;[49] in the narrative of Hezekiah they are a key to trusting Yahweh during the Assyrian attack,[50] while the horror of Manasseh's policies is focused by referring to Yahweh's words to David.[51] The reign of Solomon, both the building of the temple and the prophetic announcement of looming division on his death, is likewise frequently linked with Davidic promises.[52] The repeated references are a pointer to the exile being the result not of Yahweh's faithlessness to his promises or of weakness but of the people's apostasy. But when all kings ultimately fall short, what is the future of the Davidic covenant?

Three kings are highlighted as being incomparable in a positive feature: Solomon for 'wisdom' to rule justly, Hezekiah for 'trust in Yahweh' and Josiah for wholehearted 'love of God in accord with the Law'.[53] Although each proves to have limitations, they point to

[46] Hezekiah (2 Kgs 18:1–6) and Josiah (2 Kgs 22:1–2).
[47] Solomon (1 Kgs 3:3; but compare 11:4–6, 33), Asa (1 Kgs 15:11–15), Jehoshaphat (1 Kgs 22:41–44), Joash (2 Kgs 12:1–3), Amaziah (2 Kgs 14:1–4), Azariah (2 Kgs 15:1–4), Jotham (2 Kgs 15:32–35).
[48] Rehoboam (1 Kgs 14:21–24), Abijah (1 Kgs 15:1–5), Jehoram (2 Kgs 8:16–19), Ahaziah (2 Kgs 8:25–27), Ahaz (2 Kgs 16:1–4), Manasseh (2 Kgs 21:1–9), Amon (2 Kgs 21:19–22), Jehoahaz (2 Kgs 23:31–32), Jehoiakim (2 Kgs 23:36–37), Jehoiachin (2 Kgs 24:8–9) and Zedekiah (2 Kgs 24:18–20).
[49] 1 Kgs 15:4–5; 2 Kgs 8:19.
[50] 2 Kgs 19:34; 20:5–6.
[51] 2 Kgs 21:7–8.
[52] 1 Kgs 3:6; 5:5; 6:12; 8:15–20, 24–26, 66; 9:5; 11:12–13, 31–38.
[53] 1 Kgs 3:12; 2 Kgs 18:5; 23:25; see G. N. Knoppers, '"There Was None Like Him": Incomparability in the Books of Kings', *Catholic Biblical Quarterly* 54 (1992), pp. 411–31.

an ideal of future Davidic kingship, while the end of Kings (2 Kgs 25:27–30) 'hints that the unconditional aspects of the Davidic promise may even still, after awful judgment has fallen, remain in force'.[54]

The culminating fulfilment of the Davidic promises is a key component of New Testament proclamation. Jesus Christ is the descendant of David who is constantly obedient to his Father; he is the Son of David who reigns forever.[55] It is to the 'Son of David' that blind people and a Canaanite woman call;[56] this is the appellation given to Mary for her child[57] and on his entry in Jerusalem on Palm Sunday;[58] and it is 'the Root of David' that will ultimately triumph over all forces of evil.[59] Kings opens with David's aged weakness and death, while the New Testament affirms that the greater 'Son of David', 'David's Lord', has been raised from the dead and reigns forever.[60] The recurring promises in Kings are made by a God who keeps his word, who acts through a descendant of David to overcome the results of human rebellion.

(ii) God's word through prophets

Intertwined with the story of Kings key roles are played by prophets. Elijah and Elisha feature in a major section,[61] with several other prophets mentioned throughout. A recurring phrase is 'according to the word of Yahweh which he spoke through (prophet's name)' or similar,[62] the writer thereby explicitly drawing attention to fulfilment of an earlier word. The framework of the regnal formulae may provide chronological movement but history is seen as the realization of God's words: it is his purposes announced by prophets that come to pass. Further, the only prophetic succession, that of Elijah-Elisha, is 'outside of royal time'.[63] The kings of Israel and Judah may think they are in control, but it is prophets who announce reality, commonly linked with Yahweh's demand for a life of obedience to his commands, the path of doing what is just and right.

[54] I. W. Provan, 'The Messiah in the Books of Kings', in *The Lord's Anointed: Interpretation of Old Testament Messianic Texts,* edited by P. E. Satterthwaite, R. S. Hess and G. J. Wenham (Carlisle: Paternoster; Grand Rapids: Baker, 1995), p. 76.

[55] Matt. 1:1–17; Luke 1:27, 32, 69; 2:4; Acts 13:22–23.

[56] Matt. 9:27; 15:22; 20:30; Mark 10:47–48; Luke 18:38–39.

[57] Luke 1:32.

[58] Matt. 21:9; Mark 11:10.

[59] Rev. 5:5; 22:16.

[60] Mark 12:35–37; Acts 2:25–36; 13:32–37; Rom. 1:3; 2 Tim. 2:8.

[61] 1 Kgs 17 – 19, 21; 2 Kgs 1 – 8; almost a quarter of Kings.

[62] The identical Hebrew phrase is translated variously in NIV.

[63] Cohn, 'The Literary Structure of Kings', in Lemaire and Halpern, p. 116, noting that 2 Kgs 2 is 'not only at the center of the book', but also comes after the summary of Ahaziah's reign (2 Kgs 1:17–18) and before Jehoram's reign of (2 Kgs 3:1–3).

The extent of the pattern can be seen in the following table, the left column giving the predictions (a couple preceding Kings), and the right fulfilment, generally including the recurrent phrase noted above:

1 Sam. 2:21–36	1 Kgs 2:27
2 Sam. 7:12–13	1 Kgs 8:20, 24
1 Kgs 11:29–39	1 Kgs 12:15
1 Kgs 13:1–3	2 Kgs 23:16–18
1 Kgs 13:20–22	1 Kgs 13:26
1 Kgs 14:6–16	1 Kgs 14:18; 15:29
1 Kgs 16:1–4	1 Kgs 16:12
Josh. 6:26	1 Kgs 16:34
1 Kgs 17:14	1 Kgs 17:16
1 Kgs 21:21–24 (qualified in 27–29) and 2 Kgs 9:4–10	2 Kgs 9:30–37; 10:17
1 Kgs 22:17	1 Kgs 22:35–38
2 Kgs 1:6, 16	2 Kgs 1:17
2 Kgs 21:10–15	2 Kgs 24:2

Brueggemann's comment on Jeremiah 1:1–3 is well illustrated by the place of prophets in Kings:

> The word of the Lord is not a romantic or floating spiritual notion . . . The word of Yahweh . . . intrudes into the neat chronology of the kings to give us early notice that another governance is here that will unsettle the neat, fixed chronology. . . . The known world . . . is ending precisely because of Yahweh's governance.[64]

Can the mirror of this past recurrent pattern shine light on world events today? So much of the telling of world history is of changing fortunes of nations or peoples, of leaders and political parties, of the rise and fall of great powers, of battles won or lost, of revolutions that change the direction of nations or disasters that destroy the *status quo*. Kings has all of these. All the events commonly recorded are important, but they are the arena in which God is working, often in surprising ways. Yahweh's word through prophets and his Son[65] gives another perspective. The whole Bible presents the great narrative of God's purposes from creation to new creation, a purpose focused in Christ, 'to bring unity to all things in heaven and on earth under Christ' (Eph. 1:10). Kings shouts out the reality of God's

---

[64] W. Brueggemann, *Jeremiah 1–25: To Pluck Up, To Tear Down* (Edinburgh: Handsel; Grand Rapids: Eerdmans, 1988), pp. 22–23.
[65] Heb. 1:1–2.

involvement, shaping history in his direction. It is the same God at work today in the brutal, unsettling realities of life. It is those who hear and follow the word of the Lord who understand history, past, present and future; they are the ones who courageously speak God's word and live it out in trust and hope.

It is easy for those in authority to think that they control people and affairs – for the exiles this was the Babylonians. The Kings writer repeatedly reminds his hearers that it is Yahweh who is sovereign; his word is not thwarted. To a people whose king is a captive comes the reminder of the independent role of prophets as God's spokespersons. This confidence is expressed well by Paul, 'I am suffering even to the point of being chained like a criminal. But God's word is not chained' (2 Tim. 2:9), words I heard echoed by Pastor Martin Niemoller, a World War One U-Boat commander become Lutheran pastor and imprisoned in Nazi Germany.

b. Living the covenant relationship

Another constant motif is the necessity of keeping the covenant requirements, especially as presented in the book of Deuteronomy. (It is for this reason that the books, Joshua, Judges, Samuel and Kings are sometimes referred to as 'Deuteronomistic History'.) There are frequent reminders of the importance of keeping Yahweh's 'decrees and commands', especially sole worship of Yahweh.[66] The worship of other gods by God's people has come to the fore again in recent years, making the Kings narrative strikingly relevant. For example, at the Third Lausanne Congress on World Evangelization, Capetown, 2010, Chris Wright stated that 'idolatry of the Church' is 'the biggest single obstacle to world mission'.[67] In this way the negative examples of Kings and the prophetic warnings continue to speak. Deuteronomy 28 is a list of blessings and curses associated with the covenant and several references in Kings to 'my decrees and my commands' are in warnings or statements of implementation of the curses.

Some see Kings as a negative book, narrating nothing more than the outworking of the covenant curses because of the people's failure to obey Yahweh.[68] Others have pointed to a note of hope. The covenant promises the possibility of renewal beyond judgment

---

[66] 1 Kgs 2:3; 3:14; 6:12; 8:58, 61; 9:4; 11:11, 33–34, 38; 14:8; 15:5; 18:18; 2 Kgs 17:13–16, 19, 34–40; 18:5–6, 12; 22:13; 23:1–3.

[67] He specified three idols: 'power and pride, popularity and success, and wealth and greed' <http://www.lausanne.org/articles/calling-the-church-back.html> (accessed 25 March 2011).

[68] Especially so in Noth's groundbreaking work, *The Deuteronomistic History* (see above n. 30).

if the people turn to God. In Kings this is seen most clearly in Solomon's prayer at the dedication of the temple: the final petition states the reality of rebellion and exile – and the possibility of forgiveness (1 Kgs 8:46–53). There is hope as God has not given up on his people. As they turn back to him, which implies a willingness to follow his 'commands', there is 'grace in the end'.[69] A cluster of hope is also evident in 2 Kings 13 – 14. Strikingly, in Kings, of only two kings is it explicitly said that 'he humbled himself', leading to God's announcement that 'I will not bring disaster in his day'. The good king Josiah may have been expected (2 Kgs 22:19–20), but the other is the worst king of Israel, Ahab (1 Kgs 21:29). The spectrum of extent of disobedience is embraced by God's forgiveness.[70]

Here is the wonder of the gospel: restoration of relationship beyond rebellion and forgiveness of the disobedient. At the time of the exile Jeremiah and Ezekiel were to strengthen this good news by announcing the renewing work of the Spirit that empowers the life of faith leading to obedience, so enabling enjoyment of the covenant relationship.[71]

c. The temple and the presence of God

The four long chapters 1 Kings 5 – 8 have much detail of the temple built by Solomon and the prayer at its dedication. Thereafter comes the sad tale of various kings who gave some of the temple wealth to foreign rulers as security for a treaty arrangement or as spoils of war.[72] While a few kings built up the temple and its treasury,[73] the culmination of apostasy was the complete sacking of the temple in 597 and 587 BC.[74]

---

[69] J. G. McConville, *Grace in the End: A Study in Deuteronomic Theology* (Grand Rapids: Zondervan, 1993), and his more detailed '1 Kings 8:46–53 and the Deuteronomic Hope', *Vetus Testamentum* 42 (1992), pp. 67–79 (reprinted in Knoppers and McConville, pp. 358–69).

[70] A motif of repentance and God's grace is more prevalent in Chronicles. The vocabulary of the oft-quoted 2 Chr. 7:14 occurs in passages that have no parallel in Kings and there are kings whose trust or repentance are not in Kings, e.g., Rehoboam (2 Chr. 11:13–17; 12:6–12), Abijah (13:3–21) and Manasseh (33:11–13).

[71] Jer. 31:31–37; Ezek. 36:24–32; Rom. 7 – 8. Significantly Romans, with its major treatment of 'justification by faith' begins and ends with Paul describing his commission to bring about 'the obedience that comes from faith' among the Gentiles (Rom. 1:5; 16:26).

[72] 1 Kgs 14:26 (Solomon's son!); 15:18; 2 Kgs 12:18; 14:14; 18:14–16.

[73] 1 Kgs 15:15; 2 Kgs 12:4–16 (but see v. 18); 22:4–7.

[74] 2 Kgs 24:13; 25:13–17. The frequent details of loss of treasures matches the writer's emphasis that obedience of Yahweh's commands is more important than provisions for an ornate building (see on 1 Kgs 9:1–9, pp. 103–106).

The temple was the place Yahweh chose 'as a dwelling for his Name',[75] yet there is a relativizing of its significance right at the beginning, in two ways. In his word to Solomon both before and after his building of the temple, Yahweh acknowledges the building, but almost in passing, as the focus is, 'follow my decrees, observe all my laws and keep all my commands and obey them', with a warning that God could make the temple 'a heap of rubble'.[76] The link between disobedience and the judgment of destruction and exile is made clear. There is, however, another affirmation that could be heard as an unexpected way forward for the exiles. In his prayer of dedication Solomon asks, 'But will God really dwell on earth? The heavens, even the highest heaven, cannot contain you. How much less this temple I have built!' (1 Kgs 8:27). Yahweh's temple may be destroyed but he still reigns.

The future of the temple and the presence of God are taken up in the New Testament. The destruction of the temple being rebuilt by Herod was on the lips of Jesus, in two complementary contexts. In response to his disciples' comment on the impressive building in progress he replied that 'not one stone here will be left on another', but 'my words will never pass away'.[77] In response to questions on his authority after driving out moneychangers, Jesus' answer was, 'Destroy this temple, and I will raise it again in three days,' which John goes on to explain, 'The temple he had spoken of was his body.'[78] Jesus also stated that 'something greater than the temple is here.'[79] This is taken further as temple imagery is used of the Christian church, the 'dwelling place of the Holy Spirit'.[80] Again, our attention is drawn from the symbol to the reality of the presence of God in Christ, and to the corollary of consistent lifestyle of the people of God. Likewise Stephen's questioning of the temple as integral to worship (Acts 7:48) 'seems to allude to Solomon's exclamation in 1 Kgs 8:27',[81] leading into a quote from Isaiah 66:1–2; it is 'the earth' (not temple) that is God's 'footstool'. The accounts in Kings, with their variety of situations and responses, together with the New Testament, can help us reflect on what is involved in worshipping and keeping the words of God who is present.

[75] 1 Kgs 5:3, 5; 8:15–21; compare Deut. 12:5, 11.
[76] 1 Kgs 6:11–13; 9:3–9.
[77] Matt. 24:2, 35 and parallels.
[78] John 2:19–22; compare Matt. 26:61; 27:40; Mark 14:58.
[79] Matt. 12:6.
[80] 1 Cor. 3:16; 2 Cor. 6:16; Eph. 2:21; Rev. 3:12; 21:22. See G. K. Beale, *The Temple and the Church's Mission: A Biblical Theology of the Dwelling Place of God*, New Studies in Biblical Theology (Leicester: Apollos; Downers Grove: InterVarsity Press, 2004).
[81] M. Zetterholm, 'The Book of Kings in the New Testament and the Apostolic Fathers', in Lemaire and Halpern, p. 562.

d. A diverse cast: flawed heroes and failed reforms

We noted above the evaluation of kings, with certain kings as exemplars, for good (David) or ill (Jeroboam). Further, much space is given to Hezekiah (2 Kgs 18 – 20) and Josiah (2 Kgs 22 – 23). Sadly, however, 'the events in the history of both Israel and Judah which have the potential of redemption are colored by the presence of ultimate failure.' [82] Whether it be Solomon, or Elijah, or Jehu's purge, or the reforms of Hezekiah and Josiah, there is always some negative aspect. While we might say simply, 'that is what happened', the writer conveys another message that focuses hope in God rather than humans. In light of the tendency to look in biblical narrative for moral examples, it is crucial to remember that the main emphasis in the text is on 'God, who works for, with, through, and sometimes in spite of people'.[83] God works in a society and with people who are not perfect. That is one feature that enhances the ongoing relevance of the narrative!

The exile is not the result of the forces of history, bad luck, fate or the arbitrary nature of life. It is because Yahweh, the one and only God, has been active.

> The covenantal demand . . . implies a break with the determinism of contemporary religions, and offering in its place the freedom, responsibility, and open future that comes from the belief in one God who is at once omnipotent, holy, and disposed to bless. This entails . . . the capacity to criticize any power or institution that happens to have the ascendancy at the time . . . [The Deuteronomic idea of history[84]] implies the possibility of a personal relationship between Yahweh . . . and the human race, within which each is a responsible agent making free choices . . . in such a way as to be involved with him in the construction of their lives and destiny.[85]

God through Kings invites us to journey with him as he relates to the people of Israel in the movement of the reversal of blessing. Within are pointers to the path to future blessing that God wishes to bring, not only for them but for peoples of all nations through all time. As we read today we join with others who through the centuries and now around the globe have allowed the experiences of the past to illumine the present.

---

[82] Hobbs, p. xxviii; also J. G. McConville, 'Narrative and Meaning in the Books of Kings,' *Biblica* 70 (1989), pp. 31–49.

[83] S. Greidanus, *The Modern Preacher and the Ancient Text* (Leicester: Inter-Varsity Press; Grand Rapids: Eerdmans, 1988), p. 217.

[84] That presented in the book of Deuteronomy.

[85] J. G. McConville, *Grace in the End*, pp. 130–131.

THE KINGS OF ISRAEL AND JUDAH

UNITED MONARCHY

SAUL	ca 1020–1000
DAVID	ca 1000–960
SOLOMON	ca 960–930

JUDAH (South)		ISRAEL (North)*		
Kings	Prophets	Kings	Prophets	OTHER EVENTS
REHOBOAM 930–913		JEROBOAM I 930–909		Shishak (Egypt) invades Judah (ca 925)
Abijah (Abijam) 913–910				
Asa 910–870		Nadab 909–908		Beginning of ASSYRIAN revival
		Baasha 908–886		
		Elah 886–885		
		Zimri (7 days) 885		
		Omri 885–874		Rise of ARAMEAN power
JEHOSHAPHAT 870–848		AHAB 874–853	Elijah	
		Ahaziah 853–852	Elisha	
Jehoram (Joram) 848–841	(Brothers-in-law)	Joram (Jehoram) 852–841		
Ahaziah 841		JEHU 841–814		Jehu pays tribute to Assyria (841)
Athaliah (queen) 841–835				
Joash (Jehoash) 835–796		Jehoahaz 814–798		
		Jehoash (Joash) 798–782		Assyrian power weakens
Amaziah 796–767		JEROBOAM II 782–753	Amos	

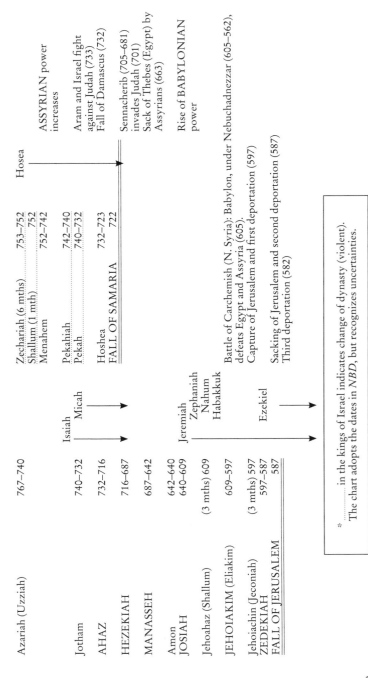

Azariah (Uzziah)	767–740	Zechariah (6 mths) 753–752	Hosea
		Shallum (1 mth) 752	
		Menahem 752–742	ASSYRIAN power increases
Jotham	740–732	Pekahiah 742–740	
	Isaiah	Pekah 740–732	Aram and Israel fight against Judah (733)
AHAZ	732–716		Fall of Damascus (732)
	Micah	Hoshea 732–723	
		FALL OF SAMARIA 722	
HEZEKIAH	716–687		Sennacherib (705–681) invades Judah (701)
MANASSEH	687–642		Sack of Thebes (Egypt) by Assyrians (663)
Amon	642–640		
JOSIAH	640–609		Rise of BABYLONIAN power
	Jeremiah		
	Zephaniah		
	Nahum		
	Habakkuk		
Jehoahaz (Shallum)	(3 mths) 609		
JEHOIAKIM (Eliakim)	609–597		Battle of Carchemish (N. Syria): Babylon, under Nebuchadnezzar (605–562), defeats Egypt and Assyria (605).
			Capture of Jerusalem and first deportation (597)
Jehoiachin (Jeconiah)	(3 mths) 597		
ZEDEKIAH	597–587	Ezekiel	
FALL OF JERUSALEM	587		Sacking of Jerusalem and second deportation (587)
			Third deportation (582)

* ———— in the kings of Israel indicates change of dynasty (violent).
   The chart adopts the dates in *NBD*, but recognizes uncertainties.

37

Chronology

Kings introduces the reigns of each king of Israel and Judah with details of length of reign and synchronization with the kings of the other kingdom. Any attempt however to add these up or to correlate the two kingdoms soon runs into inconsistencies.

Various solutions have been proposed.[1] Amongst several technical factors, two stand out:

(1) *The method of counting regnal years*: two methods are known in the ancient Near East, both based on the New Year. In Mesopotamia the period from accession to New Year was an 'accession year', with the following year 'the first year', the next New Year to New Year the second, and so on, with the year in which death occurs another year. Egypt however used the so-called 'non-accession' method with the period of reign up to the first New Year being 'one year' and the next New Year to New Year the second. There are also differences as to when New Year occurred, spring (March/April) or autumn (September/October), the latter generally being seen in Israel and Judah. A common view is that Israel used 'non-accession' counting and Judah 'accession'. Thus, for instance Nadab, who is said to have reigned *two years* (1 Kgs 15:25), may have actually reigned less than twelve months, his reign including a New Year. This explains how he *became king of Israel in the second year of Asa king of Judah* (1 Kgs 15:25), and his successor Baasha *in the third year of Asa* (1 Kgs 15:33).

(2) *Co-regencies*: it was not uncommon for a king's son to begin reigning as co-regent while his father continued to be king. The total number of regnal years can include the period of co-regency, one way to reconcile some of the synchronization between the kings of Israel and Judah and dates given during the reign of Hezekiah.

---

[1] Konkel, pp. 673–684, lists eleven significant studies published in the period 1990–2004! Refer to the excellent summaries in *DOTHB*: K. A. Kitchen, "Chronology", p. 186, and B. E. Kelle and B. A. Strawn, "History of Israel 5: Assyrian Period", p. 461, noting slight differences in dates, an illustration of uncertainty.

A. Solomon's reign
1 Kings 1 – 11

1 Kings 1:1 – 2:46
1. Solomon becomes king

1. Transition is imminent (1:1–4)

King David was very old. The simple statement signifies time for change. Like the start of Joshua (1:1) and Judges (1:1), Kings opens with a link to the previous book. Similar to Moses and Joshua's long and successful leadership, for forty years David had been king over Judah – thirty-three years for the combined Israel and Judah (1 Kgs 2:11). But what is to follow?

That the focus of chapter 1 is on kingship is shown by the designation of key characters. Not only is *King* the first word but David is always *King David* (nine times),[1] *the king* (thirty nine times)[2] and only once *our lord David* (v. 11). The first instance of simply *David* is in 2:1, after the issue of succession is resolved. Alongside are references to Adonijah seeking to become *king* (six times),[3] the promise that Solomon is to be *king* (four times)[4] and statement that he has become *king* (seven times),[5] or the question as to which is to be *king* (vv. 20, 27). The seventy instances of the noun *king* or the related verb is the most in any chapter in the Bible. The narrative has movement as various questions arise. Will David act as king in his last days, and if so, how? What will happen because Adonijah wants to be king? What about Solomon?

In recent years it has become common to talk about 'succession planning' in organisations and companies. As groups have become

---

[1] Verses 1, 13, 28, 31, 32, 37, 38, 43, 47. There are only sixteen instances in all of 2 Samuel. Statistics in this paragraph relate to MT. EVV may vary.

[2] Verses 2 (3x), 3, 4 (2x), 9 (2x), 13, 14, 15 (3x), 16 (2x), 19, 20 (2x), 21, 22, 23 (3x), 24, 25, 27 (2x), 28, 29, 31, 32, 33, 36 (2x), 37, 44 (2x), 47.

[3] Verses 5, 11, 13, 18, 24, 25.

[4] Verses 13, 17, 30, 34.

[5] Verses 39, 43, 45, 51 (2x), 53 (2x).

aware of increasing complexities and turbulence with the ending of isolation from global influences, many have seen the wisdom of planning. Churches and missionary organisations that have enjoyed a long period of stable leadership wisely plan, with prayerful mentoring and training of potential leaders for the next generation. There is concern that what is believed to be the God-given vision and ethos of the organisation continues with strength, especially when the group has been the result largely, under God, of the vision and drive of a key person. What happens when that person becomes *old*? There are two extremes: that nothing has been done, or that the successor is a clone when change is needed. The pattern of Jesus training his disciples for their tasks after his ascension is often cited as a model, as is Paul's encouragement of the young Timothy.

In the case of Moses, Joshua had spent many years alongside, the benefits evidenced in Joshua's ensuing leadership. However, while Joshua ended his life with stirring farewell speeches (Josh. 23 – 24), Judges is a sad story of chaos in the following generations. Throughout that period leadership was in the hands of 'judges/leaders' raised up by God (Judg. 2:16), with the only instance of a dynastic situation, that of Gideon's son Abimelech, being a mockery (Judg. 9). 1 Samuel starts with Eli the priest whose sons were moral failures (1 Sam. 2:12–17). It continues to tell how, surprisingly, Samuel appointed his own sons as 'judges/leaders', but they acted unjustly, seeking selfish gain and unwanted by the people (1 Sam. 8:1–5). A dynastic model has not had a good record! The first king, Saul, had been succeeded by David, chosen by God from a different family and tribe. With David comes a change: after centuries of raising up leaders, Yahweh promised that he would establish for David a *house* (dynasty; 2 Sam. 7:11–16). The past experience of leaders' sons raises the questions: what kind of person will the next king be, and which son will be king?

David's record of family relationships, including the raising and training of his sons, is not a pleasant story (2 Sam. 11 – 20). Further, there has been not even a hint as to his successor. It would seem that David's negligence in the family included not preparing one. While *very old* indicates time for significant transition to the next generation,[6] the account of David's weakening condition points to impending death with uncertainty as to whether anything can be expected. Coverings do not keep him warm and a young woman does not arouse him. That Abishag is to *lie in your bosom* (NRSV) is to be read in the context of a court where the king has a number of

---

[6] The phrase is used elsewhere of Abraham (Gen. 24:1) and Joshua (Josh. 13:1; 23:1).

wives and concubines (2 Sam. 5:13; 15:16),[7] but the phrase also echoes Nathan's description of the ewe lamb who used to 'lie in the bosom' of the poor owner, a parable concerning Uriah's wife, Bathsheba (2 Sam. 12:3; cf. 12:8). Before Bathsheba appears later in the chapter, we are reminded of the event that brought her to the court. David may be the king chosen by God, he may have had great victories and been 'a man after the LORD's heart' (1 Sam. 13:14; Acts 13:22), but he was also a person of moral failure and now physical infirmity. Biblical narrative never glosses over human weakness and sin: God works in and through imperfect people, and, as we will see, in and through human machinations and conflict.

The writer may be suggesting more by opening the book on David's deathbed. Leithart describes well two possibilities, the rest of Kings illustrating both:

> Does this foreshadow the eventual death of the Davidic monarchy and of Israel, thrown into the grave of exile? Or does 1 – 2 Kings *begin* at a deathbed to show that history moves on after death, to suggest a hope for resurrection?[8]

Early readers are experiencing the death of exile, but just as the book will go on to speak of Yahweh's gracious involvement after David's death, so there is hope after Israel's. God is consistent in character, so the telling of his actions in the past gives confidence for the future. That Kings is now part of the Law, Prophets and Writings[9] is an expression of the faith of the Jews[10] after exile; that it is included in the Christian canon of the Old and New Testaments points to its foreshadowing of the God who raises from the dead. God's action in the death and resurrection of Jesus is a focusing of his deeds throughout history – he continues to bring life where death seems to be the end.

2. Adonijah acts (1:5–10)

A feature of national histories is that death, or impending death, of a current leader can be a time of violence and bloodshed, the result of family feuds and vendettas, of regional jealousies and personal

---

[7] Monson, pp. 11–12.

[8] Leithart, p. 30.

[9] The threefold division in the Hebrew Bible gave rise to the acronym *Tanakh* from the beginning letters of the Hebrew for each section: *Torah* ('Law, teaching'), *Nevi'im* ('Prophets') and *Kethuvim* ('Writings').

[10] It is common in English to speak of 'Jews' from the exile on (Hebrew *yĕhûdî*, Greek *Ioudaios*). 'Judaean' is used in some contexts.

ambitions. As we read through Kings we will meet instances of all. The opening chapter describes a 'particular history [that] is *an arena for God's purpose*... [with] the practice of politics that is calculating, manipulative, and at the brink of violence.'[11] The experience of suffering, violence and oppression often leads to asking, 'Where is God?' The biblical narrative is a reminder that God is in the midst, there working out his purposes. This does not make everything good, but God brings good (Rom. 8:28), seen most clearly in the human actions surrounding Christ's death.

Adonijah, although David's fourth born, is the oldest surviving son (2 Sam. 3:2–5). Amnon, the eldest, had been killed by Absalom, the third son, following the rape of his sister Tamar (2 Sam. 13:23–29), while Absalom in turn died during his revolt against David (2 Sam. 18:9–17). Nothing else is known of Kileab, the second, so he was probably dead. Adonijah may have believed the throne was rightfully his as the eldest, but in the ancient Near East 'primogeniture is not always the rule... In some cultures, brothers had priority over sons. In others it was up to the king to designate his successor, and in some cases the subjects had to consent.'[12] That David himself had been the youngest in his family continues a biblical pattern where the eldest does not have priority in God's purposes, but will this be so in the Davidic line?[13] Adonijah decides to take pre-emptive steps: he is not waiting for David either to designate a successor or to die. He may well have thought that David was now so ineffective that action was needed – and he was used to getting his own way. As had the older Absalom when he briefly seized power, Adonijah gets *chariots and horses ready, with fifty men to run ahead* (v. 5; 2 Sam. 15:1), and like Absalom he too was *very handsome* (v. 6; 2 Sam. 14:25) and invites others to a sacrificial meal (v. 9; 2 Sam. 15:11–12). The details of the people invited, including *all the royal officials of Judah,* and of those excluded, show that 'Adonijah turns to people who had been with David before he became king in Jerusalem... These are the conservative elements, the "old guard" in David's regime based in Hebron.'[14] The poignancy of the situation involving a family split is shown by the repetition of 'brother': he invited *all his brothers,* but *his brother Solomon* he did not invite.

David's success had been bringing together the tribes of Judah (south) and Israel (north), with Jerusalem in between as a neutral 'city of David' (2 Sam. 5). There his key personnel had come both

[11] Brueggemann, p. 20 (emphasis his).

[12] Walton, Matthews and Chavalas, p. 355.

[13] David, 1 Sam. 16:11–13: cf. Jacob, Gen. 25:26; Joseph, Gen. 37:5–11; Ephraim, Gen. 48:13–14, 20; Judah, Gen. 49:8–10.

[14] Seow, p. 18.

from the old Judahite core and from a wider background, including as priests both Abiathar and Zadok. Adonijah's actions show that it was David who held the whole together (compare the tensions evident in 2 Sam. 19:9 – 20:22). Although Adonijah's name ('Yahweh is my lord') spoke of Yahweh, the covenantal God of all the tribes to whom he is sacrificing animals, regional and tribal loyalty (and 'the old guard') take precedence in his thinking and actions.

Reading his divisive but calculated power-grabbing action in its broader context, along with comparison with Absalom, can lead us to reflect on personal attitudes and motivations in times of decision and response to change: what is the place of family and regional or national allegiances in comparison to belonging to Christ, in whom there is 'neither Jew nor Gentile, neither slave nor free, nor is there male and female, for you are all one in Christ Jesus' (Gal. 3:28)?

3. Nathan the prophet takes control (1:11–27)

It is not David or Solomon who respond to Adonijah's initiatives, but *Nathan the prophet,* the first of a succession of prophets in Kings. The book may be called Kings, but throughout prophets often take the lead. That in itself may challenge our own perceptions as to who are the 'history makers'.[15] Is it those with political power, commonly associated with military and economic might, or people who are open to the word of God and understand his purposes?

Previously Nathan had spoken face-to-face with David (2 Sam. 7:2; 12:1, 25) but now an indirect approach seems necessary. Further, there is no mention of direction from Yahweh. While Nathan's plan can seem to be shrewd manipulation, safeguarding his own position which is threatened by Adonijah's exclusion, it can also be read as what he sees as best for the kingdom based in Jerusalem and covering both Israel and Judah. Mixed motives are a feature of human behaviour, but it is through such that God works.

Nathan first enlists Bathsheba's involvement, focusing on the threat to hers and Solomon's life, and it is only after she approaches David that he enters to corroborate her story. Repetition is a pointer to importance: in a printed text bold or italic type can show emphasis, but in a text that is meant to be heard emphasis comes by repetition of details. The threefold description of the crisis of Adonijah's coup, with variation (vv. 11–14, 17–21, 24–27), brings to the fore David's inactivity regarding the promise to Bathsheba concerning Solomon. The earlier statement that David *had never rebuked* Adonijah (v. 6;

---

[15] A term introduced by W. Brueggemann in 'Making History', *The Other Side,* October 1986, pp. 21–25.

NRSV 'displeased') suggests that David's leniency would have let things go on, either because Adonijah was now his favourite or else he was too tired to act – to go against past patterns would require much effort. As with Nathan, Bathsheba's motivation and attitude are unclear. The only mention of Yahweh is in the context of David's oath.

Bathsheba, as the one to whom the promise was made, is to remind David and warn him of the consequences of failure to keep his word. Pointedly she says, *the eyes of all Israel are on you, to learn from you who will sit on the throne of my lord the king after him.* While Adonijah's focus is Judah, David is king of *all Israel*, and it is his responsibility to let the people know his choice of Solomon. Nathan's rebuke is indirect: he asks whether in fact David has designated Adonijah as successor, *without letting his servants know* (v. 27; note the twofold *your servant* in v. 26). As in approaching David after the murder of Uriah (2 Sam. 12), 'Nathan directly addresses the failure of the king without violating royal prerogative or arousing the anger of the king.'[16] Previously he had used a parable evoking response, here he challenges by asking for an answer to a question (vv. 24, 27).

The storytelling approaches a climax, its style maintaining hearers' interest (and that of later readers of a printed Bible). At the same time, in its portrayal of characters and relationships it provides a mirror reflecting light on other situations. We are confronted with the consequences of leadership that has become weak, lacking the heart to discipline favourites or confront cliques, but we also see a prophet who knows how to confront appropriately. Sometimes it is appropriate to challenge a person directly with statements reminding of past promises and present responsibilities. That can best be done when there is a personal relationship of trust or affection between the people involved: Bathsheba is able to warn of her own personal danger, and expect that the appeal will be heard. At other times effective use of questions is the best way to disarm and call for response, particularly in situations of power inequality. Questions mean the listener becomes active.

Asking questions was a common feature of Jesus' relating to people. Often, with his disciples, or people who came to him, they were educative, but were also effective in situations of antagonism.[17] Centuries earlier the Greek philosopher Socrates was renowned for his dialogical style, engaging his pupils, an approach counsellors

[16] Konkel, pp. 54–55.
[17] For example, disciples (Matt. 16:13–16, 26; 17:25; 18:12; 20:21–22); interested people (Matt. 8:7; 19:17; John 1:38); conflict (Matt. 9:4–5; 12:29; 19:4–5; 21:23–27; 22:41–45; John 10:32; 18:34).

and communicators are rediscovering, particularly in a postmodern world. Graham Johnston has written on the significance for preachers:

> 'In inductive preaching, you unroll your idea in such a way that listeners have to work to get it themselves.'[18] When a preacher actively engages the minds of listeners, not only is their attention captured, but they receive more thorough[ly] the joy of discovery.[19]

In the light of our passage we could add, 'or the pain of realising an unpleasant truth and its consequences.' Nathan knew what questions to ask to evoke response.

4. David makes Solomon king (1:28–40)

We noted above the varied use of 'king' in the chapter. All came together in v. 13: 'Go in to *King* David and say to him, "My lord the *king*, did you not swear to me your servant: 'Surely Solomon your son shall be *king* after me, and he will sit on my throne'? Why then has Adonijah *become king*?"' Repetition has highlighted the drama: will King David, old as he is, truly act as king and announce clearly to the people who will be king after him?

The answer is unmistakable as David makes an oath in the presence of Bathsheba. She who initially had been the object of David's lust, and whose husband had been a pawn to sacrifice, is now the recipient of the words that guaranteed her safety and the future of her son. By invoking again the name of *the* LORD, as he had done previously (vv. 13, 17), David affirms that as *king* he is subject to God. The addition, *[Yahweh] has delivered me out of every trouble*, is unexpected. It appears to be a recognition that in Bathsheba and Nathan's intervention Yahweh has stepped in to the current crisis, rescuing David, and Israel, from the trouble caused by his inactivity regarding Adonijah.

The key turning point (highlighted by verse 28 beginning a new section in Hebrew Bibles) comes with David giving orders: *King David* is now exercising royal power. Three key people are to be involved in the coronation: *Zadok the priest, Nathan the prophet and Benaiah son of Jehoida.* Zadok was first named as priest along with Abiathar in the list of royal officials after David had made Jerusalem his capital (2 Sam. 8:17) and the two are linked together

---

[18] Johnston is here quoting Fred Craddock.

[19] G. Johnston, *Preaching to a Postmodern World* (Grand Rapids: Baker; Leicester: Inter-Varsity Press, 2001), p. 152.

elsewhere (2 Sam. 15:24–29, 35; 17:15; 19:11; 20:25).[20] While Abiathar had been with David from early days (1 Sam. 22:20), separation from both David and Zadok came as he supported Adonijah (vv. 7, 19, 25). Benaiah, 'a valiant fighter' (2 Sam. 23:20–23), was officer in charge of the royal guard, *Kerethites and Pelethites* (v. 38), mercenaries originally from Crete and Philistia,[21] while Joab who sided with Adonijah was a son of David's sister (1 Chr. 2:15–16) and leader of the army (2 Sam. 8:16; 20:23). While Adonijah had key priestly and military support, only for Solomon was a *prophet* involved.

Adonijah had organized for himself a gathering outside the city, at a spring about 650 yards (600 m) south of the Gihon Spring, on the boundary of the territories of Judah and Benjamin where the Hinnom and Kidron valleys meet, and his entourage of chariots and runners was a symbol of power. Solomon however was to be crowned with ceremonies associated with royalty, riding on the royal mule (2 Sam. 18:9), a more expensive animal than a horse.[22] The ceremony was to take place at the *Gihon* Spring ('the Gusher'),[23] source of Jerusalem's water supply and just below the temple – and well within earshot of Adonijah's party. Solomon's support base is the leadership of Jerusalem, the city of David: he is to be *ruler over Israel and Judah* (v. 35).

The symbolic riding on *King David's mule* (v. 38) leads on to the prophecy of Zechariah 9:9 and its fulfilment in Jesus' entry into Jerusalem on Palm Sunday (Matt. 21:1–11 and parallels). Jesus is no usurper, but the one who has been designated 'son of David' (Luke 1:32). He is a ruler who welcomes all – rejected by elitist religious leaders (yet challenging their understanding[24]), he was acclaimed by the blind (Matt. 9:27; 20:30–31), a desperate Canaanite woman (Matt. 15:22) and by the followers and children on Palm Sunday (Matt. 21:9, 15).

The use of *ruler* (v. 35; *nāgîd*), as well as *king* (*melek*), is significant. A 'king' in the ancient Near East generally had absolute power, so *ruler* (NRSV, *prince*) is a reminder that it is Yahweh who is King, to whom the ruler/prince is accountable to do what is just and right.

[20] For further discussion on Zadok see D. W. Rooke, 'Zadok, Zadokites', *DOTHB*, pp. 1012–1016.

[21] Also 2 Sam. 15:18; 20:23; Walton, Matthews and Chavalas, pp. 344, 356; Monson, pp.14–15.

[22] Walton, Matthews and Chavalas, p. 356.

[23] As Gihon is the name of one of the rivers of Eden (Gen. 2:13), J. A. Davies, '"Discerning between Good and Evil": Solomon as a New Adam in 1 Kings', *Westminster Theological Journal* 73 (2011), pp. 39–58, sees this as one of several verbal associations between the Solomon narrative and Genesis 1 – 3. He observes also that Adonijah was at 'the Stone of Zoheleth', suggesting 'Serpent's Stone' (v. 9).

[24] Matt. 22:42–45.

'Ruler' occurs at significant turning points in the history of Israelite kingship: at the anointing of Saul (1 Sam. 9:16; 10:1); at the announcement that Saul's kingdom will not continue and that Yahweh would appoint another as 'ruler . . . because you have not kept the LORD's command' (1 Sam. 13:14), with reference to David (1 Sam. 25:30; 2 Sam. 5:2; 6:21; 7:8); after Solomon, regarding Jeroboam, the first ruler of the northern kingdom of Israel (1 Kgs 14:7; 16:2); and in relation to Hezekiah, after the fall of the northern kingdom (2 Kgs 20:5). Kings has frequent reminders that kings of Israel and Judah are to obey God, the first being David's charge to Solomon (2:2–4). 'While the *melek* "sees his power from Yahweh as susceptible to his own arbitrary manipulation", the *nagid* is "no more than the willing subject of the divine monarch". Kings in Israel do not cease to be "prince" (*nagid*) in Yahweh's eyes.'[25]

Both Zadok and Nathan *anoint* Solomon *king* (vv. 34, 45), while Benaiah adds his commitment to both David and Solomon (vv. 36–37). The ceremony is accompanied by joyous, ground-shaking shouts of loyalty from *all the people* (vv. 39–40). Something of the exuberant acclamation has been captured by George Frideric Handel in an anthem composed for the coronation in 1727 of George II of Great Britain, and sung at every British coronation service since, accompanied by the brilliance of the trumpets, with oboes and bassoon prominent – Handel's equivalents of the *trumpet* and *pipes*. Based on verses 38–40, the anthem's words, 'And all the people rejoic'd and said: "God save the King, long live the King, may the King live for ever"' are appropriate prayerful expressions of loyalty in many modern nations, without identifying the nation as the continuation of Israel and Judah.

The contemporary challenge is how appropriately to express publically and nationally that all, leaders and people, are subject to God. This was straightforward for Israel, at least in ritual if not in life, as it can be for an established church-state relationship, as in England. So there a coronation is a religious service, with an anointing by the Archbishop of Canterbury. While in the USA there is constitutional separation of church and state, the inauguration of the President includes prayers by religious leaders. Similarly, in Australia parliamentary sessions open with the Lord's Prayer. Political discussion in Britain and the USA from the seventeenth century spoke of 'the sovereignty of the people', although since 1954 the USA Pledge of Allegiance includes 'one nation under God' – the people themselves

---

[25] J. G. McConville, *God and Earthly Power: An Old Testament Political Theology, Genesis – Kings* (London: T.&T. Clark, 2006), p. 137, with quotes from D. F. Murray, *Divine Prerogative and Royal Pretension* (Sheffield: Sheffield Academic Press, 1998), p. 299.

are subjects. How this is worked out in multi-faith contexts, whether Christians are a majority or minority, is a larger question than can be covered here. In all contexts followers of Christ are given the clear injunction to pray 'for kings and all those in authority', with which is associated 'that we may live peaceful and quiet lives in all godliness and holiness' and that God 'wants all people to be saved' (1 Tim. 2:1–4). To join, like the people at Solomon's coronation, in loyal prayer for leaders is to affirm God's intention that they fulfil his gracious, saving, just purposes for all people. Leaders, for their part, are to recognize that their rights are limited, for all human beings are 'in the image of God'[26] and as such only God can claim full allegiance (Gen. 1:26; Matt. 22:15–21 and parallels).

5. The end of Adonijah's *coup d'état* (1:41–53)

Adonijah hears the joyous shouting and assumes that Jonathan brings *good news.*[27] In describing Jonathan as *a worthy man*, Adonijah is probably hoping to have him on his side, after all Jonathan's father is *Abiathar the priest*. Years earlier however Jonathan had been loyal to David during Absalom's rebellion (2 Sam. 15:36) and now pointedly speaks of *our lord King David* as he recounts what happened. He adds new details (vv. 46–48) of the actual accession to the throne, of *the royal officials* (NRSV: *king's servants*) who *congratulate our lord King David* – we can observe the repeated terms of allegiance. (Adonijah had invited only officials who were 'men of Judah' [v. 9].) David may be weak, *on his bed* (v. 47), but Jonathan's report culminates in the worship given by David, praising *the LORD, the God of Israel,* again with the inclusive 'Israel'. Yahweh who delivers 'out of every trouble' (v. 29) has enabled David to see this deliverance, with a secure successor.

The passage ends with a reversal of the coup as Adonijah is not killed, as he feared, but is given the option of living as a loyal subject, as he is told to *go to your home*. (This is short-lived, see 2:13–25.) 'All's well that ends well' is a popular saying, but it has been a tortuous route to David's decisive action, Solomon's accession and safety for Adonijah as a loyal subject. David has seen Yahweh's action in the process and so gives thanks.

The mirror of the narrative may help us see God's hand in messy situations we are (or have been, or will be) involved in, whether due to our own inactivity or wrongdoing or the scheming and

---

[26] The OT has democratized the prevalent ancient Near Eastern ascribing of this term only to kings (G. J. Wenham, *Genesis 1–15* [Waco: Word, 1987], pp. 30–31).

[27] The LXX has the verb *euangelizō*, used in the NT for announcing the good news of Christ.

self-centred injustice of others. The narrative however continues. The peaceful resolution is only temporary – a common experience known by all! Solomon's rule will fall short of God's requirements, our circumstances will change, but Yahweh is still present as the one who *delivers out of every trouble*. David can rejoice that God *has allowed my eyes to see a successor on my throne today*. A thousand years later, Paul could celebrate the message of God's wisdom that

> none of the rulers of this age understood it, for if they had, they would not have crucified the Lord of glory . . . :

> 'What no eye has seen,
>   what no ear has heard,
> and what no human mind has conceived' –
>   the things God has prepared for those who love him –

> these are the things God has revealed to us by his Spirit.[28]

David may 'see a successor' but by the Spirit we are able to see the mystery of Christ crucified, the one 'greater than Solomon' (Matt. 12:42; Luke 11:31). We can look forward to seeing more of the glory that is to come, 'at the renewal of all things, when the Son of Man sits on his glorious throne' (Matt. 19:28).

6. David's last words to Solomon (2:1–12)

'Last words' from key people are a feature of biblical narrative, looking to the future: Jacob (Gen. 49:1–28) and Moses (Deut. 33) gave blessings, while Joshua (Josh. 24:1–28) and Samuel (1 Sam. 12) challenged the whole people at times of transition. David's words are spoken to Solomon alone, but again they present directions for the future.

Two disparate components are juxtaposed. The first is similar to previous leaders' 'last words', with promises of Yahweh linked with human response and so relevant for all future generations (vv. 2–4). Starkly different is the second with no mention of God, its practical advice being of the kind that could be replicated in similar contexts through to today (vv. 5–12). Both aim to secure the continuity of the Davidic dynasty, but they reflect two sides of David's character, and the character of many leaders since, a combination of sincere piety and pragmatic calculating politics.

---

[28] 1 Cor. 2:8–10, including an adaptation of Isa. 64:4.

a. Strength in obedience (2:1–4)

Be strong echoes Yahweh's words to Joshua (Josh. 1:7, 9). Depending on our own cultural experiences varied images come to mind as to what is involved in 'strong leadership'.[29] What kinds of advice might flow from those images? It is likely that what follows here, as also for Joshua, is unexpected: *observe what the LORD your God requires* – strength and courage are required to *walk in obedience to him* (NRSV, 'in his ways'). Significantly, temptations that Jesus faced were in the area of leadership and whether he would walk in the ways of his Father. Satan tempted him to use his power for his own material comfort and to follow an alternative, and easier, route to rule over the 'kingdoms of the world' (Matt. 4:1–10). The later words to Peter, 'Get behind me, Satan!' come after Peter rebukes Jesus for saying he was to suffer, die and be raised – for Peter (as for Satan) the path to being 'the Christ', the anointed King, avoids the cross. Pointedly Jesus goes on to say that the path for followers is also the way of the cross (Matt. 16:13–28). Christ's 'strength', showing compassion, mercy and love of enemies, was regarded as weakness in a context of the Roman Empire. There, success came through military and economic might, associated with arrogance and ruthlessness, and insensitivity to the needs of others, especially the weak and powerless. In subtle ways, from various sources, pressure can come to put the comfort and security of oneself or one's group to the fore, taking short cuts to what is seen as a 'good' end. God however does not leave us to our own resources: his Spirit is promised as enabling power (Acts 1:8; Rom. 8), so, to David's injunction to *be strong*, Paul can add 'in the Lord and in his mighty power' (Eph. 6:10).

David continued in his charge to state the result of walking in Yahweh's ways: *so that you may prosper in all you do and wherever you go* (v. 3). Another suitable translation of *hiśkîl*, instead of 'prosper', is 'be successful' (NLT; as in NIV Josh. 1:7–8). All societies and cultures tell stories of 'success', with today's mass media bombarding with images. That is one reason why the Gospel narrative of Jesus Christ has to be heard repeatedly, to saturate our minds with the greatest 'success' story of all. At the end of the Sermon on the Mount Jesus himself compares the person 'who hears these words of mine and puts them into practice' with the wise man who built his house on the rock, so remaining firm in the turmoil of life (Matt. 7:24–27). The way of Christ alone leads to lasting success.

---

[29] Leadership values will be explored further in discussing choices faced by Rehoboam (1 Kgs 12).

Another alternative translation of *hiśkîl*, 'understand' or 'gain insight', was adopted in the LXX translation made in the second century BC.[30] In Hebrew 'the form *hiśkîl* refers both to the "deed" and to the "consequence of the deed," i.e., both to the state of being prudent and to the success deriving from such prudence.'[31] In the garden of Eden the woman saw that the tree was desirable for 'gaining wisdom' (the same verb): the temptation was to gain understanding and resultant success independently of obeying God. It is not only that one is 'wise' and so acts appropriately but it is in the following of God's ways that wisdom is gained; 'hearing' and 'doing' belong together.

So that links 'success, prosperity, understanding' as the result God desires for those who are already his people. Blessings come with and flow out of obedience, acting in accordance with the way we have been created, not only as humans but as those to whom Paul says, 'By grace you have been saved through faith; . . . created in Christ Jesus for good works, which God prepared beforehand, that we should *walk* in them' (Eph. 2:8–10, RSV). C. S. Lewis, in a much-quoted sermon preached in 1941, helpfully compared two kinds of rewards, depending on whether there is a 'necessary connection': 'Money is not the natural reward of love . . . but marriage is the proper reward for a real lover . . . An enjoyment of Greek poetry is certainly a proper, and not a mercenary, reward for learning Greek.' The key is that 'the proper rewards are not simply tacked on to the activity for which they are given, but are the activity itself in consummation'.[32]

This first injunction to Solomon is later repeated to him by Yahweh in similar words before, during and after the building of the temple (3:11; 6:11–13; 9:4–5). From the beginning we are given a lens through which to look at the whole narrative. Solomon's reign will exhibit many commonly-accepted elements of success and prosperity, admired exuberantly by the Queen of Sheba (10:6–9). Readers however know that these did not last and that beneath the surface prosperity much was rotten. There is only one way to genuine and lasting success: to *walk* in Yahweh's ways is the path to the blessings God wishes to give.

b. Pre-emptive action (2:5–12)

Turning from verses 1–4 to verses 5–9 is like listening to a sermon on Sunday that honours God and is uplifting, but finding difficulty

---

[30] The same Greek translation is in Deut. 29:9; Josh. 1:7–8; 1 Sam. 18:14–15.

[31] K. Koenen, '*śākal*', *TDOT*, vol. 14, p. 122.

[32] 'Weight of Glory' in C. S. Lewis, *Transposition and Other Addresses* (London: Geoffrey Bles, 1949), and *The Weight of Glory and Other Addresses*, intro. and ed., W. Hooper (New York: Macmillan, 1980).

in applying it to the relationships and situations of Monday – and sometimes the attempt is given up as impossible. As we read this component of David's advice to Solomon the bare narrated facts are straightforward, but evaluation is contentious. Here is life in the raw, when all characters involved are less than perfect.

The book of Samuel has shown a David who is capable of brutal removal of those who endanger his plans: he planned a massacre of Nabal and his household (1 Sam. 25) and cold-bloodedly ordered Uriah's murder (2 Sam. 11:14–25). More legitimately he was an admired warrior, attracting the loyalty of many (1 Sam. 18:5; 22:1–2). Quite differently, a peacemaking character is widely portrayed in his refusal to act against Saul, 'Yahweh's anointed' (1 Sam. 24, 26) and in his gracious reconciliation with those who rebelled or fought against him,[33] and he grieves over Absalom's death (2 Sam. 18:33). Noticeable is his frequent willingness to leave it to Yahweh to act.[34] The two characteristics are brought together in 1 Samuel 24 – 26: two accounts of his sparing Saul frame the Nabal encounter.[35] Nabal's insolent treatment of David's men led to angry plans to destroy Nabal and his household, prevented only by the wise intervention of Abigail to whom David says, 'May you be blessed for your good judgment and for keeping me from bloodshed this day and from avenging myself with my own hands' (1 Sam. 25:33). David recognizes the avenging side of his character that is to be controlled.

It comes as a surprise at the end of David's life to see the over-turning of his previous peacemaking actions. *Joab is a son of Zeruiah*, David's sister, as are Abishai and Asahel (1 Chr. 2:15–16). David's relationship with the three over decades has been tumultuous, with Joab as David's army commander, apart from a brief period after Absalom's death when David appointed Amasa (2 Sam. 19:13).[36] The brothers show loyalty, but their violent actions exasperate David, threatening his conciliatory approaches ('What does this have to do with you, you sons of Zeruiah?', 2 Sam. 16:10; 19:22). It is easy to

[33] Abner, commander of Saul's army, 2 Sam. 2:8; 3:6–21; Amasa, Absalom's army commander, 2 Sam. 17:25; 19:13; Shimei who cursed him, 2 Sam. 16:5–14; 19:16–23.
[34] 1 Sam. 24:12; 25:33, 39; 2 Sam. 3:39; 15:25–26; 16:12.
[35] R. P. Gordon, 'David's Rise and Saul's Demise: Narrative Analogy in 1 Samuel 24 – 26', *Tyndale Bulletin* 31 (1980), pp. 37–64. D. M. Gunn, *The Story of David: Genre and Interpretation* (Sheffield: JSOT, 1978) analyses the intertwining in 1 and 2 Samuel of David as king (political sphere) and as man (private sphere, husband and father), with incidents of 'giving' and 'grasping' in both. David proves to be most successful when his action is attuned to giving.
[36] Immediately prior to this Joab bluntly confronted David for 'humiliating' his army in his long grieving over Absalom (2 Sam. 19:1–8) and subsequently Joab treacherously killed Amasa (2 Sam. 20:8–10).

imagine Joab, a skilful but hawkish military commander, being frustrated at David's refusal to press home victory, and so taking the initiative himself and killing opponents. At the same time Joab as the loyal commander implemented David's strategy that led to Uriah's death (2 Sam. 11:14–25). Perhaps disappointment in David was a factor in his supporting Adonijah's failed coup (1:7). Now David tells Solomon to deal with Joab: he cites both an incident thirty-three years previously when the leaders of Israel came to make peace with David and acclaim him as king (2 Sam. 3:22–38) and a more recent incident, in which Joab treacherously killed Amasa, Absalom's former commander who had replaced Joab as David's commander (2 Sam. 20:4–10). What is surprising is that 'hitherto, David has apparently never felt compelled to take any action he is now contemplating'.[37] No longer does he leave it to Yahweh to act. We are left to wonder whether David became too tired to think of continuing peacemaking, an example of compassion fatigue, or now sees that policy as a mistake that cannot be continued.

A similar change of attitude happens with *Shimei son of Gera, the Benjaminite*. David remembers his first encounter with Shimei, 'from the same clan as Saul's family', who was continually 'cursing . . . and throwing stones at him and showering him with dirt' as David was fleeing from Jerusalem after Absalom's conspiracy. Abishai, one of the sons of Zeruiah, had wanted to kill Shimei but David said, 'Leave him alone' (2 Sam. 16:5–13). Upon Absalom's death, David sought peace with all who had rebelled, and so when Shimei came seeking clemency, despite Abishai again asserting that Shimei should be put to death, David acts as 'king' and says, '"You shall not die." And the king promised him on oath' (2 Sam. 19:16–23). The next mention of Shimei is his non-involvement (as a Benjaminite) in Adonijah's coup (1:8), and so there is no sign of disloyalty to David. Again, we wonder why David is now vindictive. His direction to Solomon fulfils the letter of his oath, but not its spirit. Previously it was non-Israelite enemies who David defeated, but with people of Israel and Judah, members of God's people, he worked for reconciliation and peace. Now he is advising the death of individual Israelites.

In between directions regarding Joab and Shimei is the positive treatment of the family of *Barzillai of Gilead*. At the time of Absalom's revolt, after David established a camp across the Jordan, Barzillai and others provided material needs for David's company (2 Sam. 17:27–29). Later Barzillai declined David's invitation to go to Jerusalem, with David promising provision, but sent his servant Kinham (possibly a son; 2 Sam. 19:34–40). David is under no

---

[37] Provan, p. 33.

obligation, but the generosity is to continue. Again the question, why is this action included here?[38]

One likely interpretation is that David, as throughout his reign, is concerned for the future of the united kingdom of Israel and Judah. He had endeavoured all his life to keep the peace, to govern fairly for all, and the conciliatory moves had that goal. The account following David's return as king after Absalom's revolt points however to ongoing tensions between north and south (2 Sam. 19:41 – 20:22), and Adonijah's failed coup had its support amongst Judahites only. Possibly David's age and inactivity caused old tensions to come to the surface. If David found controlling Joab difficult, how much more would Solomon? Shimei as a Benjaminite may also have been seen as a potential threat to unity. Did David regret his oath? 'Certainly David does have personal revenge on his mind. But killing Shimei also lets the populace know that pro-Saul, anti-David sentiments will not be tolerated.'[39] On the other hand, the family of Barzillai from across the Jordan has potential for ongoing support if there were difficulties.

David's words and Solomon's implementation will mean that the 'kingdom was now established in Solomon's hands' (v. 46). The juxtaposition of verses 1–4 and verses 5–9 could thus be read as an endorsement of the king's 'employing the sword against evildoers'.[40] There are however pointers to a deliberate contrast. Twice Solomon is told to use his *wisdom* to remove potential enemies (vv. 6, 9), yet later when Yahweh appears to Solomon and grants 'wisdom' his commendation is that Solomon has *not* 'asked for the death of your enemies but for discernment in administering justice' (3:11)! The pragmatic wisdom of David and Solomon is contrasted with that given by Yahweh.[41] When that is put alongside David's rejection of longstanding conciliatory approaches regarding Joab – he has not forgotten events from thirty years ago – and his casuistic treatment of the oath made concerning Shimei (and subsequently Solomon's own methods), it is rather more likely that the biblical writer wants us first to hear the charge to 'walk' in the Lord's ways, as that is how one best follows the example of David, the way to true insight

---

[38] The only other biblical references to Barzillai are in the parallel genealogies of Ezra 2:61 and Neh. 7:63. Amongst the priests who returned after the exile were descendants of 'Barzillai (a man who had married a daughter of Barzillai the Gileadite and was called by that name)'.

[39] House, p. 98.

[40] So Leithart, p. 37.

[41] R. P. Gordon, 'A House Divided: Wisdom in Old Testament Narrative Traditions', in *Wisdom in Ancient Israel*, edited J. Day, R. P. Gordon and H. G. M. Williamson (Cambridge: Cambridge University Press, 1995), pp. 94–105. Gordon notes also that the last recorded activity of Solomon is seeking the life of his rival Jeroboam (11:40).

and success, while at the same time reminding readers who have seen the capture and exile of the Davidic king that in some ways the dynasty was flawed at the beginning. 'There is a private side to David and Solomon that contrasts with the oft-stated portrayal of David's righteousness and fidelity to YHWH and Solomon's reputation for great wisdom.'[42]

Reading the final words of David can highlight the universality of flawed personalities: we are 'sinners saved by grace'. It can help us reflect on how easily human behaviour can mix together a desire to serve God and walk his ways and a 'doing what is best' using methods that fall short of the way of Christ.

7. Solomon removes threats to his power (2:13–46)

After David's death Solomon's *rule was firmly established* (v. 12), the block of verses 13–46 telling how that happened (note v. 46b). The story in chapter 3 of Solomon receiving 'wisdom' from God is well-known, but first the writer tells how Solomon initially exercises *his* 'wisdom' (vv. 6, 9): he seeks to ensure the security of his own position by removing or neutralizing likely trouble makers.

David had not mentioned Adonijah (a reminder of his previous failure to discipline, 1:6), but that is the first threat to remove (vv. 13–25). Solomon had promised safety if Adonijah 'shows himself to be worthy' (1:52–53), but now Adonijah acts recklessly, even audaciously. He claims that *all Israel looked to me as their king* (v. 15), when in reality his approach had been Judah-centric. As a result of a spoilt upbringing, did he suffer from self-delusion as to his own importance, the rightful heir whose expectations have been thwarted, a person still to be reckoned with because of his standing as the oldest son and support from Abiathar and Joab? Certainly these factors are to the fore in Solomon's response (v. 22). How much harm is done when people who have been used to power as 'second in charge' feel thwarted when someone else, whom they believe less qualified, is appointed as next leader? Paul's words about pride are not spoken lightly: 'For by the grace given me I say to every one of you: Do not think of yourself more highly than you ought, but rather think of yourself with sober judgment, in accordance with the faith God has distributed to each of you' (Rom. 12:3).

Asking to have *Abishag* as wife was more than desiring a very 'beautiful young woman' (1:2–3). It was a blatant claim to status, symbolic of the power of the throne. Earlier examples are recounted during the reign of David: after Saul's death Ish-Bosheth saw in

---

[42] Sweeney, p. 61.

Abner's relationship with Rizpah, Saul's concubine, a challenge to his own reign (2 Sam. 3:6–11); the prophet Nathan spoke of how Yahweh had given Saul's 'house and wives' to David (2 Sam. 12:8); and Absalom's rebellious assumption of kingship was demonstrated in his publicly taking David's concubines (2 Sam. 16:20–22). Wives and concubines were associated with royal power, commonly linked with political and economic alliances.[43]

The central person in the account is *Bathsheba, Solomon's mother* (v. 13), the inclusion of the relationship having twofold significance. First is a contrast with Adonijah's being *the son of Haggith,* and not of Bathsheba, crucial in David's choice of Solomon; but secondly, the king's mother had special status, although her specific functions are unclear (also vv. 19, 22).[44] In her dialogue with Adonijah and then with Solomon, it is possible to see a naivety: her words throughout, whether to Adonijah or to Solomon, appear supportive, accepting at face value Adonijah's affirmation that he comes *peacefully.* Her own fears concerning Adonijah during the attempted coup, her involvement with Nathan in the stratagem for approaching David (1:11–21), and readers' awareness of previous incidents involving concubines suggest rather that her failure to say anything negative to Adonijah is a shrewd response to his own deluded naivety. She knows her son and how he is likely to respond. There is irony in Adonijah's *he will not refuse you* (v. 17) and Solomon's *I will not refuse you* (v. 20): Solomon's angry response, refusing her spoken request, is best seen as doing what she actually wanted, removing a threat, not only to her son but herself (cf. 1:21). 'Bathsheba's well conceived strategies with both David and Solomon succeed in winning the kingdom for Solomon.'[45] If a question is thus raised concerning Bathsheba's honesty, there is correspondingly doubt regarding Solomon's integrity: he does not keep his word made even to his mother. Solomon acts swiftly, strengthening his resolve with an oath in the name of Yahweh who *has founded a dynasty for me as he promised* (v. 24), not the last time a ruler has used religious justification for a brutal action protecting his own position. His action has been debated. The fifth century Theodoret of Cyr commented that

[43] Walton, Matthews and Chavalas, pp. 357–358; J. D. Levenson and B. Halpern, 'The Political Import of David's Marriages', *Journal of Biblical Literature* 99 (1980), pp. 11–28.

[44] One component of the regnal formula for kings of Judah is the naming of the king's mother (e.g., 14:21; 15:10). An overview of possible functions is given in A. Salvesen, 'Royal Family', *DOTHB*, pp. 845–850.

[45] R. L. Cohn, 'Characterization in Kings', in Lemaire and Halpern, p. 96. House lists several disparate interpretations of Bathsheba's words and actions, arguing that she 'makes prudent moves in the halls of power' (p. 100).

Some people blame Solomon because he killed his brother. Now the ways of life of people are different . . . An apostolic or prophetic perfection cannot be expected from Solomon, but only those actions that are appropriate to kings . . . He was concerned for the tranquillity of his kingdom.[46]

Here is recognition of variety of situations in which people act, yet it can readily be used to excuse behaviour as 'what everyone in my position does'. David's initial words as given by the narrator (vv. 3–4) do not allow for differing standards. As in Solomon's words, seeing God at work in bringing about a present position can easily slide to regarding as approved by God one's own subsequent actions to protect that position. Much of Kings will tell of human efforts to ensure security that ultimately fail because of lack of trust in Yahweh that means following his ways.

The next recipient of Solomon's attention is a close supporter of Adonijah, *Abiathar the priest* (v. 26; see 1:7). At least Solomon recognized faithful service, especially at the time of David's flight from Absalom and subsequent return.[47] Solomon banishes him to his home in Anathoth, a rural village 3 miles (5 km) northeast of Jerusalem.[48] To the writer of Kings this is more than a political act, demoting a disloyal priest: it is the first of many instances where Yahweh's word spoken through a prophet is fulfilled (1 Sam. 2:27–36; 3:11–14).[49]

Understandably *Joab* fears for his own life (v. 28). His relationships with David and Solomon have been mixed: he may have *conspired with Adonijah* but he had been loyal to David at the time of *Absalom*'s conspiracy, although he had killed Absalom contrary to David's orders (2 Sam. 18:5, 9–15). Like Adonijah (1:50) he clings to the *horns of the altar*, claiming sanctuary.[50] The relevant law however provides sanctuary only for unintentional killing, and continues 'but if anyone schemes and kills someone deliberately, that person is to be taken from my altar and put to death' (Exod. 21:14). Thus Solomon explicitly justifies the order to kill Joab. Readers will be aware of the irony in his words, *so clear me and my whole family of the guilt of the innocent blood that Joab shed* (v. 31): Joab himself had carried out David's orders to see that the innocent

---

[46] Cited in Conti, p. 11.

[47] 1 Sam. 23:6–12; 2 Sam. 15:24–29, 35–36; 20:25.

[48] Centuries later Jeremiah was identified as 'one of the priests at Anathoth' (Jer. 1:1).

[49] See introduction, pp. 30–32.

[50] 'Monumental stone altars some six feet square, with horns at the corners large enough for one to cling to and thus be immovable' have been excavated at Beersheba and Dan; W. G. Dever, 'Archaeology and the Question of Sources in Kings', in Lemaire and Halpern, p. 535.

blood of Uriah was shed (2 Sam. 11:14–25)! This undercuts Solomon's 'claiming to occupy the high moral ground', contrasting *Joab and his descendants* with *David and his descendants, his house and his throne* (v. 33). 'But *Realpolitik* is, of course, often dressed up in respectable clothing and presented as something better than it is.'[51]

With three potentially disloyal leaders removed – political, religious and military – the loyal *Benaiah* and *Zadok* are confirmed in their positions (v. 35). A potential threat remains in *Shimei* (v. 36), the only other person David specified (vv. 8–9). At first Shimei abides by Solomon's strict conditions: being confined to Jerusalem prevents him stirring up dissension, since to *cross the Kidron Valley,* going eastward, would be the route to his home territory of Benjamin. His breaking the conditions three years later seems to be unpremeditated and excusable, since the direction is westward and there is no hint that he sought to stir up any trouble (vv. 39–40). Solomon however sees an opportunity to act, another exercise of his 'wisdom'.

In reviewing this chapter, how are David and Solomon walking in the ways of Yahweh? We have noted questions concerning words and actions. Where is God? Yahweh is mentioned only in David's reference to Yahweh's earlier promise (v. 4), in Solomon's words justifying Adonijah's death on the ground of that promise (vv. 23–25), in Solomon's invoking Yahweh's 'repaying' in the cases of Joab (v. 32) and Shimei (v. 44), and his seeing Yahweh as giving 'peace' (v. 33). There is a messy mix of God's promises and justice being used to support human action, all moving towards the goal that *the kingdom was now established in Solomons hand* (v. 46). The only positive reference appears to be in the narrator's alerting to the fulfilment of prophecy (vv. 26–29).

David's charge, *Be strong . . . observe what the* LORD *your God requires* (vv. 2–3), has no outworking in the rest of chapter 2. Solomon's 'strength' has been evident in decisive removal of fellow Israelites who are seen to be a threat. It is left to the subsequent narrative for the charge to be renewed, by Yahweh himself. At this stage, his 'wisdom' is hardly informed by 'the ways of Yahweh' but by the last instructions of his father.

For readers today, the account provides a mirror to human behaviour in complex situations of power and leadership, with examples of questionable 'wisdom'. No direct answers are given, but we are helped to see below the surface and consider human motives and rationalizations, to see the ease with which God's words can be used to serve human ends. In fulfilment of prophecy we also see God at work in the midst of all.

[51] Provan, p. 39.

1 Kings 3:1–3
2. Setting the scene

Prior to continuing the narrative, the writer describes the setting with themes that will be threaded through following chapters. Ominously we read first that *Solomon made an alliance with Pharaoh king of Egypt and married his daughter. He brought her to the City of David* (v. 1). The writer has no interest in political or economic factors: his concern is elsewhere.[1] Kings has many links with Deuteronomy, where Egypt is the oppressor from which Yahweh rescued the people. The king is forbidden to encourage trade with Egypt (Deut. 17:16), but now the arch-enemy has become a key ally. Later we read that Pharaoh had captured Gezer, a Canaanite city strategically placed on the way from Jerusalem to the coast, and 'gave it as a wedding gift to his daughter' (9:16): 'a stunning role reversal . . . an Israelite king who depends upon the Egyptian Pharaoh to complete the conquest of Israel'.[2] More importantly the wording emphasizes the marriage relationship,[3] 'Pharaoh's daughter' occurring in significant places in the Solomon narrative (7:8; 9:16, 24; 11:1; see further below). Solomon's marrying of foreign wives who influence him is not only in the latter part of his life (as if often said by preachers, commenting on 11:1–2), but is brought to our attention at the beginning.

A description follows of *sacrificing at the high places* (v. 2); there *he burned incense*. While worship at 'high places' is later repeatedly

---

[1] K. A. Kitchen, 'External Textual Sources – Egypt', in Lemaire and Halpern, pp. 374–375, discusses historical background and economic benefits.

[2] Sweeney, p. 79. The Israelites had not been able to 'dislodge the Canaanites living in Gezer' (Josh. 16:10; Judg. 1:29). The alliance did not last: towards the end of Solomon's life rebellious Jeroboam found refuge with Shishak of Egypt (11:40), and early in the reign of Solomon's son, Rehoboam, Shishak attacked Jerusalem and carried off temple treasures (14:25–28).

[3] *hithattēn* is not the usual verb for making an alliance (cf. NIV, NLT) but refers to marriage relationships, hence NRSV 'made a marriage alliance' (similarly NJPSV).

denounced,[4] here a reason is given, *a temple had not yet been built for the Name of the* LORD (v. 2). It is likely that the mention of Solomon going to *the high places* (v. 3), introduced by *except*, is to be read negatively, although *the most important high place* at *Gibeon* was in a different category as there Yahweh appears to him (vv. 4–5).[5] Verse 2 points forward to Solomon's building of the temple, a major part of the following narrative, with the change of location affirmed in the summary after the temple is built, that Solomon 'sacrificed burnt offerings and fellowship offerings on the altar he had built for the LORD, burning incense before the LORD along with them' (9:25).

Finally we are told how *Solomon showed his love for the* LORD *by walking according to the instructions given him by his father David* (v. 3). 'Love' for Yahweh is frequent in Deuteronomy,[6] expressing commitment and loyalty, while 'the instructions' are most likely Yahweh's statutes[7] that David kept (as in 3:14; 11:33–38), and that David had enjoined on Solomon (2:2–4). This is a repeated motif, with increasing warning to Solomon and ultimate judgment (v. 14; 6:11–13; 9:1–9; 11:9–11, 33, 38). Solomon's failure, and its early seeds, may be alluded to in the unusual choice of 'love' (*'āhab*), the word occurring in Kings only in the Solomon narrative[8] and only here in all of Samuel-Kings of 'loving Yahweh'. While 'love' is here directed to Yahweh, 'it reappears twice in 1 Kings 11 (vv. 1 and 2) in relation to Solomon's other great "loves" – the foreign women, of whom Pharaoh's daughter is one . . . how fragile this love [of God] did indeed turn out to be.'[9]

1. Seeing chapters 1 – 11 as a whole

It is easy to read biblical narrative as disconnected units, missing the overall plot and purpose. With maybe a detour or two, modern stories often go in a straight line to the climax and resolution, although good literature and drama exhibit more subtlety. Hebrew literature often arranges material with 'frames' (that is, similar subject matter or language at the beginning and end of a whole unit), with

---

[4] 12:31–32; 13:2, 33; 14:23; etc.

[5] The Chronicles account of Solomon's reign is more positive throughout. It does not mention 'high places' and explains that the 'Tent of Meeting' was at Gibeon (2 Chr. 1:3).

[6] Twenty three times; Deut. 6:5; 10:12; 11:1, 13, 22; etc.

[7] 'Instructions' translates *ḥuqqôt*, often translated 'decrees' or 'statutes'.

[8] Also 5:1 [MT 15], Hiram's 'friendship' with Solomon; 10:9, Yahweh's 'love'; 11:1–2, Solomon's 'love' for foreign wives. In 2 Sam. 12:24, where Solomon is named, we read 'Yahweh loved him'.

[9] Provan, p. 46.

blocks inside the frame parallel to each other, sometimes in a reversing pattern around a central block. A chiastic structure[10] encourages readers to see the whole, with connections between individual blocks. Like jewels in a setting, the placing of individual jewels influences the beauty of the whole, with light reflected from one jewel affecting how others are seen. The centre or turning-point is often important. This is the case for 1 Kings 1 – 11.

The diagram shows the balancing components, with reversing or chiastic structure around a centre:[11]

A   Davidic succession and removal of opposition (chs 1 – 2)
    B.1 Pharaoh's daughter; no temple for sacrifices and incense (3:1–3)
                      Yahweh appears to Solomon (3:4–15)
    B.2 Wisdom used for the benefit of others (3:16 – 4:34)
        C   Preparations for building the temple (ch. 5)
             (Hiram, vv. 1–12; conscripted labour, vv. 13–18)
        D   Building the temple (ch. 6)
                 Yahweh speaks to Solomon (6:11–13)
            E   Solomon's own palace; Pharaoh's daughter (7:1–12)
        D′   Temple furnishings, the Ark and dedication (7:13 – 8:66)
        C′ After building the temple (9:1–23)
                 Yahweh appears again to Solomon (9:1–9)
            (Hiram, vv. 11–14; conscripted labour, vv. 15–23)
    B.1′ Pharaoh's daughter; temple for sacrifices and incense (9:24–25)
    B.2′ Wisdom and riches used for his own benefit (9:26 – 11:13)
                    Yahweh speaks to Solomon (11:1–13)
A′ Solomonic succession and Yahweh brings opposition (11:14–40)

The repeated mention of 'Pharaoh's daughter' at key points, one being in the centre of the description of the temple building, is one pointer to structure. Two other instances are in 3:1–3 and 9:24–25, the similar

---

[10] 'Chiastic', with the noun 'chiasm', is named for the crossover pattern from the Greek letter *chi*, χ. With any number of components, the pattern may be A–B–C–C′–B′–A′ or, with a centre, A–B–C–B′–A′. See P. Overland, 'Chiasm', *DOTWPW*, pp. 54–57.

[11] Detailed argument, interacting with and building on other proposals, is in my 'Pharaoh's Daughter, Solomon's Palace and the Temple: Another Look at the Structure of 1 Kings 1–11', *Journal for the Study of the Old Testament* 27 (2003), pp. 355–369.

subject matter with key words providing a frame.[12] Outside that is another frame: chapters 1 – 2, narrating the removal of opposition to Solomon, is balanced by 11:14–40, describing adversaries and the break-up of the kingdom (by God!). Further 9:26 – 11:13 is a block describing how Solomon falls short of being the ideal king of Deuteronomy 17:14–20.

Many commentators note the large central block on the temple (chs. 6 – 8; D – D'), but often overlook that mention of 'Pharaoh's daughter' is in the middle (E). An added contrast between Yahweh's intention and Solomon's alliance with Egypt is evident: the temple building account (D) begins with a date, 'in the four hundred and eightieth year after the Israelites came out of Egypt' (6:1), balanced in D' by the narrator's mention of the exodus in 8:9 and Solomon's fourfold mention, as an *inclusio* in his 'blessing' (8:16, 21) and at the climax of the dedication (8:51, 53). Yahweh's deliverance from Egypt is acknowledged in praise and prayer, but the marriage alliance and prominence given to 'Pharaoh's daughter' show failure to live out the deliverance in political life, the compromise having consequences in syncretism (ch. 11).

Exiles in Babylon would later look back with longing to the golden era of Solomon and the building of the temple. His wisdom is honoured not only in Kings but also in Proverbs. Now as the story of Solomon is told the Kings writer seems to be saying:

'Yes, the temple was magnificent' (giving much detail);
'Yes, Solomon's wealth and wisdom were unsurpassed' (telling the stories with wonderment), *'but . . . '*

He is encouraging us to look beneath the surface. There is something more important than wisdom and wealth alone, even than building magnificent worship structures. If that is all, destruction will follow. His strategic placing of Yahweh's words and his description of what Solomon does with his wisdom and wealth are a mirror for later readers. Solomon's activities embraced the whole gamut that would be expected for a ruler, but while he succeeded in building a temple and led in active worship, he failed to obey Yahweh's words in other areas of life. The narrative enables us to reflect on what is good and God-honouring and on what leads nevertheless to failure. 'What good will it be for someone to gain the whole world, yet forfeit their soul?' (Matt.16:26).

[12] 'Pharaoh's daughter', 'city of David', 'built', 'house', 'wall/(supporting) terraces', 'offering sacrifices', 'burning incense'. 9:24 starts in Hebrew with the emphatic *'ak* ('surely, but'; cf. NRSV), often omitted in EVV, and 'Pharaoh's daughter' has an emphatic position before the verb. Taken together with the balancing of content between ch. 5 and 9:1–23, this shows that 9:24 is set apart from the preceding.

1 Kings 3:4 – 4:34
3. Receiving and demonstrating wisdom

1. Solomon receives wisdom from Yahweh (3:4–15)

Throughout the ancient Near East rulers were patrons of the worship of the national/city god, building temples and providing the wherewithal for maintenance of worship structures, including sacrifices. Throughout Kings we read of kings of Israel and Judah fulfilling similar roles and here Solomon is generous as he brings *burnt offerings* at the main centre, *Gibeon*, about 6 miles (9 km) north of Jerusalem (v. 4).[1] There *the LORD appeared to Solomon*, the first instance of an appearance direct to Solomon (cf. to Samuel, 1 Sam. 3:21).[2]

Given the preceding mention of the *temple* (twice, vv. 1–2) and *sacrifices* and *offerings* repeatedly (vv. 2–4), and the juxtaposition in Yahweh's earlier words to David concerning David's son that Yahweh would 'establish his kingdom' (as in 2:46) and 'he is the one who will build a house for my Name' (2 Sam. 7:11–12), it might be expected that the vision would concern the temple. That however is not the case. As with David, Yahweh has other priorities – a continuing and necessary reminder to later readers.

---

[1] This, its parallel, 2 Chr. 1:2–6, and 1 Chr. 16:39; 21:29 (in David's reign) are the only references to Gibeon as an important cultic centre; see S. S. Brooks, 'Gibeon', *DOTHB*, pp. 332–332.

[2] J. A. Davies ('"Discerning between Good and Evil": Solomon as a New Adam in 1 Kings', *Westminster Theological Journal* 73 [2011], pp. 39–58), sees Solomon being given 'the mantle of a prophet'. He notes that no prophet is mentioned during Solomon's reign (that is framed by references to Nathan in ch. 1 and Ahijah in 11:29–39), that Solomon 'sees' and also 'the word of Yahweh came to Solomon' (6:11), said elsewhere of prophetic messages. Yet 'he is a flawed individual, who does not put into practice . . . the message he proclaims' (e.g., in the prayer of ch. 8).

Opportunity is given to Solomon to articulate *his* priorities: *Ask for whatever you want me to give you* (v. 5). The story of Aladdin's lamp is known by many from childhood and in modern adult life gurus abound who affirm the power of the mind to 'make your dreams come true'. Sadly what is desired is often for personal power and happiness. Christians, however, can turn to similar words of Christ, 'Ask and it will be given to you' (Matt. 7:7), importantly within the Sermon on the Mount, so asking for what is needed as we 'seek first [God's] kingdom and his righteousness', following the way of Christ.

Solomon begins by affirming Yahweh's *great kindness* to David (twice in v. 6; NRSV 'great and steadfast love'[3]), culminating in *a son* succeeding him. He is right in that affirmation, but to say that the *kindness* was *because* of David's being *faithful* and *righteous* reflects a common distortion. While blessings and obedience are associated, Yahweh's promise in initiating the covenant with David was that, even if David's successor 'does wrong', there may be punishment but he would *not* remove his 'love' (2 Sam. 7:14–15). Subsequently there are several places where Yahweh's favourable action is linked with the promise to David in spite of current behaviour.[4]

Solomon describes himself as *a little child*, expressing his inexperience,[5] and he knows that the people are not 'mine' but those whom *you have chosen*, they are *your people* (vv. 7–9). Similarly in the dedicatory prayer for the temple Solomon repeatedly refers to 'your people Israel' (seven times in 8:30–52). As king he is a vice-regent, accountable to God whose people they are, an important perspective for any person in leadership. His first priority is the well-being of God's people. As king he will make many decisions, in governing and in implementing justice (unlike many nations today there is no separation of powers between legislative, executive and judicial bodies). For these he will need *a discerning heart to govern your people and to distinguish between right and wrong* (v. 9). LXX translated literally, 'a heart to hear': the gift of being open and able to listen to others is to be highly prized in leadership.

Solomon's words summarize important dimensions of leadership, not least in the Christian church. Foremost is the steadfast love and

---

[3] *hesed* is a rich word, variously rendered in English as 'covenant love, steadfast love, kindness, loving-kindness, mercy, faithfulness'. As a term of commitment to a relationship, it goes beyond legal requirements and is often used in contexts of coming to aid. See D. A. Baer and R. P. Gordon, '(H2874) *ḥāsad* II, etc.', *NIDOTTE* 2, pp.211–218. In 2 Sam. 7:15 NIV has 'love'.

[4] E.g., 1 Kgs 11:32; 15:4–5; 2 Kgs 8:19; 19:34; 20:5–6; 21:7–8.

[5] On the basis of chronological details he already had a son, Rehoboam (11:42; 14:21). The same description is used of the Edomite Hadad when he fled to Egypt (11:17).

kindness of God who brings a person to leadership, building on all that has gone before in the life of the person and of the group. A corollary is that the group is not 'mine', but 'yours'. It may be natural to use a phrase such as 'my church' as shorthand for 'God's church in which he has made me an under-shepherd' (see 1 Peter 5:2–4), but the longer phrase is needed to resist subtle temptations of power.

Yahweh's granting of the request is of major importance in Solomon's life. In the context of Solomon's own words and of surrounding chapters, a number of features stand out. That Solomon has not asked for *long life or wealth for yourself* (v. 11) is matched by the promise of *both wealth and honour – so that in your lifetime you will have no equal among kings* (v. 13); but *long life* is conditional, *if you walk in my ways* (v. 14 NRSV; cf. 2:3). Between these statements is God's unexpected inclusion that Solomon has not *asked for the death of your enemies* (v. 11) and the addition to *discerning heart* of the adjective, *wise* (v. 12). In the preceding chapter Solomon has used his 'wisdom' to bring about the death of his enemies!

The contrast between two 'wisdoms', that encouraged by David and that given by Yahweh, is evident. The former focused on self-protection, the latter on justice for all – the first example of such wisdom will be on behalf of a prostitute and her child (vv. 16–28). A thousand years later James asks the question, 'Who is wise and understanding among you?' and contrasts the wisdom that is 'earthly, unspiritual, demonic' with 'the wisdom that comes from heaven' that is 'first pure; then peace-loving, considerate, submissive, full of mercy and good fruit, impartial and sincere'. It is 'peacemakers who sow in peace [who] reap a harvest of righteousness' (Jas 3:13–18). Jesus' own words that 'wisdom is proved right by all her children' (Luke 7:35) is associated with his being welcomed by the common people. The way of Christ, exemplified in his own life, was to 'love your enemies' (Matt. 5:44), reinforced when Paul wrote to the church at Rome that 'as far as it depends on you, live at peace with everyone' leaving any avenging to God (Rom. 12:18–19).[6] When so many human plans are to remove enemies and troublemakers, it requires godly wisdom to know how to be a peace-maker. That way will always mean *walking* in the ways of Christ.

Part of Solomon's obedience is explicit as he returns to Jerusalem and there *stood before the ark of the Lord's covenant* (v. 15), the place where Moses placed the 'tablets' on which the Decalogue was written (Deut. 10:1–5). There he submits to Yahweh's rule, accepting his own obligations. Now he *sacrificed* there, the place of future worship.

[6] See further discussion on the purge of Jehu (2 Kgs 9 – 10).

2. Wisdom used to benefit the powerless (3:16–28)

After the granting of wisdom, the next narrated action of Solomon is exercising justice for people who are socially on the fringe and most disadvantaged. True wisdom combines worship of Yahweh alone and the doing of what is just and right for all. The narrative highlights social distinctions by using no names, only status terms, 'woman', 'prostitute' and 'king'. At that time, as universally today, a woman became a prostitute due to slavery or to social and economic necessity. A woman without a protecting male (husband, father, brother, brother-in-law, or adult son) was in a precarious situation. This is one reason why God 'sustains the fatherless and the widow' (Ps. 146:9).

The story is well-known and its power is due in part to the literary style. 'It combines vivid character contrasts and poignant human interest with the intellectual challenges of a mystery story . . . Dialogue dominates . . . In the first half we listen with the king . . . In the second half, the king's shocking command drives the action of the story. We hear it along with the women.'[7]

Initially the women are identified as *prostitutes*, but thereafter they are *women*: they are not defined by their activity. One speaks and we warm to her story (vv. 17–21), but it becomes an example of 'a law-suit where the first to speak seems right, until someone comes forward and cross-examines' (Prov. 18:17). If the woman was asleep how did she know how the baby died? Could her story be fabricated? The other woman simply denies the claim (v. 22). We have been told there are no independent witnesses (v. 18): *no one* translates the Hebrew 'no stranger', most likely referring to the absence of any clients since they were without family members. There is an irresolvable impasse, the equal balance between the two statements evident in what the women say and then in Solomon's almost verbatim repetition (vv. 22–23).

The surprise is Solomon's dramatic order – the only action in the whole narrative is *they brought a sword for the king* (v. 24). The 'sword' that has killed enemies (2:8, 32) is, with God's 'wisdom', being used in the cause of justice. Solomon's unexpected words show his decision relates solely to the *living baby* and *his mother*, 'the bonding relationship between a mother and her child, which he presumes to be present by virtue of the fact that the case has come before him'.[8] Without witnesses there is no basis for cross-examination and a modern court might reject the plaintiff's case since there is no proof.

[7] Walsh, pp. 78–79.
[8] Konkel, p. 82.

In ancient Near Eastern systems . . . recourse could be had to supra-rational means . . . evidentiary oath (also found in Kings: 1 Kgs 18:10–11) and the oracle (Exod 22:8) . . . The king does not, however, resort to supra-rational methods. It is his wisdom, divinely granted but nonetheless using human means, which replaces sacral investigative procedures . . . The divine gift of wisdom enables Solomon to make judgments normally reserved for the divine court.[9]

The text however leaves readers with one uncertainty. Solomon says, 'Give to *her* the living child' (so Hebrew). We can rightly assume that Solomon is pointing to the woman who spoke first in verse 26, as he uses her words; NLT's 'give him to the woman who wants him to live' making this explicit. NRSV and NIV's *to the first woman* goes further as it tends to point readers to the woman who spoke in verses 17–21, whereas this is not specified: we do not know the true circumstances of the other baby's death. Focus is on the wisdom of Solomon who sees beyond two arguing prostitutes to a mother and her child. With such an unexpected response by Solomon it is no wonder *all Israel . . . held the king in awe* (v. 28).

The description ends with a key phrase: *because they saw that he had wisdom from God to administer justice*. It was affirmed throughout the ancient Near East that a king's central role was to do justice. For example, around 1700 BC Hammurabi, king of Babylon, wrote that the supreme gods 'named me to promote the welfare of the people . . . to cause justice to prevail in the land, to destroy the wicked and the evil, that the strong might not oppress the weak'.[10] It is said of David that he 'reigned over all Israel, doing what was just and right for all his people' (2 Sam. 8:15), while 'doing what is just and right' is consistently given elsewhere as the king's major responsibility (e.g., 1 Kgs 10:9; Ps. 72:1–3; Jer. 22:3, 15; Ezek. 45:9).[11] This chapter has shown that to so act requires 'God's wisdom', a point made also in the opening purpose statement of the book of Proverbs: 'for gaining wisdom . . . for . . . doing what is right and just and fair' (Prov. 1:2–3).

It is possible to administer 'justice' in a way that is heartless and socially discriminatory. Throughout history and across nations examples abound of legal processes that function for the benefit of those with power, whether of political connections, status, intellect

---

[9] R. Westbrook, 'Law in Kings', in Lemaire and Halpern, pp. 449–450.

[10] 'Code of Hammurabi', *ANET*, p. 164; *COS* 2.131, p. 336.

[11] M. Weinfeld, *Social Justice in Ancient Israel and in the Ancient Near East* (Jerusalem: Magnes; Minneapolis: Fortress, 1995), comprehensively analyses wide-ranging sources.

or wealth, with those who are on the fringes of society, the poor and powerless, often experiencing injustice that is perpetuated rather than corrected. The story of Solomon's wise exercise of justice has placed to the fore an example of not only hearing a case but also looking beyond social stereotypes and prejudices to the person: he sees beyond 'prostitute' to caring 'mother'. In Western society in the twenty-first century 'the wisdom of Solomon' is needed in the resolution of an increasing number of situations of conflict, especially family disputes involving the custody of children or division of property, one article using the title 'Splitting Babies'.[12] Whose interests are at heart in the dispute, the feuding parents or the child? Judges are called to administer laws, and so wisdom is needed in both framing laws and making judicial decisions so that compassionate discernment is exercised. While 'wisdom' is needed for all in positions of leadership – and so we are to pray for 'kings and all those in authority' (1 Tim. 2:2) – it is relevant for daily life as we make our judgments concerning other people. Significantly in Israel the 'doing of what is right and just' is a responsibility of all, not only kings: God said of Abraham that he was to 'direct his children and his household after him to keep the way of the Lord by doing what is right and just' (Gen. 18:19), a basis for many prophetic proclamations.[13]

Sadly Solomon later in life, and kings after him, fell far short of the ideal, yet there is a message of hope. '"The days are coming", declares the Lord, "when I will raise up for David a righteous Branch, a King who will reign wisely and do what is just and right in the land"' (Jer. 23:5). In Jesus Christ we see the 'wise' King who was 'a friend of tax collectors and sinners' (Matt. 11:19), and who 'will proclaim justice to the nations' (Matt. 12:18). In all Christ is and does, above all on the cross, we see 'the wisdom of God' (1 Cor. 1:24).

3. Wisdom in ruling all Israel (4:1–28)

The statement is easily made, *King Solomon ruled over all Israel* (v. 1), but implementation is another matter. A governing body, be in a monarchy, aristocracy or democracy, whether secular or ecclesiastical, requires structure and supporting personnel, with associated costs. There are both internal and external relationships to consider and negotiate. The narrator now lists details of Solomon's administration, evidence of wisdom at work in a clear structure, with an intertwining of religious, political and economic aspects. As lists of administrative arrangements, palace provisions and ruler's abilities

---

[12] K. Walker, 'Splitting Babies: Religion making custody disputes even messier', *Christianity Today* (November 2009), p. 18.

[13] E.g., Isa. 5:7; 56:1; 58:2; Jer. 4:2; Ezek. 18:5; Amos 5:24; Mic. 6:8.

are known in both Egyptian and Mesopotamian records,[14] 'Solomon is being compared to other rulers in his efficiency, power, wealth, and wisdom.'[15] At the same time details reveal seeds of future problems. Further, historical details peculiar to that context provide a comparison that can shine light on aspects of all rule and government.

a. Administering all Israel (4:1–20)

First is a list of key officials, the names pointing to a time on in Solomon's reign.[16] Structurally the first four names are set apart, probably as the closest officials, an inner cabinet. *Azariah* is *priest*, the position later designated as 'high priest'.[17] By now both *Zadok* and *Abiathar* (v. 4) are old (David had reigned for forty years and the temple was finished in Solomon's eleventh year).[18] Two *secretaries* (or 'scribes') follow: 'since they controlled the written material flowing both in and out, they could serve as royal "chief of staff" and confidant of their employer.'[19] The traditional 'writing' background is seen still in 'Secretary' appearing in titles of senior government and business positions, for example, in the UK and USA, as well as of people in lesser positions who 'write' on behalf of someone else. While *Jehoshaphat* is described as *recorder*, a person in this role was part of the high level delegation sent to the Assyrian field leader by Hezekiah (2 Kgs 18:18) and the office is known in surrounding nations as a 'herald'.[20]

The next group, all linked by *and*,[21] appear at a second level. *Benaiah* played a key role from the beginning of Solomon's reign (2:25, 35). Two new developments are seen in the offices of *Azariah son of Nathan*, to be *in charge of the district governors* (v. 5), a group to be named below, with their 'districts' (vv. 7–19), and of *Adoniram* who was to be *in charge of forced labour* (v. 6), a term that speaks of work imposed by the state. This was commonly forced on subject

---

[14] Walton, Matthews and Chavalas, pp. 359–361.

[15] Seow, p. 49. A. Lemaire, 'Wisdom in Solomonic historiography', in *Wisdom in Ancient Israel*, edited J. Day, R. P. Gordon and H. G. M. Williamson (Cambridge: Cambridge University Press, 1995), pp. 110–113, summarizes eight themes in 1 Kgs 3 – 11 'shared by the historiography of the ancient Near East at the start of the first millennium'.

[16] See N. S. Fox, 'State Officials', *DOTHB*, pp. 941–947, and his major work, *In the Service of the King: Officialdom in Ancient Israel and Judah* (Cincinnati: Hebrew Union College Press, 2000).

[17] 2 Kgs 12:10 [MT 11] 'the great priest'; 25:18: 'the head priest'.

[18] Cf. 1 Chr. 6:8–10; 'son' is used often in Hebrew in the sense of 'descendant'.

[19] D. W. Baker, 'Scribes and Schools'. *DOTHB*, p. 885.

[20] Sweeney, pp. 84–85.

[21] The conjunction *wĕ* 'and' is lacking in the listing of the first three offices, setting them apart.

peoples, e.g., the Israelites in Egypt (Exod. 1:11) or peoples defeated by Israel (Deut. 20:11; Josh. 16:10; 17:13). New under Solomon was that he 'conscripted labourers from all Israel' (5:13–14).

The division of *all Israel* into twelve districts[22] was for taxation purposes, each month in turn a district supplied *provisions for the king and the royal household* (v. 7), including *barley and straw for the . . . horses* (vv. 27–28). It has been long noted that MT has no mention of Judah, all the areas described being in Israel. In verse 19 MT refers to the 'land of Gilead, the land of Sihon . . . and there was one officer in the land' (my translation), but the last phrase in LXX is 'and one officer in Judah' (followed by NLT)[23]. It is likely however that LXX is a later correction, since the person is unnamed and if over Judah would be the thirteenth officer. A more likely solution is that the summary phrase refers to Adoniram having overall charge.[24] What is striking is that, apart from the dubious LXX, there is no mention of Judah, and twelve regions are named for twelve months. It looks as if Solomon treats the people of Israel differently from his own tribe of Judah, unless, as is possible, places mentioned in verse 10 are in Judah.[25] Indisputable is that the boundaries are not determined by traditional tribal areas, at times breaking up such areas but including newly conquered land, and the number 'twelve' relates to months of the year rather than the number of tribes. Further, the people overseeing the tax collection are not local elders but related to the court, a common policy in most nations throughout history.[26] We can see a (deliberate?) breaking down of old tribal loyalties, with no sense of representative leadership. It is one nation, with a central monarchical government, with criterion for division being provision for the needs of the burgeoning ruling structures.[27] Samuel had warned the people that having a king would have costs in terms of people and provisions (1 Sam. 8:11–18); now they were experiencing the reality.

---

[22] 'District' is added for sense: there is no specific word in Hebrew, although areas are defined.

[23] Also DeVries, pp. 64–65, 72.

[24] The word translated 'governor' in v. 19 (*nĕṣîb*) differs in form from 'district governors' in vv. 5, 7, 27 (*niṣṣābîm*); Provan, p. 57; compare Wiseman, p. 93.

[25] Provan, p. 56, but contrary is Sweeney, pp. 90–91.

[26] *Ben-Abinadab* and *Ahimaaz* were sons-in-law of Solomon (vv. 11, 15) and *Baana* (v. 16) is *son of Hushai*, David's 'friend' (2 Sam. 15:37). *Benaiah*, previously in charge of David's guard, was promoted (v. 4; 2 Sam. 8:18; 20:24), *Azariah* and *Zabud*'s father may be the same as Nathan the prophet (v. 5), while *Jehoshaphat* continued his role under David (v. 3; 2 Sam. 8:16; 20:24), as did *Adoniram/Adoram* (v. 6; 2 Sam. 20:24).

[27] *NBD*, p. 1117, Brueggemann, p. 60 and J. Bimson et al., eds, *The New Bible Atlas* (Leicester: Inter-Varsity Press, 1985), p. 43, have maps. Sweeney, pp. 88–95, provides lengthy analysis of the place names, but Provan, pp. 55–56, has some different interpretations.

At this stage all works well: the population grows, with *as numerous as the sand on the seashore* (v. 20) a fulfilment of the words to Abraham (Gen. 22:17; also Gen. 32:12). The phrase has also described enemies amassed against Israel (Josh. 11:4; Judg. 7:12; 1 Sam. 13:5): Israel was conscious of being surrounded by larger nations and so the statement is a measure of both standing and security for *Judah and Israel*. In a setting where the people *ate . . . drank* and *were happy* there can be easier acceptance of new government structures and taxation, including conscription of labour for national projects. Later in Solomon's reign precisely these changes were to be the cause of revolt. The literary balancing of 3:12 – 4:34 and 9:26 – 11:13 (B.2 and B.2' in the diagram on p. 61) is a way of contrasting the initial implementation and later excesses.

As groups grow in size – nations, churches, voluntary organizations, businesses – change is necessary in administrative structures, generally including increase in 'paid positions' and financial arrangements. Similar to clothes worn in the growth from infancy to adulthood, shape changes as well as size. What 'worked' when the group was small is no longer effective, what could be handled on a voluntary and part-time basis is no longer the case. Leaders today can 'marvel at the complexity of a kingdom requiring such a sophisticated system',[28] and pray for wisdom like Solomon in devising appropriate structures for unity and growth, and yet there can be resistance as people feel something is lost. Change is most welcomed when it is seen that 'we are all in this together' and when the result is good for all. In the early church 'when the number of disciples was increasing' a divisive issue was resolved by new structures that respected all: no group was regarded as less important, leaders were representative and the result was continuing growth (Acts 6:1–7).

Later developments in Solomon's reign (see on 9:26 – 11:13) will be a reminder that new structures bring temptations as well as strengths: they are not immune from being used for personal benefit at a disproportionate cost to the wider community. For the present, however, all the people are *very contented* (v. 20, NLT).

b. Wealth from the nations (4:21–28)

A major factor contributing to the nation's prosperity was *tribute* from the nations that David had subdued (another fulfilment of the promise to Abraham, Gen. 15:18), so lessening the burden on the twelve districts while enhancing Solomon's position. Wealth from client-states and colonies has been enjoyed by various nations

[28] Nelson, p. 40.

throughout history, sometimes to the detriment of the subservient peoples – and here we are not told the impact on tributaries. Peace throughout Solomon's whole reign was another contributing factor as battles have their economic cost. Again all the people benefit: from *Dan to Beersheba* (north to south) they were able to live *in safety*, feeling secure (v. 25). The idyllic picture of each person being *under their own vine and . . . fig-tree* is a common description of both enjoyment and security.[29] 'The vine and fig provided some shade as well as fruit and enjoying them indicated some long-term prospects – each took several years to become productive.'[30]

While contrast is obvious between the simple enjoyment of rural life and the luxuries of the palace establishment, with its *finest flour* and both *stall-fed* and *pasture-fed* cattle, with a variety of game (vv. 22–23), there is no evidence of oppression. It was universal practice for royalty to live at a different standard, as Samuel had reminded those wanting a king (1 Sam. 8:11–18), and the people were content and enjoyed *peace*. Nevertheless an ominous detail is the number of horses (v. 26), for apart from 'display chariots'[31] the main value was in warfare. While on the one hand a measure of Solomon's wealth, the equivalent today of amassing extensive and expensive military equipment, Deuteronomic legislation for the king affirmed that he 'must not acquire great numbers of horses for himself' (Deut. 17:16; see further on 1 Kgs 10:26). The concern is hinted at by the writer in referring again to *horses*: the ongoing defence budget was paid for in *their quotas of barley and straw* (v. 28). Israel indeed now has a king 'such as all the other nations have' (1 Sam. 8:5), but as subsequent history shows, that did not guarantee their survival. Solomon learned from those around and his wise administration provided peace and contentment for the people – for the present. Could he have foreseen how radically different would be the ways of 'one greater than Solomon' (Matt. 12:42), who 'though he was rich, yet for your sake became poor, so that you through his poverty might become rich' (2 Cor. 8:9)? The impression is that Solomon's approach was that of 'trickle down', while Christ shares his wealth with all, and in a lasting and deeper way says, 'Peace I leave with you; my peace I give you. I do not give to you as the world gives. Do not let your hearts be troubled and do not be afraid' (John 14:27).

---

[29] 2 Kgs 18:31; Mic. 4:4; Zech. 3:10; contrast Isa. 34:4; Joel 1:12; Hab. 3:17; Hag. 2:19.

[30] Walton, Matthews and Chavalas, p. 360.

[31] D. M. Master, 'Institutions of Trade in 1 and 2 Kings', in Lemaire and Halpern, p. 508.

4. God's wisdom for all of life (4:29–34)

'Wisdom' has a long and wide tradition in Egypt and Mesopotamia, whether in the court and scribal schools, or in the oral culture of the village and family and desert communities.[32] The writer seeks to assure us that the wisdom *God gave Solomon* surpasses all, comprehensively listing both possible contenders to superiority[33] and his versatile range. People came to *listen* (v. 34; 10:1–13) to him speak *proverbs*, a diversity of generally short sayings or aphorisms, with 'comparisons' drawn from life (e.g., Prov. 10:1 – 22:16),[34] *songs* (cf. Song 1:1), and encyclopaedic knowledge of the natural world.[35]

The chapter has told of Solomon's administrative structures and rich provision for the court, but it is because of his God-given *wisdom* that *from all nations people came to listen . . . , sent by all the kings of the world* (v. 34). In the whole narrative from Joshua to Kings the Hebrew root *ḥkm* ('wise', etc.) occurs once in Judges (5:29), six times in 2 Samuel 13 – 24, but twenty-one times in 1 Kings 2 – 11 and nowhere else in those books. Chapter 3 told of the wisdom God gave, different from wisdom Solomon had previously exercised in removing enemies, and ended with 'all Israel' recognizing that 'he had wisdom from God to administer justice' (3:28). Neither 'wisdom' nor 'God' has been mentioned in 4:1–28, but in verses 29–34 the narrator has returned to the wisdom *God gave*, with *wisdom* or 'wise' used eight times. In verse 29 two phrases are linked with *wisdom*, both alluding to Solomon's initial request: he had asked for a hearing heart so that he might 'discern' (3:9); now it is said God gave him *very great insight* (the noun is related to the verb 'discern') and *breadth of understanding* ('breadth of heart'), an unusual phrase referring 'to an expansive capacity to comprehend all knowledge . . . largeness of vision and perspective beyond self-interest'.[36] God has given Solomon more than he asked for, and his *wisdom* has attracted the nations.

Given the overall relationship between Kings and Deuteronomy, a comparison is where Deuteronomy speaks of the nations being

---

[32] R. Hess, 'Wisdom Sources', *DOTWPW*, pp. 894–901, surveys wide influences on Israel.

[33] The named individuals in v. 31 are listed in 1 Chr. 2:6 as sons of Zerah, son of Judah and Tamar (Gen 38:30). Psalm 89 is ascribed to Ethan the Ezrahite.

[34] *māšāl* means 'likeness'. 'As today, wisdom can often be the result of research and gathering of information' (Walton, Matthews and Chavalas, p. 361). There is scope for collecting, adapting and fresh composition; see K. A. Kitchen, 'Proverbs 2: Ancient Near Eastern Background', *DOTWPW*, pp. 552–566.

[35] Collections of scientific listing of plants and animals are known in the ancient Near East; Gray, pp. 145, 148.

[36] Brueggemann, p. 67.

attracted by 'wisdom' in a passage which also links with the concurrent injunction to Solomon to 'walk in my ways, keeping my statutes and commandments' (3:14, NRSV):

> See, I have taught you decrees and laws as the LORD my God commanded me, so that you may follow them in the land you are entering to take possession of it. Observe them carefully, for this will show your *wisdom and understanding to the nations*, who will hear about all these decrees and say, 'Surely this great nation is a *wise and understanding* people.' What other nation is so great as to have their gods near them the way the LORD our God is near us whenever we pray to him? And what other nation is so great as to have such righteous decrees and laws as this body of laws I am setting before you today? (Deut. 4:5–8; emphasis added)

Solomon is demonstrating much wisdom in diverse areas, but the question remains as to his, and our, showing wisdom among the nations by continually following God's ways. God's abundant gift to Solomon is a demonstration of James' words: 'If any of you lacks wisdom, you should ask God, who gives generously to all without finding fault' (Jas 1:5).

1 Kings 5:1 – 8:66
4. The temple – building and dedicating

Within the Solomon narrative (chs 1 – 11) forty per cent relates to the building and dedication of the temple (chs 4 – 8). Both the quantity and specifics, along with its central placing, seek to communicate a relevant message to hearers in exile who have recently seen the destruction of the four-hundred-year-old temple. There is a presentation of its grandeur and of Yahweh's blessing, together with indications of relativizing its importance. Included are statements concerning the relationship of the temple to God's presence and to his priorities of obedience, alongside material that at least raises questions regarding Solomon's motivations and values.

1. Preparations (5:1–18)

Unlike the tabernacle there are no divine instructions regarding architecture, whether design or materials. Solomon simply recalls Yahweh's permission given through the prophet Nathan to David (v. 5; see 2 Sam. 7:12–13). Opening details tell of provision of materials from *Hiram king of Tyre*, and of workers, whether supplied by Hiram and paid by Solomon or conscripted from Israel. Again we see contrast with the tabernacle: there we read of the people of Israel themselves contributing in generous abundance and of key Israelite artisans chosen by God and 'filled with the Spirit of God' (Exod. 31:1–11; 35:4 – 36:7). The permanent larger temple building Solomon wished to construct required materials and expertise not available within Israel. Some readers of this exposition will know of churches whose first building was a simple structure erected by volunteers and paid for by generous and sacrificial giving, but for whom a later, more elaborate building required resources, whether physical, financial or human, from outside the group. The biblical accounts of both tabernacle and temple refer to God giving 'wisdom' (*ḥokmāh* can include practical skills): Bezalel and all the artisans involved in the tabernacle received 'wisdom' (Exod. 31:3, 6; NIV, 'skill') while *the LORD gave Solomon wisdom, just as he had promised him* (v. 12), related to his continuing relationship with Hiram. A larger construction requires different God-given skills and we can be thankful to God for wisdom and skill given for large projects today, involving wider negotiations, diverse construction personnel and sourcing of finances.

a. Help from Hiram of Tyre (5:1–12)

Tyre, the major Phoenician port, around 50 miles (80 km) north of Jerusalem, was renowned as a commercial centre, wealthy through extensive trading activity around the Mediterranean coastlands and inland. Its main centre was on an island and easily defended ('fortified city', Josh. 19:29; 'fortress', 2 Sam. 24:7).[1] Its prosperity and influence increased under the reign of Hiram, whose alliance with David he now seeks to continue with Solomon.[2] A parallel is evident between Solomon's current request and Hiram's previous benevolence towards David soon after David became king: 'Hiram king of Tyre sent envoys to David, along with cedar logs and carpenters and stonemasons, and they built a palace for David' (2 Sam. 5:11). *bayit* ('house') is commonly translated 'palace' when referring to a king's residence and 'temple' for 'God's house' (as in vv. 3–5): Hiram had helped David build his 'house', now Solomon asks for assistance to build 'a house' *for the Name of the LORD my God* (v. 5). We are reminded of David's initial concern that he was 'living in a house [palace] of cedar, while the ark of God remains in a tent' (2 Sam. 7:2). Solomon initiates God-sanctioned plans to rectify the imbalance with a request that leads Hiram to describe Solomon as a *wise son* of David (v. 7). The language has another element of continuity with reference to David and *the LORD his God* (v. 3) shifting to *the LORD my God* (vv. 4–5; see also 2:3; 3:7): Solomon's commitment to Yahweh is firm. At this stage only one building, the *temple*, is in view, although 3:1 has already mentioned building 'his own house and

---

[1] A later description of Tyre's wealth-producing activities and confidence in her security is an oracle at the time of the fall of Jerusalem (Ezek. 27). The vivid language is taken up in the description of 'Babylon' in Rev. 18:9–20 which details material prosperity through commerce rather than military might.

[2] The phrase, *he had always been on friendly terms with* (v. 1), uses *'āhab*, sometimes translated 'love', known in treaty documents to refer to being an ally or loyal treaty partner (see v. 12). See also on 3:3, p. 60.

the house of the LORD' (NRSV), the order there raising questions as to Solomon's priorities (see further on 7:1, the next mention of Solomon's 'house').

After some negotiation, Hiram supplies the raw materials while Solomon pays for labour, both Hiram's men and Israelites. Payment to Hiram is by *providing food for my royal household* (v. 9), not the Phoenician workers, but the labour force remains joint (compare vv. 14, 18 with Hiram's request in v. 9). The provision (v. 11) was substantial: 'the annual payment amounted to a quarter less than the total Solomon received for his own court, but in different commodities (4:22–23)',[3] appropriate given Israel's solid agricultural base. It foreshadows the grandeur of the building where no expense is spared.

The narrative highlights Solomon's *wise* initiative and direction of the whole process (vv. 7, 12). While Hiram's approach provides the setting, action in the whole chapter leading to building is driven by verbs of which Solomon is the subject. Like any king in the ancient Near East he is to build a temple for the nation's God, although the writer is careful to speak of the 'house' as being not for Yahweh but for *the Name of the LORD*, 'a way of speaking about the presence [of Yahweh] without overcommitting Yahweh and compromising Yahweh's presence'.[4]

b. Conscripted labour (5:13–18)

The human resources are great. The work force was not voluntary but *conscripted* from each of the regions of *all Israel*, working in three month cycles of *one month* away in Lebanon and *two months* back home. To this were added *carriers* and *stonecutters* at some undefined *hills*, with their *foremen*. Skilled people came not only from Israel and Tyre but also from *Byblos* further north, for shoddy workmanship could not be tolerated. *High-grade stone* that had been carefully *dressed* (hewn squared and straight) was required. Further the timber included *cedar* from Lebanon (v. 8), famed throughout the ancient world for its strength and beauty, its height making it ideal for large structures.

The picture is of massive size, efficient organization and quality materials, fitting for a temple in Jerusalem where buildings expressing national identity are focused. While much is to be admired, there are community costs. The necessary social disruption during building can only be imagined: apart from family life, agricultural production had to continue for some years for livelihood and payment to

---

[3] Wiseman, p. 100.
[4] Brueggemann, p. 75.

Hiram's court (6:37–38). The sum of the figures given is around one-seventh of the 'eight hundred thousand' plus 'five hundred thousand' in David's census (2 Sam. 24:9). The twentieth century has witnessed mobilization during world wars, while at the micro-level many community projects, including church buildings, have involved people rearranging personal activities. Sacrifices and disruption are accepted for perceived benefit and common purpose, generally articulated by a leader whose vision and commitment inspire. Solomon provided the vision, but we do not know how willingly it was embraced by the general population. Not only was the temple a new direction for the Israelites, one of the changes associated with monarchy, but people differ in their response to change depending on both cultural background and personality.[5] Further, in all societies dramatic changes to forms of taxation (proportionate conscription can be seen in that way) are met with mixed reactions! Leadership requires decisions as to when to move forward, irrespective of likely opposition. The temple eventually became a valued focal point of religious life, but for the present an unspoken question remains: what will be the long-term effect of extensive conscription? That comes to the fore near the end of Solomon's reign.

Solomon has for the present acted 'wisely' in marshalling resources, both internal and external to the people of God. He is beginning a massive national project to provide a fitting 'temple for the Name of the LORD'. That the writer uses the word 'wise' (v. 12) points to commendable features in Solomon's project leadership that can be an inspiration to others. Sadly, later parts of the narrative will alert readers to how even 'wise' actions have dangers that can lead to ultimate failure. Part of wisdom is going forward aware of dynamic complexities.

This opening chapter on the 'temple' has already suggested issues that have continued in the Christian church from the beginning, with various resolutions: the function of buildings and relationship to God's presence and God's honour; comparison between the quality and appearance of secular residences and other edifices and that of church buildings; and ways in which 'created artefacts [including architecture] are expressions and, as expressions, promote the worldview of their creator, whether intentionally or not'.[6] Times of political, cultural or ecclesial change are often reflected in

---

[5] It is common to speak of a range from 'innovators' and 'early adopters' to 'never adopters', e.g., A. Malphurs, *Pouring New Wine into Old Wineskins* (Grand Rapids: Baker, 1993), p. 84. Malphurs analyses personality types but does not discuss cultural influences.

[6] P. M. Phillips, 'Rhetoric', in *Words and the Word*, edited by D. G. Firth and J. A. Grant (Leicester: Apollos, 2008), p. 243.

buildings, illustrated by the Emperor Constantine's building of the Church of St John Lateran in Rome after the Edict of Milan (313), the spate of cathedral building in medieval Europe, and varied architectural styles resulting from theological and ecclesiological differences after the Reformation. Religious buildings are more than provision of space for activities, as their shape, materials and style express beliefs and values of the builders. We will return to explore these matters at the conclusion of the whole section on the temple (the end of chapter 8).

2. Solomon builds the temple (6:1–38)

To Christian readers, it may appear that the details of chapters 6 – 8 have been included in the final form of Kings simply to provide Jewish exiles with a record of past glory. How can this inform Christian life and witness today? There are clues however that more is being said than 'this is what the temple was like in all its glory'. Details are presented in ways that highlight ongoing realities: events of the past are told in such a way as to inform the future.

a. Chronological perspective (6:1, 37–38)

Unlike chronological details elsewhere throughout Kings, which record length and comparative dating of kings' reigns with no more significance than delineating consecutive events, here is a statement that is more than chronological. The narrator mentions that *the Israelites came out of Egypt* before saying Solomon *began to build the temple of the Lord* (v. 1). The rest of Kings will describe how worship of Yahweh in the temple and confidence in the associated Davidic kingship were separated in both regal and popular attitudes from the lifestyle commensurate with being God's redeemed people, living in covenant relationship. From the start the writer places the temple within the wider context of Yahweh's covenant relationship with Israel, flowing from their deliverance from Egypt, a reminder flagged at significant places in the temple narrative (vv. 11–13; 8:9, 16, 21, 51, 53, 56–58). That wider context both explains the later destruction as resulting from the people's neglect of the covenant and provides hope, since Yahweh's delivering grace towards his people preceded, and so is independent of, the temple.

The specific dating of *the four hundred and eightieth year* (v. 1) has been given different interpretations. It appears often in debates concerning the date of the exodus, with those favouring a fifteenth century BC date treating it literally while others see it as equivalent to 12×40 years, i.e., twelve generations, compatible with a thirteenth century exodus.[7] There may well be a comparison with the period from the building of the temple to the time at the end of Kings, approximately 400 years, so that the building of the temple is near the mid-point between exodus and exile.[8] The number itself ensures association of exodus, temple, and probably exile. One cannot speak of temple apart from exodus, and the exile can only be understood in terms of how people looked at both temple and exodus. Such schematization of historical periods may be compared with Matthew's three periods of fourteen generations, with key turning points (Matt. 1:17): one cannot talk of Jesus Christ apart from his being 'son of David, son of Abraham'.

Another dating appears at the end of the chapter, with verses 37–38 resuming some of the details in verse 1 and bringing a completion. The dates provide a literary frame for the account of the building of the temple structure, concluding *the temple was finished in all its details according to its specifications* (v. 38). Chapter 7 however continues with more details, concluding *all the work King Solomon had done for the temple of the LORD was finished* (7:51). The chronological notes of verse 38 seem out of place (and are in a different location in LXX), yet their link with the following verse (7:1) proves to be significant as the seven and a half years to build the temple is immediately associated with thirteen years for the palace. They serve to shift attention from the temple to other buildings: 7:1–12 is placed in the centre of the temple narrative, a jarring insertion raising questions as to Solomon's attitudes and values (see below on 7:1–12, pp. 86–87).

The literary frame thus alerts readers: Solomon's building the temple is to be seen in light of the exodus and of his other activities. Building a temple – or today any other religious activity, including buildings – cannot be separated from the wider context of the whole of life lived in relationship with a redeeming, covenant-making God.

b. The temple exterior (6:2–10)

Building descriptions always vary – depending on the interests of speaker and hearers. Layout, materials and decoration all have their place, but selection will always be involved. The writer provides some broad details along with close attention to parts. The description of the temple exterior itself is brief, with no mention of location

---

[7] The latter view notes the common OT use of '40 years' as a schematic period, with a generation actually around twenty five years. LXX has 'four hundred and fortieth year', perhaps matching the eleven generations 'which intervened between Aaron and Zadok (I Chr. 5.29)' (Gray, p. 159). Others see '480' as resulting from calculations using years mentioned in Deuteronomy to 1 Kings (e.g., Sweeney, p. 108).

[8] Jones, pp. 162–63; Wiseman, p. 104; Konkel, pp. 136–37.

or orientation. While broad features are clear, the meaning of some architectural terms is problematic, and the way components fit together is at times debatable.[9]

First comes the big picture, the dimensions of a tripartite oblong structure, with a *portico* (*'ûlām*; NRSV: 'vestibule'), *main hall* (*hêkāl*; NRSV: 'nave') and *inner sanctuary* (*dĕbîr*; in v. 16 also named 'the holy of holies', i.e., *the Most Holy Place*). Similar structure and architectural features are known in temples from the era in Syria, that at 'Ain Dara being the largest, 125 ft (38 m) in length.'[10] With dimensions of 60 cubits length, 20 cubits wide and 30 cubits high (88 ft × 29 ft × 44 ft; 27 m × 9 m × 13.5 m) the area covered is four times that of the tabernacle (30 cubits × 10 cubits). The tripartite structure can be compared to the great hall and throne room in a royal palace, so symbolizing access to the divine presence in the divine palace. The king could go no further than to stand by the columns in the porch (2 Kgs 11:14; 23:3) while priests could enter the *main hall*, with more restricted entry to the *inner sanctuary*.

The cutting and dressing of stones off-site could be related to an earlier prohibition of the use of iron tools in constructing sacred buildings or altars (Deut. 27:5; Josh. 8:31) but may reflect a note of reverence.[11] What is known is that the stones were large (7:10):

> The temple was built to last . . . That it was built of massive stone walls signified the notion that Yahweh was to dwell there indefinitely . . . They encouraged those who saw them to rely more on the outward symbols of Yahweh's presence than on . . . the heartfelt loyalty to his covenant that his spokesmen continually demanded.[12]

c. An unexpected word from Yahweh (6:11–13)

An important message interrupts the narrative. In the midst of enjoying the description of the temple, remembering its grandeur, readers are jolted into recognizing something greater than the temple. Yahweh's words have a surprising twist: *As for this temple you are*

---

[9] Several commentaries and dictionary articles discuss details, including differences between MT and LXX and relationship to 2 Chr. 3 – 4. Unclear architectural features include those translated in NIV as *narrow windows* (v. 4), *structure, side rooms* (vv. 5, 10), and *stairway* (v. 8).

[10] J. M. Monson, 'The Temple of Solomon: Heart of Jerusalem', in *Zion, City of Our God*, edited by R. S. Hess and G. J. Wenham (Grand Rapids: Eerdmans, 1999), pp. 1–22, and 'The New 'Ain Dara Temple: Closest Solomonic Parallel', *Biblical Archaeology Review* 26, 3 (2000), pp. 20–35; and V. Hurowitz, 'Solomon's Temple in Context', *Biblical Archaeology Review* 37, 2 (2011), pp. 46–57, 77–78.

[11] Walton, Matthews and Chavalas, p. 362.

[12] DeVries, p. 97.

building, is followed by no explicit mention of the temple! Solomon's mind (and the reader's) may be focused on the temple, but God has other concerns: these are the only divine words in all of chapters 5 – 7 and their import is unmistakable.

As I write, the state in which I live is experiencing another burst of major resource projects involving billions of dollars, with all the spinoffs relating to employment and general economic prosperity. There is an air of confident expectancy, although some are rightly concerned about housing and other social costs and impact on people of low income. At this stage of Solomon's reign there is excitement in national development. He has been providing leadership in negotiations with Hiram, organizing the labour force and other matters relating to the temple (and other building projects, 7:1–12) and ruling the nation, but there is danger that he (and later hearers and readers) forget what is central: *follow my decrees, observe my laws and keep all my commands and obey them* (v. 12).

Solomon may have thought that everything else he was doing was ensuring the future of the nation – every other king in the ancient Near East sought the continuing favour of their god by building a magnificent sanctuary[13] and as mentioned above the very solidity of the temple structure symbolized permanence; but he is reminded, as was said to the first Israelite king, 'to obey is better than sacrifice' (1 Sam. 15:22). The temple that is to be a place for 'the Name of the Lord', bringing honour and glory to him, cannot replace keeping the covenant; beauty and material glory are never substitutes for obedience. In Yahweh's earlier words to Solomon, covenant faithfulness had been the path to his 'long life' (3:14); here it is the path 'through you' to bring the blessing of Yahweh's presence to *my people Israel*. The people now in exile had tied divine presence to the temple (Ps. 46; Jer. 7:4), but here they are reminded of a different perspective: *I will live among the Israelites* is based on following his ways (v. 13). Here is a glimmer of hope, a way forward in the despair of exile: God's presence with them is independent of a temple.

Why is it that throughout human history people have acted as if what God (or a god) most requires is worship (with its buildings, ritual and sacrifices)? There is much in both Old and New Testaments about worship (although little detail in the New), but always with qualification. Worship that is not linked with justice and reconciliation on the human level is abhorrent to God, and loving behaviour is more important than correct ritual and magnificent buildings.

The human quest for beauty is good: it is being 'like God' who saw all he had created as 'very good' and who in the garden provided

[13] Monson, p. 28.

trees that were not only 'good for food' but firstly 'pleasing to the eye' (Gen. 1:31; 2:9). It can be God-honouring to desire a building that is a physical reminder of his existence and greatness, yet God is more concerned with building his people as a covenant-keeping community known by its lifestyle of doing what is just and right, that shares with and cares for all, especially its weaker and less powerful members. People are drawn to God by the beautiful lifestyle of his people, not by the buildings they erect (Deut. 4:5–8; Matt. 5:14–16).[14] At the same time, the buildings we erect say much about our lifestyle and values! This passage, and its wider context of the history of Israel and Judah, can provide input as we ask, 'Do our buildings help or hinder our doing God's will?' In the midst of lives full of doing many 'good' things, Yahweh's words provide a reality check as to priorities.

d. The temple interior (6:14–38)

After Yahweh's words the earlier (v. 9a) statement is repeated: *Solomon built the temple and completed it* (v. 14). The statement divides descriptions of work in different materials, with verses 2–8 in *stone*, and verses 9b–10, 15–36 in wood, some items being overlaid with *gold*.[15] At verse 15 attention moves inside the temple. While some exilic hearers may have remembered the appearance of the temple exterior, no ordinary Israelite had ever seen the interior. The description is of almost unimaginable beauty and grandeur, the wealth it represented being far greater than anything they had ever seen – and certainly beyond their current experience. The buildings of Nebuchadnezzar's Babylon may be much larger than the temple, but nothing could match the splendour now to be described of the house 'for the Name of the LORD'.

For the exiles this was now all in the past, although its glory fore-shadows the future. Centuries later Christians were given another picture of reality beyond their visual experience as John recorded his 'revelation' of the scene in heaven with all its grandeur. As we journey with Israelite hearers into the temple our minds can take time to reflect on '"what no eye has seen, what no ear has heard, and what no human mind has conceived" . . . God has prepared for those who love him' (1 Cor. 2:9, adapting Isa. 64:4).

---

[14] In Matt. 5:16 'good' is *kalos*, often translated 'beautiful', not another common word, *agathos*. The 'beautiful deeds' of Matt. 5:16 match the 'beautiful deed' of anointing Jesus' feet that is also to be spoken of 'wherever this gospel is preached throughout the whole world' (Matt. 26:10, 13).

[15] Walsh, p. 103. The pattern continues in ch. 7 with bronze material made by Hiram/ Huram, then work in gold by Solomon.

First come *panelling* with *cedar* and floors covered with *juniper*[16] (v. 15) before moving to the *cedar boards* that *partitioned off . . . the Most Holy Place* (v. 16). A pause before entering the *inner sanctuary* notes the decorative timber carving portraying *gourds and open flowers* (v. 18). 'Gourds' were also cast in bronze to decorate the Sea (7:24) while 'open [blossoming] flowers' are alongside 'cherubim' and 'palm trees' in carvings on the doors (6:29, 32, 35). These symbols of fertility and fecundity 'suggest the garden of Eden to symbolize the role of the temple as the center of creation'.[17]

A text that is read aloud determines the narrative pace: our guide fixes our gaze with ten verses on *the inner sanctuary*, six being on the *cherubim*. The inner sanctuary was to contain not an image of Yahweh but *the ark of the covenant of the LORD* (v. 19) as had also been the case for the tabernacle (Exod. 26:34). At this stage nothing more is said of the ark, attention remaining on its setting. Later will come the reminder that *the ark of the covenant* contained 'nothing . . . except the two stone tablets that Moses had placed in it at Horeb, where the LORD made a covenant with the Israelites after they came out of Egypt' (8:9).

Even though *cedar* has its own beauty, the ark's inner sanctuary setting is even more magnificent with all covered *in gold,* whether *overlaid* with plating or 'gilded with liquid gold'[18] (*gold* and *overlaid* each occur six times in three verses, verses 20–22). Gold had been extensively used in the tabernacle also, there donated willingly by the people (Exod. 25:3–7; 35:20–22).

Wood covered *in gold* continues with the making of *a pair of cherubim* (v. 23),[19] wild *olive wood*[20] being hard and finely grained, widely used for fine statuary. Winged creatures with composite faces are a feature of thrones in the ancient Near East,[21] but there is no divine image on the throne in Yahweh's temple. The pair would

---

[16] Most likely the Phoenician juniper, *Juniperus Phoenicia* (*HALOT*); LXX, 'pine'; NRSV: 'cypress'. 'Typically they used hardwoods that polished to a fine finish with nice grain or fragrant odor. A number of these woods are also impervious to bugs or mildew' (Walton, Matthews and Chavalas, p. 424).

[17] Sweeney, p. 114; Leithart, p. 56, discusses ways in which 'sanctuaries are also recapitulations of the garden of Eden'.

[18] Konkel, p. 127.

[19] The transliterated Hebrew plural form, *cherubim*, is traditional in English, rather than 'cherubs', which as a result of artistic representations has come to have connotations of beautiful or innocent children.

[20] *'ăṣê-šemen* 'trees/wood of oil' is not the common term for olive trees, *zayit* (both occur in Neh. 8:15, showing a distinction), and is more likely to be the 'wild olive' or 'oleaster', unrelated to true olive (*Helps for Translators: Fauna and Flora of the Bible* [London: United Bible Societies, second ed., 1980], pp. 157–158).

[21] *NBD*, p. 1184; O. Keel, *Symbolism of the Biblical World: Ancient Near Eastern Iconography and the Book of Psalms* (Winona Lake: Eisenbrauns, 1997), pp. 167–171.

dominate the room, towering over a human, each being 10 cubits high and wide (14.5 ft [4.5 m]); the inner sanctuary is a 20 cubit cube). They join the two smaller cherubim already on the ark (Exod. 25:10–22; cf. the 'four living creatures' under the throne in the vision of Ezek. 1, 10). In the subsequent description of walls and doors *cherubim* carvings, always mentioned first, are included along with plant imagery (vv. 29, 32, 35). Even as the guide leads us from the inner room we are reminded that the temple has one purpose, to be a 'house' (*temple*, v. 38) for Yahweh who is 'enthroned between the cherubim' (1 Sam. 4:4; 2 Sam. 6:2; 2 Kgs 19:15).

Being 'the house of the LORD' (v. 1) the temple is radically different from church buildings designed to provide a facility for services of worship and congregational meetings. As previously in the tabernacle, the most splendidly lavish section of the temple was 'seen' only by God: the best skills and materials are presented to God for his sole enjoyment. The choirmaster at St Paul's Cathedral in Melbourne was once asked why the choir practiced so hard and used new material for weekday evensong when few people were present. His answer was direct: 'We are not performing for a congregation but for God, and we want to give him the best.' It is a sign of a self-centred society when a 'service of worship' is evaluated on the basis of 'what I get out of it'. God in his grace and mercy does bless us in worship and speaks to us through his read and preached Word, and a major outcome of gathering is mutual encouragement (Heb. 10:24–25), but the very words 'service' and 'worship' have their focus on God and his presence, a truth to which the beauty of the Most Holy Place points.

The opening chapter on the construction ends with a feature combining the two major components, *stone* and *cedar*, 'perhaps an architectural buffer against earthquake damage', a style known elsewhere.[22] Solomon knows the risks and takes precautions: the temple is beautiful, solid and secure. Later worshippers were to sing: 'Though the earth give way and the mountains fall into the heart of the sea . . . the city of God, the holy place where the Most High dwells, God is within her, she will not fall' (Ps. 46:2–5). That psalm continued to be sung after the exile as a hymn of trust in 'the God of Jacob' (Ps. 46:7, 11): he has been our God well before the temple was built and he continues after the temple is destroyed, 'God the Lord of hosts is with us evermore'.[23]

---

[22] Walton, Matthews and Chavalas, pp. 362–363.
[23] The concluding line of each verse of the hymn based on Ps. 46 by R. Bewes, 'God is our strength and refuge' © R. T. Bewes/Jubilee Hymns.

3. Solomon's palace and Pharaoh's daughter (7:1–12)

In the middle of the temple details comes a section about Solomon's palace and another reference to Pharaoh's daughter (see 3:1). Chronologically and thematically it would seem to belong better with 9:10, which says that the two buildings took twenty years, that is, the sum of seven years for the temple and thirteen years for the palace (6:38; 7:1). Its placement here however serves as a contrast, raising questions as to Solomon's piety: his commitment to building a temple for Yahweh is undoubted, but was it simply the religious component of a monumental national centre of both temple and palace, the latter being larger and matching the temple in grandeur? The building of the palace required extending the labour corvée and payments to Hiram, a cost to the general population. While its larger size is understandable due to the activities that took place in it, the location of the description and mention of Pharaoh's daughter (v. 8) suggest all is not right (see earlier analysis of the structure of chapters 1 – 11).[24]

The contrast is expressed intentionally by the chiastic Hebrew sentence structure of 6:38 – 7:1 (obscured by the much later chapter division and further in some Bibles by a heading; there is no paragraph division in MT):

> . . . the house was completed according to all its matters and
> specifications
> and he built it in seven years,
> and his house Solomon built in thirteen years
> and he completed all his house.[25]

The chiastic structure continues with the following description being in the reverse order of chapter 6, so comparing the two buildings: first come structures built with *cedar* (vv. 2–8) and then details of *high-grade stone* (vv. 9–10), concluding with a combination (vv. 11–12).

The Palace of the Forest of Lebanon (v. 2), separate from Solomon's residence (v. 8), is as high as the temple (30 cubits) but more than four times the area (100 × 50 cubits compared to 60 × 20). Its name suits the large number of cedar columns, although the overall structure is unclear.[26] A key public area was *the throne hall, the Hall*

---

[24] In LXX this block is placed after MT 7:52 (7:38–50 in LXX). A. S. Turkanik, *Of Kings and Reigns* (Tübingen: Moht Siebeck, 2008), p. 21, n. 34, cites Van Keulen's argument that the translator and the Jewish historian Josephus shared a motive to 'protect Solomon against the charge that he showed lack of piety'.

[25] My translation.

[26] For varying reconstructions, see Wiseman, pp. 111–112, DeVries, p. 102, Sweeney, pp. 116–118.

of Justice, where he was to judge (v. 7). The quality of the whole complex, including residences for himself and Pharaoh's daughter, matches that of the temple. Together they become 'visual architectural backing for the Jerusalem elite – an ostentatious show of their wealth, their piety as servants of Yahweh and their ability to dictate how Yahweh should be worshipped'.[27]

Early in his reign Solomon 'judged' in the case of the two prostitutes (3:16–28), but after the temple narrative all we read is of Solomon's wealth and trading. The trend towards a greater interest in status symbols than in doing justice is expressed vividly in Jeremiah's critique of a later Davidic king, Jehoahaz (Shallum), son of Josiah:

> 'Does it make you a king
> to have more and more cedar?
> Did not your father have food and drink?
> He did what was right and just,
> so all went well with him.
> He defended the cause of the poor and needy,
> and so all went well.
> Is that not what it means to know me?'
> declares the LORD. (Jer. 22:15–16)

David's palace had been built of cedar (2 Sam. 5:11; 7:2), but Solomon's is 'more and more'. At this stage Solomon is faithful and generously provides for the temple, but the positioning of the description of the palace complex in the middle of the temple account is one way the writer points to the seeds of destruction being present at the very beginning of the temple worship, seeds that were to bear their poisonous fruit in injustice, oppression and apostasy.

The juxtaposition of temple and palace brings to the reader today a reminder of the questions and tensions that arise living in a world that is far from what God intends. How does trust in God influence 'standards of living' and questions as to what is 'appropriate' for 'my position in society'? How are these related to public worship and necessary financial involvement? This passage does not provide answers, but it at least leads us to see the questions. Subsequent chapters provide further illumination as we read of both Solomon's piety at the temple dedication and his future royal actions.

---

[27] P. M. Phillips, 'Rhetoric', p. 247; see DeVries, p. xxvi.

4. Nothing but the best (7:13–51)

After describing items built from stone and then wood, some covered with gold, the narrator turns to *bronze* (vv. 13–47) and *gold* (vv. 48–50). Throughout *Solomon* takes initiative as *King* (vv. 13, 40, 45–46, 51). He turns again to *Tyre*, recruiting *Huram*,[28] a metalsmith whose mother is an Israelite (interaction between the northern tribes and Phoenicians had been close for centuries). Mention of family background may be a way 'to ease troubled consciences . . . this man was nonetheless a true Israelite',[29] but the key factor in the commission was his skill: he was *filled with wisdom, with understanding and with knowledge to do all kinds of bronze work* (v. 14). By using a description almost identical to that of Bezalel who was in charge of the tabernacle construction (Exod. 31:3), the writer highlights that he is a superb artisan, the best available.

Two bronze pillars (vv. 15–22) were prominent at the entrance, with an overall height of three-quarters of that of the temple – 23 cubits (33 ft / 10 m), roughly three storeys high. The capitals were dominant, with decorations of *pomegranates* and *lilies*, common symbols of fertility of the land.[30] Free-standing pillars are known in a number of Phoenician and Assyrian structures, and common to all interpretations is representation of power and strength. Various suggestions have been made concerning the pillars' names and significance (v. 21): *Jakin* means 'he establishes or upholds' and *Boaz* 'in him is strength' or 'may strength be in him'. One proposal is that each word begins a longer inscription, for example, 'He (Yahweh) will establish the throne of David' and 'In the strength of Yahweh shall the king rejoice'.[31] Sweeney however comments that 'when read from right (north) to left (south) [the direction of Hebrew writing], the names produce the phrase "in strength he establishes," which suggests that the columns symbolize the foundations of the earth and the stability of creation (Mic. 6:2; Isa 24:18; . . . "pillars of the earth" in Job 9:5; Ps 75:4; and "pillars of heaven" in Job 26:11).'[32] This has the merit of complementing other cosmic imagery in the architecture. A widespread continuing cultural phenomenon is the use of tall pillars at the entrance of major buildings, commonly supporting an

[28] MT has 'Hiram'; 2 Chr. 4:11, 16 has the variant 'Huram', adopted by NIV in Kings to lessen readers' confusion with Hiram, king of Tyre.

[29] DeVries, p. 110.

[30] Pomegranates decorated the tabernacle (Exod. 28:33–34) and the hem of priestly robes (Exod. 39:24–26).

[31] Gray, p. 188, building on R. B. Y. Scott, 'The Pillars, Jachin and Boaz', *Journal of Biblical Literature* 58 (1939), pp. 143–147; adopted by Walton, Matthews and Chavalas, p. 363.

[32] Sweeney, p. 122.

overhang, seeking to convey to all who enter an image of power and stability. Architecture involves symbolism and beauty as well as function.

The Sea (vv. 23–26) is a very large water container, separate from the *ten bronze basins* placed on *ten movable stands of bronze* (vv. 27–39). The name and size (diameter of 10 cubits, i.e., half the temple width, and height of 5 cubits) give it prominence far greater than only providing water for washing.[33] The 'sea' is a widespread eastern Mediterranean image of threatening chaos, a place from which the beast Leviathan comes. In the Ugaritic epic, for example, Baal, with the help of Anat, has to defeat and kill the god Yam ('Sea') and the 'snake with seven heads' before being enthroned.[34] In contrast Yahweh reigns supreme over the 'waters' or 'sea'. While for surrounding cultures reference was primarily to the physical realm of 'sea' and 'floods' or 'raging waters', in the OT the imagery embraces Yahweh's victory over Pharaoh in the 'sea' at the time of the exodus and hence in prophecy and prayer his deliverance in the future. The 'sea' is not an enemy to be defeated but part of creation which serves God from the beginning of creation; similarly Yahweh is sovereign over forces of chaos in history that threaten order.[35]

The *Sea* thus visually reminded worshippers of Yahweh's rule over all creation, the image of strength enhanced by the *twelve bulls*, in groups of three facing each compass direction (v. 25): 'Perhaps the bulls symbolize the twelve tribes,[36] but this is uncertain. The four cardinal points of the compass symbolize all creation, and the bulls symbolize strength and virility.'[37] Exilic hearers, who feel that the forces of chaos have won, are encouraged to imagine the scene, but also remember that the bronze *Sea* was *made*, it itself is not the reality it symbolizes. Unlike the human artifact, the truth to which it pointed has not been destroyed: Yahweh ruled over all creation before Hiram's work and he continues to rule.

Centuries later the young Christian church faced a time of turmoil with persecution. In a vision John saw two pictures of a 'sea'. First he saw in front of the heavenly throne 'what looked like a sea of glass, clear as crystal. In the centre, around the throne, were four

---

[33] 2 Chr. 4:6: 'to be used by the priests for washing' (similar to the 'bronze basin' of the tabernacle, Exod. 30:18–19). The height of 7.3 ft (2.5 m) seems impracticable, although it may serve as a reservoir (Jones, pp. 183–184).

[34] COS 1.86, pp. 246–252; W. Beyerlin, ed., *Near Eastern Religious Texts Relating to the Old Testament* (London: SCM, 1978), pp. 198, 203–206.

[35] E.g., Gen. 1:2; Job 26:12; Ps. 29:3, 10; 74:13–15; 89:9–10; 93:3–4; 104:5–13, 25–26; 144:7; Isa. 27:1; 51:9–10.

[36] Adopted by Walton, Matthews and Chavalas, p. 426, and developed theologically by Leithart, p. 57.

[37] Sweeney, p. 122.

living creatures' (Rev. 4:6; cf. 15:2). The allusion to the temple 'sea' is a reminder that God reigns supreme, sovereign over what others may view as the threatening chaos of history. Later he saw another use of 'sea' imagery, using the potent Near Eastern imagery of chaos: the 'beast' comes out of the sea (Rev. 13), but after his defeat, in the 'new heaven and new earth . . . there was no longer any sea' (21:1), there is no longer any potential source of threat.

> Holy, holy, holy! All the saints adore Thee,
> Casting down their golden crowns around the glassy sea;
> Cherubim and seraphim falling down before Thee,
> Who was, and art, and evermore shalt be.[38]

The worship of God involves activity and so various bronze implements are listed (vv. 27–45), cast in a location where the clay was most suitable (vv. 46–47). The skilled work of Huram makes them objects of beauty as well as utility, decorative details mentioned a number of times: the *movable stands* had *lions, bulls and cherubim . . . wreaths of hammered work . . . and palm trees* (vv. 29, 36). In addition to all of this Solomon himself provides items, the sixfold use of *gold* highlighting the splendour (vv. 48–50). Finally come items prepared in advance by David (v. 51), the impression being that they are minor in comparison.

All is ready for bringing up the ark and dedicating the temple. Temple and furnishings are grand and splendid, made possible with pagan help in supplies and craftsmanship. Here is a case study in contextualization, the process whereby the faith and life of God's people is related to the living context.[39] David's initial desire to build a temple arose not from a divine command, but from pre-existing cultural practice: kings honoured their God by building a temple. This was something God allowed, and blessed as 'the glory of the LORD filled his temple' (8:11), and later the temple became a key theological concept taken up in the NT (see further discussion at the end of ch. 8). The temple's design and ornamentation have many similarities with neighbouring cultures, influenced in part by the active Phoenician involvement. The imprint of specific Israelite faith is seen in the 'inner sanctuary', with 'cherubim' and 'ark' but no divine image, and probably also in the 'Sea'. The quality of materials communicated significance in terms of cultural values.

---

[38] R. Heber (1783–1826).
[39] For 'contextualization' in missiological practice, see D. J. Hesselgrave and E. Rommen, *Contextualization: Meaning, Methods and Models* (Grand Rapids: Baker, 1989).

The symbolism and imagery of [the temple's] features drew their meaning from the culture of the time, just as word symbols in language derive their significance from the culture in which they are used . . . Similarities are essential to establishing communication, the differences are vital to the concept intended.[40]

The history of Christian architecture illustrates similar relationships to cultural patterns, beginning from early Christian adaptation of the structure of public buildings of the Greco-Roman world.[41] With global expansion of the church there has often been transplanting of architecture – for decades in Australia church buildings copied those from England ('this is what churches should look like') despite differences in climate (why build steep roofs for non-existent snow to fall off?). Occasionally there is radical evaluation of architecture in terms of cultural communication. One such example, decades ahead of its time, was built in Hong Kong in the 1930s at Tao Fong Shan, the Christian Mission to Buddhists, by the Norwegian missionary Karl Reichelt. In the style of a Chinese temple, its architectural language communicated to Buddhist monks, without compromising Christian faith.[42] A worthwhile, and sometimes salutary, exercise is to look at the architecture and symbolism of church buildings where one is personally involved and to ask what cultural values and symbols are expressed in the materials, structure, furnishings and decorations and what is communicated to people in the surrounding community. Buildings as 'created artefacts . . . promote the worldview of their creator, whether intentionally or not'.[43] The account of Solomon's temple provides a mirror for contemporary reflection.

5. The ark brought up and the temple dedicated (8:1–66)

The temple is finished and all is ready *to bring up the ark of the LORD's covenant from Zion, the City of David*.[44] Only when that is

---

[40] Konkel, p. 151 and n. 102; pp. 137–140 details similarities in architecture and symbolism.

[41] A concise overview of church architecture through the centuries is 'Buildings and Beliefs' and 'Building for Worship' in *A Lion Handbook: The History of Christianity* (Oxford: Lion, rev. ed., 1990), pp. 44–47, 158–161.

[42] E. J. Sharpe, *Karl Ludvig Reichelt, Missionary, Scholar and Pilgrim* (Hong Kong: Tao Fong Shan Centre, 1984); N. R. Thelle, 'Karl Ludvig Reichelt 1877–1952', in *Mission Legacies*, edited by G. H. Anderson *et al.* (Maryknoll, NY: Orbis, 1994), pp. 216–224.

[43] P. M. Phillips, 'Rhetoric', p. 243; see also pp. 246–248 on the rhetoric of architecture.

[44] After the ark was taken from Shiloh during battle with the Philistines (1 Sam. 4:3–4) it was never again in the tabernacle. It was eventually brought to Jerusalem by David and placed in a tent (2 Sam. 6:17), although the 'tabernacle' was then at Gibeon (1 Chr. 16:39; 21:29; 2 Chr. 1:5).

accomplished successfully can the temple be dedicated. The account divides naturally by subject matter: the bringing up of the ark and the authenticating presence of *the glory of the LORD* (vv. 1–13), leading to Solomon's blessing of the people (vv. 14–21), his prayer of dedication (vv. 22–53), his further blessing of the people (vv. 54–61) and concluding celebrations (vv. 62–66). The chapter is framed by Solomon's summoning of the people (vv. 1–3) and his sending the people away (v. 66).

Two important threads run throughout. The first is the involvement of *all Israel*. Hitherto the people have had part in the temple only as forced labour (5:13) and Solomon's administration is independent of pre-monarchic leadership (see on 4:1–19). In contrast the totality of Israel is mentioned frequently in this chapter, including in verses 1, 3 the traditional pre-monarchic leadership: *Israel* occurs five times in verses 1–5; *the whole assembly of Israel* verses 14 (twice),[45] 55; and *all Israel* in verses 62, 63, 65. The *covenant* was made with *the Israelites/my people Israel* who were brought *out of Egypt* (vv. 9, 16 [twice]; cf. vv. 21, 53) and repeatedly Yahweh is *the God of Israel* (vv. 15, 17, 20, 23, 25, 26), while in the middle of the prayer is a welcome to *the foreigner who does not belong to your people Israel* (v. 41). 'Israel' occurs 35 times in the Hebrew of this chapter. The only OT chapter with more is Judges 20 (42 times), narrating the Israelite punitive attack on the Benjaminites, a sad picture of disunity, while the next highest is 1 Kings 22, where 'Israel' is the northern kingdom. 1 Kings 8 stands out in portraying unity in worship at the temple, a foreshadowing of even greater unity embracing Jew and Gentile in the 'holy temple' of which Christ is the 'chief cornerstone' (Eph. 2:19–22).

Secondly comes repeated mention of *David*, beginning with the ark being brought up from *the city of David* (v. 1). In the centre Solomon acknowledges the relationship between Yahweh and David and Yahweh's promises ('David' occurs eight times in verses 15–26), while at the end the people *went home, joyful and glad in heart for all the good things the LORD had done for his servant David and his people Israel* (v. 66), joining together the two motifs.

The temple may have been built by Solomon, but it is the unifying centre for all Israel; it is the temple of Yahweh the God of Israel, who brought his people out of Egypt, and who in the temple fulfilled promises to David for the good of the people and who welcomes the foreigner. *The whole assembly of Israel* is not Solomon's subjects but Yahweh's *people* (thirteen times in verses 30–52), Solomon's royal

---

[45] The second instance is in NIV *them*.

role being to enable and encourage by example the worship of all the people. At this stage nothing but good is said about the temple and its place in the life of the people within the broader context of God's dealings with them from the exodus on. The conclusion is a prayer for enabling obedience of the covenant requirements (vv. 58, 61). Temple and kingship cannot be separated from obedience, a connection that was soon forgotten.

We see here a model for corporate worship of the covenant-making, promise-keeping God: a placing of the present in the broad sweep of God's saving purposes for all peoples, and a wholistic linking of praise and prayer to the God of grace with commitment to obedience. The dedication of a new church building comes with many emotions, and it is easy to focus on benefits the building brings to the congregation. The flow of this chapter and its varied content encourage wide-ranging prayer and celebration before the Lord our God. Recently our local church moved to larger facilities for worship and my wife and I were asked to 'write a psalm for the congregation', with the suggestion of Psalm 66 as base. It proved to be highly significant as the psalm enabled explicit placing of the history of the congregation and the present move within the broad context of God's purposes for his world, and to join our thanksgiving and commitment with that of God's people through the ages, across the globe and into the future.

a. The ark is brought up (8:1–13)

David had brought the *ark*, with careful and joyful celebration accompanied by sacrifices, to the *City of David*, the narrow fortress between the Kidron and Tyropoeon Valleys (2 Sam. 6:12–19). With temple building finished on the higher ground around 1,500 ft (450 m) to the north, the *ark* is carried up, again accompanied by sacrifices. While other nations would bring an idol in procession to its new home, Israel brings Yahweh's throne and symbol of the covenant. The importance is conveyed by the style of narration, with emphasis through repetition and extended description. So in verses 6–9, for the first time in this chapter, the full name, *the ark of the LORD's covenant,* appears; its new location is given both descriptors, *the inner sanctuary* and *the Holy Place,* and the relative positions of *ark* and *cherubim* are stated twice. All that can be seen regularly, and that only by priests, however, are the non-removable *poles* (Exod. 25:12–15), a visible reminder of the ark inside. All builds up to the contents that display the centre of Israelite faith and life: *the two stone tablets that Moses had placed in it at Horeb, where the LORD made a covenant with the Israelites after they came out of Egypt.*[46] Central to the temple and to the ark representing Yahweh's kingship is the covenant relationship, initiated in an act of deliverance.

The ark is no more mentioned in Kings.[47] It is as if the narrator has given all this detail as another way of reminding exilic hearers of what is central, namely the covenant and Yahweh's reign, transcending the temple. At the same time, the narrative marks a transition: the 'roving ark' now has a 'fixed home' (vv. 13, 21) and 'by presenting the temple as enduring, the Deuteronomist portrays worship at the temple of Jerusalem as definitive for succeeding generations'.[48] One result however was that the temple itself became a major focus of security rather than the covenant relationship to which it pointed through the ark and its contents. The sole mention of the ark in the prophetic books is Jeremiah's description of a future when the ark will not be missed because of an intimate relationship with God (Jer. 3:16). For Christians the disappearance is given a different resolution: the ark reappears in the heavenly temple in Revelation 11:19, 'accompanied by the marks of the theophany at Sinai'.[49] In the vision the ark's symbolism is again to the fore: 'now at the climax [of history] the symbol of [God's] covenant faithfulness is publicly displayed'.[50] God keeps his word.

God's seal upon the installation of the ark in the Most Holy Place is described dramatically in terms matching those used of the tabernacle:

Exodus 40:34	1 Kings 8:10
Then the cloud covered the tent of meeting, and the glory of the LORD filled the tabernacle.	The cloud filled the temple of the LORD.

[46] A close parallel is a copy of an Assyrian treaty (covenant) document discovered in the inner room of a temple at Tayinat on the Antioch plain (identical architecture to Solomon's temple); Hurowitz, 'Solomon's Temple in Context', p. 56; C. Elias, 'U of T researchers shed light on ancient Assyrian tables' <http://www.news.utoronto.ca/humanities/u-of-t-researchers-shed-light-on-ancient-assyrian-tablets.html>, April 8, 2010.

[47] The ark's disappearance has resulted in many traditions and claims, summarized by C. L. Seow, 'Ark of the Covenant. C. 3. Disappearance', *ABD* 1, pp. 390–391. Lack of information fuels speculation and imagination, whether for a film such as *Indiana Jones and Raiders of the Lost Ark* (1981) or tales of the Knights Templar discovering the ark at the time of the Crusades.

[48] G. N. Knoppers, 'Prayer and Propaganda: Solomon's Dedication of the Temple and the Deuteronomist's Program', *Catholic Biblical Quarterly* 57 (1995), p. 242 (reprinted in Knoppers and McConville, p. 384).

[49] C. C. Rowland, 'The Book of Revelation', in *The New Interpreter's Bible*, vol. 12 (Nashville: Abingdon, 1998), p. 644.

[50] L. Morris, *Revelation*, Tyndale New Testament Commentaries (Leicester: Inter-Varsity Press, second ed. 1987), p. 150.

Exodus 40:35	1 Kings 8:11
Moses could not enter the tent of meeting because the cloud had settled upon it, and the glory of the LORD filled the tabernacle.	And the priests could not perform their service because of the cloud, for the glory of the LORD filled his temple.

Solomon's response is to affirm Yahweh's age long practice to *dwell in a dark cloud* (v. 12), *'ărāpel* being elsewhere the 'thick/deep darkness' on Sinai (Exod. 20:21; Deut. 4:11; 5:22) and in David's description of Yahweh's intervention (2 Sam. 22:10 = Ps. 18:9). Genesis explicitly refers to 'darkness' (a different word) before the first act of creating 'light' and so with the temple symbolizing the cosmos, the darkness of the windowless Most Holy Place 'indicates that YHWH remains separate from the created world'.[51] Solomon's expectation is that here Yahweh *would dwell . . . forever* (v. 12–13).

The *glory of the LORD* is here his presence made visible, with universal import, as Habakkuk was to proclaim:

> The LORD is in his holy temple;
> let all the earth be silent before him.[52]

This was looking forward to the time when

> The earth will be filled with the knowledge of
> the glory of the LORD
> as the waters cover the sea.[53]

Solomon's 'forever' expectation did not eventuate as he envisaged. A couple of years before the temple was razed Ezekiel in a vision saw the 'glory of Yahweh' leaving the temple because of the pollution of pagan worship, violence and oppression, but after the cleansing of the exile he saw the 'glory' returning to the new temple in the middle of the land (Ezek. 10; 43:1–5).

This trajectory of movement through the centuries is taken up in NT descriptions of the coming of Christ: 'The Word became flesh and made his *dwelling* among us. We have seen *his glory*, the *glory* of the one and only Son, who came from the Father, full of grace and truth' (John 1:14, emphasis added). God's 'dwelling', the living presence of 'his glory', is personal, in the midst of people, no longer untouchable and physically separated, but reaching out to touch even tax collectors, sinners, Samaritans and people possessed with

---

[51] Sweeney, p. 132.
[52] Hab. 2:20
[53] Hab. 2:14.

demons or having skin diseases. Ethical corollaries follow as the glory of God seen in the person of Christ is also to be evident in the lives of all in Christ who 'bear much fruit' (John 15:8; 17:22–23).

Solomon's expectation that the temple would be *a place for you to dwell forever* (v. 13), seemingly dashed in the experience of the exile, is to reach its glorious realization when people 'will see the Son of Man coming in a *cloud* with power and *great glory*' (Luke 21:27, emphasis added) and when in the 'new Jerusalem ... God's dwelling place is now among the people, and he will dwell with them. They will be his people, and God himself will be with them and be their God' (Rev. 21:2–3).

b. Solomon and God's promise to David (8:14–21)

Solomon turns to address the people, giving thanks to God who has kept his promises to David. Solomon brings together Yahweh's deliverance of his *people Israel out of Egypt* (vv. 16, 21), his choosing David as ruler of God's people (v. 16), and Solomon's succession and completion of David's plan for a temple (vv. 17–20).[54] Davidic kingship and temple building are framed by references to the exodus and *covenant* (vv. 16, 21); all are kept together.

After speaking in v. 13 of the temple as a place for Yahweh to *dwell* (the word may be translated 'sit', as on a throne),[55] five times in this section it is stated that it is Yahweh's *Name* that is there (vv. 16–20).[56] Still today we have difficulties with language to describe God as both 'here with us' (immanent) and yet far beyond us (transcendent and omnipresent). 'Name' is a way of identifying Yahweh with the temple: he has endorsed that by the presence of his glory; it is here that people will gather in his presence,[57] bringing sacrifices to him and calling on his name in prayer (vv. 29–30, 33, etc.), but he does not 'live' there in any way that limits his freedom and power. His

---

[54] A comparison is an inscription Nabopolassar, king of Babylon (626–605 BC) placed when 'dedicating his temple to Marduk, the Etemenanki: "At that time Marduk, the lord, ordered me firmly to found the base of Etemenaki. . . O Marduk, my lord, look joyously at my pious work! By your noble command, that will never be changed, may the work, the work of my hand, last forever! As the bricks of Etemenaki are firm forever, establish the foundation of my throne for all time to come"' (T. W. Cartledge, *1 & 2 Samuel* [Macon, GA: Smyth and Helwys, 2001], p. 448; quoting text from T. Ishida, *The Royal Dynasties in Ancient Israel* [New York: de Gruyter, 1977]).

[55] Knoppers, 'Prayer and Propaganda', p. 241, in Knoppers and McConville, p. 383.

[56] Also vv. 29, 44, 48; and 3:2; 5:3, 5; 9:3, 7; 2 Kgs 23:27.

[57] Similar language is in the key statement that Yahweh will choose a place 'to put his Name there for his dwelling' and that 'there, in the presence of the LORD your God' you 'shall eat and shall rejoice' (Deut. 12: 5, 7).

ark is there, and so his *Name*, but God himself cannot be constrained by a building (see further below on v. 27).

c. Solomon's prayer of dedication (8:22–61)

Solomon next turns to Yahweh in prayer. The opening petition (vv. 23–30) 'makes no request except for divine attentiveness to his prayer ... Solomon's invocation is actually altruistic. The prayer he offers exploits his special position, as king, to intercede in behalf of his people'.[58] His prayer is based upon Yahweh's will and promises in two areas.

First, Yahweh has hitherto kept his promise regarding David and so can be petitioned in confident hope to continue in the future (vv. 24–26), although twice human response is included, *your servants who continue wholeheartedly in your way* (v. 23) and *if only your descendants are careful in all they do to walk before me* (v. 25). Significantly the last word of the opening petition is *forgive* (v. 30), with the following petitions taking up the reality of disobedience and its consequences for *there is no-one who does not sin* (v. 46). Secondly, the temple that Solomon has built is *this place of which you said, 'My Name shall be there'* (v. 29), implementing the command of Deuteronomy 12:10–14 following the promised rest in the land. Thus Solomon can pray that Yahweh's *eyes be open to this temple night and day ... Hear the supplication of your servant and of your people Israel when they pray toward this place* (vv. 29–30).

Solomon's actions and language succinctly express again God's being present and yet transcendent (see above on vv. 14–21). Solomon has *spread out his hands toward heaven* (v. 22) and yet he speaks of prayer *toward this place* (vv. 29–30). Yahweh is incomparable *in heaven above or on earth below* (v. 23), indeed *the heavens, even the highest heaven, cannot contain you* (v. 27), and yet with the presence of *My Name* it can be expected that he will constantly be looking and listening (*eyes ... open* and *hear*, vv. 29–30).

It could be said that the statement of Yahweh's transcendence and freedom is obvious, yet history illustrates an inordinate emphasis upon buildings, and attachment to them as a focus of religious commitment, sometimes with the corollary that God will protect 'his' building. Sadly human beings have a tendency to tie God to material objects (or intellectual constructs) which, with their associated religious activities, become the primary focus, even talismans, downplaying obedience in life and society, highlighted in Jeremiah's

---

[58] Knoppers, 'Prayer and Propaganda', p. 245, in Knoppers and McConville, pp. 387–388.

temple sermon (Jer. 7, 26) and in Jesus' repeated affirmation of the words of Hosea, 'I desire mercy, not sacrifice' (Hos. 6:6; Matt. 9:13; 12:7).

The affirmation that God and his promise-keeping nature precede and are not tied to the temple is particularly relevant and encouraging to people in exile. As they hear the narrative of the temple dedication they are reminded of its secondary nature. Further it is *from heaven*[59] that God hears and answers, still the case when there is no temple. A thousand years later God's mobility and the human origin of the temple are to be themes of the unpopular speech of Stephen (Acts 7).

Nevertheless God is willing to allow and to bless specific places where he is honoured. Buildings, whether a 'temple' or a Christian church building, are important and can be an aid to the service of God and a witness to, or reminder of, his presence. A building can however become too important and a substitute for true witness to God's character: the temple was destroyed, both at the exile and in 70 AD. The absence in the NT of any command (or prohibition) regarding places of worship is a reminder to Christians that buildings are secondary to the main requirements of discipleship. Our faith is in the promise-keeping God whose presence is not constrained. Buildings are useful and blessed by God when they enhance, rather than hinder, worship of God, discipleship and witness in changing circumstances.

Solomon's prayer (vv. 31–51) has seven petitions describing situations where things are not right. Each petition has a similar structure:

- *When...* (something that is wrong; vv. 31, 33, 35, 37, 41, 44, 46)
- *and when they pray* (or other action or attitude linked with the temple; vv. 31b, 33b, 35b, 38, 41b–42, 44b, 47–48)
- *then hear from heaven,* and act to restore (vv. 32, 34, 36, 39–40, 43, 45, 49–51).

Emphasis is overwhelmingly on the grace of God. He is asked to *forgive* (vv. 30, 34, 36, 39, 50) and to restore all kinds of relationships. The petitions involve all people, individually and corporately: *anyone* (v. 31), *your people (Israel)* (vv. 33, 35, 44, 50), *anyone among your people Israel* (v. 38), and *the foreigner* (v. 41).

Now notice that Solomon did not only pray for his people but also for the foreigners and strangers who distrusted the nation of

---

[59] Verses 30, 32, 34, 36, 39, 43, 45, 49. In vv. 39, 43, 49 'heaven' is 'your dwelling place', the term used in v. 13 of the temple.

Israel and were often hostile to it, so that the son of David might show the God of David to everyone in general, by praying for his enemies and by speaking ahead of time to us those future words: 'But I say to you, Love your enemies and pray for those who persecute you.'[60]

Circumstances are all-embracing, mainly parallels to the covenantal curses in Deuteronomy 28: a legal dispute that cannot be resolved (v. 31), defeat by an enemy (v. 33), drought (v. 35), other disasters whether caused by natural events or besieging armies (v. 37), a foreigner who is attracted by 'your name' (v. 41), battles (v. 44), and exile (v. 46). The comprehensive sweep could well be a model for the prayers of God's people today.

The prayers are often linked with repentance, a turning to God,[61] heightened in the seventh and longest petition (vv. 46–51), 'a complex series of wordplays on the roots "take captive" (*šbh*); "return, repent" (*šwb*); and "dwell" (*yšb*)'.[62] Amazingly, in the context of joyous dedication the final petition concerns the possibility of worshippers rebelling against God and being handed over to their enemies as captives![63] Here however is a clear statement of hope beyond exile:[64] there is no mention of defeat of the captors, but rather a plea for *their captors to show them mercy* (v. 50), nor is there explicit mention of return from exile (as for instance in the prophets), although it might be implied in references to the exodus. Rather 'Kings rests content with its message that even in exile God will not abandon his people'; in repentance they can look to his grace.[65] The phrasing of the plea for continuity of relationship demonstrates that 'the true nature of Israel depends, not on institutions, not even on possession of the land, but on loyalty to Yahweh'.[66]

Significantly the final plea and the summary of all pleas are based not on the Davidic promise and the temple (as in vv. 23–30) but on

---

[60] Attributed to the fourth century Syrian writer Ephrem; quoted in Conti, p. 60.

[61] *šûb* 'turn' is used of 'turning from' God or sin and 'turning (back) to' him and, in another verbal form, of God 'bringing back/causing to return'; see vv. 33, 34, 35, 47–48.

[62] Walsh, p. 114.

[63] The description of the people as Yahweh's *inheritance* (vv. 51, 53) is elsewhere in Kings only in a word of judgment at the time of Manasseh (2 Kgs 21:14).

[64] See also on 2 Kgs 13.

[65] J. G. McConville, 'I Kings 8:46–53 and the Deuteronomic Hope', *Vetus Testamentum* 42 (1992), p. 79 (reprinted in Knoppers and McConville, p. 369). See also his *Grace in the End: A Study in Deuteronomic Theology* (Carlisle: Paternoster, 1993).

[66] J. G. McConville, *God and Earthly Power: An Old Testament Political Theology, Genesis–Kings* (London: T.&T. Clark, 2006), p. 163.

God's electing action in the exodus (vv. 51, 53).[67] God's deliverance is not exclusive, as the fifth plea had been on behalf of *the foreigner*, with the reason being *so that all the peoples of the earth may know your name and fear you* (v. 43). The global goal is one to which Solomon returns in the final blessing.

The continuing flow of verses 56–61 is important. Again there is praise of Yahweh's faithfulness to his promises culminating in the temple (v. 54), this time leading to prayer that Yahweh turn the hearts of king and people towards obedience (vv. 58, 61). Following is the prayer that Yahweh meet *each day's need* for king and people (v. 59) – but that is not the end in view. The culmination is so *that all the peoples of the earth may know that the* LORD *is God and that there is no other* (v. 60). The temple, and associated prayers and ritual, are both a blessing to Israel and a means of blessing to 'all peoples on earth' (Gen. 12:3). Almost a millennium later Jesus was to enter the temple area and begin 'driving out those who were buying and selling there', quoting the words of Isaiah (56:7), 'My house will be called a house of prayer for all nations' (Mark 11:15–17). 'This [v. 60, together with vv. 41–43] is the most remarkable of all the passages with a universal vision in the historical books.'[68] The universal vision is the basis of the challenge addressed to *your hearts* (v. 61, shifting from 'our, us' in preceding verses): 'The missional hope . . . is turned into a missional challenge to the people that they must be as committed to God's law as God is committed to such a worldwide goal.'[69]

Forgiveness, strength to obey, deliverance, provision of daily needs in a setting of God's name known in all the earth – each has some equivalence in the Lord's Prayer. Petitions in both prayers involve personal and corporate needs which God in his grace meets, but all are in the larger setting of God's reign 'in heaven' over all the earth which is yet to hallow 'your name', yet to do God's will 'on earth as . . . in heaven'.

d. Concluding acts of dedication (8:62–66)

The dedication and accompanying festival were corporate acts by both *the king and all the Israelites* (vv. 63, 65). Hopes were high as

---

[67] The ascription 'Sovereign LORD' (*'ădōnāy yhwh*; NRSV Lord GOD) occurs in Kings only here, and in Samuel only in David's prayer after Yahweh announced his covenant with David (2 Sam. 7:18–29, seven times). Its use seems to be more than stylistic: at the end of Solomon's prayer it highlights Yahweh's sovereignty over king and people and relativizes the importance of the king.

[68] C. J. H. Wright, *The Mission of God: Unlocking the Bible's Grand Narrative* (Nottingham: Inter-Varsity Press, 2006), p. 229.

[69] Ibid, p. 386.

the people returned to their homes *joyful and glad in heart* (v. 66) – 'those who have met with the Lord do experience great joy. . . [as in] the shepherds (Luke 2:20), the wise men from the east (Matt. 2:10–11) and Jesus' disciples (John 1:41–45)'[70] – but exilic hearers knew that the nation tragically divided after Solomon's death and four hundred years later the temple would be destroyed. The petitions of Solomon's prayer now were real to their situation, and Yahweh was still God reigning in heaven to whom they could turn in prayer.

The petitions of Solomon's prayer, and even more of the Lord's Prayer, are still applicable for people in a range of situations. The basis for confidence is not the worth of the one praying but the God who delivers. For Solomon, this was the God of the exodus, the God of Israel, the God of David and his God. Today we can look to the fulfilment in God's saving work in Christ, the son of David, and to the ongoing faithfulness of God as his Spirit enables witness 'to the ends of the earth' (Acts 1:8). In the midst of the darkness of exilic experiences we are able to turn to the God who 'demonstrates his own love for us in this: while we were still sinners, Christ died for us . . . [nothing] in all creation, will be able to separate us from the love of God that is in Christ Jesus our Lord' (Rom. 5:8; 8:39).

In reading the account of the temple building and dedication (chs 5 – 8) many aspects have encouraged reflection on contemporary situations, including input from NT material. NT references to the temple are quite varied.[71] The Gospel of Luke begins and ends in the temple, Jesus and the early disciples worshipped in the temple, the first miracle after Pentecost enabled a lame man to enter the temple (Acts 3:1–10),[72] and Paul went there when he returned to Jerusalem with gifts for the poor; yet Jesus himself pointed beyond the temple, describing his own body as the temple that would be raised (John 2:19–21; cf. Matt. 26:61; 27:40 and parallels) and at his death the veil of the temple, protecting the Most Holy Place, was torn (Matt. 27:51). Paul speaks of the Christian church as 'God's temple' since 'God's Spirit lives in you' (1 Cor. 3:16–17; also 2 Cor. 6:16–17), a 'holy temple' that builds together Jewish and Gentile believers, breaking down barriers (Eph. 2:21), while the 'body' of

---

[70] Gotom, p. 426.

[71] See B. Chilton, P. W. Comfort and M. O. Wise, 'Temple, Jewish', *DNTB*, pp. 1167–1183.

[72] 'According to current Jewish practice his physical condition marks him as an "outsider" to the temple community (cf. Lev. 21:17–20; *mSabb*. 6:8). By contrast, his healing and entrance into the Temple for prayer symbolize the dawning of a messianic epoch'; R. W. Wall, 'The Acts of the Apostles', in *The New Interpreter's Bible*, vol. 10 (Nashville: Abingdon, 2002), p. 77.

the individual believer is 'a temple of the Holy Spirit, who is in you' (1 Cor. 6:19). How amazing is the contrast: in the temple, as in the tabernacle, the most beautiful and magnificent part was prepared by people in advance and made solely for God's presence and enjoyment; but now God takes the initiative as 'the Word became flesh and made his dwelling among us' as we are in our uncleanness and sinfulness. Now the Spirit dwells in a temple that is a building in progress (Eph. 2:22), both in growing Christ-likeness, producing fruit that is beautiful (2 Cor. 3:18; Gal. 5:22–23), and in the addition of new 'living stones' (1 Pet. 2:5). 'Our task as the covenant community, the church is to be God's temple, so filled with his glorious presence that we expand and fill the earth with that presence until God finally accomplishes the goal completely at the end of time!'[73]

The description of the physical magnificence of Solomon's temple is amenable to a modern society attracted by visual images of material success, but the temple's destruction may then be seen as a parable of what has happened in many Western nations to the perceived status of the Christian church. A TV documentary series, 'Addicted to Money',[74] contrasted the nineteenth century skyline of London peppered with church spires and the prominence of buildings of banking and finance in the twenty-first century. Solomon's prayer and the frequent mention of following God's ways point to different values, focused in Christ, and reinforced by Pauline use of temple imagery.

'Since the NT represents a new world view a new architecture is needed – although this time that architecture is not instantiated within a physical building but in the corporeality of Jesus and his followers.'[75] The glories and values of this age pale into insignificance in light of 'the glory of God seen in the face of Christ' (2 Cor. 4:6) and the wonder of the work of the Spirit transforming 'with ever-increasing glory' all who are in Christ (2 Cor. 3:18) – that is the 'temple' that is to be looked at in awe and wonder and praise, the place where the Spirit of God dwells and to which others are drawn.

---

[73] G. Beale, *The Temple and the Church's Mission* (Leicester: Apollos; Downers Grove: InterVarsity Press, 2004), p. 402, summarizing his main point.

[74] D. McWilliams, 'Addicted to Money' (Electric Pictures, 2009; http://www.davidmcwilliams.ie/addicted-to-money) surveys the causes, results and prospects of the Global Financial Crisis that began in 2008.

[75] Phillips, 'Rhetoric', p. 248.

1 Kings 9:1 – 11:43
5. After building the temple

1. All is not well (9:1–23)

The temple dedication reads as a high point in Israelite history and
one might expect much positive action to follow. At first there is
affirmation by Yahweh, but that quickly moves to warning. The
account of Solomon's activities also provide a mixed picture. There
are signs that at core all is not well as God's word penetrates surface
appearances.

a. Yahweh appears again to Solomon (9:1–9)

After the joyful end of the temple celebrations Yahweh appears again
to Solomon. At Gibeon God had given him more than he had asked
for (3:9, 12–14); similarly now in answer to Solomon's prayer (8:29)
Yahweh does more in affirming he has *consecrated* (set apart as holy)
the temple, by *putting my Name there forever* as well as guaranteeing
that *my eyes and my heart will always be there*, ready to answer their
prayers (v. 3). He also responds to Solomon's prayer concerning the
continuity of the Davidic dynasty (vv. 4–5; cf. 8:25–26), but expands
Solomon's short 'if only your descendants are careful in all they do
to walk before me faithfully as you have done' (8:25) by adding the
qualities of *integrity of heart and uprightness* and explicitly mentioning *do all I command and observe my decrees and laws* (v. 4). Yahweh's
words are a reminder of his previous admonitions to Solomon (3:14;
6:12) and recall Solomon's words relating to all the people (8:58, 61).

The message is a continuing refrain: although Yahweh has *consecrated* the temple, priority for king and people is to be obeying his
commands. Obedience is not a footnote but central to the body of
the text of relationship with Yahweh. Such is not a form of legalism
but an expression of the structures God has built into his creation,

'inescapable givens that have to do with human quality and cov-enantal neighborliness'[1] and relationship with the Creator.

What follows is unexpected: no sooner is the temple completed than a warning comes of its destruction (vv. 6–9)! Solomon and all Israel may have been worshipping Yahweh at the temple dedication, but here are warnings of apostasy, a turning from following God (the Hebrew construction emphasizes the action, suggesting a deliberate and persistent stance). Hitherto Yahweh has addressed Solomon (*you* is singular in vv. 3–5), but in verse 6 the audience is widened with *you* being plural, embracing all Israel, all who hear this word across the generations of *your descendants*. Persistent apostasy will lead to separation from *the land I have given them,* the use of *cut off* contrast-ing with the earlier Davidic promise that 'there will not be cut off to you a man on the throne of Israel' (2:4).[2] Even though Yahweh has *consecrated* the temple *for my Name* (v. 7; cf. v. 3), he will *reject* it ('cast out from my sight'; cf. v. 3). The nation which was meant, by its obedience, to be a beacon of 'wisdom' among the nations (4:34; Deut. 4:5–8) will become *an object of ridicule,* and the magnificent temple building to which foreigners were to come (8:41–42) *a heap of rubble.*[3] The phrase *become a byword and an object of ridicule* (v. 7) occurs within the covenant curses in Deuteronomy 28:37, joining other language from that chapter taken up in the prayer of 8:31–53: when turning away (v. 6) is persistent, the 'sin' that was often referred to by Solomon as needing forgiveness[4] will reach its inevitable outcome.

Solomon's prayer had not mentioned the worship of other gods, but the core of disobedience is named here: they *embraced other gods* (v. 9; cf. v. 6). One either serves and relies on Yahweh, the God *who brought their ancestors out of Egypt,* lived out in following his ways, or turns to other gods. At the heart of human disobedience from the Garden of Eden on is a failure to trust Yahweh, a belief that other paths are the way to success in life, a following after other gods. Paul wrote of those who 'exchanged the truth about God for a lie, and worshipped and served created things rather than the Creator' (Rom. 1:25), 'things' which may be physical objects or human ideologies and systems.[5]

---

[1] Brueggemann, p. 131.

[2] Sweeney, p. 139. NIV, NRSV: 'fail'.

[3] Based on *le'iyyîm,* a widely adopted emendation of MT's *'elyôn* 'something high', 'supported by the Old Syriac, and Aquila's Greek version and by the Old Latin' (Gray, p. 236, n. h), and also Targum Jonathan.

[4] 8:33, 34, 35, 36, 46, 47, 50.

[5] Ezekiel has much about Israel's worship of other gods, even in the temple. In LXX words related to 'idols' were commonly translated by *enthymēma* ('thoughts, inven-tions') or *dianoēma/dianoia* ('thoughts'), so drawing attention to wrong and futile 'thinking' and consequent actions; J. Olley, *Ezekiel* (Septuagint Commentary Series; Leiden: Brill, 2009), pp. 25, 27, 311–312.

Yahweh's words to Solomon are a crescendo of warning (3:11–14; 6:11–13; 9:3–9). Why is this so, especially now after the building of the temple? Yahweh is promising his continuing presence and establishing of the throne, but the unexpected introduction to the vision points to incipient problems in human response. The occasion is not simply *when Solomon had finished building the temple of the* LORD (v. 1) – that alone could have introduced the vision. Included are *the royal palace*, which had been an unexpected interruption in the temple narrative (7:1–12), *and had achieved all he had desired to do* (v. 1; lit. 'and [finished] every desire of Solomon in which he delighted'). The final phrase is most striking.[6] The noun *ḥēšeq* ('desire') is rare[7] but the related verb (used as well as the noun in verse 19) is a strong word describing elsewhere a person 'desiring' a woman (Gen. 34:8; Deut. 21:11) or God (Ps. 91:14; NIV 'love') and God 'setting his affection on' Israel (Deut. 7:7; 10:15). In contrast, Solomon's 'desire' is on things (repeated in v. 19b, after vv. 10–19a). The accompanying verb in v. 1, *ḥāpēṣ* ('take delight in, desire'), appears elsewhere in the Solomon narrative with regard to Hiram giving Solomon whatever he 'desires' (5:8–10 [MT 22–24]; 9:11) and the Queen of Sheba receiving from Solomon 'all she desired' (10:13), while she herself, amazed at Solomon's 'wisdom and wealth' praises 'the LORD your God, who has delighted in you'. Yahweh has given Solomon 'wealth' as promised (3:13), but the wording in verse 1, reinforced by verses 10–28, shows that Solomon's 'desire' is not towards God and his ways but on increasing material wealth, evidenced in buildings. Solomon needs the warning.

It is common to speak of Solomon being led astray by 'foreign women' (11:1, 4),[8] but here are signs that he is being led astray by material wealth and power, with 'conspicuous consumption'[9] that enhances his status. He is able to build *all* he desires, but at what cost? Jesus spoke of the impossibility of serving both 'God and money' (Luke 16:13), strikingly illustrated by Solomon and challenging much of the present world. Today we see the results of embracing the god of money, the quest for wealth and associated status symbols and power, evident in social and economic disruption and injustice at both micro-levels (individual, family and community

---

[6] Surprisingly not commented on by many; see Gray, p. 237.

[7] The noun is only here, v. 19 (par. 2 Chr. 8:6) and Isa. 21:4, 'longing for' twilight, probably as relief.

[8] Cf. NIV's insertion of *however* in 11:1 (not in Hebrew), so suggesting that the marriages were the sole factor in Solomon's failure.

[9] This term was coined by T. Veblen, in *The Theory of the Leisure Class* (New York and London: Macmillan, 1899) to describe the use of money or resources to display a higher status than others.

breakdowns) and macro-levels (poverty, slavery and sweatshops, trade imbalances and environmental pollution), along with impoverishment of spirit. *Disaster* (v. 9) is already seen in ways in which humanity falls short of what God desires for the world he has created. Such worship leads to ultimate *disaster* of being 'shut out from the presence of the Lord and from the glory of his might' (2 Thess. 1:9).

The priority expressed and the implied criticisms in the warning of verses 6–9 suggest another look at the preceding account of the building of the temple. Detail was mainly of 'the ornateness and splendour of the temple' rather than features 'having cultic value'.[10] Further, when Solomon responds to the presence of 'the glory of the LORD' (8:11), his early words are 'I have indeed built a magnificent temple for you' (8:13) and in the following prayer he 'frequently mentions that he built the Temple (8: 20, 27, 44, 48)'.[11] It appears that Solomon's focus was on the magnificence of the building rather than its worship aspects. This may explain why Yahweh apparently does nothing to protect such wealth on the several occasions when temple wealth is given to, or taken by, invading kings.[12] The writer is saying to people in exile, and beyond, that God's interest is not in the material wealth supplied but in heart allegiance shown in obedience.

b. Solomon, Hiram and conscripted labour (9:10–23)

This block has been seen as a catalogue of 'Solomon's Other Activities',[13] a miscellany of projects in international relationships, buildings in Jerusalem and beyond, efficient organization of non-Israelite labour and fulfilment of temple obligations and trade. It demonstrates Solomon's wide-ranging expertise and success and 'on the face of it, the text is a celebration of the king and his remarkable achievements. If we remember that Israel, only two generations before, was a disadvantaged hill country with a peasant population, the work of Solomon must necessarily be received as exotic and astonishing.'[14]

The narrating contains clues to a different perspective, one that points to failure leading initially to the division of the kingdom on Solomon's death and ultimately to the end of the Davidic dynasty.

---

[10] A. Crane, 'Solomon and the Building of the Temple', in *Text and Task: Scripture and Mission*, edited by M. Parsons (Milton Keynes: Paternoster, 2005), p. 34.

[11] A. Crane, ibid., p. 40.

[12] 1 Kgs 14:26 (Solomon's son!); 15:18; 2 Kgs 12:18; 14:14; 18:14–16.

[13] The heading in NIV (also Wiseman, p. 125); compare 'Solomon's Pursuits' (House, p. 155).

[14] Brueggemann, pp. 127–128.

Yahweh has provided his criteria for success (vv. 3–9) which include 'nothing about trade or buildings or alliances or organization. It all turns on the single point of Torah obedience . . . If Torah has to do with *love of God* and *love of neighbor*, then the massive expansionist enterprise of Solomon is to be judged harshly as a deep failure.'[15] This is borne out by the juxtaposition of the two blocks, so that verses 1–9 provide a bright light to reveal what may be overlooked in the dazzling list of accomplishments.

Prior to the temple building we read of relationships with Hiram (5:1–12) and the use of conscripted labour for the temple building (5:13–18). Those two elements feature first in the current block. Here however Hiram may have been treated poorly. In exchange for timber and gold, Solomon gives him *twenty towns in Galilee* (v. 11), which Hiram regards as inferior but Solomon makes no change.[16] Solomon's action 'is striking. Having been granted the land of Israel by YHWH . . . , Solomon gives part of the land to Hiram, a Phoenician/Canaanite monarch'.[17] Whereas Joshua with trust in Yahweh had conquered the land, Solomon gives away, as part of a deal made because of *gold* (vv. 11, 13). What were the thoughts of the Israelite inhabitants of those towns, pawns in the hands of a king? Proverbs, attributed to Solomon, provides ironic commentary repeating the injunction of Deuteronomy 19:14: 'Do not move an ancient boundary stone set up by your ancestors' (Prov. 22:28; cf. 23:10). Further, in the pre-temple negotiations Solomon sought timber and food, now the focus is on *gold* (vv. 11, 14, 28). 'Why, indeed, is there no mention of gold at all in the description of Solomon's glory in chapters 4 – 5, where prosperity is described rather in terms of *food*? And why does gold appear in such abundance here, after the solemn warning of 9:6–9 about "turning away from God"?'[18]

Next is the account of conscription of non-Israelites as forced labour (vv. 15–23). Conscripted labour is mentioned in 5:13; 9:15, 21; 11:28: the first and last speak of Israelites, while 9:22 says *Solomon did not make slaves of any of the Israelites.* While Israelites had previously been conscripted on a rotational basis for the temple, now the indigenous Canaanite population is slave-labour for Solomon's many building projects. In addition to the role of Israelites in state projects (vv. 22–23), they continued to be conscripted for other

[15] Ibid., p. 128.
[16] R. Westbrook, 'Law in Kings', in Lemaire and Halpern, pp. 462–463, argues that Solomon's action is not 'stinginess' as Hiram's language is typically diplomatic usage 'so as to obtain a better deal'.
[17] Sweeney, p. 142.
[18] Provan, p. 85.

projects as is evident from 11:28 (cf. 12:4).[19] They are also involved in building facilities for Solomon's expanding military preparedness, *chariots* and *horses* (v. 19). The subservience of the remaining indigenous Canaanite population is mentioned in earlier periods,[20] but servitude is greatly increased under Solomon for his royal building projects, including *store cities* (v. 19), a striking resemblance to the Israelites' experience in Egypt under an earlier Pharaoh (Exod. 1:11). As if to remind us of that event, in the middle of the account of slave-labour comes mention of Pharaoh defeating Gezer (which the Israelites have been unable to do) and providing it as a dowry for his daughter. Solomon, king of Israel and Judah, is becoming more like Pharaoh of Egypt in his activities and policies.

Solomon's successes, suitably updated, would receive praise in many parts of the world today, with people wanting to know his secrets and emulate his initiative. Practices in diplomacy that get 'the best' for his country, trade relationships that build up his wealth (with some spinoff to the nation), and building projects with cheap slave labour all have similarities in the modern world. This chapter injects a voice often suppressed, or deemed 'old-fashioned' and not relevant to new situations. The Israelite experience of exile opened up a willingness to hear again the priority of the moral and social values implicit in the covenant, with undivided allegiance to God and care for all. Likewise today it is often 'failure' of current practices and ideologies that lead to reassessment. In the mid-1970s in Hong Kong university student leaders who had blindly followed the ways of Maoism, as expressed in the Chinese Cultural Revolution, were devastated with the overthrow of the 'Gang of Four' (Mao's wife and others). They turned to Christian students and asked about their faith in Jesus Christ as Lord.

Solomon's life journey, and the visions he was granted, are a salutary contemporary warning: the enticements of symbols of material wealth and their beguiling promise of a better life, evident in the diversity of marketing and advertising techniques, create a 'desire' for things that is a turning away from a 'desire' for God (Ps. 91:14). The temptations of trappings of power and status lead to treating others as objects for one's own advancement, be they 'Hirams' or 'non-Israelites'. Jesus relativized 'Solomon in all his splendour' in speaking of God's provision as his followers desire

---

[19] The relationship between different forms of conscripted labour is much discussed. The common word for conscripted labour, *mas*, is in 4:6; 5:13, 14 [MT 27, 28]; 9:15; while in 9:21 a longer *mas-ʿōbēd* 'forced labour of serving', i.e., 'slave-labour', occurs and 11:28 has *sēbel* 'forced labour' (carrying burdens). See Provan, pp. 88–89; Konkel, p. 199; Sweeney, p. 145; DeVries, p. 132.

[20] Deut. 20:11; Josh. 16:10; 17:13; 2 Sam. 20:24.

something more valuable, the 'kingdom [of God] and his righteousness' (Matt. 6:25–34). A place of worship can be a place where, like Solomon, we hear the word of God reminding of his great acts of deliverance, his ongoing presence and promises, fanning into a flame a 'desire' to *walk before me faithfully with integrity of heart and uprightness.*

2. Pharaoh's daughter, sacrifices and gold (9:24–28)

Mention of Pharaoh's daughter and her move to a palace near the temple seems at first to intrude into a passage on projects and organization, especially as the building of the *terraces* (v. 24b) was mentioned in verse 15. As in 3:1–4, however, what was *sacrificed* and *burning incense* are placed next to *Pharaoh's daughter* (vv. 24–25), marking a transition in the narrative and highlighting tensions in Solomon's reign by now juxtaposing a further element, *gold* (vv. 26–28). Pharaoh's daughter, as well as being a reminder of close ties with Egypt, will reappear in 11:1 in the account of the 'foreign women' who led Solomon astray to worship other gods. At least here he is faithful in offering sacrifices to Yahweh at the designated times each year, a requirement for every male.[21] The concluding phrase of v. 25, *fulfilled the temple obligations*, is unclear. A literal translation might be 'and he finished the house (temple)',[22] 'underlin[ing] the point that the temple was not truly regarded as "finished" by the authors of Kings until it was ready for worship'.[23] Appropriately as king, Solomon in this aspect is setting an example for all to follow.

Again Solomon obtains help from Hiram: Solomon may have built the ships but, as Phoenicians, Hiram's *men* provided the expertise needed at sea. Focus is on one item only, *gold* (v. 28): God has fulfilled his promise that he would give Solomon 'wealth' (3:13), but what is Solomon doing with the wealth?

These three sections (vv. 24, 25, 26–28) provide a striking juxtaposition: Pharaoh's daughter, sacrifices to Yahweh and gold. Each is significant in Solomon's life, each having attractions and making demands. Similar juxtaposition is the experience of many. Relationships, whether in marriage, friendship, work or as citizens of a nation, bring benefits, along with potential either to enhance or to

---

[21] Exod. 23:14–19; 34:18–26; Deut. 16:1–17.
[22] So NRSV, NLT and REB. Cf. the same verb in 7:51, '*when* all the work . . . *was finished*'.
[23] Provan, p. 89. House, supporting NIV's rendering, comments: 'Solomon met all the religious obligations set by the Mosaic law and implied by the building of a central sanctuary' (p. 159).

lead away from wholehearted, undivided loyalty to Christ. Since the garden of Eden we experience both 'it is not good for the man to be alone. I will make a helper' and she 'gave some to her husband, who was with her, and he ate it' (Gen 2:18; 3:6). Likewise, an essential part of life is God's provision of material needs, but now mixed with self-centred allure of wealth and possessions, with promises of enjoyment, status and security. The tension is evident in the exhortation in Deuteronomy 8:10–14: 'When you have eaten and are satisfied, praise the LORD your God for the good land he has given you' is associated with 'Be careful that you do not forget the LORD your God, failing to observe his commands ... Otherwise, when you eat and are satisfied, when you build fine houses and settle down, and when your herds and flocks grow large and your silver and gold increase and all you have is multiplied, then your heart will become proud and you will forget the LORD your God, who brought you out of Egypt, out of the land of slavery.' Solomon provides a case study.

As we journey with Solomon through the narrative we are encouraged to reflect on our own heart. Our wealth may be nowhere near Solomon's nor our relationships akin to being married to Pharaoh's daughter, but the starkness portrayed can illumine our greys. At this stage Solomon is faithfully worshipping Yahweh but questions are being raised as to his priorities. Jesus was to point to sad results: 'The seed falling among the thorns refers to someone who hears the word, but the worries of this life and the deceitfulness of wealth choke the word, making it unfruitful' (Matt. 13:22).

3. Wisdom, wealth, wives – and God (10:1 – 11:13)

In his first appearance Yahweh promised Solomon 'a wise and discerning heart, so that there will never have been anyone like you, nor will there ever be' and in addition 'both wealth and honour – so that in your lifetime you will have no equal among kings' (3:12–13). God keeps his word as *King Solomon was greater in riches and wisdom than all the other kings of the earth ... the wisdom God had put in his heart* (10:23–24). But how are the wisdom and wealth used and for whose benefit?

Already the narrator has given cause to question how well Solomon followed God's opening injunction to 'walk in obedience to me and keep my decrees and commands' (3:14). Initially, Solomon used his God-given wisdom on behalf of two people on society's fringe (3:16–28) and under his wise administration 'the people of Judah and Israel ... ate ... drank and were happy' (4:20). His worship of Yahweh, leadership and diplomatic skills and wealth were further evident in the building of the temple, but the account after the temple building tells a mixed story. There is praise of his wisdom by non-Israelite rulers, illustrated by the queen of Sheba's visit (10:1–13; also 10:24), but no mention of benefit to the wider population. His increasing wealth is described in detail, but all is focused on Solomon and his court.

The three components of 9:24–28, Pharaoh's daughter, temple sacrifices and gold, help us read what follows. There is much on *gold* (the word occurs fourteen times in chapter 10), with the temple or its sacrifices mentioned only in passing (vv. 5, 12). We see Solomon's power and 'honour' (promised in 3:13) as other rulers bring tribute. The language will show how far Solomon has turned away from the Deuteronomic rules for a king (Deut. 17:14–20), culminating in the first mention that Solomon had more foreign wives beyond Pharaoh's daughter and that he turned to other gods (11:1–8). The account of Solomon's reign provides an early example of the threefold alluring challenges of money, sex and power (see further after 11:1–13).[24] Kings and a queen may see him as successful, a ruler with wisdom, wealth and power, but Yahweh's final words to Solomon (11:9–13) are a judgment of failure: the kingdom which David and Solomon ruled is to be 'torn away', with only Judah remaining (11:9–13).

The contrast between human and divine criteria for success is clear: 'There is a way that appears to be right, but in the end it leads to death' (Prov. 14:12; 16:25). Solomon receives much, but is led astray by his own 'desire' (see on 9:1, 19), which 'gives birth to sin; and sin, when it is full-grown, gives birth to death' (Jas 1:15).

a. Wisdom, wealth and the queen of Sheba (10:1–13)

The visit of the *queen of Sheba* is rightly seen as the climax of God's promise to Solomon. Here is 'Solomon in all his splendour' (Matt. 6:29). She has come most likely from around Yemen, the south-western corner of Arabia,[25] and her *very great caravan* with its gifts for Solomon is evidence both of his standing and power and of the wealth Sheba gained through trading, probably as far as Mesopotamia, India and Africa.[26] To *test . . . with hard questions* or 'riddles'[27] is evidence that she came to explore trading arrangements, possibly

[24] A modern, now classic, work is R. Foster, *Money, Sex and Power: the Challenge of a Disciplined Life* (London: Hodder and Stoughton, 1985).

[25] Assyrian texts name a number of queens from the region in subsequent centuries while an earlier tradition links Sheba with Ethiopia (Sweeney, pp. 149–150).

[26] Walton, Matthews and Chavalas, p. 429.

[27] *ḥîdôt* is a term for 'riddles' such as asked by Samson (Judg. 14:12), but can include 'difficult diplomatic and ethical questions . . . to see if he would be a trustworthy business partner' (Wiseman, p. 129).

because of Solomon's expansion of trade in the region (9:26–27). Her praise of Solomon is quite explicit: his fame is linked to *his relationship to the* LORD (v. 1), possibly an allusion to the temple;[28] his *wisdom* and display of wealth leave her breathless (vv. 3–5) and in astonishment she exclaims, *Praise be to the* LORD *your God* (v. 9). Here is true praise, that she saw beyond Solomon and honoured the Giver.

The text however has undercurrents that question not Yahweh – he has fulfilled his word – but Solomon. Is there a hint in the order of the content of verses 4–5, with a detailed listing of what she could see as she is feted in *the palace he had built* before mentioning briefly *the burnt offerings he made at the temple of the* LORD (the only mention of the temple in the whole chapter apart from verse 12 where again *the royal palace* is associated). It appears that worship has become an expression of *Solomon's* glory, suggested previously by the placing of building of the palace in the middle of the temple building account.

The mirror of the passage can bring to light other rulers or communities (or even local churches) trying to outdo one another in the 'wealth' of their worship (buildings, music, facilities, liturgy), so that the worship draws attention to humans rather than to God. There is a thin line between 'giving the best to God' and self-centred pride in what *we* are doing.

The queen of Sheba's amazed *how happy* speaks of *your people*[29] and *your officials* (10:8), but absent from this chapter is mention of any benefit to the general population (unlike the earlier descriptions in 4:20–25). The wealth that comes to Solomon remains his, not the nation's. It is the Queen of Sheba, a foreigner, who has a wider perspective as she speaks of *the* LORD's *eternal love for Israel* in making Solomon king, adding the key role of a king, *to maintain justice and righteousness* (v. 9; see on 3:9, 28). Early in his reign Solomon's 'justice' was admired by 'all Israel' (3:28), but what the queen of Sheba has seen herself are answers to *hard questions* (vv. 1, 3) and display of royal wealth, amply detailed in this chapter. Her praise in this context can be seen by readers as something that Solomon needs to act on!

Jesus cites her visit 'from the ends of the earth to listen to Solomon's wisdom' as a pointed challenge to those who were unwilling to listen to 'something greater than Solomon' (Matt. 12:42 // Luke 11:31). Significantly the other OT group that will 'stand up at the judgment with this generation and condemn it' is also foreign, the people of

[28] Hebrew for the phrase is literally 'with regard to the name of Yahweh'.
[29] This is not the usual *'am* used of God's 'people' in ch. 8 but the plural *'ănāšekā* 'your persons, men'. LXX and Syriac have 'your wives', based on *nāšekā*, followed by NRSV; also Gray, p. 258, DeVries, pp. 134, 136.

Nineveh (Matt. 12:41 // Luke 11:30). Those outside God's people may see with fresh eyes that have not been dulled by familiarity and compromise.

b. Gold and horses (10:14–29)

The writer conveys a sense of wonderment at the wealth of Solomon, describing in detail the material and quantities brought to him by the *queen of Sheba* (vv. 2, 10) and by *Hiram's ships* (vv. 11–12, 22). This builds into a dazzling crescendo with detailed description of the gold for the throne and the decorations and household articles of the palace (vv. 14–22), with the loud summary of verses 23–25: he was *greater in riches and wisdom than all the other kings of the earth.* There is no disdaining of wealth or beauty, but there is no question that the wealth is predominant and that *the wisdom God had put in his heart* is resulting in his fame before other kings, with no mention of the general populace of Israel. Solomon is acting like the rulers of other nations, and they admire him.

The final item in the catalogue of Solomon's wealth and trading is *chariots and horses* (vv. 26–29), used mainly in warfare.[30] 'The implication is clear that Solomon had stationed sufficient forces on his borders to insure adequate protection and a strike force capable of quick retaliation or punitive campaigns.'[31] Like nations that parade the size and superiority of their military resources, both human and hardware, and who trade in armaments, Solomon builds up and trades in the ancient equivalent, *chariots and horses*. He even sold to the *Arameans*, who later are to attack Israel!

Reading in the wider biblical context provides another perspective. Deuteronomy 17:14–20 is quite specific in its guidelines for kingship. The key positive command, adherence to the laws of Yahweh (Deut. 17:18–19), has been mentioned a number of times in the Solomon narrative.[32] It is preceded by four specific prohibitions (Deut. 17:16–17):

- The king must not acquire many horses for himself. Elsewhere God's people were to trust in him, not horses (Deut. 20:1; Ps. 20:7).
- Further he must not cause the people to return to Egypt to acquire horses. Significantly the exodus included the destruction of Pharaoh's horses in the sea (Exod. 15:1, 19, 21; Deut. 11:4).

[30] On breeding of horses and mutual trade in Egypt and Anatolia, see K. A. Kitchen, 'External Textual Sources – Neo-Hittite States', in Lemaire and Halpern, pp. 367–368.
[31] Walton, Matthews and Chavalas, p. 431.
[32] See on 2:2–3; 3:3, 14; 6:11–13; 8:58, 61; 9:4–9.

- He must not acquire many wives for himself, or his heart will turn away (marriage was linked with political alliances, then as throughout history in all cultures).
- He must not acquire silver and gold for himself 'muchly' (to coin a word to render the Hebrew *mĕ'ōd*).[33]

The Kings description of Solomon's glory explicitly lists the breaking of all four, three having been mentioned thus far, with the 'wives' to follow:

- Solomon excelled himself with horses, with *chariot cities* throughout the country (10:26; also 4:26; 9:19).
- He had them bought from Egypt (10:28–29; and the wife given most prominence is Pharaoh's daughter).
- He had many wives, who 'turned' him to worship other gods (11:1–10; 'turned away' occurs four times).
- In the account of his wealth in 10:1–13 *mĕ'ōd* occurs four times (vv. 2 [twice], 10, 11; EVV 'very', 'large', 'great'), and large amounts of gold are enumerated in verses 14–22. There is so much gold that *silver was considered of little value in Solomon's days*, and so much *silver* that it was *as common in Jerusalem as stones* (vv. 21, 27).

A feature of verses 14–29 is the amount of enumeration. Measurement has always been part of human life, and numbers are given for diverse items throughout the Bible. The world God has created is such that exact measurement and mathematical models are powerful tools, able to be used for both betterment and destruction of human life. Ever since the garden of Eden 'wisdom' can either be 'a tree of life' when based on 'the fear of the LORD' (Prov. 1:7; 3:18) or sought as a way to control life circumstances and others independently of God. One can read the enumeration of Solomon's wealth with a sense of wonder at the magnificent superabundant blessings God gave, in the same way that tourists may marvel at the grandeur of a palace. It can also be read as an expression of Solomon's self-centred acquisition for his own glory, suggesting power and control over his kingdom with religious faith being a formality. The temptations are real in a world where, globally and personally, economic measures and scientific and technological advances are seen to provide solutions. Science

---

[33] The relative dating of the Deuteronomic laws and periods of Israelite monarchy is much debated. D. L. Christensen, *Deuteronomy 1:1 – 21:9, Revised*, Word Biblical Commentary, 6A (Nashville: Nelson, 2001), pp. 377–389, and J. G. McConville, *Deuteronomy*, Apollos OT Commentary 5 (Leicester: Apollos, 2002), pp. 283–284, provide summaries with bibliographies.

developed dramatically in the decades around 1800, but the Scottish essayist, Thomas Carlisle, wrote in 1833 that 'The Progress of Science . . . is to destroy Wonder, and in its stead substitute Mensuration and Numeration.'[34] A different stance is expressed in the 1874 inscription over the entrance of the Cavendish Laboratory in Cambridge: 'The works of the Lord are great, sought out of all them that have pleasure therein' (Ps. 111:2).[35]

c. Solomon turns to other gods (11:1–13)

Solomon's marriage to *Pharaoh's daughter* is mentioned yet again (see on 3:1), another drumbeat to remind readers of the link with Egypt (most recently mentioned in 10:29). David either made subject or entered in alliances with Moab (2 Sam. 8:2), Ammonites (2 Sam. 10; 12:26–31) and Edomites (2 Sam. 8:13–14), while Sidon is part of the territory ruled by Hiram (2 Sam. 5:11–12), but it was Solomon who sealed those alliances with marriages. The large number of *wives*, all of *royal birth*, and *concubines* is a measure of Solomon's standing amongst the surrounding nations, 'a symbol of wealth and political power'.[36] Further, he maintained relationships by providing facilities for worship of their gods (vv. 7–8). According to the practices of the ancient Near East all was praiseworthy, showing a mastery of international politics and diplomacy.

The biblical writer however saw a sign of weakness and failure for it contradicted the Deuteronomic warning (Deut. 7:1–6). It could be said that Solomon trusted in political alliances, sealed by marriage, rather than wholeheartedly in Yahweh, a negation of 'be strong' of 2:2–3. In fact, the warning became reality as *his wives turned his*

---

[34] In *Sartor Resartus*, quoted in R. Holmes, *The Age of Wonder* (London: HarperCollins, 2008), p. 436.

[35] 'Magna opera Domini exquisita in omnes voluntates ejus'; placed at the insistence of the first Professor of Experimental Physics, James Clerk Maxwell, and continued on the doorway of the new building (1974). In a personal email (26 October 2001) Joseph Kaung of the Divinity School of Chung Chi College, The Chinese University of Hong Kong, commented: 'A Chinese historian Ray Huang who wrote a book on Capitalism and the 20th Century (only Chinese version is available) placed Venice as the birthplace of modern capitalism. His definition of capitalism is "management through numbers". He used this idea to explain why capitalism did not flourish in China as China was not able to be governed or managed by quantification. In that sense, Solomon would be the prime example in Bible for being able to have life measured in numbers. The economic globalization process moves exactly in this direction which is not a blessing for university or church which values quality more than quantity.'

[36] I. A. Phiri, in an overview of biblical material in both Testaments and its relevance in Africa today, 'The Bible and Polygamy', in *Africa Bible Commentary*, edited by T. Adeyemo (Nairobi: Word Alive; Grand Rapids: Zondervan, 2006), p. 430.

heart after other gods (v. 4). While this statement has been read as blaming the wives, just as Adam blamed Eve (Gen. 3:12), God places the responsibility squarely with Solomon (vv. 9–10; cf. Gen. 3:17–19). He obviously continued to worship Yahweh (as in 9:25; 10:5), but *his heart was not fully devoted to the* LORD *his God, as the heart of David his father had been* (v. 4). David, despite serious failings, above all relating to Bathsheba and Uriah, had remained undivided in his worship of Yahweh, whereas Solomon lacked in commitment. The Deuteronomic charge to all Israelites was to 'hold fast to . . . the LORD',[37] to 'love' him[38]; instead Solomon *held fast to them* (foreign women) *in love* (v. 2). The persistent nature of his turning from following Yahweh is shown by repetitions: *turn* (vv. 2, 4, 9), *follow* (vv. 5, 6, 10), and *heart* (v. 4, three times; v. 9), the heart being the centre of both willing and reasoning, of conscious decision-making.

For the fourth time Yahweh speaks to Solomon.[39] The heightening warnings of the previous occasions now become judgment. Yahweh is 'slow to anger' (Exod. 34:6), and 'patient with you, not wanting anyone to perish, but everyone to come to repentance' (2 Pet. 3:9), but a time for judgment does come when warnings are persistently neglected or rejected. Seriousness is expressed in the narrator's introduction (vv. 9–10), repeated in Yahweh's words (v. 11a), giving solid reason for Yahweh taking deliberate action, stated vividly and emphatically: *I will most certainly tear the kingdom away from you and give it to one of your subordinates* (v. 11). The image strikingly repeats that used to Saul in announcing that 'The LORD has torn the kingdom of Israel from you today and has given it to one of your neighbours' (1 Sam. 15:28; 28:17) and will be symbolically enacted by the prophet Ahijah to Jeroboam (vv. 29–31). 'What the family of David receives as a gift from Yahweh . . . is taken away by the same action of Yahweh . . . The powerful in Israel are always again relearning respect for the overriding claim of Yahweh' (cf. Dan. 4:25).[40]

There is however mitigation, based on two previous actions of Yahweh, the promise to *David*, who as well as being *your father* is also *my servant* (vv. 12–13), and the choosing of *Jerusalem* (v. 13).[41] This brings to the fore an issue that will continue in Kings and which

[37] Deut. 10:20; 11:22; 13:4; 30:20.
[38] Deut. 6:5; 11:1, 22; 13:3.
[39] Previously 3:5–15; 6:11–13; 9:1–9, the first and third being visions.
[40] Brueggemann, p. 143.
[41] 'The place [Yahweh] will choose . . . to put his Name there for his dwelling' recurs in Deuteronomy (12:5, 11, 14, 18, 26; 14:23–24, etc.). Yahweh's endorsing of the temple as that place has been affirmed (1 Kgs 8:10–11; 9:3), and now there is expansion to the city.

confronts the exiles: what is the relationship between the Sinai covenant relationship with its obligations (evident in v. 11) and the Davidic covenant and its association with Jerusalem (as in vv. 12–13)? For the present there is 'middle ground somewhere between rigid law and boundless grace'.[42] Yahweh's relationship continues in the rump Davidic kingdom of Judah, but the parallel to his 'tearing away' the kingdom from Saul also points to his ongoing relationship with the one who will be given the ten tribes that are 'Israel' (see below on Jeroboam, pp. 123–127).

d. How did Solomon go wrong?

Commentators and preachers commonly focus on 11:1–13: 'That Solomon clung in love to his foreign wives suggests that his character was flawed by an inordinate desire for women.'[43] Further, this happened *as Solomon grew old* (11:4–6). Certainly the implementation of God's judgment is related to his worshipping of other gods alongside Yahweh (11:9). Nevertheless, we have noted how, through both structure and language, the writer shows the seeds of the problem right from the beginning. Solomon's action in marrying Pharaoh's daughter is inappropriate on the basis of the covenant, and yet he is keen to serve Yahweh and be the best king he can, especially in chapters 5 – 8. Thereafter the narrative suggests that he was caught in the trappings and benefits of power.

An answer may be in another statement in Deuteronomy 17:20. In between two statements about following God's laws is the phrase 'not consider himself better than his fellow Israelites'. Solomon received wealth, but it was focused in the royal establishment. One way he became wealthy was through the forced labour required for all the building operations – someone had to do the work. Food supplies and servants were needed for the palace – someone had to pay for the government. Labour forces alone would have meant major social disruption, made explicit after Solomon's death when the people from the north complained to Solomon's son, Rehoboam, 'Your father put a heavy yoke on us' (12:4), a contrast to the earlier enjoyment of peace (4:20). Solomon's schemes of grand buildings for himself and his armies (horses and chariots) and provision of the necessary food supplies were at the cost of the labour of the majority of the people. Wealth was used not to alleviate the conditions of the people but to enhance the quality of life of Solomon himself and his large court. A millennium later John saw a wealthy city ('Babylon',

---

[42] Provan, p. 92. See Introduction pp. 28–30 on the Davidic promise in Kings,
[43] Rice, p. 87. Cf. NIV's 'however' (not in Hebrew).

a cipher for Rome), describing its beauty with wonder and awe yet ending with the cost, 'human beings' (Rev. 18:11–13). Issues of acquisition of wealth at the expense of others' lives are perennial – and God's judgment is clear.[44]

Descriptions point to wisdom misdirected to enhance his own comfort and reputation. Did he justify this by saying it brought more fame to Yahweh, as instanced by the Queen of Sheba's words (10:1, 9) and a luxurious temple (10:12), although his own palace was more grand (10:16–22)? Looking into the mirror today may suggest others who justify injustice on the basis of 'gifts to the church'. 'Through his disregard of Torah . . . Solomon's wisdom, if not always degenerating into folly . . . nevertheless is not used for the benefit of the people. His justice turns to tyranny.'[45] How different is the One 'greater than Solomon' (Matt. 12:42), 'the wisdom of God' (1 Cor. 1:24), who shares his riches with all, becoming 'poor, so that you through his poverty might become rich' (2 Cor. 8:9).

Until 11:1–9 the narrator is not too harsh on Solomon: details are there, criticism is implied, but it is recognized that Solomon is acting as kings do! His father David, with all his failures, still clung to Yahweh and served him. He had begun to deal with the practicalities of ruling, but to Solomon, the second generation, fell the task of setting up the kinds of structures and associated lifestyle that belong with monarchy. Administrative and tax-gathering structures were required. A labour force had to be organized for government service and state building projects. Relationships with other nations had to be negotiated and defence requirements met. The list continues.

Many nations have come into being through wars of independence or revolutions. The initial leader soon finds that turning from war and struggle to the realities of government is not straightforward. At a local level, all leadership of growing churches and organizations brings with it challenges as to patterns to follow. In facing new situations of growth, Solomon had the model of surrounding nations. There was always a palace and, close to the palace and under royal patronage, a temple for the chief god of the city or nation. Egypt had a developed bureaucratic system. The adopting of cultural

[44] D. Cadbury, *Chocolate Wars: From Cadbury to Kraft, 200 Years of Sweet Success and Bitter Rivalries* (London: HarperPress, 2010), is a challenging account of ways in which the Cadbury family (Quakers, along with the Rowntree and Fry families) for almost 200 years saw their business as a way not to personal wealth but to improvement of the living conditions of workers and the poor, including workers on cocoa plantations. She concludes with questions concerning the priorities of current ownership having global shareholders with no community links.

[45] K. I. Parker, 'Solomon as Philosopher King? The Nexus of Law and Wisdom in 1 Kings 1–11,' *Journal for the Study of the Old Testament* 53 (1992), p. 86.

patterns is evident throughout the history of the church in all cultures, whether the lifestyle of 'princes' in the Middle Ages or business corporations and use of media in the modern West. Each has been accompanied by voices of critique.

The text tells how Solomon's leadership was exercised through the wisdom that God gave him, yet reading the same text raises questions as we seek to allow the text to illuminate our own situations. Was Solomon so involved in the processes of ruling and the trappings of power and status that they dominated? Did he think he was still serving Yahweh faithfully because he was growing in prosperity and fame? Did he get caught up in his own importance and fail to listen to the advice of others? (It will be 'the elders who had served his father Solomon' who will counsel Rehoboam to 'be a servant to the people' and lighten the yoke [12:6–7].)

The text, like any narrative, does not answer all questions. It points to complexities and ambiguities in human response to God's gifts. It challenges us to look at our own situation. It questions values and priorities, providing cautionary lights along our own roads, giving another perspective on what has become 'normal' but may be going in the wrong direction. I was personally challenged some years ago when Chinese students from the theological institution where I was teaching in Hong Kong attended an international conference. Their comments on return were that 'Western Christian leaders warned us from Asia of the dangers of syncretism with Asian religions but they failed to see their own syncretism with materialism, with its focus on money, numbers, and technology.' The temptations are subtle and the shift away from biblical priorities often gradual.[46] In 2006, at an international conference in Central Asia, a Korean leader commented that, with increasing economic standards, church growth in South Korea and in the cities of China had slowed, as Christians were drawn into the quest for more security and a 'higher standard of living' (that phrase itself is illuminating in that it generally refers to material possessions). Others commented on a similar phenomenon in their own countries. Writing in a context of ministry in Manhattan, Tim Keller explores ways in which 'money, sex and power . . . are vying to be counterfeit gods', with 'a cultural analysis, using the category of idolatry, to help Christians see how they get sucked in'. The story of Solomon demonstrates well Keller's succinct statement that 'sex, work, and money . . . are great goods. They are intrinsic to our being made in God's image. If God is second place

---

[46] B. C. Birch and L. L. Rasmussen, *The Predicament of the Prosperous* (Philadelphia: Westminster, 1978) include, along with biblical material, analysis of the shift over recent centuries from a covenantal Protestant work ethic to an individualistic capitalist work ethic with different goals and attitudes.

in your life and one of them is first, you're cooked. These things are candidates for first place because they are so great.'[47]

The people of God are not left without guidance. Within the Deuteronomic guidelines for kingship is:

> When he takes the throne of his kingdom, he is to write for himself on a scroll a copy of this law ... It is to be with him, and he is to read it all the days of his life so that he may learn to revere the LORD his God and follow carefully all the words of this law and these decrees. (Deut. 17:18–19)

Writing out requires time and attention to detail, a reading of the whole, and is a good way to learn.[48] Christians have now the full range of the Scriptures, a God-breathed resource requiring regular, systematic reading and putting into practice (2 Tim. 3:16), best done in a setting of mutual encouragement for reading. This is not simply building up 'Bible knowledge' but a grappling with implications for life in society (Heb. 10:23–25). Solomon may be an example of a person whose life is so full of doing and enjoying good things that 'following Yahweh's ways' becomes something to which mental assent is given, but learning of and reminding oneself of those ways have low priority. The Christian church in the early centuries took seriously the final command of Jesus to 'make disciples ... teaching them to obey everything I have commanded you' (Matt. 28:19–20), with a systematic, ongoing practice of teaching inquirers and new believers using the Gospels, inculcating the way of Christ. There is strong evidence that lifestyle changes were a key factor in the expansion of the church in the Roman empire: it was Christ-like lifestyle that attracted 'the nations'.

> In an age of bondage, of increasing disorder, of a deepening gulf between privileged people and poor people, of life-disfiguring addictions and compulsions, the church was growing because it and its members had a freedom and fullness of life in Christ that could not be hid ... This newness in the practices of its corporate life and the behaviour of its members towards non-members was intriguing, inviting, question-posing.[49]

---

[47] T. Keller, *Counterfeit Gods* (New York: Dutton Adult, 2009). Quote from an interview in *Christianity Today*, November 2009, p. 71.

[48] Christensen, *Deuteronomy 1:1 – 21:9, Revised*, p. 388, tells of his own experience in writing out the whole book a number of times.

[49] A. Kreider, 'Worship and Evangelism in Pre-Christendom', *Vox Evangelica* 24 (1994), p. 10; see also his *The Change of Conversion and the Origin of Christendom*, Christian Mission and Modern Culture (Harrisburg, PA: Trinity Press International, 1999).

Through the Scriptures, the Spirit of God indeed brings freedom and life.

Running through the narrative is the presence of Yahweh. He appears to Solomon and gives wisdom and warning, and he keeps his promises of wealth and fame. Even though right at the start is the potential problem of Pharaoh's daughter, God deals in grace with Solomon as he is. Yahweh's desire to bless is evident as he continues to give both wisdom and wealth, but with increasing warnings as the gifts are misused. Wisdom is to issue in justice for all, to be praised by both the Queen of Sheba and the powerless prostitute. Wealth is to be shared, not a means of self-aggrandizement. There can be no divided worship of Yahweh *and* other gods: the only true God requires total trust and allegiance, and a character that reflects his own, maintained through consistent meditation on his word.

4. Adversaries and succession (11:14–43)

At the beginning of his reign Solomon had removed David's enemies (2:5–46), but now Yahweh raises up adversaries, two associated with David (11:14–28). Previously Yahweh had commended Solomon because he had not 'asked for the death of your enemies' (3:11) but at the end Solomon seeks the death of Jeroboam (11:40) – Solomon has reverted to the 'wisdom' he had before Yahweh's gift (2:6, 9).[50] Solomon had written to Hiram that 'the LORD my God has given me rest on every side, and there is no *adversary* or disaster' (5:4), but now relationships are fractured. Yahweh himself raises up as an *adversary*,[51] not only *Hadad the Edomite* (v. 14) on the southeast but also, to the north, *Rezon* who ruled in *Aram* (Syria)[52] (vv. 23, 25), both associated with forces David had defeated. Lasting peace could be secured not by Solomon's wisdom, wealth, diplomacy and military strength but only by his following Yahweh's ways.

a. Neighbouring adversaries (11:14–25)

The accounts of *Hadad* (vv. 14–22) and *Rezon* (vv. 23–25) are striking and unexpectedly detailed. Walsh argues that 'an ancient Israelite reader' would see ways in which Hadad's life has parallels with Moses and Rezon's with David: 'The same Yahweh who raised

---

[50] See on 2:5–12, pp. 54–55.

[51] Hebrew *śāṭān* is used in Kings only in 5:4, and of Hadad and Rezon, so linking the three verses.

[52] Syria is the Greek name that continues in the name of the modern nation. Throughout the OT the term for the region (people) is Aram(aean), although some English versions use Syria(n).

up Moses as Israel's savior, the same God who raised up David to be Israel's ideal king, now raises up adversaries to oppose Solomon . . . [All] become part of the sacred history of Yahweh's dealings with Israel.'[53]

Solomon's relationship with Pharaoh has surfaced several times,[54] but surprisingly Pharaoh is also treating very generously a refugee *from the royal line of Edom*, Israel's long-standing enemy, thoroughly defeated by David.[55] Here too Pharaoh provides a royal wife. Upon hearing of David and Joab's death Hadad desired to return, although dissuaded by Pharaoh. We are not told what he did on return but the pairing with *Rezon* (v. 25) suggests some kind of guerilla warfare that would have threatened at least the shipping trade based at Ezion Geber (9:26).[56] While, as suggested, Israelite readers saw parallels with Moses, Christian readers can look to another child who was taken as a refugee to Egypt and who lived there safely until the murderous threat ended with the death of a ruler, the Idumean[57] Herod, king of the Jews (Matt. 2:13–23). That child would be not an adversary of the Davidic king but himself the Son of David, who came to bring peace.

Zobah was north of Damascus, its defeat by David mentioned along with other Aramean kingdoms (2 Sam. 8:3–10). Like David, *Rezon* attracted a band of men and eventually *took control* of *Damascus*, founding what soon became the most powerful Aramean dynasty and state, and is next met in the biblical narrative in the reign of Asa of Judah (15:18–20) when Judah seeks Aram's aid against Israel! Such are the pragmatic twists of allegiances.

There is no description of what Hadad and Rezon did, except being adversaries; for Rezon *as long as Solomon lived*. The significance of their inclusion is in the assertion that their antagonism was not merely a matter of changing balances of power and political alliances, but the action of Yahweh. He may be the God of Israel, but that does not restrict his power or locus of involvement. Solomon may have seen Hadad and Rezon as minor nuisances on the fringes of his empire, but Yahweh's action in judgment foreshadows what the exilic hearers had experienced, the destruction of Jerusalem and its temple by Nebuchadnezzar and the forces of

---

[53] Walsh, p. 140; similarly Leithart, pp. 87–88, Sweeney, p. 157.

[54] 3:1; 7:8; 9:16, 24; 10:28–29; 11:1.

[55] 2 Sam. 8:13–14; cf. Num. 20:14–21; 24:17–19; 1 Sam. 14:47.

[56] For historical and cultural setting of Hadad and his period in Egypt, see K. A. Kitchen, 'External Textual Sources – Egypt', in Lemaire and Halpern, pp. 372–373.

[57] Idumea is the Grecized form of 'Edom', although during the Greco-Roman period its region was to the west of the Dead Sea. Edomite territory, until the exile, was to the east, with subsequent movement westward. The Idumeans were subjugated by the Jews around 125 BC and forcibly converted.

Babylon. That too was the judging action of Yahweh who had announced, 'I will summon all the peoples of the north and my servant Nebuchadnezzar king of Babylon' (Jer. 25:9), but who later announced the end of exile and return to Jerusalem, 'I will raise up Cyrus', the Persian emperor (Isa. 45:13). 'All human rule is subject to Yahweh. . . . This sovereignty of God in human affairs is set against the fickleness of human rule, its tendency to tyranny, its self-deluding pretentiousness.'[58]

Centuries later in the birth of a child in a manger God was to confront the pretensions of a Caesar Augustus, a child who was called 'Lord' and 'Saviour', bringing peace to earth (Luke 2:11, 14). That child's later death and resurrection enabled the early Christians not to fear the arrogance of human rulers and to follow Christ boldly. At that time 'the kings of the earth rise up and the rulers band together against the Lord and against his anointed one' (Acts 4:26, citing Ps. 2:1–2), but God has shown his power in the resurrection and the exaltation of Christ 'far above all rule and authority' (Eph. 1:21). Human rule is to be respected and prayed for (e.g., Rom. 13:1–7; 1 Tim. 2:1–2), but its authority is relativized under the sovereignty of God.

In the messy world of national and international politics, armed conflict and arrogant dictatorships, to say 'the Lord raised up' with regard to a specific individual is to be done with great caution (history provides examples of misuse of such attribution), yet the examples of Hadad and Rezon can remind us that God is involved in the history of his world, seen definitively in Christ.

b. Jeroboam, an adversary from within (11:26–40)[59]

The introduction of *Jeroboam* immediately flags his significance in the ongoing drama. In MT word order his family and tribal identification comes first – he is an *Ephraimite*, from the dominant tribe in the north, and unusually his mother, now a widow, is named[60] – followed by the terse juxtaposition of *one of Solomon's officials* (lit. 'a servant of Solomon') and he *rebelled against the king*. This is ominous: Solomon had been told that Yahweh *will most certainly*

---

[58] J. G. McConville, *God and Earthly Power: An Old Testament Political Theology, Genesis–Kings* (London: T.&T. Clark, 2006), p. 166.

[59] The narrative concerning Jeroboam and Rehoboam is quite different in LXX, with two accounts. For English translation see *NETS;* and for analysis, R. P. Gordon, 'The Second Septuagint Account of Jeroboam: History or Midrash?', *Vetus Testamentum* 25 (1975), pp. 368–393.

[60] *Zeruah* means 'skin disease, leper' and may be a deliberate change from Zeruiah (also the name of David's sister), so denigrating Jeroboam's line (J. R. Soza, 'Jeroboam', *DOTHB*, p. 545).

tear the kingdom away from you and give it to one of your sub-
ordinates (v. 11; lit., 'your servant'). All is not right in Solomon's rule
and Jeroboam is a ready candidate as the one to whom the kingdom
will be given.

The writer's perspective is shown as he relates how Jeroboam
rebelled against the king. He describes Jeroboam as *a man of*
standing, pointing to characteristics praised in battle,[61] and one who
did his work . . . well (lit. 'doer of a task'). Even as a *young man* his
leadership capabilities were recognized, with Solomon promoting
him to be *in charge of the whole labour force of the tribes* ['house']
of Joseph, i.e., the tribes of Ephraim and Manasseh (v. 28). Then
unexpectedly comes the dramatic detailed prophecy of *Ahijah* (vv.
29–39), followed only by a concise statement that Jeroboam *fled to*
Egypt because Solomon *tried to kill* him (v. 40). That Shishak
provided sanctuary is another indication of Solomon's deteriorating
relationship with Egypt, Shishak likely being the successor to the
Pharaoh who gave his daughter in marriage to Solomon. Within five
years of Solomon's death Shishak attacked Jerusalem (14:25–26).[62]
The alliance in which Solomon had confidence is proving to be
shaky, even dangerous.

In light of verse 27 we might have expected specific details of
Jeroboam's rebellion – we can only assume he led a protest by the
forced labourers. What is given is a long prophecy of division.
Jeroboam next appears after Solomon's death along with the Israelites
who seek alleviation from his oppressive policies (12:2–4). The writer
is emphatic that Jeroboam's success is due not to his capabilities or
actions but to Yahweh's decision, that division after Solomon's death
is primarily the result not of Rehoboam's arrogant dismissal of the
Israelites' concerns (12:12–16) but of Yahweh's judgment on
Solomon. The prophet *Ahijah* is from *Shiloh* (v. 29), the ancient
worship centre which was Samuel's base (1 Sam. 1:3; 3:21), and his
symbolic action is reminiscent of the occasion when Saul grabbed
Samuel's robe and 'it tore', a symbol that his kingdom would be
given to another (1 Sam. 15:27–28). The disposition of the kingdom
is Yahweh's prerogative, the message repeatedly telling what *'I'* will
do (vv. 31–36; reinforcing vv. 11–13). In various ways the narrator
asserts that history is governed by God and his word made known
through prophets, not by human machinations and struggles. God
is acting in judgment on Solomon, extended to include the people
(v. 33), for worship of other gods and failure to keep *my decrees and*

[61] The phrase *gibbôr ḥāyil* mainly, but not always, describes warriors, e.g., groups
of men (Josh. 1:14; 6:2; 8:3, etc.), Gideon (Judg. 6:12), Jephthah (Judg. 11:1), Boaz
(Ruth 2:1), Kish, Saul's father (1 Sam. 9:1), and Naaman (2 Kgs 5:1).

[62] Monson, pp. 53–54.

laws.[63] *Israel* is now to be ruled by Jeroboam (v. 37), although a descendant of David will continue *in Jerusalem* (v. 36; contrast Yahweh's original appointment of David as ruler over 'my people Israel', 2 Sam. 7:8). Pointedly the charge and promise to Jeroboam (vv. 37–38) are full of language used previously to David and Solomon (2 Sam. 7:11–15; 1 Kgs 2:2–4; 3:14), with one qualification, *not forever* (v. 39). There is hope for future restoration of the Davidic kingdom, a promise to be held on to by exilic readers who are experiencing only a glimmer of continuation (2 Kgs 25:27–30).

The future for Jeroboam and Israel at this stage is as bright as that which had applied to David. Yahweh is establishing the kingdom and the same conditions apply to the north as for the remnant Judah: *walk in obedience to me* ['in my ways'] *and do what is right in my eyes* (v. 38). While the rest of the account of Jeroboam and of the kingdom of Israel will be of failure, at the very commencement is affirmation that Yahweh is concerned for all his people, Israel and Judah. He has laid the foundation on which Israel is to build.

What kind of heritage does one generation of leaders leave for the next? The history of groups – whether nations, corporations, churches or families – demonstrates persistence through generations of patterns of religious commitment, of personal and corporate values, of social and political behaviour. The role of founders, and of leaders at significant transitions, is a major factor. Anyone seeking to bring change needs to be aware of such patterns and their origins. Jesus chose disciples to 'be with him' (Mark 3:14), to observe his ways over a long period, and to 'make disciples . . . teaching them to obey everything I have commanded you' (Matt. 28:19–20). So the pattern of Christ became a dominant component of the teaching of the church in the early centuries, although a major shift in practice came when Christianity became the official religion of the Roman empire.[64]

David, for all his failures, was a faithful servant of Yahweh, open to words of judgment and correction, showing genuine repentance and ongoing commitment to Yahweh's ways. This was the direction of his whole life and so it is said that *he did keep*[65] *my commands and decrees* (v. 34 NRSV). Solomon received this heritage (2:2–4), but

---

[63] MT has plural verbs throughout v. 33, although 'they' is left unspecified and the end of the verse has 'David *his* father'. NIV, NJPSV follow the plural (with 'Solomon' clarifying 'his'). Other versions, e.g., NRSV, NLT, follow LXX which has singular throughout, referring to Solomon alone.

[64] See Kreider, *The Change of Conversion*.

[65] Hebrew *šāmar* is used widely meaning 'watch over, guard, protect, keep'. With commandments as object it is sometimes translated 'obey' (as NIV, vv. 34, 38), but it is more than mere conformity. Common is the idea of 'pay careful attention to' (K. N. Schoville, '*šmr* #9068', *NIDOTTE* 4, pp. 182–184).

diverted to pursue other values and priorities. Failure to worship Yahweh alone, not paying attention to his ways, had as corollary oppressive policies that seemed to have as their goal the glory of Solomon rather than 'justice' for all (3:9, 28). Such was the heritage tragically passed on to Rehoboam and his contemporaries. When God and his revealed ways are not central in one's vision the result is breakup of social cohesion.

'A healthy lifestyle' has become a popular concern today, with attention to diet and exercise, along with medical treatment using pharmaceuticals. In the physical realm benefits of conformity to 'laws' are recognized. As Creator Yahweh knows what is good for the well-functioning of society and so has given to his people laws that can bring about and maintain 'a healthy community lifestyle', well-being, harmony and peace for all.[66] When such laws are flouted societal disruption and harm result. In a wide-ranging investigation, epidemiologists Richard Wilkinson and Kate Pickett examined a range of social phenomena such as life expectancy, mental health, obesity, teenage births, violence, imprisonment, and children's educational performance in twenty-three developed countries.[67] They found a clear correlation between the degree of inequality and the level of health and social indicators: the greater the income disparity in a country the lower was life expectancy across all groups, the higher the amount of violence and drug-taking, and similar. Readers of Scripture should not be surprised, given the emphasis in both Old and New Testaments on community members caring for each other, sharing resources, together with words against self-centred unjust behaviour. Solomon's reign saw rapid increase in economic disparity between Jerusalem, with its court establishment, and the rest of the country. Two centuries later during the reign of Jeroboam II a similar disparity was to develop in the northern kingdom of Israel, also associated with empty religiosity and syncretism, leading to the prophetic message of Amos.

Solomon's reign was marked by regal policies that went against the injunctions of Deuteronomy, Yahweh's laws and decrees, in both worship and economics: the result was the rupture of the united kingdom. God's judgment was made known then by prophetic message. Readers today can reflect on those policies and

---

[66] George Ellis, a leading cosmologist and 2004 recipient of the prestigious Templeton Prize for Progress Toward Research or Discoveries about Spiritual Realities, has argued that just as the universe has a physical structure so it has a moral structure. See his (with N. Murphy) *On The Moral Nature of the Universe: Cosmology, Theology, and Ethics* (Fortress Press, 1996; also in Russian and Chinese).

[67] R. Wilkinson and K. Pickett, *The Spirit Level: Why More Equal Societies Almost Always Do Better* (London: Allen Lane, 2009).

the prophetic message in the light of subsequent history, refracted through the life, message, ministry, death and resurrection of Jesus and example of the early church, and illustrated from current secular research. Jeroboam was told that the way to an enduring dynasty was through doing *what is right in my eyes* (v. 38). Jesus was to say that the 'everyone who hears these words of mine and puts them into practice is like a wise man who built his house on the rock', standing fast through storm and flood (Matt. 7:24–25).

c. Death and succession (11:41–43)

The account of Solomon ends with the first instance of a standard pattern for recording death of a monarch and succession. Much more could have been told but what the narrator has given provides a perspective to illumine the exilic situation, pointing not only to Yahweh's judgment but also to his ongoing covenant relationship. There is hope for the future in turning back to him, following his ways and looking to his grace (8:46–51).

As we have moved through the story of Solomon the narrative has shone light not only on the exilic context of early hearers but also on the life of God's people today. Some of that light has been refracted through NT references to 'wisdom that is from above' (see on 3:4–15; 10:1–13), to Solomon and his wealth (for varying aspects see on 9:1–9, 10–23, 24–28; 10:1–13, 14–29) and to the temple (see on 8:1–13, 62–66). Of note is NT perspective in its explicit references to Solomon. Matthew 6:29 is part of 6:19–34 commencing, 'Do not store up for yourselves treasures on earth', and warning that 'You cannot serve both God and money'; rather God supplies what is needed and so our priority is to 'seek first his kingdom and his righteousness'. The parallel comparison in Luke 12:27 is in a passage which commences with the parable of the rich fool, and goes on to enjoin 'Sell your possessions and give to the poor', concluding 'for where your treasure is, there your heart will be also' (Luke 12:13–34). Solomon's glory becomes warning, with the implication that in the end he was a 'rich fool'.

Other NT references to Solomon are in the genealogy of Jesus (Matt. 1:6–7), pointing to Jesus as the fulfilment of the promise concerning the Davidic king, reinforced by the statement that the 'Queen of the South' came to 'listen to Solomon's wisdom, and now something greater than Solomon is here' (Matt. 12:42; Luke 11:31). The only other reference is in Stephen's provocative retelling of the history of God's people in which his mention of Solomon's building the temple is immediately followed by, 'However, the Most High does not live in houses made by human hands' (Acts 7:47–48). In saying 'made by human hands', Stephen may be deliberately using the derogatory word used of idol worship,[68] as well as alluding to the quoted words of Jesus, 'I will destroy this temple made by human hands and in three days will build another, not made with hands' (Mark 14:58).[69]

Thus whether wisdom, wealth or temple, Solomon's life and activities are a warning, each aspect being transformed in light of Christ. He is the 'wisdom of God' (1 Cor. 1:21), who 'became poor' so that we 'might become rich' (2 Cor. 8:9). He is the 'temple' into whom we are being built (Eph. 2:21). As such we show the glory of God as we receive from him 'wisdom that comes from heaven' (Jas 1:5; 3:17) and generously share the riches he provides (2 Cor. 9:6–15). The story of Solomon exposes the temptations that come in the midst of complex situations to misuse God's good gifts, to turn aside after counterfeit gods.

Here is a cautionary account of a leader who 'showed his love for the LORD' (3:3), who built a magnificent temple and regularly offered sacrifices (3:15; 8:62; 9:25; 10:5), but nevertheless whose 'heart turned away from the LORD, the God of Israel, who had appeared to him twice' (11:9). Past decisions do not guarantee present attitudes, and so Paul's words concerning earlier behaviour of the Israelites could well be adapted here: 'Now these things occurred as examples to keep us from setting our hearts on evil things as [he] did' (1 Cor. 10:6). Mutual encouragement in perseverance is evident in the NT (e.g., Heb. 10:24–25; 1 Cor. 15:58), together with seniors sharing experience with those who are younger (e.g., 1 – 2 Tim.; Titus). It was my privilege as an undergraduate to be secretary of the Sydney University Evangelical Union. The president, Lawrence Chia, a Singaporean, was challenged by statistics showing how many student leaders were no longer active in Christian service a decade after university. With his initiative committee members continued to meet regularly for prayer and encouragement through the transitions of graduation, beginning professional life and marriage and family. We would all see this as a significant factor in our continuing ministries and witness.

Early in his reign Solomon is commended for his answer to God's question, 'Ask for whatever you want me to give you' (3:5), but later 'all he had desired to do' (9:1) is related to royal buildings and 'he held fast to them [foreign women] in love' (11:2). A millennium later Christ says to his disciples, 'Ask and it will be given to you' (Matt. 7:7), significantly in the context of the broad lifestyle and attitudinal

---

[68] Greek *cheiropoiētos* is used in LXX, Lev. 26:1, 30; Isa. 2:18; 10:11; 19:1; 21:9; 31:7, etc., overwhelmingly of idols.

[69] I. H. Marshall, *Acts* (Tyndale NT Commentaries; Leicester: Inter-Varsity Press, 1980), p. 146. See also Acts 17:23; Heb. 9:11, 24.

teaching of the Sermon on the Mount. With confidence, James writes in a context of facing trials that test faith and of being tempted by evil desires, 'If any of you lacks wisdom, you should ask God, who gives generously to all without finding fault, and it will be given to you' (Jas 1:5), and Paul, in a context of generous giving for the poor in Jerusalem, affirms, 'My God will meet all your needs according to the riches of his glory in Christ Jesus' (Phil. 4:19). In Christ there is both forgiveness and generous provision as we follow his way through all stages of life.

B. Division – the first 160 years
1 Kings 12:1 – 16:28

1 Kings 12:1 – 14:20
6. Leadership: power, pragmatism and God's evaluation

Rehoboam his son succeeded him as king is the end of chapter 11, but Yahweh's word through the prophet Ahijah has led us to expect that in some way Jeroboam will become king of the dominant region of Israel. Human interactions and Rehoboam's arrogant decisions that bring this about, and Jeroboam's fateful policies as he begins his reign, are the content of chapter 12, while 13:1 – 14:20 provides God's evaluation in dramatic ways.

1. Rehoboam and power (12:1–24)

a. How will Rehoboam lead? (12:1–15)

Almost all of Rehoboam's life has been spent during the reign of his father, Solomon.[1] What has he learnt? How is he to exercise power and authority? The opening alerts to core issues. It is to *Shechem* in the north, not Jerusalem, that *all Israel* come to crown Rehoboam. Shechem is associated with their ancestor Jacob, also named Israel (Gen. 33:18–20; 35:10), and was where the covenant renewal ceremony under Joshua was held and Joseph's bones buried, both actions bringing to a culmination the exodus from Egypt (Josh. 24). It was the location of an earlier, abortive attempt to institute kingship, rejected because 'the LORD will rule over you' (Judg. 8:22–27; 9:1–57). Identity, as the 'descendants of Israel/Jacob' who had been brought out of Egypt by the covenant-making God, was deeper than being 'subjects of a king'. Further, as yet there was no clear procedure

---

[1] According to 14:21 he was 41 years old when he began to reign, while in 11:42 Solomon reigned 40 years.

for dynastic succession, illustrated by Solomon's becoming king rather than Adonijah (ch. 1). As in many nations, at different eras in history, succession was determined by a recognised body of elders. The *whole assembly of Israel* (cf. 2 Sam. 5:1–3) will eventually reject Rehoboam and crown Jeroboam (vv. 3, 20). Solomon had weakened the old tribal loyalties in his administrative districts (see on 4:7–19) and Rehoboam has grown up under that structure, but now he has to consider where *he* stands with regard to 'Israel'. Will he reign in terms of the covenant?

The Israelites have a major concern, with Jeroboam summoned possibly as their spokesperson.[2] In vocabulary reminiscent of the Egyptian oppression[3] they request that *the heavy yoke* (repeated) and *harsh labour* imposed by Solomon be lightened (vv. 3–4). How tragic that Solomon's rule is described as a return to the slavery from which Yahweh had delivered them, but Rehoboam has an ideal opportunity. It was common for Mesopotamian kings at the beginning of a reign to lessen taxes, remit debts and set people free from forced labour.[4] How much more should this be so for a people whom Yahweh had delivered from slavery. That was the tenor of the counsel of the elders who had advised Solomon. Their model of kingship was to be *a servant* who will *serve* the people, who in turn become *servants* of the king (vv. 6–7), the pattern of mutuality in Deuteronomy 17:20. Rehoboam rejects their advice in favour of an arrogant and tough authoritarian model recommended by his peers, with *heavy yoke* used three times and additional imagery of *scorpions* twice (vv. 8–14).[5] Rather than being the first among equals (Deut. 17:20), he acts as the one above all.

What dynamics are at work? Some of the elders would have spent time with David and were involved from the early years of Solomon. They had experienced servant leadership and perhaps had more understanding of the covenant tradition. They may well have been distressed by Solomon's rule later in his reign. The immature younger men[6] have known only the latter years of Solomon's rule. They have enjoyed the luxury of the court (10:5, 8), benefitting from cheap labour! They may have known a religion of only costly buildings

---

[2] MT has the whole people involved throughout, with Jeroboam mentioned only in vv. 3, 12, both instances together with 'the whole assembly' or 'all the people'.

[3] Exod. 1:14; 2:23; 5:9; 6:6, 9; with 'yoke' used in Lev. 26:13. Solomon's impositions are outlined in 4:7–19; 5:13–18; 11:27–28.

[4] M. Weinfeld, 'The Counsel of the "Elders" to Rehoboam and Its Implications', in Knoppers and McConville, pp. 516–539 [reprint of *MAARAV* 3/1 (1982), pp. 27–53].

[5] 'Scorpions' are a feature of the barren wilderness through which God led the people (Deut. 8:15).

[6] The Hebrew *yĕlādîm* is commonly 'boys'.

and elaborate ritual, rather than a concern for the well-being of all, 'administering justice' (3:11, 28), and wish to safeguard their own position. Power and privilege are not easily relinquished.

Analogous to the hardening of Pharaoh's heart at the time of the exodus, with a matching of human and divine actions (Exod. 7:13), we are reminded that God's judgment is at work (v. 15). 'This is not to excuse Rehoboam. He is culpably stiff-necked to the point of rupturing the kingdom. But the rupture itself is not to be regretted, since Yahweh purposed it.'[7]

Kingship then may be different from modern societal structures; nevertheless, the confrontation has relevance in a variety of relationships involving power differences, both public and private. Paul's exhortations on household relationships in the first century (wife-husband, child-parent, slave-master) are introduced by a phrase of mutuality, 'Submit to one another out of reverence for Christ' (Eph. 5:21).[8] Christ himself 'came not to be served, but to serve' (Mark 10:45), while in willing response we serve him 'whose service is perfect freedom'.[9] In the elders' plea for mutuality, rulers and ruled serving one another, initiative comes from the ruler, the one with the notional authority or superior situational power. The stronger provides the example: the king does not order subjects to 'serve', rather the people willingly respond because they see him 'serving' them. There is awareness of being together, with differing responsibilities.

b. Long-lasting division results (12:16–20)

Rehoboam's choice to *not listen* (vv. 15–16) fractures the fragile political unity, forged especially by David (2 Sam. 5:1–5). The cry of verse 16 echoes that of rebellious Sheba during David's reign (2 Sam. 20:1): there the action of a 'troublemaker', here in accord with Yahweh's will (v. 15; 11:29–39). *Israel* is now divided: while it was *all Israel, the whole assembly of Israel* (vv. 1, 3) who had sought relief, now the great majority continue as *Israel* (v. 16) and only some *Israelites* who live in the region of Judah remain under Rehoboam's rule (v. 17). The language highlights how Rehoboam is left with only a piece of cloth, torn from the whole.

Rehoboam is unwilling to surrender his territory and workforce so easily. His intention in sending *Adoniram* (v. 18) is unclear,

---

[7] Walsh, p. 165.

[8] This is the concluding participial phrase of a series accompanying 'be filled with the Spirit' ('speaking, singing, making music, giving thanks, submitting'). In some Bible versions the linking of v. 21 with both what precedes and what follows is obscured by paragraphing, and more so by subject headings.

[9] *Book of Common Prayer*, Collect for peace.

whether to negotiate or to bring fear. Either is possible given Adoniram's long-standing position (also in 4:6; 5:14), but to the Israelites he is the hated taskmaster and is *stoned to death*, the standard capital punishment. Hebrew sentence structure suggests that Rehoboam made his *escape* while the stoning was occurring: had he underestimated the depth of opposition to royal policies? The *rebellion* first mentioned in 11:26 reaches its climax as Jeroboam is *made king over all Israel* (vv. 19–20). 'Politically and theoretically speaking, Jeroboam is the legitimate ruler of the whole kingdom . . . Nevertheless, in his sovereign grace God has decreed that Rehoboam should hold Judah.'[10] The 'not forever' of Ahijah's prophecy (11:39) continues *to this day* – for the writer, return to a single kingdom under the *house of David* (vv. 19–20) is still to come.

c. Rehoboam obeys Yahweh's word (12:21–24)

Rehoboam's response is seen repeatedly in history: reassert authority by military might. Is he not *Rehoboam son of Solomon* (v. 21) who like David had reigned over Judah and Israel? His orders however are countermanded by God who likewise says, *Rehoboam son of Solomon,* but adds, *king of Judah* (v. 23)! Orders through the prophet *Shemaiah* are to king *and* all the people of *Judah and Benjamin*: *Go home,* that is, dismissing the soldiers, for it is not right to *fight against your brothers* (using a word common in Deuteronomy). Rehoboam may have thought that the rebellion was the action of Jeroboam and fellow northerners, but he and the people now hear that it is *my doing* (v. 24). Rehoboam is bluntly reminded who is really in charge of the future of Davidic rule. This time all, king and people, *obeyed the word of the LORD,* at least temporarily. Sadly, despite God's word that this is not to be, warfare continued between the two nations (14:30; 15:7). The enticing lure of using military force to gain control is potent.

While the division is an act of divine judgment, early hints of future reunion (11:39) will be strengthened as later prophets present a vision of the uniting of Israel and Judah under one Davidic king.[11] Again military force to restore unity is prohibited: unity is not to be imposed, but will occur willingly as people give their allegiance to a 'shepherd' who cares (2 Sam. 5:2; 'shepherd' imagery for rulers was common throughout the ancient Near East). During the exile the prophet Ezekiel pronounced God's judgment upon 'shepherds of Israel who only take care of yourselves' and announced that God

---

[10] Provan, p. 106.
[11] E.g., Isa. 11:12–13; Jer. 3:17–18; 33:14–26; Ezek. 37:15–28.

himself would 'search for my sheep and look after them', especially the lost, injured and weak and 'place over them one shepherd, my servant David'. Our thoughts go to Jesus who looked on 'the crowds', the great majority of anonymous ordinary people, who were 'harassed and helpless, like sheep without a shepherd', and who is himself 'the good Shepherd' who unites people in one flock in himself. In turn, Christian leaders are shepherds who care and lead by example, not coercion. Christ provides the model.[12]

2. Jeroboam: the path of pragmatism (12:25–33)

Jeroboam is now king of the larger of two nations, the one carrying the traditions of *Israel*, but how is he to rule? God through Ahijah had promised that 'you will rule over all that your heart desires' with 'a dynasty as enduring as the one I built for David'. There was however a condition: 'if you do whatever I command you and walk in obedience to me and do what is right in my eyes by obeying my decrees and commands, as David my servant did' (11:37–39). God's way forward is for Jeroboam to trust in his promise and to obey him.

Despite becoming king, Jeroboam shows no sign of any trust. 'King Jeroboam of Israel, who had proof that God was true, when he got the kingdom God had promised, was so warped in mind as not to believe in him.'[13] Jeroboam's very first recorded actions as king are fortification and ritual innovations out of fear that his support base is weak (vv. 25–27). Disobedience and lack of trust are inseparably linked. Beginning with Adam and Eve, humans have acted as if 'I know better than God what is good for me, I cannot rely on God and his word'.

Rather than moving forward trusting and obeying Yahweh, Jeroboam makes his own plans, instituting religious practices that astutely support the political scene. He is worried about his subjects going to the temple in Jerusalem, only a few miles from Israel's southern border. For Jeroboam – and he feared, also the people – the temple was closely identified with Davidic kingship: its location in Judah, Rehoboam's father as the builder, proximity to the palace and royal patronage were more to the fore than any thought of the temple being the location of the ark of the covenant, the place where Yahweh 'chose to put his name'.

His answer is to build on ancient tradition: Bethel in the south, just 12 miles (20 km) north of Jerusalem, was a sanctuary with roots back to Abraham and Jacob, while Dan at the northern extremity

---

[12] Ezek. 34; Matt. 9:36; John 10:11, 14–16; 17:20–23; Acts 20:28; 1 Pet. 5:2–4.
[13] Augustine, *City of God* 17.2, as quoted in Conti, p. 81

features in a narrative in the time of the judges.[14] Bull-calves are images of fertility known amongst Canaanites and Assyrians as 'pedestals on which the invisible god stood'.[15] Jeroboam sees a need for public ceremony, an annual religious festival to match in grandeur that at the temple, so he institutes a celebration a month earlier than the major Feast of Tabernacles. He seeks success by cleverly building on features of long-standing cultural practices.

The biblical writer sees differently. All the reforms are because Jeroboam *thought to himself* (v. 26), and then *seeking advice* (v. 28; from whom is unstated). It is true that 'wisdom is found in those who take advice' (Prov. 13:10), but that cannot be separated from the fact that 'the fear of the LORD is the beginning of wisdom, and knowledge of the Holy One is understanding' (Prov. 9:10). The language of verse 28 – *Here are your gods, Israel, who brought you up out of Egypt* – echoes Aaron's words in the rebellion at Mount Sinai which aroused God's anger (Exod. 32:4, 8, 11). Some interpreters have defended Jeroboam on the grounds that the calves were not actually images of Yahweh. However,

> Whatever Jeroboam *thinks* he is doing with his calves, it is idolatry from the point of view of these passages [Deut. 4:15–24; 1 Kgs 14:9]; and it is clearly associated with the worship of Canaanite deities in 1 Kgs. 14:15. Sincerity – if that is what it is – is not enough.[16]

The calves are what *the king made*, the priests are those he *appointed . . . even though they were not Levites*, and the *festival* in *the eighth month* the one *he instituted*. This is *his* chosen path to success, to take control of the situation (so he thinks). 'The living God was being commandeered and crafted through state propaganda to serve the needs of national security – a form of idolatry that did not perish with Jeroboam.'[17] He is not the first, nor the last, to use religion for personal political goals or in the cause of patriotism. Absent is any indication of seeking Yahweh's will. Only much later, with his son's illness, does he send for 'Ahijah the prophet . . . the one who told me I would be king over this people' (14:2).

Recent years have seen a resurgence of religious values in the political realm, whether in countries where Islam is dominant or in Western nations that have sought to keep church and state separate

---

[14] Gen. 12:8; 28:10–22; 35:1–15; Judg. 18. Monson, pp. 59–60.
[15] Wiseman, p. 143.
[16] Provan, p. 112.
[17] C. J. H. Wright, *The Mission of God* (Nottingham: Inter-Varsity Press, 2006), p. 156.

(although this should never mean that the Christian faith has no place in political decisions). While in the USA overt expression of religious faith has been more common, in Britain and Australia politicians across the spectrum have been willing to speak of how their personal faith and politics interact.[18] Many have a genuine desire to be God-honouring, although for some the question remains whether religion is being used primarily for personal or political gain.

Pragmatism, with selective use of religion to bolster a person's own position, is not limited to politics; for example, businesses may parade Christian connections. The biblical account of Jeroboam shines light on situations in all organisations, whether in government, business or the church. Today no nation can be described as 'God's people' – it is to Christians on the fringe of Roman society that Peter wrote, 'you are . . . a holy nation, God's special possession'.[19] The relationship between church and state, including the role of the state in religion, has seen many variations and still comes to the fore when one form of organised Christianity becomes dominant.

The past two millennia have seen many situations where national leaders have sought to control and change the church to fit in with national or personal goals. In the name of patriotism, or because of prestige, power and security provided, church leaders have followed or even initiated the change. It is easier to move with dominant cultural trends than to oppose, particularly when national pride and personal status are involved. Perhaps none has been as extreme as the situation in Germany where

> On 13 November, 1933 twenty thousand German Christians[20] had attended a mass meeting in the Berlin Sports Palace . . . complete with swastikas, flaming torches, brass bands, *Sieg Heils*, and Nazi hymns. The Old Testament was denounced for 'its Jewish morality', the censorship of the New Testament was urged and an appeal went up for the removal of 'Rabbi Paul' from the theological scene. A heroic Aryan Jesus, whom one bishop had triumphantly claimed as an archetypical Storm Trooper, was to take the place of the Jewish preacher from Nazareth.[21]

[18] For example, R. McCloughry, ed., *Belief in Politics* (London: Hodder & Stoughton, 1996).

[19] 1 Pet. 2:9–10; using words addressed to the Israelites in Exod. 19:5; Isa. 43:20–21; and Hos. 2:23.

[20] 'The Faith Movement of German Christians' was a merger of groups within the larger German Protestant Church who wanted a 'German Christianity' and who saw National Socialism as a way of overcoming 'godless Bolshevism'.

[21] M. Craig, *Candles in the Dark: Seven Modern Martyrs* (London: Hodder & Stoughton, 1993), p. 31, in a chapter on Dietrich Bonhoeffer, who was active in opposing such trends.

Political leaders are pleased when religious leaders endorse their policies, but cry 'keep out of politics' when there is criticism. Whether it is good or bad to be involved seems to depend on whether 'religion' supports the politics of the speaker!

The Jeroboam account highlights subtle interplay between religious practice and ethnic or national identity. Jeroboam was appealing to long-held traditions over against the comparatively recent Jerusalem temple – his becoming king was popular due to antipathy towards Judah or Judaean rule. His actions illustrate how division focuses on differences.

For the previous few hundred years the Israelites had been spiritually united. Despite tribal antipathies and worship of other gods (as seen in Judges), as 'descendants of Israel' they all worshipped Yahweh, the God who had brought his people out of Egypt, the ark of the covenant being a central symbol of his rule. Now they were politically divided. For Jeroboam, as for many rulers throughout history, a spiritual centre – as a focus of authority outside the realm – was seen as a threat. Assertion and protection of national identity were more important than spiritual unity that transcended national boundaries.

Political or organisational division leads to a focus on differences. To see good in the other, and especially to focus on the larger unity, is often seen as disloyalty and an indication of being 'not really one of us'. The church historian Kenneth Latourette describes the result of the break-up of the Roman Empire from the sixth century AD, the Roman state having provided a 'framework of unity':

> When that framework fell apart, the bond of love which ideally characterizes Christians did not have sufficient strength to hold the Church together. The ostensible grounds for the divisions which emerged were doctrinal and administrative . . . However, the cleavages were largely along the cultural, racial, and national seams in the fabric which Rome had once held together.[22]

The history of conflict in the world and of divisions in the church demonstrates how differences are made a badge of honour. When religion or theology mixes with cultural and social identity the result can be volatile, with religion distorted for the social cause. Viewpoints that highlight commonality with others are threatening, for they make reasons for being distinct less important. Even at a micro-level, local churches may seek to run a multiplicity of activities for 'our

---

[22] K. S. Latourette, *A History of Christianity* (London: Eyre and Spottiswoode, 1954), p. 276.

members and their families' so as to guard against people moving to another local church. Divisions generally major on secondary matters. Jeroboam's early actions are a mirror to expose motives and priorities, to point to what happens when pragmatism and self-protection are put before trust and following God's ways.

3. The man of God from Judah: the folly of going one's own way (13:1–34)

Similarly to the narrative of Solomon (chs. 1–11; see p. 61), the literary arrangement of the story of Jeroboam gives a clue as to what is central:[23]

A   Introduction: Jeroboam and Solomon (11:26–28)
B1   Prophecy of Ahijah (11:29–40)
B2   Fulfilment of prophecy (11:41 – 12:24)
    C   Jeroboam's sin (12:25–33)
        D   The Man of God narrative (13:1–32)
    C'   Jeroboam's sin (13:33–34)
B1'   Prophecy of Ahijah (14:1–16)
B2'   Fulfilment (in part) of prophecy (14:17–18)
A'   Conclusion: death of Jeroboam (14:19–20)

Chapter 12 ended literally, and in terms of Jeroboam's self-expectations, at a high point: *he instituted the festival for the Israelites and went up to the altar to make offerings* (12:33). Then comes a dramatic turn of events: *Look! a man of God is coming from Judah by the word of Yahweh to Bethel and here is Jeroboam standing on the altar to make an offering* (v. 1, my translation keeping MT order and syntax). Jeroboam has his plans, with no expectation of Yahweh's action – he is in the middle of making an offering! Yahweh however cannot be controlled by Jeroboam's agenda.

The following narrative is central to the account of Jeroboam: *the word of the* LORD is dominant throughout[24] and the behaviour of the *man of God*[25] who *came from Judah* (v. 1). Its consequences are more important to the future, and to the hearers, than Jeroboam's

---

[23] Based upon R. L. Cohn, 'Literary Techniques in the Jeroboam Narrative', *Zeitschrift für die alttestamentliche Wissenschaft* 97 (1985), pp. 23–25.

[24] The phrase occurs eleven times in the chapter (so NIV), the most of any chapter in the Bible. Hebrew has 'word' nine times, vv. 1, 2, 5, 9, 17, 18, 20, 26, 32, and 'mouth' = 'command' twice, vv. 21, 26.

[25] This term occurs elsewhere for a prophet, e.g., Samuel, 1 Sam. 9:6–10; Shemaiah, 1 Kgs 12:22; and Elijah, 1 Kgs 17:18, 24; 2 Kgs 1:9–13 and here enables differentiation between two anonymous prophets.

achievements in his twenty-two year reign. The many linguistic and thematic associations between parts of the story show it to be a literary unity, with close parallels between verses 1–10 and 20–25a, and between verses 11–19 and 25b–32.[26] The key concern is obedience to Yahweh's commands.

a. Confrontation at the altar (13:1–6)

Jeroboam, king of Israel by Yahweh's will, is supposedly offering to Yahweh on his newly built altar at Bethel but 'the word of the Lord was brought by someone from Judah'.[27] Further, that word announces doom for the priesthood and *altar* at the hands of a Davidic king (v. 2; the fulfilment is recounted in 2 Kgs 23:15–18), backed up with an authenticating *sign*, splitting of *the altar* (vv. 3, 5). Jeroboam tries a common strategy for avoiding an unwelcome message, especially when it comes from a 'foreigner': *Seize him* (v. 4). Two centuries later the chief priest at Bethel during the reign of Jeroboam's namesake tried scorn for another messenger from the south (Amos 7:10–15), and religious leaders tried to remove Jesus through crucifixion. Rejection of the messenger can never alter the truth of the message! Rejection simply ensures judgment, in this case immediate: Jeroboam's arm *shrivelled up* – the arm that had earlier been 'raised' against Solomon[28] is powerless – and the *altar was split apart*. The narrator ensures the significance is unmistakeable by repetition of language: *according to the sign given by the man of God by the word of the LORD* (v. 5). There can be no doubt as to the authenticity of the prophet and the word of judgment. Further, Jeroboam's continuing authority and power, symbolized by his 'arm', depends upon Yahweh's mercy. But what has Jeroboam learnt? An answer will be in verse 33.

b. The actions and fate of the man of God (13:7–32)

Focus shifts to the man of God in a narrative that raises many questions. First we learn that he has been *commanded by the word of the LORD: You must not eat bread or drink water or return by the way you came* (v. 9). No reasons are given, the focus throughout

---

[26] J. K. Mead, 'Kings and Prophets, Donkeys and Lions: Dramatic Shape and Deuteronomistic Rhetoric in 1 Kings xiii', *Vetus Testamentum* 49 (1999): 191–205; Cohn, 'Literary Techniques', notes the symmetry in the narration: vv. 11, 25; 13, 27; 14, 28; 19, 29.

[27] Seow, p. 106.

[28] The only other reference to Jeroboam's 'arm' is in 11:26–27: he 'raised his arm' (NIV, NRSV 'rebelled') against Solomon.

being on obedience to a known command of Yahweh. The prohibition of eating and drinking may be due to cultural aspects of meals together, signifying fellowship and having some things in common. The nineteenth-century commentator Bähr argued that:

> By not eating or drinking in that place, where that sin (Jeroboam's) fully showed itself, he was to prove that . . . there could be no fellowship between those who kept Jehovah's covenant and those who had broken it. If he ate and drank in that place, he nullified . . . by appearing as one who himself did not fear to transgress the express command of Jehovah.[29]

Christian readers might see a similarity in Paul's advice to the Corinthian believers concerning sharing in meals involving meat offered to idols (1 Cor. 10:14–33).[30] At the same time it was Christ's eating 'with tax collectors and sinners' that aroused criticism from religious leaders whose priorities were different from his – he directed them to God's desire for 'mercy, not sacrifice' (Matt. 9:11–13; 12:7) – and the question of Jewish Christians eating with Gentiles was a major issue for the early church (Acts 10, 15; Rom. 14). In each instance, whether the time of Jeroboam, NT contexts or today, at issue is obeying 'an express command' – now including the example of Christ and the resolution of the early church. A key element is the attitudes and priorities conveyed by eating or not eating.

'The ban on the return route might serve to avoid further contact with a cursed place and people'[31] but 'way' is to be a key motif throughout the narrative.[32] It is a drumbeat culminating in the statement that *Jeroboam did not turn from his evil way* (v. 33 NRSV). The physical journey of the man of God points to the path of obedience or else to destruction.

Jeroboam's invitation introduces the command as both known to and obeyed by the man of God. The clear will of God has priority over the possibility of food after his journey and *a gift* from the king (v. 7), yet more challenges are to come from *a certain old prophet living in Bethel* (v. 11), probably associated with the sanctuary (cf. Ahijah with Shiloh, 11:29). He hears what has happened – and so knows about the confirmed sign – and takes deliberate action to invite the man of God back to Bethel for a meal. Even when he is

---

[29] Quoted by D. G. Deboys, '1 Kings xiii – a "new criterion" reconsidered', *Vetus Testamentum* 41 (1991), pp. 210–212. See also Wiseman, pp. 146–147.

[30] Refer to commentaries for issues involved within the cultural setting of Corinth.

[31] Wiseman, p. 147,

[32] *derek* occurs twelve times in the chapter, translated in NIV variously as 'way, road, journey'. The final instance, v. 33, is also in the singular (NIV, NLT translate as plural).

told of the command from Yahweh he counters with another message, himself falsely invoking the name of Yahweh. But why was he *lying to him* (vv. 18)? Possibly, enticing the man of God to eat and drink is an attempt at corruption, buying a change of message (perhaps also Jeroboam's motive; Micah 3:5–7 tells of prophets whose message depends upon the payment). Again the narrator does not state any reason or motive for the prophet's persistence and lie, for what is important is the man of God's response as he *returned with him and ate and drank in his house.* Yet again no reason is given for the man of God's decision, focus remaining on the act of disobedience.

In a surprising twist, the lying prophet receives and communicates a genuine *word of the LORD* (v. 20). He announces unnatural death for the man of God, judgment for what is described bluntly, *you have defied the word of the LORD* (vv. 21–22; cf. v. 26). There are more surprises as even the death has strange features. Normally a *lion* would maul its victim, along with his donkey, but here *both the donkey and the lion* are standing beside the corpse (v. 24; repeated in vv. 25, 28). This exceptional phenomenon leads to a change of attitude by the *old prophet*: the strangeness of the death reinforces that the word he had received was indeed from Yahweh and also that here was someone special, and so he recognizes the status of the man of God. The old prophet had conveyed Yahweh's word that *your body will not be buried in the tomb of your ancestors* (v. 22), but now it is carried and buried in the prophet's *own tomb* and the man of God is mourned as *my brother* (v. 30). His identifying with the man of God in his own burial (v. 31; also 2 Kgs 23:17–18) is more than some form of regret or reparation for being instrumental in the death; rather he identifies with and endorses the man of God's message. The consequences of the man of God's disobedience were a further sign of the certainty of Yahweh's judgment on the disobedience seen in *the altar in Bethel and . . . all the shrines in the high places in the towns of Samaria* (v. 32).

Is not death too strong a punishment for what appears to be a minor misdemeanour? And what about the actions of the donkey and lion? These are added to our questions, but they are not the narrator's and so are unanswered. Twists in the story, repetition of key phrases and multiple unusual features all reinforce the key message concerning obedience of God's known word, confirmed by signs, and the consequence of disobedience.

The prophet's lying word and the man of God's response bring to the fore a perennial question: what criteria can distinguish the message of a true and a false prophet? This passage illustrates the guidelines in Deuteronomy 13:2–6: ultimately 'obedience to the commandment of God is the only criterion, prophets were supposed to encourage obedience to the law'.[33] The question still remains for Christians, seen, for example, in John's 'do not believe every spirit, but test the spirits to see whether they are from God, because many false prophets have gone out into the world' (1 John 4:1). John's criterion was acknowledging 'Jesus Christ has come in the flesh' (4:2), leading to the life of God within the believer issuing in love, which is the 'command' given us (4:15–16, 21); indeed, 'Whoever who does not love does not know God' (4:8). A true prophet proclaims Christ and lives, by the Spirit, the command of love. For the hearer, any message that leads away from Christ and a life of love is false, while for the speaker, 'the preacher-prophet must be so committed to the transcendent truth of what he proclaims that his very own life is affected by it.'[34]

Alongside is the reality that here is a story of a true prophet who disobeyed, yet his failure did not mean the failure of God's word. To the contrary, the consequences of his disobedience confirmed the word. 1 John can also be put alongside as we reflect on the narrative's twists and turns: John too affirms the contradiction between being 'born of God' and keeping on sinning (1 John 3:6; 5:18), while recognizing the universality of sin and the forgiveness and cleansing that comes with confession (1 John 1:8–10). There can be no minimizing the importance of absolute obedience to the known will of God, yet no human messenger can claim perfection: 'In all of history there was only one Prophet who kept God's rule in every minutia . . . He too was doomed to die, but for the sins of others rather than for sins of his own.'[35]

c. Jeroboam persists despite warning (13:33–34)

The opening phrase is general, maintained in NIV's *after this* which leaves untranslated the common word *dābār*, 'word, event, thing'. It could refer to simply the prophetic 'word', to what Jeroboam had experienced directly, or more likely to the whole preceding narrative. The story of the man of God is framed by the two accounts of rebellion (v. 33 repeats the action of 12: 31, complementing the preceding mention of the Bethel altar and other cult places).

A key word in the chapter is *šûb*, 'turn, return': it occurs sixteen times,[36] giving 'the whole story a feeling of repeated reversals in

---

[33] D. W. Van Winkle, '1 Kings xiii: True and False Prophecy', *Vetus Testamentum* 39 (1989), p. 42.

[34] DeVries, p. 174.

[35] Ibid.

[36] The most of any chapter in the OT apart from Jer. 3 (also 16 times).

both physical and moral direction'.[37] The climax comes as *Jeroboam did not turn from his evil way but he turned and made priests from the ordinary people* (v. 33, my translation). The placing of the story draws a parallel between the man of God's disobedience and Jeroboam's *evil ways*, and a contrast between the old prophet's change of heart and Jeroboam's failure to 'turn'. What is clear is that once God's word is heard it must be obeyed (v. 21 has the significant phrase, *you ... have not kept the command the* LORD *your God gave you*). Rebellion has consequences: Jeroboam experiences the grace of God (v. 6) but does not learn from the confirming sign and the restoring of his hand (which could be read as pointing to restoration of the kingdom if he changed his policies), so the fate of the man of God foreshadows that of Jeroboam (vv. 33–34; 14:1–20). The death of the man of God is a warning for, like him, Jeroboam had been commissioned by God. Jeroboam had been promised that 'I will build you a dynasty as enduring as the one I built for David', but the condition was 'if you do whatever I command you and walk in obedience to me' (11:38). His persistent rebellion leads now to the opposite: 'God's agent can become God's victim if he does not remain true to his calling.'[38]

Tragically, Jeroboam's fate foreshadows that of Israel. For readers of the whole book in exile, this chapter has close verbal links with the accounts of the end of the northern kingdom in 2 Kings 17 and of Josiah's reforms in 2 Kings 23.[39] Like the man of God 'Israel too had received a command from Yahweh, as revealed in the Mosaic Torah and reiterated repeatedly by his servants the prophets. Like him, she had rebelled against the mouth of the Lord by turning from her divinely appointed way, thus sealing her ultimate downfall and destruction.'[40]

God in his grace was willing to bless Jeroboam. He was willing to heal an arrogant rebel who turned to him with plea. Ultimately, however, to pay no attention to warnings and to persist in rebellion leads to destruction. The only way forward, now as then, is to follow the way made known by God.

---

[37] Walsh, p. 190.

[38] Cohn, 'Literary techniques', p. 33.

[39] Certain phrases occur only in these blocks: 'towns of Samaria' in 13:32 and 2 Kgs 17:24, 26; 23:19; 'priests of the high places', 12:32; 13:2, 23; 2 Kgs 17:32; 23:9, 20; and 'shrines of the high places', 12:31; 13:32; 2 Kgs 17:29, 32; 23:19.

[40] W. E. Lemke, 'The Way of Obedience: I Kings 13 and the Structure of the Deuteronomistic History', in *Magnalia Dei: The Might Acts of God*, edited by F. M. Cross, W. E. Lemke and P. D. Miller, Jr (Garden City, NY: Doubleday, 1976), p. 317.

4. Another prophecy of Ahijah, now against Jeroboam (14:1–20)

Only one other event in the life of Jeroboam is narrated, also described at length – but all Jeroboam does is send his wife in disguise to the prophet Ahijah, *the one who told me I would be king over this people* (v. 2). Yahweh also sends: the key actor in the drama is the prophet who, without moving from his own home, is *sent* with Yahweh's word which the queen is to convey (vv. 4–16). In the final outcome, the death of the son, we are told that *all Israel mourned for him*, but Jeroboam and his queen participate only in the undefined, *they buried him* (vv. 17–18). In the narrator's eyes Jeroboam who began centre stage has become insignificant. Yahweh, through his word spoken, determines the future; a prophet who receives and fearlessly communicates that word is the key agent.

Jeroboam's future is unclear: his son is ill. Although not specified it is likely that *Abijah* is crown prince (hence the response of *all Israel* in verse 18). Like later kings Jeroboam seeks help from a prophet,[41] but even here he endeavours to be in control, manipulating the message through having his wife look like an ordinary Israelite[42] concerned about the royal son and so receiving a more favourable message. With all that has happened in past dealings with a prophet, has Jeroboam learned nothing? Does he think that Ahijah will be supportive, since he alludes to the early promise, although omitting the condition?

'God cannot be mocked' (Gal. 6:7). The narrator pointedly tells in detail how God enables the blind and aged prophet to greet the queen before she even speaks, uncovering the *pretence* (vv. 4–6). Instead of a favourable message concerning Jeroboam's son the immediate announcement is a *harsh message* (NJPSV) concerning the king himself. Jeroboam's recounting of the original encounter simply mentioned *I would be king*, with no inclusion of Yahweh (v. 2). He is now to be reminded that the appointment was Yahweh's action ('*I*' is the subject of four verbs in verses 7–8) and that unlike David he had failed to acknowledge *the* LORD as *the God of Israel*. He has not simply *made for* himself *other gods*, which he may have considered as simply including others alongside Yahweh, for even his son's name is *Abijah* ('my [heavenly] father is Yahweh'). Rather such action positively *aroused my anger*,[43] to worship other gods

---

[41] 17:17–24; 2 Kgs 1:2; 4:22, 40; 5:3; 8:7–15; 20:1–11.

[42] The level of gift brought is appropriate from a commoner; cf. 1 Sam. 9:7–8; 2 Kgs 8:8–9.

[43] The verb *k's* (hif'il), 'vex, provoke to anger', is used regarding the worship of other gods in Deut. 4:25; 9:18; 31:29; 32:16, 19, 21; Judg. 2:12 and frequently hereafter in Kings (14:15; 15:30; 16:2, 7, 13, etc., through to 2 Kgs 23:26). A poignant example in human relationships is Peninnah's behaviour towards Hannah (1 Sam. 1:6–7, 16).

being in reality to turn *your back on me* (v. 9). The action of 'turning' (a key element in chapter 13) has been deliberate: to turn to other gods is to turn away from God.

The judgment is brutally unmistakable. Ahijah's first message had promised continuity of dynasty, 'if . . . ' (11:38), but that Jeroboam has *done . . . evil* (v. 9; verb *rā'a'*) is to be met by Yahweh bringing *disaster* (v. 10, noun *rā'â*); the dynasty will be *cut off* (cf. 8:25; 9:5, 7). The shocking description of a horrible end brings together the vulgar language of 'every one who urinates against a wall' (so Hebrew, see AV/KJV; NIV, 'male')[44] and *dung*,[45] along with the corpses being devoured by *dogs* and *birds*.[46] The picture is not pleasant – nor is Jeroboam's *evil*. The only slight amelioration is that, although the son will die *when you set foot in your city*, yet *all Israel will mourn for him and bury him* (vv. 12–13; fulfilled in vv. 17–18). The reason is stated simply, without detail: *he is the only one in the house of Jeroboam in whom the LORD, the God of Israel, has found anything good.* In some way he remained true to his name, Abijah. There is an alternative to judgment where there is devotion to Yahweh.

The agent of Yahweh's cutting off (v. 10) is to be a new king that *the LORD will raise up for himself* (v. 14), just as he had *raised . . . up* Jeroboam (v. 7). The future however is shaky; Israel will be *like a reed swaying in the water* (v. 15). There were to be eight violent changes of dynasty in less than two hundred years (see chronological chart, pp. 36–37). Judgment is not only on the royal household (vv. 10–13) but on *Israel* as a whole. Centuries previously Joshua had warned the people of consequences of 'turning away': Yahweh will remove them from 'this good land, which the LORD your God has given you' (Josh. 23:13, 15–16; cf. Deut. 11:17).[47] Just as Yahweh will reverse the 'raising up' of Jeroboam by 'cutting off', so Israel that has been 'planted' in the land (Exod. 15:17) he will *uproot* (cf. Deut. 29:27).[48]

---

[44] Also 1 Sam. 25:22, 34; 1 Kgs 16:11; 21:21; 2 Kgs 9:8; 18:27, all in contexts of killing opponents.

[45] Dung is still used in some countries as fuel, cf. Ezek. 4:12, 15. The description is used for Jezebel's corpse, 2 Kgs 9:37, and Babylon's victims, Jer. 8:2; 9:22; 16:4; 25:33. 'Vulgarity and scatology are weapons in the rhetorical arsenal of prophecy' (Leithart, p. 105; citing also Ezek. 16, 23; Matt. 7:6; Phil. 3:2; 2 Pet. 2:22).

[46] Dogs were never pets in Israel. To not be buried was the ultimate shaming and punishment and is one of the covenantal curses (Deut. 28:26). See also 1 Sam 17:44, 46 (Goliath's taunt of David and David's reply); 1 Kgs 16:4 (Baasha and his house); 21:19, 23–24; 22:38; 2 Kgs 9:10, 36 (Ahab and Jezebel).

[47] Nine times in Deuteronomy 'the land' is 'good', normally followed by 'which the LORD our/your God is giving' (1:25, 35; 3:25; 4:21, 22; 6:18; 8:7, 10; 9:6; 11:17.

[48] Later prophetic messages announce Yahweh's 'replanting' in the land after exile, Jer. 24:6; 31:27–28; 32:41; 42:10; Ezek. 17:23; Hos. 2:23; Amos 9:15.

Not only Jeroboam (v. 9) but also *they aroused the LORD's anger*
(v. 15). The parallel is closer with the word translated *because* (v. 16,
bigĕlal) recalling the word for *dung* (v. 10, *gālāl*). There is likely
deliberate ambiguity[49] and 'the sentence could also be translated,
"Yahweh will give Israel up for the dung of the sins of Jeroboam . . . "
God's opinion of Israel's sin is no less insulting than it is of
Jeroboam's.'[50]

For the first time in Kings we read of *Asherah poles* (v. 15),
although their presence in Canaanite worship and the command to
destroy them is in Exodus 34:13 and Deuteronomy 7:5; 12:3, and
prohibition of their association with Yahweh worship in
Deuteronomy 16:21. Their destruction is a key component of the
Gideon narrative (Judg. 6:25–30), but henceforth they will be often
mentioned in Kings. Asherah was a popular fertility goddess and
extrabiblical evidence of her syncretistic association with Yahweh is
in inscriptions from Kuntillet 'Ajrud in north-east Sinai and Khirbet
el-Qom near Hebron.[51] 'Asherah' is used for both the goddess and
her wooden cult-symbol (whether made or planted, hence AV/KJV
'groves')[52] and clearly her worship had much popular appeal.
Significantly Jeroboam is judged for making *other gods, idols made
of metal* (v. 9; see 12:28–30), while the people are *making Asherah
poles*, albeit with Jeroboam's approval, as he 'built shrines on high
places' (12:31; 13:32).

The fulfilment of prophecy is *as the LORD has said* , the narrator
reinforcing this key theme in Kings. All that remains to be said is
the standard concluding formula (vv. 19–20). Much more could
have been told concerning Jeroboam's twenty-two year reign – and
many national histories tell of wars and accomplishments of rulers
– but the narrator is not an annalist. He is preaching to a subsequent
generation, following the end of Israel less than two hundred years
after Jeroboam's death, and after Jerusalem too has been destroyed.
He focuses on patterns set centuries before the final disaster. They

---

[49] The combination meaning 'because' occurs only eleven times in OT. As the more
usual *ya'an* (about ninety times) is used in vv. 7, 13, ambiguity here appears
deliberate.

[50] Walsh, p. 198.

[51] There is confusion of names and blurring of distinctions regarding key Canaanite
goddesses. In Ugaritic myths Asherah is El's wife, the mother-goddess, and Anat, the
goddess of war and love, is Baal's consort, but Baal is linked with Asherah in 1 Kgs
18 and with Ashtarte, another Ugaritic fertility goddess, in 1 Sam. 7:4; 12:10. J. Day,
'Asherah (Deity)', *ABD* 1, pp. 483–487; Walton, Matthews and Chavalas, p. 179;
D. T. Tsumura, 'Canaan, Canaanites', *DOTHB*, pp. 122–132, and A. H. Curtis,
'Canaanite Gods and Religion', *DOTHB*, pp. 132–142.

[52] The usual LXX translation is *alsos* 'grove, especially sacred', followed by the
Vulgate.

were people who needed to hear that what had happened was *as the LORD has said* through prophets from the very beginnings of both kingdoms. While there is a glimmer of hope when people turn back to Yahweh, to be a key component of the proclamation of exilic prophets, for the writer of Kings the message of the nature of persistent rebellion and Yahweh's response needed to be heard first.

The account of Jeroboam ends. In the space of two and a half chapters (and twenty-two years) the hopes expressed in Jeroboam's appointment have been dashed. He was commissioned to follow the example of David in 'doing what is right in my eyes' (11:38) but henceforth he himself will be cited in the formula used for all subsequent kings of Israel: 'he did evil in eyes of the LORD, following the ways of Jeroboam and committing the same sin Jeroboam had caused Israel to commit' (15:34, etc.). He and his peers would have evaluated his reign differently, dismissing the prophetic critique as unjustified and extreme in failing to recognize political and cultural realities, but history vindicated Yahweh's word through his prophets. He had fine attributes, recognized by Solomon (11:28) and by the people in making him king (12:3, 20), his religious policies looked pious, but no amount of personal qualities and piety can substitute for obeying the known will of God.

The mirror of judgment brings to the fore attitudes, priorities and perspectives that continue in human society and in God's response. Some have been noted already. Central to the whole narrative is Jeroboam's active worship of other gods, promoting their altars. It is common today to see individual and community concerns regarding ecological pollution, the despoliation of land and water, and the decimation of species, and many nations have acted against the damage to physical health from tobacco and chemical pollutants or poor diet. Christians have a responsibility to act in all these matters: the 'good land' Yahweh gave to Israel points to the 'good creation' given to mankind, along with responsibility (Gen. 1:27–31). Yahweh's judgment on Jeroboam is a strong reminder of areas of ethical and spiritual pollution that are even more pernicious in the damage caused to human lives and the rest of creation and which likewise result in God's judgment (Rom. 1:18–32).

Here is a message to the Christian church, God's people, to examine corporate and personal priorities and practices. The church in her lifestyle based on undivided allegiance to Christ as Lord models God's purposes for the whole of creation. It is relevant here that in the many oracles against nations in prophetic books the basis of judgment is commonly arrogance and ill-treatment of others, including Israel, rather than religious practice. It is God's people who are judged for syncretism.[53]

In the confrontation of Jeroboam and prophets we see a question that persists throughout history: who determines future directions and events? The narrative focuses on ways in which the patterns set by Jeroboam, the policies he implemented out of a concern for national identity and his own security, continued for centuries – with disastrous results. His encouragement of syncretism suited the general populace. Human decisions, particularly those by people in positions of authority in any group, large or small, do have lasting impact through generations.

That however is not the final word: the narrator of Jeroboam's reign shouts out to people in exile at a time of national weakness that God continues to work out his purposes in and through human interaction, through their response to his word. His word spoken comes to pass. It is Yahweh who is 'the great King over all the earth' (Ps. 47:2); it is the Lamb who is 'Lord of lords and King of kings' (Rev. 17:14; 19:16). Pilate thought that he was in control in Jerusalem, implementing the might and authority of great Rome, to be confronted by the apparently weak and unarmed Jesus. He was defeated by Truth that was beyond his comprehension (John 18:38). He could provide a guard for the tomb, but it was powerless before the God who raised Christ from the dead (Matt. 27:65–66; 28:4, 11–15). Modern nations are not the people of God, a caution against seeing specific events as 'God's judgment',[54] yet the reality of the supreme rule of God and of eschatological judgment on nations is a major component of the New Testament that encourages faith (Matt. 25:31–46). The sign of the resurrection, followed by the Spirit's coming at Pentecost, is guarantee of the future (Eph. 1:3–23). It is those who know and submit to the Word of God who have understanding of ultimate outcomes.

5. A tale of two kings – in review

Kings has opened with the account of Solomon and Jeroboam, two kings who set patterns for the future. Both received uninitiated positive promises of God for the future success of dynasties, along

---

[53] This can be readily seen in Amos 1 – 2. See T. G. Smothers, 'A Lawsuit Against the Nations: Reflections on the Oracles Against the Nations in Jeremiah', *Review and Expositor* 85 (1988), pp. 545–554; J. W. Olley, 'The God of Heaven: A Look at Attitudes to Other Religions in the Old Testament', *Colloquium: The Australian and New Zealand Theological Review* 27 (1995), pp. 76–94.

[54] Konkel, pp. 257–259, has a helpful discussion of 'interpreting the signs', referring *inter alia* to the sacking of Rome in 410, the Black Death in thirteenth century Europe, the 1755 Lisbon earthquake and the 2001 attacks on the World Trade Center in New York.

with reminders that enjoyment of blessing required following in Yahweh's ways. Both however failed, following paths that seemed right in their own eyes. Both were more concerned for their own status and security as kings, Solomon gradually but Jeroboam from the beginning of his reign. Both were involved in religious structures: Solomon's temple, while blessed by Yahweh as the place where his 'Name' dwells, was also a building that served the purposes of the throne and became in the eyes of the people a false security; Jeroboam's innovations placed worship in the service of the state and was to lead to the nation's downfall. Both separated the worship of Yahweh from following his commandments.

Of both it could be said that the seed of the Word was sown, but 'the worries of this life, the deceitfulness of wealth and the desires for other things come in and choke the word, making it unfruitful' (Mark 4:19). Jeroboam, with fearful concern for his own security (12:25–27), joins those who 'have no root, they last only a short time. When trouble or persecution comes because of the word, they quickly fall away' (Mark 4:17).

In a succinct manner the words of Jesus, 'You cannot serve both God and money' (Matt. 6:24 // Luke 16:13), bring together major aspects of the lives of Solomon and Jeroboam. 'Solomon in all his glory' and Jeroboam making 'two golden calves' both fail to serve Yahweh alone, turning to other sources of security and status – syncretism is a turning away from God. Here are examples of reliance on natural abilities, whether the kind of wisdom that knows how to handle situations (2:6, 9) or leadership qualities (11:28), and of misusing for selfish purposes the gifts of God, whether Solomon's wealth and wisdom 'from above' or Jeroboam's position as king. For both, syncretism flows from concern to ensure one's position, beginning for Solomon with marriage to Pharaoh's daughter and continuing with other political marriages and increase in trade, military might and wealth, and for Jeroboam with insecurity and fear of internal rebellion. Their lives can be a mirror shining a light to expose attitudes and priorities that are contrary to following Christ with undivided allegiance.

Throughout the narrative God's words and actions encourage obedient trust. The prophetic words Solomon and Jeroboam received play their role within the much larger revelation of God and his will and purposes. That those words came to pass encourages ongoing commitment to Christ and his ways. We can rely on God to act according the word he has spoken 'through the prophets at many times and in various ways, but in these last days . . . to us by his Son' (Heb. 1:1–2).

1 Kings 14:21 – 16:28
7. Two nations and eight kings: similarities and differences

The policies and actions of Solomon and Jeroboam have radically transformed the life of the Israelites from that experienced under David's rule. With a leapfrogging arrangement of the account of now divided kingdoms (see Introduction, p. 21), after the end of Jeroboam's reign (14:19–20), the story returns to the kings of Judah. The reigns of Rehoboam, Abijah and Asa (14:21 – 15:24) take us beyond the death of Jeroboam, so the narration then switches back in time to Jeroboam's successors as king of Israel, Nadab, Baasha, Elah, Zimri and Omri (15:25 – 16:28), three of whom become king through a bloody coup. That will be followed by a major section covering the reign of Omri's successor, Ahab of Israel, and the activities of the prophet Elijah.

Founding leaders of any social grouping set institutional structures, behavioural patterns and values that persist through generations, 'an ongoing inheritance that can both imprison and inspire'.[1] Jeroboam's 'ways' were characteristic of all subsequent kings of Israel. In Judah on the other hand patterns for the Davidic monarchy were influenced by both David and Solomon. Thus in this block, while Rehoboam and Abijah are condemned, Asa 'did what was right in the eyes of the LORD, as his father David had done' (15:11). The story of the Judahite kings through to the end will demonstrate how a king is not bound by patterns set by his father, whether good or bad. The narrative illustrates how each generation is accountable – change is possible.[2]

---

[1] J. Herron, *Byzantium* (London: Penguin, 2007), p. xv.

[2] That the narrative addresses a live issue in the exile is shown by Ezekiel's reply to the exiles' complaint that they are being punished for the sins of previous generations: 'The parents eat sour grapes, and the children's teeth are set on edge' (Ezek. 18:2).

1. Three kings of Judah (14:21 – 15:24)

a. Rehoboam (14:21–31)

Rehoboam's reign had not begun auspiciously, with his arrogant authoritarian stance leading to rebellion, although in not attacking the seceding Israel he had 'obeyed the word of the LORD' (12:1–24). Now, as his reign is formally introduced, a contrast is set up within the standard introduction. The city where he reigns is pointedly described as *the city the LORD had chosen out of all the tribes of Israel in which to put his Name* (v. 21)[3]. Rehoboam is to be subservient to Yahweh and yet as we read that Rehoboam's mother *was an Ammonite* (v. 21), we wonder about the future since Solomon had married Ammonites, leading him to 'follow Molek the detestable god of the Ammonites' (11:5, 7).

Unlike introductory statements for subsequent Judahite kings, there is no explicit evaluation of Rehoboam: the indictment concerns *Judah* as a whole.[4] The story to be told may centre on kings, but it is about Yahweh and his people. Just as not only Jeroboam but also Israel *aroused the LORD's anger* (vv. 9, 15), so too *Judah did evil* (v. 22). The message is shouted at the listeners, people of Judah in exile, saying in effect: 'right from the beginning of your separate existence you were worse than any previous generation and no different from the original inhabitants of Canaan' (vv. 22–24). Israel's judgment was for *making Asherah poles* (v. 15), Judah's *evil* is described in much more detail (although other passages show the same practices in the north)[5]. The description of worship practices[6] echoes Deuteronomy 12:2–7, where the announcement that Yahweh will choose a place 'to put his Name there for a dwelling' is preceded by the command to destroy other places and objects of worship: the presence of the temple in Jerusalem (v. 21) makes Judah's behaviour more reprehensible. Implicit is the threat that Judah will experience the same fate as the nations that Yahweh had driven out before the Israelites (v. 24; cf. 9:6–9; Deut. 28:63).

Whereas Israel's action aroused *anger* (the verb *k's*, see on v. 9), Yahweh's response to Judah is described more strongly, *stirred up his jealous anger* (v. 22), a phrase which itself stirs up mixed reactions

---

[3] Later instances of the introductory formula have simply 'Jerusalem'. 'The city of David', referring to the lower section (9:24), is used in the formulaic royal burial details (v. 31; 2:10; 22:50; 2 Kgs 8:24; etc.).

[4] Cf. 15:3, 11.

[5] See the summary after Israel's end, 2 Kgs 17:7–23; also Hos. 4.

[6] Brief explanatory comment on each practice is given by Walton, Matthews and Chavalas, pp. 371–372.

today! Here is the only instance in Kings of *qn'* associated with Yahweh, but the related adjective 'jealous, zealous' is part of the revelation of Yahweh's character in Exodus 34:14 (also Exod. 20:5). Its secular usage is often in a marriage context, describing a husband's 'jealous' reaction when his wife is unfaithful (e.g., Num. 5:11–31), all too often associated with anger or fury which is warned against as dangerous.[7] While commonly translated as 'jealous' in passages such as Numbers 11:29, where Joshua is 'jealous' to protect Moses' position, 'zeal(ous) for Yahweh' describes strong, even violent, actions by Phinehas, Elijah and Jehu against those seen to be encouraging the worship of other gods (Num. 25:11, 13; 1 Kgs 19:10, 14; 2 Kgs 10:16). Sin-distorted expressions of jealousy (e.g., Jas 1:20) create problems for many in using this word of God, although in matters of 'anger' the NT knows of an anger without sin (Eph. 4:26) and Paul speaks of leaving it to God to exercise 'wrath' (Rom. 12: 19). In all OT instances of *qn'* very strong feelings are involved, with an 'intolerant demand for exclusivity' in a relationship, in the case of Yahweh, 'between Yahweh and his worshippers'.[8] Yahweh's passionate response resembling a 'jealous' husband is vividly portrayed in Hosea 2 and Ezekiel 16, but he is just as passionate regarding restoration, described in Hosea 2:14–23 and intensified in the repeated *qn'* in Zechariah 8:2, 'I passion for Zion a big passion, a fierce passion I passion for her.'[9] The Stoic notion of 'divine impassibility' has often influenced Christian theology, but the biblical presentation of the passionate commitment of God is such that

> we are nearer a true knowledge of Him in such terms than in the bloodless definitions of theological philosophy. Elsewhere Scripture takes ample care of what such definitions seek to safeguard, but it never takes the warmth out of love, the fire out of anger or the audacity out of grace.[10]

How are the mighty fallen![11] Solomon's alliance with Pharaoh of Egypt, including profitable trade in horses and chariots (10:28–29), seemed already shaky near the end of his reign with Solomon's enemies finding royal protection in Egypt (11:17–22, 40). Within five

---

[7] E.g., Prov. 6:34; 14:30 [(NIV 'envy'; NRSV, NJPSV 'passion'); Song 8:6.

[8] E. Reuter, '*qn'*', *TDOT* 13 (2004), pp. 47–58, is a comprehensive discussion (quote from p. 54).

[9] Literal translation by J. Goldingay, *Old Testament Theology, Volume 2: Israel's Faith* (Milton Keynes: Paternoster; Downers Grove: InterVarsity Press, 2006), p. 122.

[10] D. Kidner, *Love to the Loveless*, The Bible Speaks Today (Leicester: Inter-Varsity Press, 1981), p. 104, on the 'passionate intervention' of Hos. 11:8–9.

[11] An apt phrase, originally used by David in lamenting Saul and Jonathan (2 Sam. 1:19, 25, 27 AV/KJV).

years Shishak attacked the whole region,[12] the narrator focusing on the removal of accumulated treasures in the temple and palace, mainly made of gold (7:51; 10:14–17). Rehoboam is reduced to substituting shields of bronze (not even of silver which Solomon had 'made . . . common', 10:27). The writer of Chronicles gives more detail, including a prophetic message to Rehoboam leading to his humbling himself (2 Chr. 12:1–12), but the writer of Kings focuses on dramatic reversal: there is no independent act of Yahweh to protect his temple. The transition from gold to bronze took less than five years, the sole event which the narrator chooses to record from Rehoboam's seventeen-year reign. Such is the unreliable transience of self-vaunting human glory.

The concluding formulaic statement mentions *warfare* between the two kings, possibly an uneasy truce or border skirmishes showing the fragility of the peace of 12:22–24. Unusually the Rehoboam account is framed with mention of his Ammonite mother (vv. 21, 31), making that the defining characteristic of his reign. From his royal upbringing Rehoboam had learnt arrogant abuse of power and privilege (12:1–19) and syncretistic worship. Even though he fulfilled his royal patronage as *he went to the LORD's temple* (v. 28) his rule did nothing to encourage change in the people's behaviour.

b. Abijah/Abijam[13] (15:1–8)

Abijah's reign is brief, possibly only a few months over a year,[14] so much that the continuing *war . . . throughout Abijah's lifetime* was predominantly *between Rehoboam*[15] *and Jeroboam* (NRSV v. 6), the reference to *Abijah* at the end of verse 7 reading like a footnote. No other incidents or activities are mentioned,[16] but the writer uses his

---

[12] Shishak is equated with Shoshenq I whose own records list over 150 cities; Walton, Matthews and Chavalas, p. 433; *ANET*, pp. 242–243, 263–264.

[13] NIV's *Abijah* ('My Father is Yahweh') follows LXX which accords with 2 Chr. 12:16 – 14:1. NRSV and other versions follow MT's 'Abijam' ('My Father is Yam', the sea-god in Ugaritic myths), most likely resulting from corruption of the final letter in early Hebrew script (Gray, p. 347, DeVries, p. 187). The identity and details of Abijah's *mother* are much discussed, with his successor Asa having the same *mother* (15:9; NIV's 'grandmother' is one solution), but 2 Chr. 13:2 has a different name (NIV footnote). Another question is whether his wife's father's name, *Abishalom*, is a variant of Absalom, David's son. A succinct outline of issues and possibilities is given by Sweeney, p. 191.

[14] On counting of regnal years see Chronology, p. 38.

[15] So most Hebrew mss; see NIV note.

[16] Chronicles recounts at length a major battle where Abijah defeated Jeroboam, including capture of Bethel, because 'the people of Judah . . . relied on the LORD, the God of their ancestors' (2 Chr. 13:18).

reign as an opportunity to focus on Yahweh's ongoing promise to David.

Unlike the northern kingdom where Jeroboam's dynasty was 'cut off' (14:10–11), and despite the description of Judah's sin (14:22–24), the Davidic dynasty continues, *a lamp in Jerusalem* (v. 4; cf. 11:36; 2 Kgs 8:19). 'Lamps' are a common symbol of continuing divine presence (1 Sam. 3:3) and of the continuity of a ruler (2 Sam. 21:17; also ancient Near Eastern practice), with a 'burning coal' a symbol of family continuity (2 Sam. 14:7; also known in Old Babylonian). Even today an 'eternal flame' is a symbol of continuing remembrance.[17] God's promises to David were of heightened concern in the exile (most desperately in Psalm 89) and many passages look to the future. For exilic readers the promise recorded here is one expression of hope: the lamp continues to shine. In Psalm 132:17, in answer to the plea that he will 'remember' David, God promises that 'I will make a horn grow for David and set up a lamp for my anointed one'. Such background enhances the contrast between statements of Revelation 18:23 and 21:23: to Babylon, 'the light of a lamp will never shine in you again', but of the new Jerusalem, 'the Lamb is its lamp'.

c. Asa (15:9–24)

Asa's long reign saw dramatic reversal of the practices of Rehoboam's reign (vv. 11–13; cf. 14:23–24). In his religious policies he *did what was right in the eyes of the LORD, as his father David had done* (v. 11), a particularly appropriate statement closely following what has just been said about David (v. 5).[18] First mentioned is *he expelled the male shrine prostitutes* (v. 12; cf. 14:24).[19] Sacred prostitution, associated with the goddess Asherah, was a fertility practice, possibly sympathetic magic, known in Ugarit and continued by the Phoenicians, but for the people of Yahweh Deuteronomy 23:17 forbade both male and female shrine prostitution.[20] Asa also *deposed . . . Maacah from her position as queen mother* (v. 13). *Gĕbîrâ* 'mistress, Lady'[21] is used

---

[17] Walton, Matthews and Chavalas, p. 367; D. Kellermann, '*nēr*', *TDOT* 10 (1999), pp. 14–24.

[18] Said of Solomon early in his reign (3:3, 14), but later negated (11:6, 33). Comparison with David is part of the introduction to each king of Judah.

[19] Three hundred years later Josiah removed shrine prostitutes from the temple itself (2 Kgs 23:7).

[20] *qādēš* 'consecrated, holy one' ('holy' means 'separated for divine purpose', any moral connotation depending on the god for whom one is separated); D. T. Tsumura, 'Canaan, Canaanites', *DOTHB*, p. 128.

[21] Used as 'mistress' generally (Ps. 123:2; Prov. 30:23; Isa. 24:2), and specifically of Sarai in relationship to Hagar (Gen. 16:4, 8–9) and Naaman's wife in relationship to the Israelite servant (2 Kgs 5:3).

of a royal woman in Judah only of Maacah and Jehoiachin's mother (Jer. 13:18; 29:2), in Israel only in 2 Kings 10:13 presumably of Jezebel, and elsewhere as an appropriate title of Pharaoh's consort (11:19; NIV, 'Queen'). Whether all 'queen mothers' in Israel and Judah had this title or role is debatable, as are the position's particularities.[22] Whatever the case it appears that Maacah's status gave prominence to and endorsement of Asherah worship and so she was *deposed*. Family ties did not necessitate toleration of *repulsive* worship. All is positive, although the narrator, writing from a Deuteronomistic perspective, had ongoing concern over the continuation of *high places* (v. 14), seen from Solomon on (3:3; 22:43; 2 Kgs 12:3; 14:4; 15:4, 35). They were not removed until the reforms of Hezekiah (2 Kgs 18:4, 22) and Josiah (2 Kgs 23:19).

Tensions between Judah and Israel continued, so in a bold, yet costly, diplomatic move Asa bought an alliance with *the king of Aram* (Syria)[23] against Israel. The next two hundred years will see all possible combinations of alliance and hostility involving Judah, Israel, Aram and later Assyria.[24] Readers might compare shifting alliances and political landscapes in the twentieth century involving countries such as Great Britain, USA, Italy, Germany, Soviet Union, Japan, Iraq, Iran, Turkey, with changing geopolitical interests and the priority of national security. Late in Solomon's reign Rezon of Aram had been an 'adversary', hostile to the united kingdom (11:23–25), although soon after Aram and Judah were in alliance, seen in Asa of Judah's mention of *my father and your father* (v. 19a). Now however it is Aram and Israel in alliance, with Asa asking Ben-Hadad of Aram, *Break your treaty with Baasha king of Israel* – which he did (v. 19b)! We will return to the changing relationships in chapters 20, 22.

How Judah's conditions have deteriorated since the time of Solomon! Baasha of Israel is in control at Ramah, only a few miles north of Jerusalem, and, when he has to withdraw, the removal of the fortification has to be done by a corvée of Judahites (vv. 17, 22). Asa builds up the temple treasury, but then uses it all as a *gift of silver and gold* to seek Ben-Hadad's change of alliance (vv. 15, 18–19; *šōhad* is a 'gift seeking favour', and so often 'bribe', Prov. 17:8, 23). Solomon's treaties had been linked with trade and income to the palace, while Asa's is for border security. There is subsequently reduction in Israel's territory (v. 20).

[22] A. Salversen, 'Royal Family. 8. Queen Mother', *DOTHB*, pp. 848–849.

[23] For the use of 'Aram' and 'Syria' see p. 121, n. 52.

[24] H. Sader, 'The Aramaeans of Syria', in Lemaire and Halpern, pp. 273, n. 2, lists verses narrating 'tumultuous relations', and pp. 299–300 summarizes disputes over territorial claims and trade routes.

The concluding formulaic summary for Asa contains a note that *in his old age, however, his feet became diseased* (v. 23). Of only two other kings is illness noted, Azariah's leprosy (2 Kgs 15:5) and Hezekiah's disease (2 Kgs 20:1–11), both with explicit theological import. The many links in this passage with Deuteronomy support rabbinic exegesis based on the unusual *no one was exempt* in the forced labour (v. 22). This contradicted the 'exemption' of newly married men in Deuteronomy 24:5 enabling them to 'bring happiness to the wife'. With 'feet' a common OT euphemism for genitals, here is another instance of correspondence between sin and judgment.[25]

Thus, in the end, Asa is given a qualified positive report. Even his reforms prove to be partial as Jehoshaphat will have to conclude the task (22:46). Nevertheless, the 'lamp' of David (v. 4) continues to shine (contrast Israel's leadership turmoil, see below) as God works with and through imperfect people. Only one Son of David will prove to fully obey the ways of God, and his 'lamp' will shine forever (Rev. 21:23).

2. Five kings of Israel, with three coups (15:25 – 16:28)

The forty-one year reign of Asa of Judah parallels six[26] kings of Israel, three the result of coups. Only Omri will bring dynastic stability to Israel, although all are judged negatively for idolatrous worship.

a. Nadab, son of Jeroboam (15:25–32)

Nadab may have thought he was in control, seeking to expand territory westward into the coastal plain, *besieging* a *Philistine town*. His reign however was brief: between the standard framing of verses 25–26, 31–32, the narration tells only of his being overthrown as king, with *Nadab* and *Jeroboam's whole family* being *killed* by *Baasha* (vv. 27–30). The revolt may have been an outworking of inter-tribal or regional power struggles, a feature of clashes in the period of judges – and of many conflicts in history up to today. Jeroboam's family was from Ephraim in the central hill country, the dominant tribe, while Baasha is from *Issachar*, one of the tribes from the region of Galilee which included the strategic Jezreel valley.

[25] J. Schipper, 'Deuteronomy 24:5 and King Asa's Foot Disease in 1 Kings 15:23b', *Journal of Biblical Literature* 128 (2009), pp. 643–648; Sweeney, p. 195, Brueggemann, p. 192. A later critical expansion is in 2 Chr. 16:12.

[26] The narrative of the sixth, Ahab, will be explored in the next major section due to the key role of Elijah.

The narrator sees a different factor as crucial: the outworking of *the word of the* LORD *given through his servant Ahijah the Shilonite* (v. 29; cf. 14:10–11). The statement is reinforced by repeating the reason for the judgment: Jeroboam's *sins*, also involving the people, and the consequent arousing of *the anger of the* LORD.[27]

b. Baasha, and the prophet Jehu (15:33 – 16:7)

Baasha is the first Israelite king said to have reigned in *Tirzah*, although previously it had become Jeroboam's base (14:17). It remained the capital until Omri moved to Samaria (16:23–24; cf. 16:8, 15). Tirzah was 7 miles (11 km) north-east of Shechem, strategically located on a trade route and a site 'of great natural beauty with extensive gardens and groves encouraged by its abundant water supply (one of the best in Israel)'.[28] Baasha however *did evil in the eyes of the* LORD: a beautiful setting does not guarantee right honouring of the Creator, as seen in fertility cults of Canaan and varied contemporary forms of worship of 'nature'.

In the revolt and massacre Baasha no doubt thought that his success was a result of decisive, brutal action, showing to the people his power and right to reign. He was to hear differently from the prophet *Jehu* ('He is Yah[weh]'). In language similar to that spoken to Jeroboam Baasha is told that Yahweh *lifted you up from the dust and appointed you ruler over my people Israel* (v. 2; cf. 14:7). He is a *ruler* accountable to Yahweh who is King,[29] but he has failed to take any action to overthrow Jeroboam's religious innovations. *Baasha and his house* will thus suffer the same fate as *the house of Jeroboam* (verses 3–4; cf. 14:10–11).

He reigned for twenty-four years, but all that is narrated is his coup and the prophetic word of judgment, along with a vague reference to *achievements* (v. 5) and mention elsewhere of his battles against Judah and alliance with Aram (15:16–21, 32). Being appended after the usual closing formula, the final word (v. 7) is unexpected, demanding attention. His coup and massacre of Jeroboam's family have been described as 'according to the word of the LORD' (15:29; cf. 16:2), yet *the word of the* LORD that came because of *all the evil he had done in the eyes of the* LORD continues *and also because he destroyed it* ('the house of Jeroboam'). A similar tension will appear in evaluation of the later coup and blood massacre of Ahab's

---

[27] For 'arousing anger' see on 14:9, pp. 145–146.

[28] G. L. Carr, *The Song of Solomon*, Tyndale OT Commentaries (Leicester: Inter-Varsity Press, 1984), p. 146, commenting on Song 6:4, 'beautiful as Tirzah'.

[29] See on 1:35, pp. 46–47, for the use of *nāgîd* 'leader, ruler' over against *melek* 'king'.

household by Jehu.[30] That God accomplishes his purposes through wicked individuals and violent acts does not remove moral responsibility.[31] 'Peter in addressing the men of Israel on the day of Pentecost speaks in exactly the same terms as the condemnation of Baasha (Acts 2:22–23) . . . Human deeds are never regarded as divine coercion . . . At the same time, God never fails to accomplish his purposes, whatever may have been the human volition and intent.'[32]

c. Elah (16:8–14)

The account of Baasha's son, *Elah*, matches that of Jeroboam's son, Nadab (15:25–31). There are the same short reign and similar coup, this time by one of the inner court. All we know of Elah is that he reigned only months[33] and that he was *getting drunk in the home of Arza, the palace administrator at Tirzah* (v. 9)!

More than half the space reporting Elah's reign is given to *Zimri's* coup and massacre of Baasha's family, including Elah (vv. 11–13) – and more than half of that report (vv. 12b–13) brings together four components: what happened was *in accordance with the word of the Lord*, that word was spoken *through the prophet*, the *sins* of king and people, and Yahweh being *aroused* to *anger* (cf. 15:29–30).

d. Zimri (16:15–20)

News of the coup travelled fast. Zimri commanded half the chariots (v. 9), but he was sub-ordinate to *Omri, the commander of the army* (v. 16) who was with the troops about 40 miles (60 km) distant. The army's response was to *proclaim Omri king over Israel* and to move swiftly to besiege Tirzah. We can only guess as to the dynamics, but living memory in many countries today is of similar coups involving sections of armed forces, and 'the outcome is suspicion and violence'.[34] Swift action led to Zimri killing himself only seven days after his coup.

The concluding standard evaluation (v. 19) is a reminder that, as for Baasha, even though the killing of Elah was 'in accordance with the word of the Lord' (v. 12), Zimri was also accountable for his allegiance to Yahweh. It is hard to imagine Yahweh being anywhere in his thoughts!

[30] 1 Kgs 21:21–24; 2 Kgs 9 – 10 and Hos. 1:4.
[31] That regicide is sin is evident in David's responses relating to Saul (1 Sam. 24:6; 26:9; 31:4; 2 Sam. 1:1–16; 4:1–12) (Sweeney, p. 198).
[32] Konkel, p. 278.
[33] Parts of 'two years' straddling a new year (see, p. 38).
[34] Gotom, p. 436.

e. Omri (16:21–28)

Divisions within Israel continued. Other historians might have given more details of the four year turmoil[35] and the cost of lives but the biblical writer is blandly concise: *Omri's followers proved stronger than those of Tibni son of Ginath. So Tibni died and Omri became king* (v. 22). His reign marked a change in fortunes for the northern kingdom, with the Omride dynasty lasting about forty-five years, the longest to date. Again the biblical writer is focused, mentioning only the purchase of *Samaria* (v. 24) and Omri's continuation of the policies of Jeroboam, expressed now as *he sinned more* and *followed completely the ways of Jeroboam son of Nebat* (vv. 25–26).

Other biblical data and archaeological material point to accomplishments which contemporaries – not the biblical writer – would have praised as positive achievements. The move to Samaria was masterly. The royal acropolis was on a small hill about 6 miles (10 km) northwest of Shechem, well-positioned for controlling trade to the coast and up to the Jezreel valley and beyond. It was the capital until the end of the nation and remained a significant centre through to late Roman times (renamed Sebaste by Herod the Great, in honour of Caesar Augustus).[36] In the period of Omri and his son Ahab royal buildings were well-built and fortifications impressive.[37] It is likely that Omri organized the sealing of relationships with the neighbouring Phoenicians through marriage of his son (v. 31), providing commercial and security benefits. To the south east the Moabite Mesha Stele recounts how Omri 'humbled Moab for many years'.[38] At the same time Aram exerted pressures on the northern border and there were Aramean markets in Samaria (20:34). When Israel fell to the Assyrians one hundred and fifty years later, Assyrian rulers still referred to Israel as 'Omri-land',[39] and even Jehu, who had overthrown the Omride dynasty, is described as 'of the house of Omri'.[40] All counts for nothing in the eyes of the narrator: he, and the readers, knew that one hundred and fifty years later all was destroyed. Centuries later Jesus' evaluation of life-building is that 'everyone who hears these words of mine and does not put

[35] See chronology in vv. 15, 23.

[36] 'Sebaste' is Greek equivalent of Latin 'Augustus'.

[37] R. E. Tappy, 'Samaria', *DOTHB*, pp. 854–862.

[38] *ANET*, pp. 320–32; *COS* 2.23, pp. 137–138. The Mesha Stele is in the Louvre museum, <http://www.louvre.fr/llv/commun/home.jsp>.

[39] Annalistic reports of Sargon II, *ANET*, p. 285.

[40] The Black Obelisk of Shalmaneser has a representation of 'the tribute of Jehu of the house of Omri', *ANET*, p. 281; *COS* 2.113F, pp. 269–270. The obelisk is in the British Museum, <http://www.britishmuseum.org>.

them into practice is like a foolish man who built his house on sand' (Matt. 7:26).

3. Reviewing one hundred and sixty years

The accounts of the kings following Solomon do not make for pleasant reading with its sad (even boring?) repetitive telling of syncretistic religion and, in the north, of political and social instability. Much could be repeated today, with change of names and locations, as media reports tell of conflict, oppression and instability in many nations, at the cost of human lives. 'Rise, reign, sin, die. War and sin, sin and war. . . . Idolatry produces nothing new, nothing exciting, nothing fresh.'[41]

What shines through in the midst of the repetitive, dismal record of human sin is the word of God that comes to pass. History is not just a mishmash of human actions. While thus far the word has been overwhelmingly of judgment, in the midst of the tragic unreliability of human rule and rivalry is the trustworthiness of God's word spoken through his prophets. In the account of Judah that word includes promise regarding the house of David and Yahweh's maintaining of a 'lamp'. While that promise too will be tested, above all with Judah's destruction at the end of Kings, there are glimmers of hope to be brought to full flame in the coming of Christ. Further, in the reign of Asa we are shown possibilities of reform as God's word is listened to and obeyed. In the ongoing march of history God is at work and people are called to respond, to honour him with full allegiance.

---

[41] Leithart, p. 114.

C. Elijah and kings
1 Kings 16:29 – 2 Kings 2:25

1 Kings 16:29 – 19:21
8. Elijah confronts crisis[1]

1. Setting the scene, Ahab king of Israel (16:29–34)

Political stability in Israel continues with *Ahab son of Omri* reigning for twenty two years, but the biblical evaluation is scathing: *[he] did more evil . . . [he] did more to arouse the anger of the LORD, the God of Israel* (vv. 30, 33). The specifics of 'more' are introduced dramatically: 'and it came to pass – was it a light thing his walking in the sins of Jeroboam? – and (that) he took, etc.?'[2] *Ethbaal king of the Sidonians* (v. 31) had overthrown the dynasty of Hiram of Tyre (2 Sam. 5:11; 1 Kgs 5), united Phoenician cities and greatly expanded the trade around the Mediterranean and east towards Assyria, for which Tyre was famed.[3] Ahab's marriage to *Jezebel*, sealing an alliance with Ethbaal, was a boon in terms of national security and trade. The luxurious use of 'inlaid ivory' in his palace is one result (22:39).

The same marriage led however to 'the greatest peril Israelite faith had to face between the days of Moses and the Exile'.[4] The nation of Israel was only sixty years old, begun with a promise from Yahweh (11:31), but now with a queen actively promoting the worship of her Tyrian gods, especially Baal-Melqart (18:4, 19). This readily merged with the ongoing popular worship of Baal and the Asherahs of Canaan.[5] Ahab went along with her: he *began to serve Baal and worship him*, the first Israelite king to do so. More than a passive

---

[1] Parts of this section use, by permission, material from my article, 'YHWH and his zealous prophet: the presentation of Elijah in 1 and 2 Kings', *Journal for the Study of the Old Testament*, 80 (1998), pp. 25–51.

[2] Sweeney, p. 205, a literal translation of the unusual interrogative form in v. 31.

[3] H. J. Katzenstein, 'Tyre. C. Tyre in the Iron Age', *ABD*, 6, pp. 687–689; S. B. Noegel, 'Phoenicia, Phoenicians', *DOTHB*, pp. 792–798.

[4] H. H. Rowley, 'Elijah on Mount Carmel', *Bulletin of the John Rylands Library*, 43 (1960), p. 191.

[5] Judg. 2:11–13; 3:7; 10:6; 1 Sam. 7:4; 12:10. See on 14:15, p. 147.

'accompanying his wife', the heaping of phrases show active patronage: *he set up an altar for Baal in the temple of Baal that he built in Samaria* and *made an Asherah pole* (vv. 31–33). Alongside he maintained his worship of Yahweh, shown, for instance, in the naming of his sons, Ahaz-*iah* and *Je*-horam (22:51; 2 Kgs 1:17), and his interaction with Elijah. Therein was the crisis, a deliberate royal policy of keeping both going but promoting Baal.

With Ahab doing 'more evil' than previous kings we expect some 'word of Yahweh' as has been the case with Jeroboam (13:1) and Baasha (16:1), with judgment occurring 'in accordance with the word of Yahweh' (14:18; 15:29–30; 16:12). Expectation is reinforced by the recording of deaths in Ahab's lifetime of two sons of Hiel *in accordance with the word of the LORD* (v. 34; cf. Josh. 6:26): the verbal parallel of Hiel and Ahab being 'builders' (vv. 32, 34) foreshadows the untimely deaths of two of Ahab's sons 'in accordance with the word of the LORD' (Ahaziah, 2 Kgs 1:1–17; Joram/Jehoram, 2 Kgs 9:24–26).[6]

In times of crisis issues are sharpened and decisions have to be made. When whole communities are involved deep emotions are aroused, often accompanied by persecution and violence as people seek to restore some equanimity to life or protect vested interests. Whatever happens at leadership levels common people suffer or have to make their own decisions. The narrative of the next several chapters will have all these components. The very intensity focuses issues of undivided commitment to Yahweh and can shine light onto response to religious conflict today, with its socio-political dimensions. Reading today is accompanied by recognition that Israel was the people of God, a witness among the nations to his glory. So the searchlight is turned on to the life of the church which is not without its debates on allowable diversity as it witnesses to Christ.

2. Elijah outside Israel (17:1–24)

Elijah bursts on to the scene: he comes unannounced, and with an announcement. His activities dominate the narrative of 1 Kings 17 – 19, 21 and 2 Kings 1 – 2, and he remains prominent in later tradition: 'With Moses began the long line of Yahweh's intermediaries in Israel; in Elijah that line produced its quintessential hero.'[7] The narrative evokes comparison with Moses, not least in chapter 19 when Elijah goes to Mount Horeb. It was Moses and Elijah who appeared with Jesus on the Mount of Transfiguration (Matt. 17:3 and parallels), and

---

[6] C. Conroy, 'Hiel between Ahab and Elijah-Elisha: 1 Kings 16,34 in its Immediate Literary Context', *Biblica* 77 (1996), pp. 210–218.

[7] J. T. Walsh, 'Elijah', *ABD*, 2, p. 465.

the expectancy aroused by Malachi's prophesy that Yahweh would 'send the prophet Elijah to you' (Mal. 4:5) sparked questions relating to the ministry and persons of John the Baptist and Jesus.[8]

After Elijah's initial announcement to the king, the scene moves outside Israel where Yahweh provides, not only for Elijah but surprisingly for a non-Israelite widow and her son. Centuries before, Moses spent time in Midian after an initial confrontation with an Egyptian (Exod. 2:15 – 4:26) and the faith of a Canaanite woman, Rahab, was the opening incident in the account of entry into the promised land (Josh. 2). The time, place, recipient and nature of God's gracious provision do not conform to human expectations!

a. Confrontation, then being fed (17:1–6)

Elijah'a introduction is unexpected. All other prophets, before and after Elijah, are introduced by *the word of the* LORD *came to . . .* , or the prophet says, 'This is what the LORD says.'[9] We expect a word from Yahweh against Ahab (cf. 16:34), but instead we hear a word from Elijah with the self-assertion that he serves Yahweh and that there will be no rain *except at my word.* The unique introduction alerts the reader: he undoubtedly serves Yahweh fearlessly and confidently; he lives his name, 'My God is Yahweh', without flinching, but has Yahweh sent him? The following incidents show how God is with Elijah, providing for him and answering his prayers.

In announcing that there will be *neither dew nor rain in the next few years* he is throwing down the gauntlet. To say it will not rain *except at my word* directly challenges the reality and power of Baal at the point of Baal's supposed strength. Texts over more than a millennium describe Baal as 'the great storm god', the 'rider on the clouds', the god who sends the rain, restoring life after the death of summer[10] and guaranteeing fertility. If there is no rain he is submitting to the god, Mot (death).[11]

Then the word of the LORD *came to Elijah* (v. 2). Like Moses after his initial confrontation, Elijah goes eastward for a period, Yahweh's command leading to protection and provision in a life-threatening

---

[8] See the section on 2 Kgs 2:12–18, pp. 217–219.

[9] 2 Sam. 12:24–25; 24:11; 1 Kgs 11:29–31; 12:22–24; 13:1–2; 14:7; 20:13, 28; 22:14; 2 Kgs 2:21; 3:14–19; 7:1; 8:10; 9:3. The only exception is Nathan, whom Yahweh soon corrects (2 Sam. 7:3–17).

[10] Mediterranean climate is a long dry summer, with the autumnal 'early rains' leading into a wet winter.

[11] A. H. W. Curtis, 'Canaanite Gods and Religion', *DOTHB*, pp. 132–142. The epithet, 'rider on the clouds' appears often in texts from Ras Shamra (Ugarit), e.g., *ANET*, p. 132 (CTA 4.iii). A stele from Ras Shamra depicting Baal as storm god is now in the Louvre, http://www.louvre.fr.

situation. That he has to *hide* points to danger from the wrath of Ahab and his queen, while in a place where one would expect to die from starvation he is fed in a manner reminiscent of the Israelites in the wilderness: bread, meat and water (Exod. 16), except that he has both bread and meat morning and evening!

We are not Elijah, but the mirror of the story may shine light on situations of compromise for the sake of political and economic benefit, such as Ahab's. The striking nature of the narrative, that Yahweh's word comes to Elijah *after* his initial stance, is a reminder of God's frequent promises of strength and provision for those who trust him alone, a provision that may be in this life but also transcends death.[12]

b. Provision in Baal's territory (17:7–16)

The brook eventually dries up, so it may seem that Yahweh too has failed. To the contrary, Yahweh gives an even more powerful sign of his life-sustaining sovereignty. Elijah cannot stay by the brook, but surprisingly Yahweh sends him around 90 miles (140 km) to near the Mediterranean coast. *Zarephath in the region of Sidon* is the home not only of Jezebel but of her god! Elijah who has confronted Ahab is not however sent to the king: the God who *directed the ravens to supply you with food there* (v. 4) has now *directed a widow there to supply you with food* (v. 9). Here is a claim to sovereignty: Yahweh can *direct* a non-Israelite – and she obeys. Later the Arameans will learn to their loss how wrong they were in thinking that he is 'god of the hills and not a god of the valleys' (20:28), while here a widow in Zarephath, outside of Israel, will learn to her life-continuing gain that indeed *the LORD your God lives* (v. 12). God is not only concerned for kings, but also for a foreign widow.

Elijah takes a direct approach, expecting provision on the basis of Yahweh's promise. We can sense intensity as he *called* out to her (v. 10); after all he would be famished after the journey. The *water* is apparently no problem, but the cry for *bread* brings the desperate situation to light: she and her son are near to death from the famine. Elijah has confidence in God and so he orders her to go ahead, to use the little she has to make a small loaf – and, surprisingly to Western minds, he says that the first loaf is *for me*, and then *for yourself and your son* (v. 13). The time-honoured practice of Middle Eastern and Central Asian hospitality is to feed the guest, even if one's own family goes without. God's gracious provision means that she does not have to shut her eyes to the stranger who seeks hospitality. She

---

[12] E.g., Matt. 6:25–34; 2 Tim. 2:11–13; Heb. 13:1–8, each in context of opposition.

will be able to feed him, *and* have more than enough for herself and her son – and Yahweh's promise is of provision for them all throughout the period of drought. We are then told that it happened, using Kings' drumbeat refrain, *in keeping with the word of the LORD spoken by Elijah*.[13] The movement of history involves a widow and son outside the land. A person far away from centres of power and wealth, outside of what was meant to be a community of faith, believes and provides evidence of the character and activity of God.

This was a scandal to Jesus' hearers at the synagogue in Nazareth (Luke 4:23–30). Jesus' introduction to the example of Elijah and the widow, that *no prophet is accepted in his hometown*, shows that he has more in view than simply pointing to God's grace to Gentiles – although that aspect is important. The widow is an example of an 'outsider', someone on the fringe, who, when given opportunity to respond to God's gracious saving provision, believes and lives, whereas 'insiders' are not willing to believe or may be critical when 'outsiders' are welcomed – a situation borne out many times in the ministry of Jesus, and in the witness of the early church. Sadly, similar attitudes continue. Philip Yancey's *What's So Amazing About Grace?* has touched a nerve as he explores the phenomenon that 'We read, we hear, we believe a good theology of grace. But that's not the way we live. The good news of the Gospel of Grace has not penetrated the level of our emotions.'[14] The joy when the prodigal son returns is not shared by the elder brother (Luke 15:22–32). Konkel[15] tells of Lamin Sanneh, an Islamic scholar, originally from Gambia, who became a follower of Christ but met suspicion and scepticism from various churches. He persevered because 'Jesus was for real in spite of the prevarications of the church' and is now Professor of Missions and World Christianity at Yale Divinity School. God is at work in unexpected places and ways: the story of the widow of Zarephath encourages us to open our eyes and hearts to God's grace, wherever it is seen.

God's overflowing provision that not only meets our needs but enables generosity to others is a theme of Paul as he writes to the Philippian church. 'My God will meet all your needs according to the riches of his glory in Christ Jesus' (Phil. 4:19) is in a context of their being generous in supporting Paul. He expounds more fully to the Corinthians as he urges them to be generous, because of Christ's generosity. The oft-quoted – 'God is able to bless you abundantly, so that in all things at all times, having all that you need, you will

[13] See Introduction, pp. 30–32.
[14] P. Yancey, *What's So Amazing About Grace?* (Grand Rapids: Zondervan 1997), p. 15, quoting a counsellor, David Seamands.
[15] Konkel, pp. 317–319.

abound in every good work' – is again in a context of being generous: the God who supplies the seed supplies even more as it is given away.[16]

Our thoughts can also go to the feeding of the five thousand as Christ 'brought the powers of heaven irrupting once more into this world and transformed its meagre resources into more than enough to feed the multitudes'.[17] Ongoing significance can be seen in that it was as the disciples obediently distributed the bread that they found there was more than enough.[18]

c. Life-giving in Mot's territory (17:17–24)

Another crisis: the widow's only son becomes ill and stops breathing. In a response that it is almost universal, through time and across societies, she thinks that this is due to some wrongdoing[19] and that Elijah is God's agent to punish her. At stake is the character of God.

Elijah does not answer her but instead takes the son and *cried out to the LORD* (v. 20). Urgency is obvious: does God bring tragedy or life? 'When faced by "Mot", must the LORD, like Baal, bow the knee? Elijah knows the answer, even if the woman does not.'[20] The plea is made: *LORD my God, let this boy's life return to him!* (v. 21). The response is powerful in its simplicity: *The LORD heard Elijah's cry, and the boy's life returned to him, and he lived* (v. 22). In the midst of drought Baal may be in the hands of Mot (Death), but Yahweh is the living God (v. 12) who restores life.

The woman's affirmation stands out. Elijah may have burst on to the biblical stage addressing the king of Israel (v. 1), but the first person to affirm that *the word of the LORD from your mouth is the truth* is a pagan woman from Phoenicia.[21] A later comparison is that between the uncertain response of Nicodemus to Jesus and that of the Samaritan woman to whom Jesus spoke at the well: she was the first to share the good news of Jesus with non-Jews and 'many believed' (John 4:39).

God's purposes for our lives, and the way he prepares us, may often seem strange and at times taking a while to be clear. Elijah, like Moses, began in a centre of power and a time of obvious crisis, but had to

[16] 2 Cor. 9:8–10.

[17] D. Gooding, *According to Luke* (Leicester: Inter-Varsity; Grand Rapids: Eerdmans, 1987), p. 162.

[18] I am indebted for this point to Michael O'Neil in an address at the Vose Seminary Commencement Service, March 2009.

[19] The book of Job confronts this view, as does Jesus in Luke 13:1–5.

[20] Provan, p. 134.

[21] Both vv. 1, 24 in Hebrew have 'word' and 'mouth', suggesting the link.

spend a long period of limited activity far away. Moses spent forty years with one family, while Elijah spent three years either alone or with a widow and son. Elijah may have been thinking of the thousands of Israelites that needed to be challenged – as will happen on Mount Carmel – but through his presence God gave provision and life to a pagan widow and son. Kings may tell the story of kings of Israel and Judah, but in this chapter the king has been mentioned only once. After sixteen chapters about kings, hearers and readers are reminded that God cares for the widows and fatherless (Ps. 68:5).

A feature of all societies is the myriad of people, groups, organizations who promise to give 'life' and 'provisions', including peace and security. Today's bombardment of claims is persuasively presented in a variety of media. Whether political or religious leaders, economic or lifestyle gurus, medical cures, 'get rich schemes' or diverse spiritual options, promises abound of success, prosperity, health, long life: 'make your dreams come true'. The dominant picture is often of material prosperity as the way to happiness.

The drought in Elijah's time demonstrated the inability of Baal to 'deliver the goods'; it showed that following him, with consequent lifestyle and values, was not the way forward – though many continued that path, leading a hundred and fifty years later to the end of the nation. Times of crisis can be occasions for re-examination – and finding in unexpected ways the truth of Christ's words: 'I am the bread of life . . . I have come that they may have life, and have it to the full . . . I am the resurrection and the life' (John 6:35; 10:10; 11:25). Just as the story of Yahweh's life-giving, death-defeating provision for Elijah and the widow and her son has been repeated in countless situations, so there is value in telling encouraging contemporary stories of the Lord's shattering of false hopes and demonstrating that he is the God who lives and gives now life that is eternal. As we live out the life of Christ, showing his character in our behaviour to others, living out compassion and justice to all, irrespective of ethnic background, gender or social standing, sharing resources that he supplies, so his gracious provision is experienced. Then others may say of our words also, *The word of the* LORD *from your mouth is the truth.*

3. Direct confrontation (18:1–46)

a. Time to act (18:1–2a)

The drought is in its third year. For two winters the rains have failed[22] and people are desperate, although Ahab expresses concern only for

[22] See p. 165, n. 10.

his horses and mules (vv. 1, 5). Now Yahweh tells Elijah to confront Ahab so that rain will come.[23] Baal may have been given the epithet, 'rider of the clouds',[24] but that title belongs to Yahweh (Ps. 68:4; cf. 104:3; 147:8): Yahweh, not Baal, controls the rain and Ahab and the people are to know that.

b. Risk-taking obedience (18:2b–15)

We, and Elijah, are introduced first to *Obadiah*, Ahab's *palace administrator*. Although in a high office, perhaps superintendent of the royal estates and assets,[25] he *revered the LORD greatly* (v. 3 NRSV). Later Obadiah himself says, *I have revered the LORD from my youth* (v. 12 NRSV), but the narrator's prior evaluation uses the word *greatly* (18:3).[26] There is no question as to his commitment. Twice (vv. 4, 13), a way of emphasis, we read that at much risk to himself, at the time when the queen was ordering massacres, he has hidden and provided food and water for a hundred prophets of Yahweh. Here is one form of faithful witness to Yahweh, quiet and risk-taking.

Elijah however sees differently. To him Obadiah is simply the bearer of a message to Ahab (vv. 8, 15). 'Even though Obadiah has already addressed Elijah as "my lord", Elijah retorts that Ahab is actually Obadiah's "lord"' (vv. 7, 8, 10, 11, 14).[27] With the message 'Elijah is here' (v. 8) being identical with 'Behold, Yahweh is my God', Obadiah 'must profess his Yahwistic faith to the Baalist king'.[28] Obadiah is worried that Elijah's confrontational style will make matters worse (vv. 9–14)! Elijah's attitude comes through in his later statements: although he has been told about Obadiah's bravery and the prophets of Yahweh he has hidden, Elijah will soon say *I am the only one of the LORD's prophets left* (v. 22), the word order giving emphasis to 'I am the only one left' (cf. 19:10, 14).

The contrast continues. The name Obadiah means 'servant of Yahweh' and he is wary of conveying the message to Ahab – his risk-taking caring for prophets of Yahweh requires staying alive. Elijah's response pointedly commences, *As the LORD Almighty lives, whom I serve.* He will do what Yahweh has told him, even at the risk of his life, and *present myself to Ahab today* (v. 15). Recent

---

[23] Following an imperative ('go') the Hebrew cohortative singular ('I will send') normally signifies purpose or result.

[24] See above on 17:1.

[25] I. Eph'al-Jaruzelska, 'Officialdom and Society in the Book of Kings', in Lemaire and Halpern, pp. 481–483.

[26] NIV obscures the repetition, translating 'a devout believer in the LORD' and 'I have worshipped the LORD'.

[27] Walsh, p. 240.

[28] *Hinnēh 'ēlîyāhû*; Walsh, p. 242.

decades have seen debates regarding 'official' and 'unregistered' churches in Communist countries. Which is the right Christian response? Which group is 'more faithful to Christ'? Obadiah and Elijah illustrate two models for 'serving the LORD' in difficult situations, *both* commended by God (see further on ch. 19).

c. Ahab and Elijah: who causes the problem? (18:16–19)

Obadiah conveys the message and unexpectedly Ahab *went to meet Elijah* (v. 16). 'The narrator contrives a setting for the meeting far removed from the panoply of court', in keeping with Elijah's serving not Ahab but Yahweh as 'lord'.[29] What will be the result?

After their rebellion, Adam and Eve's responses exhibited awareness of a problem (they hid themselves), but they blamed others, including God: 'the woman you put here with me . . . the serpent . . . ' (Gen. 3:7–13). That has been a human characteristic ever since. Now Ahab blames Elijah, *you troubler of Israel* (v. 17). 'Presumably in the mouth of a Baalist king it means that the intransigent championing of Yahweh as sole God of Israel has aroused the wrath of Baal and caused him to withhold Israel's rain.'[30] Elijah turns back the accusation: not only have Ahab and the whole house of Omri disobeyed Yahweh's command, but Ahab himself has followed the Baals (v. 18; 16:32–33). It is not Baal who is upset, but Yahweh!

We are faced with two different interpretations of one event, the drought. That is often so. The Gospel narratives are full of differing explanations of the actions and teaching of Jesus. For some 'he is out of his mind', or 'possessed by Beelzebul . . . the prince of demons' (Mark 3:21–22). On one occasion some 'said it had thundered; others said an angel had spoken to him' (John 12:29). Diversity is most evident in the variety of responses to Christ's death and resurrection. Experiences are interpreted in the light of our past, our expectations, our worldview — and our prejudices.

Ahab's worldview allowed for both Yahweh and Baal. Baal was in charge of rain, but it was also less threatening to maintain the *status quo* in worshipping Yahweh. What were his thoughts as he heard a prophet of Yahweh ordering him, a king, to *summon the people from all over Israel*? Did he wonder what would be the consequences if Elijah was right in his condemnation? Did Elijah's boldness cause him to face up to his worship of Yahweh? Or did he feel more confident with the eight hundred and fifty prophets

---

[29] H. C. Brichto, *Toward a Grammar of Biblical Poetics: Tales of the Prophets* (Oxford: Oxford University Press, 1992), p. 132.
[30] Walsh, p. 243.

involved, which Jezebel might have thought was a show of her strength? What we know is, he took up the challenge.

d. The people must choose (18:20–40)

Ahab summons the people and prophets, but he is not mentioned again until verse 41. Elijah addresses *all the people*, it is *all the people* who respond (vv. 21, 24, 30, 39),[31] and Elijah's prayer will be that *these people will know* (v. 37). King and people are brought together, all are responsible (see the section on 14:22–24). The confrontation is set somewhere on Mount Carmel, a mountain spur on the coast, bordering Phoenicia. Its location is favourable to the worship of Baal and Asherah with lush vegetation due to the headland encouraging rainfall. It was also the site of a broken down *altar of the LORD* (v. 30).[32]

Elijah portrays the people's situation picturesquely. 'Limp' (NRSV) is preferable to *waver* (NIV, v. 21): they are hobbling around or 'hopping' (NJPSV), either at the fork of a road trying to go both directions, or perhaps on crutches. The same word is used of the prophets: 'they limped about the altar' (v. 26; NIV *danced*).[33] Elijah faces the people with a choice that to them may have been unexpected. Evidence from biblical narratives and archaeological excavations makes clear that many (most?) saw no problem in worshipping both Yahweh and Baal. Worship of a number of gods, each with their own sphere of responsibility, was common throughout the ancient world (and in some cultures today). Yahweh was the God who had brought them out of Egypt and led them in battles. In the cycles of life and the seasons, however, with the need for fertility in humans, animals and crops, one turned to Baal and the Asherahs. That had been the practice for centuries. Popular religion is often different from 'official' faith, although for Israel the practice of religious leaders and kings had itself been mixed. What was new was the militant promotion of Baal worship with Yahweh worship made difficult.

[31] NIV does not include 'all' in v. 21; cf. NRSV, NJPSV.

[32] This may be a border sanctuary, along with those at Dan (border with Arameans), Bethel (with Judah) and Gilgal (facing Moab); so also for Judah, Arad in the south (W. Zwickel, 'Priesthood and the development of cult in the books of Kings', in Lemaire and Halpern, p. 412).

[33] The same verb is behind *pesaḥ*, 'Passover', describing Yahweh's 'passing over' (Exod. 12:13, 27) and another form describes 'crippled' Mephibosheth (2 Sam. 4:4). Elijah's rhetorical question may be a deliberate wordplay: 'How long will you go limping (*pōsĕḥîm*) with two different opinions (*ḥassĕ'ippîm*)?' (cf. Sweeney, p. 227). The word translated 'opinions' occurs only here and related words suggest a translation 'crutches' (*HALOT*; Gray, p. 396; DeVries, p. 228).

In many places today Christian worship is practised alongside traditional rituals or contact with shamans or other spirit mediums, especially in times of sickness or trouble. In the secularised West the combination may be more subtle: the God and Father of our Lord Jesus Christ is seen as important in church and family life, but somehow in the worlds of business, politics, international conflict or religious diversity different rules apply: one must follow 'the way of business' or 'market forces'; 'love of enemies' is 'unrealistic'; God 'does not belong' in business or politics; faith 'belongs to your private life'. Elijah challenges every generation: if Yahweh is the only God, he is God of every sphere of life in every place in every age – but that has not been practised in daily life. It is no surprise that *the people said nothing* (v. 21).

Elijah sets the contest conditions equitably and lets the prophets of Baal go first. Lightning (linked with thunder and rain) was Baal's arrows,[34] and so Elijah gives opportunity for Baal to act where he is supposedly strongest (vv. 16–25). Baal is a god whose attention needs to be gained and Elijah taunts with comments that fit with common description of Baal's activities in Ugaritic texts, while the prophets show their seriousness by self-mutilation.[35] The times of both the morning and the evening sacrifices pass and Baal has not acted (vv. 26–29). The narrator heaps up staccato phrases to highlight the silence: 'no sound and no answerer' (v. 26), and then 'no sound and no answerer and no attentiveness' (v. 29).[36]

Elijah on the other hand is audaciously confident (vv. 30–37). He reminds the people of their covenant background, with *twelve stones* for the twelve tribes who came from *Jacob/Israel* (v. 31). He involves the people in adding water, plenty of it! His straightforward prayer, with no dramatic actions, is to the LORD, *the God of Abraham, Isaac and Israel.* Each element is a reminder of the God who has been theirs since before the exodus and entry into Canaan, a God who 'is near us whenever we pray to him' (Deut. 4:7).

His prayer is of note in its twofold petition: *let it be known today that you are God in Israel and that I am your servant and have done all these things at your command* (v. 36). Acknowledging Yahweh and his obedient messenger go hand in hand. A similar association

---

[34] Lightning as Yahweh's arrows is seen in 2 Sam. 22:15; Ps. 18:14; 77:17; 144:6; Hab. 3:11.

[35] Self-mutilation is known in similar ancient Near Eastern and hellenistic contexts (Cogan, p. 441). NIV's *frantic prophesying* (v. 29) recognizes that group 'prophesying' was often accompanied by music and rhythmical dancing leading to an ecstatic state where it was believed the gods communicated messages; cf. 1 Sam. 10:5–6; 18:10; 2 Kgs 3:15 (P. A. Verhoef, 'Prophecy', *NIDOTTE* 4, pp. 1067–1078).

[36] My literal translation.

was affirmed by Christ in speaking to his disciples as he sent them out, 'Anyone who welcomes you welcomes me, and anyone who welcomes me welcomes the one who sent me' (Matt. 10:40), and in warning them of rejection and persecution: 'they will treat you this way because of my name, for they do not know the one who sent me' (John 15:21).[37] God has chosen to make himself known through his messengers: while he speaks above all through his Son (Heb. 1:1–2), he continues through all who are in Christ, empowered by his Spirit (John 20:21–23). Today's world is full of words, with instant communication bombarding the senses through eyes and ears, a cacophony we all experience. A strong influence in personal response – what we will pay attention to and how we will react – is our attitude to the communicator and the medium. The message and the messenger may be distinguished but cannot be separated: communication is essentially relational. That is God's chosen pathway to making himself and his purposes known to the world, then through his prophets and his Son and today through his church.

The prayer continues to add the intended result of 'knowing': *that you are turning their hearts back again* (v. 37). Yahweh's sending fire is not only to demonstrate that he is *God in Israel* and that Elijah is his prophet – that is the means to turn people's hearts around. This is another prayer with the shape used in Anglican 'collects': an address ('Yahweh'), attribute (*the God of Abraham, Isaac and Israel*), petition (*let it be known today . . .*), and purpose (*so these people will know . . .*), still a useful model for both private and corporate prayer.[38] There is value in ending all petitions with 'so that . . . '.

The two appeals, to Baal and to Yahweh, are deliberately contrasted in the shape of the narrative: initial terms (vv. 22–24), actions of the Baal prophets and of Elijah (vv. 25–29a, 30–37), and responses (vv. 29b, 38). 'The omnipotence and undeniable supremacy of God is offset against Baal's ineffectualness.'[39] Yahweh's action demonstrates his power and also his accepting the sacrifice and granting the petition (cf. 1 Chr. 21:26). The people's response is immediate. With alacrity they remove the prophets of Baal at Elijah's command (vv. 39–40).

How genuine or lasting will their decision be? The narrative does not say, although subsequent chapters (and the end of the northern

---

[37] Similarly Mark 9:37; Luke 9:48; 10:16; John 7:16, 28; 12:44–45; 13:20. Cf. Exod. 14:31: 'When the Israelites saw the mighty hand of the LORD displayed against the Egyptians, the people feared the LORD and put their trust in him and in Moses his servant.'

[38] The Book of Common Prayer collects conclude with 'ground' ('in Jesus' name' or similar); C. Sherlock, *God on the Inside: Trinitarian Spirituality* (Canberra: Acorn, 1991), pp. 221–222.

[39] S. Bar-Efrat, *Narrative Art in the Bible* (Sheffield: Almond Press, 1989), p. 111.

kingdom of Israel only a century later) raise questions as to long-term effect. The worship of Baal and Asherah resurfaced (did it ever disappear?). Chris Wright helpfully points out that while in the Bible 'YHWH alone is "the God" . . . [o]ther gods are *nothing in relation to YHWH*' yet 'they are *something in relation to the worshippers*. This is precisely the paradox that Paul carefully articulates. . . "an idol is nothing at all in the world" (1 Cor 8:4). Yet in the next sentence Paul says, "For even if there are so-called gods. . . (as indeed there are many 'gods' and many 'lords'). . .".' A reality of some kind affects the lives of the worshippers, but 'not the *divine* existence that the one living God alone possesses'.[40] The demonstration on Carmel has highlighted the ineffectiveness of Baal and the supreme power of Yahweh acting towards and for his people, to which the people respond, for the present.

Jesus himself was aware of the superficiality of response based only on miracles or 'signs' (Mark 8:12; John 2:23–25; 4:48; 6:26), but still points to his 'works' as evidence (Matt. 11:4–5; John 10:25), with a theme of the Gospel of John being 'signs' (John 2:11; 20:30). While 'signs' could not command positive response and are open to interpretation (John 9:16; 12:37), many believed as a result of Jesus' acts of healing or exorcism (e.g., John 4:53; 7:31). Later Paul wrote of many Gentiles who came 'to obey God by what I have said and done – by the power of signs and wonders, through the power of the Spirit' (Rom. 15:18–19; cf. Acts 14:3; 15:12). Out of a wealth of missionary and teaching experience Charles Kraft noted that

> throughout the world many Christians who have committed themselves to Jesus Christ, and who have embraced much Christian truth, have not given up their pre-Christian commitment to and practice of what we call spiritual power. The powers of darkness that they formerly followed have not been confronted and defeated by the power of Jesus. So they live with a 'dual allegiance' and a syncretistic understanding of truth.[41]

He argued for the need of three encounters: 'power, allegiance and truth', noting how these are seen together in the NT, all needed in

---

[40] C. J. H. Wright, *The Mission of God: Unlocking the Bible's Grand Narrative* (Nottingham: Inter-Varsity Press, 2006), pp. 139–140, in a chapter, 'The Living God Confronts Idolatry' (pp. 136–188).

[41] C. H. Kraft, 'Three Encounters in Christian Witness', in *Perspectives on the World Christian Movement: A Reader*, Fourth Edition, edited by R. D. Winter and S. C. Hawthorne (Pasadena: William Carey Library, 2009), pp. 446–447; revised from 'What kind of encounters do we need in our Christian witness?', *Evangelical Missions Quarterly* 27 (1991), pp. 258–265.

balance. 'For example, a power demonstration has little, or wrong, significance unless it is related to truth.' That power is evident today in transformed lives, as well as through protection, healing, blessing, deliverance and answers to prayer. It is evident in the resurrection of Jesus Christ, the sign *par excellence* (Matt. 12:39–40; Eph. 1:19–22). Paul prays for all believers that God 'may give you the Spirit of wisdom and revelation, so that you may know . . . his incomparably great power for us who believe' and later that 'the Father. . . may strengthen you with power through his Spirit . . . so that Christ may dwell in your hearts through faith. . . and you may have power . . . to grasp how wide and long and high and deep is the love of Christ' (Eph. 1:17–22; 3:16–19). It is not enough to affirm the truths of the Gospel: through the Spirit the truths are to be a living, powerful reality in everyday life with undivided allegiance to Christ.

The challenge, 'Baal or Yahweh', with the subsequent slaying of prophets of Baal, seems foreign to many readers today. The Western world has become tolerant of diverse religious views, although religious persecution is a reality in many countries. It was different in early sixteenth-century England when Thomas Helwys made a bold plea to the king for freedom of conscience, for the state not to legislate religious belief and practice. Such freedom was not only for Christians with views different from the established church but also for 'heretics, Turks, Jews or whatsoever'.[42] Such a perspective had a major impact on the development of the USA and can only be endorsed. There is a great divide between that style of society and one in which a uniform religious or political ideology is imposed on all. 'The fact that the cross stands as the central Christian symbol must forever forbid the identification of the gospel with political power.'[43] There is however confusion: tolerance has come to imply that it does not matter what one believes and has been used even to exclude religious faith from the 'public world'. To this it must be replied that tolerance and respect of others need mean neither silence nor indifference.

In considering attitudes to followers of different religions, it is important to observe that Elijah's confrontation was *not* with pagan followers but with God's own people. He addressed Ahab and the people of Israel, not Jezebel and Phoenicians. This is characteristic of the whole Bible. The frequent warnings about worship of other gods, whether in Old or New Testaments, are to the people of God.

---

[42] T. Helwys, *A Short Declaration of the Mistery of Iniquity* (London: 1612; facsimile edition, London: Kingsgate, 1935), p. 69. For this he was imprisoned where he likely died.

[43] L. Newbigin, *A Word in Season* (Edinburgh: Saint Andrew; Grand Rapids: Eerdmans, 1994), p. 167.

The overwhelming tenor elsewhere in the Bible is that other peoples come to see the reality of God and his saving work not through confrontation, but through God's activity amongst his people and their lifestyle. The challenge for God's people amongst the nations is to live out in word and deed their relationship with the only one living, covenant-making, creator God.

e. Elijah's confident expectancy (18:41–46)

Elijah is confident as he hears with the ears of faith: *there is the sound of a heavy rain* – but as yet no cloud (vv. 41, 43). He expectantly commands the king to *go up, eat and drink* (NRSV, NJPSV), that is, participate in the meal associated with the sacrifice, here signifying for Ahab a reaffirming of the covenant with Yahweh.[44] And Ahab *went up* (NRSV, NJPSV). A positive response is seen in Elijah's action as later he catches up with Ahab's chariot and *ran ahead of Ahab all the way to Jezreel* (v. 46), joining the royal escort (cf. 2 Sam. 15:1; 1 Kgs 1:5).[45] Elijah was confident that for both king and people Yahweh was *turning their hearts back again* (v. 37). His expectations are dashed soon after (19:1), but for now he is seeing Yahweh at work in ways he expects. For the reader however, mention of *Jezreel* is an anticipation of the later confrontation (ch. 21), where again Ahab acknowledges Yahweh as he 'humbles himself' (21:27–29).

Elijah goes up *to the top of Carmel*, higher than the location of the altars. His *bent* position suggests intense prayer as he looks eagerly for sign of rain. Seven times he sends his servant before the smallest glimmer of a sign of rain, a cloud coming from the sea (cf. Luke 12:54), but that is enough for Elijah. Soon comes torrential downpour.

Yahweh is the God who 'lives' (17:1, 12; 18:10).[46] This conviction can be continued into the twenty-first century: God may act differently (such a dramatic ending to drought happens only once in the Scriptures), but he can be relied on to act appropriately and often in

---

[44] K. L. Roberts, 'God, prophet, and king: eating and drinking on the mountain in First Kings 18:41', *Catholic Biblical Quarterly* 62 (2000), pp. 632–644, builds on the repeated 'go up' ('*ālāh*, vv. 41, 42) and parallels in Exod. 24:4, 11; similarly Walsh, p. 286.

[45] Sweeney, p. 230.

[46] 'Living God' occurs in two other situations where Israelites were tempted to believe that other gods had power: Josh. 3:10 before entering Canaan, and 1 Sam. 17:26, 36 – on David's lips when confronting the Philistine Goliath. 'The living God' speaks 'out of fire', yet his hearers live (Deut. 5:26). The Persian Darius refers to 'the living God' when Daniel survives the lions' den (Dan. 6:20, 26), while the ascription is seen in Peter's confession of Christ as 'the Son of the living God' (Matt. 16:16). Other gods are powerless; they are not 'living'.

new ways in the life of his people. In a time of crisis he provided for Elijah, the widow and her son (ch. 17) and on Mount Carmel his answer to Elijah's prayer demonstrated to king and people his powerful, life-changing presence. Successive chapters will illustrate other dimensions, as do other Scriptures and the life of church through the centuries. He alone is the compassionate God who seeks to turn people's *hearts back again* to him (v. 37), providing rain and food. The one who eats and drinks with 'sinners' still invites people to 'eat' and 'drink', enjoying his bounty.[47]

4. God's ways are usually quiet (19:1–21)

The result of the Carmel victory is not what Elijah expects: Jezebel does not change but rather threatens to remove him. The Elijah who boldly gave orders to Ahab, prophets and people *was afraid* (v. 3).[48] The ensuing narrative has been a biblical example in many analyses of emotional collapse and depression: Elijah runs away (v. 3), asks to die (v. 4), and twice states that everybody else has rejected Yahweh and *I am the only one left* (vv. 10, 14).

> The narrative shows deep psychological insight in describing the generalized depression that sometimes results from stress, in this case the stress of fear coupled with the stress brought on by victorious success ... Depressed persons cannot usually be talked out of their gloom. What does sometimes help is a sense of purpose, and that is exactly what God provides with a new commission.[49]

There is value in reading the narrative in this light, noting especially how God handles the situation. Elijah runs south, far from Israel. In the desert he wants to die, saying *I am no better than my ancestors* (v. 4). The phrase is enigmatic, with no comparative phrase elsewhere. Various possibilities have been suggested. Is it simply an acceptance of mortality? Had he expected to bring about a national rejection of Baal worship where others had failed? Had he expected to do it alone, since that becomes a focus later? Given other links in the narrative with Moses, is there a mirror of Moses' despair at not being able to handle the people alone in the wilderness (Num. 11:14–15)? The idea

---

[47] Isa. 55:1–3; Matt. 9:10–11; 26:17–30; 1 Cor. 11:17–34.

[48] Modern versions follow LXX (and other ancient versions and Josephus) in reading the Hebrew as *wayyirā'* 'and he was afraid'. MT tradition, followed by AV/KJV, is *wayyar'* 'and he saw', although there is no object stated. Possibly later readers had difficulty with a fearful Elijah.

[49] Nelson, pp. 126–127.

of a limit to one person's endurance is evident in later Jewish tradition: 'It is long enough for me. How long am I to be knocked about like this?'[50] Whatever the significance, his denial of being different starkly contrasts with previous self-confidence and many readers have identified with him.

God does not answer Elijah's request to die. Rather, through *an angel* (or 'messenger') he twice gives Elijah something to eat (vv. 5–7). Martyn Lloyd-Jones has helpfully described the part played in depression of both 'tiredness, overstrain, illness' and 'reaction after a great blessing'. A good meal and sleep may be the first step to recovery.[51]

In that strength he continues his journey whose destination is *Horeb, the mountain of God* (v. 8),[52] although it is unspecified whether this is Elijah's plan or Yahweh's. Yahweh has shown his power on Mount Carmel: what will happen at Mount Horeb? Only at Horeb, after a journey of almost six weeks, does Yahweh speak directly to him, not in rebuke but with a question. He allows Elijah to express his feelings — and Elijah does! As may occur in times of depression, he focuses on himself: there is no 'you called me' or 'you told me', rather he emphasizes his zeal for Yahweh (*very zealous*). The opposition that has overwhelmed him is now not simply Jezebel (v. 2) but *the Israelites* who *are trying to kill me* (v. 10). He feels that he alone has remained loyal. Has he forgotten Obadiah and the prophets of Yahweh he hid? What has happened to the people on Mount Carmel who killed the prophets of Baal?

Yahweh's response is not first to correct Elijah. He asks him to prepare for a theophany, a specific divine manifestation (v. 11). Elijah's first self-description was as one who 'stood before Yahweh' (17:1)[53] and now he is invited to do just that (v. 11) – but such is his condition he delays. Only after the theophany *he went out and stood* (v. 13). The theophany description recalls Moses' experience on this same mountain.[54] Now however, *the LORD was not in the wind* . . .

---

[50] Aramaic Targum paraphrase of v. 4, translation by D. J. Harrington and A. J. Saldarini, *Targum Jonathan of the Former Prophets* (Wilmington: Glazier; Edinburgh: T. & T. Clark, 1987), p. 253.

[51] D. M. Lloyd-Jones, *Spiritual Depression* (Bromley: Marshall Pickering, 1965), pp. 18–19.

[52] Horeb is the name throughout Deuteronomy for Mount Sinai (the exception is Deut. 33:2, in a song). 'Horeb, mountain of God' is identified as the location of Yahweh's revelation to Moses in the burning bush (Exod. 3:1).

[53] NRSV, 'The LORD . . . before whom I stand'; cf. NIV, NJPSV: 'whom I serve', which translates the Hebrew idiom, 'before whom I stand'. To 'stand' is to be in the position of a courtier awaiting orders from a king.

[54] Exodus 19:9, 16–19; also 33:18–23; 34:5–7.

the earthquake . . . the fire. There was *a gentle whisper*[55] (vv. 11–12). Surprisingly Elijah responds to Yahweh by repeating exactly his previous words (compare vv. 9b–10, 13b–14). He has nothing further to say. The vision has made no difference. It seems that he is having difficulty turning from himself to see a fresh vision of God, as if the stillness of the desert environment and now the whisper of the presence of God have had no impact on the turbulent storm of his own thoughts. The finding of God in stillness and silence has been captured in the popular words of the Quaker John Greenleaf Whittier:

> Drop thy still dews of quietness,
>   till all our strivings cease;
> take from our souls the strain and stress,
> and let our ordered lives confess
>   the beauty of thy peace.

> Breathe through the heats of our desire
>   thy coolness and thy balm;
> let sense be dumb, let flesh retire;
> speak through the earthquake, wind and fire,
>   O still, small voice of calm.[56]

Yahweh's response is significant: there is still no direct criticism. Instead Yahweh gives him a task (vv. 15–18). God will not let him resign his commission as prophet. Elijah feels that all is lost, but Yahweh is still at work and Elijah has a part. There are three people to *anoint*, a foreshadowing of a massacre, and almost as a gentle afterthought God adds: Elijah you are not alone, there are *seven thousand in Israel – all whose knees have not bowed down to Baal and whose mouths have not kissed him* (v. 18).

[55] The writer seems to have the same difficulty in describing the 'sound' as translators (LXX 'a light breeze'; NRSV 'a sound of sheer silence'; with AV/KJV 'still small voice' narrowing the generality of Hebrew 'sound'). 'The terms *qôl*, "sound," and *dĕmāmâ*, "silence," contradict each other in a metaphorical presentation of power through a combination of presence and absence. The term *daqqâ*, "crushed, thin, fine," is an attempt to minimize the presence of the sound as much as possible' (Sweeney, p. 232).

[56] The hymn, 'Dear Lord and Father of mankind', is taken from Whittier's longer poem, 'The Brewing of Soma' (1872). In 2007 the hymn was voted second in the BBC 'Songs of Praise' poll of the nation's 'Top 10 Hymns'. Of relevance is that the hymn voted first was 'How great thou art', a Russian hymn translated S. K. Hine (©1953 Stuart K. Hine/Thankyou Music) and sixth was 'Be still, for the presence of the Lord' by D. J. Evans (© 1986 Thankyou Music) (http://www.bbc.co.uk/songsofpraise/factsheets/20070708.html). All bring together stillness and the power of God who is present.

Elijah's response is muted. He *went from there and found Elisha ... went up to him and threw his cloak around him* (v. 19). He does not 'anoint', although the cloak suggests some investiture. Elijah may be showing some reluctance,[57] but Elisha, although being well-off with obvious security, is willing to give up all, with a feast enjoyed by many. Here is a foreshadowing of those who left all to follow Jesus (Matt. 4:18–23; 9:9–10; Mark 10:28–31). There is no mention of any attempt to *go the Desert of Damascus to anoint Hazael* or *anoint Jehu*. Both will be undertaken later by Elisha (2 Kgs 8:7–15; 9:1–13). Nevertheless, Elijah has at least travelled back from Horeb, his prophetic ministry has not ended, although all that will be narrated is another confrontation with Ahab (ch. 21) and one with Ahab's son, Ahaziah (2 Kgs 1). In between we will meet other prophets who confront Ahab (chs 20, 22): Elijah is not the only faithful prophet.[58]

Depression has been known for years; 'burn-out' is a recently-named phenomenon. The narrative is brief (less than one page), but it provides encouragement to people experiencing such, and is an example of God's compassionate understanding response. There *is* a future. Many might identify with Elijah's subsequent actions as being less than enthusiastic, but nevertheless a move forward. Throughout Yahweh meets Elijah's depression and resignation with gentle and patient understanding and quiet revelation, and an expression of trust in giving a task that is new.

5. Further reflections on Elijah thus far

There is more to chapter 19 than a case study of depression. An overview of chapters 17 – 19 provides further light on matters of witness and burn-out.

Already noted have been ways in which the portrayal of the relationship of Elijah to Yahweh is unlike that of other prophets. His introduction is abrupt (17:1) with the first 'word of the LORD' to Elijah being to leave and hide east of the Jordan (17:3). In the following chapter, after Yahweh's opening word (18:1), no action or word has Yahweh expressly as the subject, except the indirect 'fire of the LORD' (18:38). Elijah is told to go to Ahab and 'I [Yahweh] will send rain', but the narration leaves open the question as to

[57] Elisha next appears at the transition in 2 Kgs 2, where the 'cloak' reappears (vv. 8–13). There Elijah leaves the cloak behind and Elisha picks it up.
[58] D. G. Firth, 'Backward Masking: Implicit Characterisation of Elijah in the Micaiah Narrative', *Old Testament Essays* 13, 2 (2000), pp. 174–185, notes *inter alia* that in 22:8 the one of whom Ahab says, 'I hate him because he never prophesies anything good about me, but always bad' is not Elijah but Micaiah son of Imlah.

whether the confrontation on Carmel was Elijah's initiative or Yahweh's. Elijah directs the action throughout, although he does refer to having 'done all these things at your command' (18:36).

To the narrator's, but not Elijah's, commendation of Obadiah (see on 18:3–15, pp. 170–171) can be added cross-links. Gregory has pointed out that, in chapter 17, Elijah is 'cared for by Yahweh's instruments' outside the land, away from Ahab, while at the same time in chapter 18, close to Ahab, 'Obadiah was serving as Yahweh's comforter to another group. Obadiah, "servant of Yahweh", was earning his name.' In both chapters 18 and 19 the narrative involves feeding and hiding in 'caves' (18:4, 13; 19:9, 13) in a context of 'intense persecution which Jezebel instigated': 'Obadiah performs a courageous act of compassion for the prophets of Yahweh ... Elijah completes a cowardly pilgrimage of fear.'[59]

Elijah's dismissal of Obadiah surfaces in his words to Yahweh from the cave, focusing on his being 'very zealous' and that he alone has been faithful (19:10, 14). Jewish hearers would see comparisons with Moses: the journey to 'Horeb, the mountain of God' and the words of Yahweh that he would 'pass by' (v. 11; Exod. 33:19, 22; 34:6) are immediate pointers alerting the hearers. Both faced a situation of the people worshipping other gods (for Moses, the golden calf). Moses interceded for the people and argued for Yahweh's continuing relationship (Exod. 32 – 34), while Elijah, at the same Horeb, focuses on himself as the only one left. Is it too harsh to say that Elijah's relationship with people is controlled by zeal for Yahweh, but not compassionate identification?[60]

There is no doubt as to Elijah's commitment to Yahweh and his burning desire to see the people worship Yahweh alone, yet he is portrayed as acting on Yahweh's behalf in places and ways that Yahweh has not explicitly ordered. He speaks and acts as if he alone is really serving Yahweh and so when things do not work out as he expects he sees no hope for the people. If he is 'the only one' and what he does fails then it is all to no avail. He has failed to bring the nation back to Yahweh, and so he may as well die. Even the assurance of Yahweh's presence with him at Horeb does not immediately change his attitude. His 'zeal', his focus on what 'I' have done, results in burn-out.

The theophany addresses Elijah's situation directly. He expects to see God in thunder and lightning – like his own confrontation with Ahab and on Mount Carmel. However, he needs to see God just as

---

[59] R. Gregory, 'Irony and the Unmasking of Elijah', in A. J. Hauser and R. Gregory, *From Carmel to Horeb: Elijah in Crisis* (Sheffield: Almond, 1990), pp. 105, 112.

[60] Conti provides quotes from Syriac church fathers who speak of Elijah's lack of compassion: Ephrem (fourth century), pp. 103, 117–118; and Isho'dad of Merv (ninth century), p. 100.

much in the sound that can barely be heard – like the surreptitious actions of Obadiah, and Yahweh's plans for three key people. Elijah's continuing commission speaks of Yahweh at work independently of Elijah, in ways the prophet could not imagine (vv. 16–18). The way forward for Elijah is to see and accept the diversity of people through whom God is at work, even Gentiles.[61]

There are clues here that can help today to guard against depression or burnout.[62] The story of Elijah alerts to subtle temptations for both individuals and groups: to believe that because I am doing things 'God's way' to 'bring God glory', the result will be success ('as I see it'); and to think that 'my way' is the only or 'the best' God-honouring way. The danger is compounded when accompanied with a belief that 'no one else is with me' or 'I alone can do it'.

In looking at the contemporary scene of renewal and reform Mark Galli praised 'the vision to transform the world. . . the passion . . . to make Christ's love and grace known to the four corners'. However, reflecting on the variety of movements through church history he wondered what would happen when things do not work out as hoped. He recalled those who have 'abandoned ministry', some having become 'bitter at the church and at God'. He argued that God 'longs for . . . people who listen for his call and lovingly respond – no matter how absurd or impossible the command'. At times 'we can rejoice that God has permitted us to see him at work' but at others 'we've only received hardship'.[63]

How can one keep together a bold, adventuresome witness for Christ, looking for change, and perseverance in the face of difficulties and seemingly little success? Paul's drive in proclamation of the gospel to Gentiles is obvious, yet his letters frequently point to 'weakness' and 'suffering' in Christian ministry over against success-criteria common in the Graeco-Roman world: 'Valid ministry must reflect a sharing both in Christ's suffering and death and in God's power in raising him from the dead.'[64] His confidence

---

[61] Three hundred years later Jews in exile had difficulty accepting that God could use Cyrus, a Persian, to set his people free (Isa. 45:9–13).

[62] Various factors contribute to depression and burn-out, not only 'spiritual', but the mirror of the Elijah narrative suggests spiritual, attitudinal components that may be relevant in individual situations.

[63] M. Galli (Senior Managing Editor, *Christianity Today*), 'Long live organic church! But what do we do if the world is not transformed', http://www.christianitytoday. com/ct/2010/januaryweb-only/11-41.0.html (7 January, 2010). Neil Cole, author of *Organic Church*, responded, discussing aspects of longevity, http://www. christianitytoday.com/ct/2010/januaryweb-only/12-21.0.html (12 January 2010).

[64] E. Ashley, 'The scandal of weak leadership: Paul's defense of ministry', in *On Eagle's Wings: An Exploration of Strength in the Midst of Weakness*, ed. M. Parsons and D. J. Cohen (Eugene: Wipf & Stock, 2008), p. 73.

was in Christ, not himself. 'Expect great things from God, attempt great things for God' has become a motto associated with William Carey.[65] In long, continuous, ground-breaking ministry in India (1793–1834) he faced much discouragement and frustration, disappointment and loneliness, but persevered because of trust in the sovereign will of God. A key is in words spoken during his final illness when he was visited by Alexander Duff, a young Scottish missionary: 'Mr. Duff, you have been speaking about Dr. Carey, Dr. Carey. When I am gone, say nothing about Dr. Carey – speak about Dr. Carey's Saviour.'[66] At a time of great discouragement he wrote, 'Well, I have God, and His Word is sure.'[67] 'A sturdy faith capable of weathering opposition and failure requires both these elements: a strong sense of call to a mission, and a recognition that God's cause in the world far transcends any individual's efforts on behalf of that mission.'[68]

The narrator, unlike Elijah, endorses Obadiah's quiet and risky behaviour in the very court of Ahad. That, together with the absence of Yahweh in the wind, earthquake and fire followed by 'the sound of sheer silence', suggests that the narrator believes Yahweh prefers the quiet service of Obadiah to the confrontational noise of Elijah. Yahweh's quiet work is seen in the narrative of chapter 17, away from Israel in foreign territory, compassionately providing for a lone prophet and a poor widow, and in 19:15–18, his choosing of other agents. Here can be seen a foreshadowing of the ministry of Christ, a pattern which sustained Paul.

Elijah was not perfect – and that has ongoing significance. God always works with imperfect people! Elijah's single-minded zeal may have had negative features, but Yahweh continued to care for him, to use him and to confirm his word. His bold confrontation was remembered and so had impact. At the end he was honoured (his ascent to heaven was unique)[69] and he and Moses were with Jesus at the transfiguration (Matt. 17:3 and parallels). On the other hand, his dramatic confrontational witness was not the only pattern God honoured.

[65] The title of his sermon based on Isa. 54:2–3 preached to the Northampton Baptist Association meeting at Nottingham, Wed 31 May 1792 (three weeks after the publication of his *Enquiry*). The sermon manuscript was not kept but details of setting and content are in S. Pearce Carey, *William Carey* (London: Hodder & Stoughton, 1923), pp. 78–86.

[66] L. Rowe, *Say Nothing About Dr. Carey* (Didcot: Baptist Missionary Society 1991), p. 1.

[67] Ibid, p. 8.

[68] D. Epp-Tiessen, '1 Kings 19: The Renewal of Elijah', *Direction* 35, 1 (Spring 2006), pp. 39–40 <http://www.directionjournal.org/article/?1418>.

[69] 2 Kgs 2.

Such a message has relevance for people in exile, serving foreign rulers away from their homeland, perhaps looking for some spectacular display of God's power. The narrative speaks today to all who believe in and serve the same God. In his gracious compassion he cares for and uses an imperfect prophet—and an imperfect people who are willing to turn to him.

1 Kings 20:1 – 22:40
9. Ahab and some prophets – leading to death

The narrative of Ahab's reign continues with three different situations where he interacts with prophets: two battles with the Arameans (chs 20, 22) frame confrontation with Elijah over murder for property (ch. 21).[1]

1. Ahab and Ben-Hadad – and prophets (20:1–43)

Elijah's brief confrontations with Ahab,[2] his self-perception as a prophet 'very zealous for the LORD God Almighty . . . the only one left' (19:10, 14) and his unexpected commission to 'anoint Hazael king over Aram' and 'Jehu son of Nimshi king over Israel' (19:15–16) have been features of the story so far. Thus when the narrative turns to *Ben-Hadad*, the current *king of Aram*,[3] and his demands on *Ahab king of Israel*, we may wonder what will happen to these two kings whose anointed successors are not in the dynastic lines and how Elijah is to be involved.

Several conversations structure the narrative, dramatic shifts

---

[1] LXX order is 17 – 19, 21, 20, 22, placing the Elijah narratives together, separated from narratives involving other prophets. The flow of MT has three chapters focusing on Elijah, with minimal interaction with Ahab (chs. 17 – 19), followed by three chapters focusing on Ahab, with God using other prophets as well as Elijah. See Turkanik, *Of Kings and Reigns*, pp. 34–36.

[2] 17:1; 18:1–2, 16–20; 18:41 – 19:1.

[3] Several Aramean kings are named Ben-Hadad ('son of Hadad' [the storm god]). One was mentioned at the time of Asa of Judah (15:18–20), and at the time of Elisha another is killed by Hazael (2 Kgs 8:7–15), who himself has a son named Ben-Hadad (2 Kgs 13:24) (Walton, Matthews and Chavalas, pp. 381, 393).

indicated by the arrival of new characters.[4] The opening scene is confrontation between Ben-Hadad and Ahab over treaty arrangements, leading to preparation for attack on Samaria (vv. 1–12). Unexpectedly[5] an anonymous *prophet*, not Elijah, enters with a message from Yahweh. The announced victory eventuates, but the prophet warns of a future attack (vv. 13–22). The initiative and strategy for that attack come not from Ben-Hadad himself but from his *officials* (vv. 23–27). Again *the man of God* enters announcing defeat of the Aramaeans (vv. 28–30a). Attention turns to Ben-Hadad's future and Ahab's leniency, which at first glance could be read as a good outcome, politically astute (vv. 30b–34). God's evaluation is different: again a *prophet* is involved, bringing a word of judgment on Ahab (vv. 35–41).

Ahab and Ben-Hadad may have thought they were the key protagonists, but the constant thread is that it is Yahweh who determines outcomes, whether in victory for Israel or in judgment on disobedience. Ahab and the people are to know that *I am the* LORD (vv. 13, 28), that God's power is not limited to *hills* or *valleys* (vv. 23, 28). Another feature, unexpected after chapters 17 – 19, is Elijah's absence and the prophets' anonymity. Elijah is not the only prophet willing to bring a message to Ahab.

a. Ben-Hadad and Ahab (20:1–12)

Ben-Hadad comes against Samaria supported by a large group of *kings* (city-state rulers and tribal chieftains).[6] He intends to force Ahab into a vassal treaty in which Ahab would be subservient, expressed by acknowledging Ben-Hadad's right to *silver and gold* (tribute or taxation) and *the best of your wives and children* (who as hostages become a guarantee of continuity loyalty) (v. 3). This can be compared to the conclusion of the battles: Ben-Hadad is defeated and taken prisoner, but Ahab nevertheless sets him free after negotiating a parity treaty, one between equals (v. 34). Ahab's action is what is to be judged.

Although Ahab is willing to enter the vassal relationship (v. 4), Ben-Hadad provokes by going beyond normal conventions. Rather than simply requiring Ahab's recognition of rights, he now says *I*

---

[4] Hebrew narrative is generally carried forward by 'and' followed by a verb and then subject. Each of vv. 1, 13, 23, 35 starts with the subject before the verb, so foregrounding the new participant.

[5] Like a spotlight, the particle *hinnēh* draws attention with a note of immediacy ('look!'; AV/KJV 'behold', NIV 'meanwhile', NRSV 'then').

[6] 'The historical setting presupposed by this narrative has been the subject of considerable debate' (Sweeney, p. 238); see also Wiseman, p. 175; Konkel, pp. 127–129.

sent to demand . . . (v. 5), as if Ahab has been rebellious, and threatens wholesale plunder of the city if Ahab does not agree to hand over speedily (*about this time tomorrow*). Ahab sees that Ben-Hadad is *looking for trouble*, 'simply looking for an excuse to attack'.[7] With the backing of key leaders (*elders of the land*), Ahab, still expressing a subordinate relationship (*my lord the king*, vv. 4, 9), is not willing to give in. After a quick exchange of taunts (vv. 10–11) Ben-Hadad begins to *attack the city* (v. 12). There is no hint of any reliance on Yahweh, so what were the *elders of the land* and what was Ahab expecting to be the result? Not what eventuated!

b. Yahweh's word intervenes (20:13–22)

This is what Ben-Hadad says (v. 2) were the first spoken words in the account. Now to Ahab comes a prophet announcing, *This is what the LORD says* (v. 13).[8] The message is simple: there are two realities, *this vast army* and '*I*' (Yahweh). God's message countermands a message coming from human pride, and his word will come to pass.

Ahab will then *know that I am the LORD*. This phrase is a feature of the exodus account,[9] and a noted theme of Ezekiel,[10] but in Joshua-Kings occurs only in this passage (also v. 28). More than simply 'know me' or even 'know I am God', it connotes 'know that I am what my name means, Yahweh', 'know I am Yahweh and not some other god (or generic god)'. Zimmerli points to the link with 'Yahweh's self-statement [Exod. 3] in which he reveals himself in his most personal mystery . . . [which] leads directly to Yahweh's promise to act historically in Israel's behalf'.[11] What he says of the phrase in Ezekiel applies here:

> The remarks preceding the statement of recognition say nothing about any sort of human effort or intellectual exercise that leads to the goal of recognition of Yahweh . . . It is always a matter of Yahweh's intervention, either in history of hostile nations or of the people of God themselves.[12]

[7] Walsh, p. 296, in an analysis of the literary structures and language of the negotiations.

[8] The standard message formula is common in the prophetic books, often translated 'thus says the LORD'.

[9] Exod. 6:7; 7:5, 17; 10:2; 14:4, 18; 16:12; Deut. 29:6.

[10] Sixty one times in MT of Ezekiel.

[11] W. Zimmerli, *I am Yahweh*, edited with an introduction by W. Brueggemann (Atlanta: John Knox, 1982), pp. 80–81.

[12] Ibid., pp. 33, 36.

Ahab wants to know the strategy and no doubt is surprised by the answer. Action is to be in the hands of *the junior officers under the provincial commanders* (v. 14). The overall literary and theological context points to these being '"servants" in a very generalized sense, taking our lead from 1 Sam. 17:33, where the contrast . . . is between the young, untrained David (*na'ar* [as here]) and the warrior Goliath'.[13] Ahab prepares, but with a backup army.

Ben-Hadad's confident bravado is highlighted by portrayal of him and the kings *getting drunk* in the middle of the day (v. 16; also v. 12). Is this why his orders are confused? In both eventualities, *Take them alive* (v. 18)! Going out at midday in full view of the enemy, with young men in front, hardly looks like an attacking strategy, but with Ben-Hadad's orders the Arameans are unprepared. The battle is quick, *each one struck down his opponent*. Ben-Hadad *escaped* but the prophet warns of another attack *next spring* (v. 22), the time when armies attack as winter rains and ripening crops provide food and water (cf. 2 Sam. 11:1). Ben-Hadad's future has not been resolved. He remains a threat.

Throughout the ancient Near East prophets were commonly involved in military strategy, but different here is the unexpected strategy and ease of victory. As always interpretations of an unusual event can differ (see above on 18:16–19). We will soon hear the Arameans' explanation but we are not told Ahab's response. His later actions (vv. 31–34) suggest no significant change. Yahweh remains simply a God to call on when needed in battles.

c. The God of hills and valleys (20:23–30a)

The next move comes not from Ben-Hadad but from *the officials of the king of Aram* (as also in v. 31). They at least recognize that their previous defeat involved divine intervention! Their theology is typically polytheistic, with gods limited to areas of responsibility or location: the previous defeat had been due to fighting where the Israelites' *gods,*[14] *the gods of the hills*, had power. Their approach to Ben-Hadad may also be political manoeuvering: they are telling their king he was not responsible for the defeat as he was against powerful gods. All he needs to do now is fight *on the plains*, somewhere west of the Golan Heights and leading into the Valley

---

[13] Provan, p. 155.

[14] Since the plural *'ĕlōhîm* 'gods' is the common word for 'God' it is possible to translate in the singular, 'their God', as does NJPSV. EVV, following AV/KJV, have traditionally translated as plural, fitting both polytheistic speakers and popular Israelite worship of multiple gods, alongside Yahweh. In v. 28 'God' is appropriate since 'Yahweh' is the complement.

of Jezreel.[15] They effectively criticize the *kings* by telling Ben-Hadad to replace them with *officers*[16] (v. 24) under his direct command. Further, fighting on the plains gives advantage to a force based on *chariots* (v. 25). This all sounds excellent military strategy and victory would seem inevitable, with the comparison of the Israelites as *two small flocks of goats* against the Arameans who *covered the countryside* (v. 27).

The scene is before our eyes, but, as in verse 13, a message from Yahweh provides the unseen perspective (v. 28). Again Yahweh's honour is at stake: the Arameans do not recognize his name or character. As in verse 13, the victory will not be Ahab's but Yahweh's: *I will deliver this vast army into your hands* ('your' is singular, i.e., Ahab). The result will be that *you will know that I am the* LORD. This time 'you' is plural: as well as Ahab and the Israelites, the Arameans could well be included, as they have outspokenly denied Yahweh's power. It also addresses readers, then and now, who are tempted to limit God's power and presence.

Mention of *seven days,* with an unexpected attack on *the seventh day,* together with the subsequent *wall* that *collapsed,* provides a literary echo of Joshua's defeat of Jericho. There too Yahweh had given dramatic complete victory and the implication is that now at *Aphek* the wall collapse is likewise no accident. The numbers in verses 29–30 are large, a feature throughout Old Testament narrative, following ancient Near Eastern practices. 'The nations around [Israel] used numerical hyperbole to glorify a given king; the writers of Israel's history did the same to glorify the King of kings . . . Thus Israel's use . . . may be seen to be both polemical and theological.'[17] This is not being 'inaccurate' but truthfully conveying meaning using rhetorical conventions understood by the readers. Even today conventions vary from culture to culture in reporting crowd and attendance sizes in ways that communicate importance or impact.

The phrase *a god of the hills and not a god of the valleys* (v. 28) is direct in its simplicity, and readers today with belief in an almighty God, creator and ruler of all, may at first say 'how ignorant' (compare Acts 17:30) or even 'how foolish'. Nevertheless the narrative provides a mirror for Western Christians influenced by the Enlightenment.

---

[15] The location of *Aphek* (vv. 26, 30) is uncertain, two proposals being east of the Sea of Galilee, on the road from Damascus to Israel, or in the valley of Jezreel (Wiseman, p. 178; Walton, Matthews and Chavalas, p. 382).

[16] *peḥâ* is generally a political term, often translated 'governor' (*HALOT*, NJPSV). Ben-Hadad may be effectively deposing the kings and taking direct rule.

[17] D. M. Fouts, 'Numbers, Large Numbers', *DOTHB*, p. 753. His article (pp. 750–54) includes other features assisting interpretation, e.g., use of *'elep* ('thousand') and, with the same consonants, *'allûp* ('chief of a thousand'; modern Hebrew, 'colonel').

Religion, with faith in God, becomes a matter for the private spheres of life, personal and family, but insignificant in or even excluded from public life: God is a god of private life but not of public discourse and activities. Added has been the impact of industrialization, with its fragmentation and compartmentalizing of life. Work situations are diverse but congregational members have in common 'church, family life and personal spirituality', and so these become the focus of sermon content and devotional literature. There is often little discussion of how God is involved in the world of work, commerce and politics. We may know how to 'stand up for God', sing his praises and proclaim the Good News when we are 'in the mountains', in familiar territory, but in public life, 'in the valleys', we may be less sure of how to live and speak as Christians. How does one speak of God, living his sovereignty and power in *all* areas of life? An encouraging sign in recent decades is increasing discussion, and debate, of ways in which the Bible and faith impact on public life. The *man of God* came to Ahab with a word from Yahweh that was specific to his situation. We can thank God for ways in which today he is equipping individuals and groups with expertise and spiritual discernment.[18] At issue is whether and how we live out belief that God's presence can be just as evident in public life as in church and family experiences. Then we can encourage one another in not being fearful of the Ben-Hadads and 'vast armies' of contemporary life but rather live confident that 'at the name of Jesus every knee should bow, in heaven and on earth and under the earth, and every tongue acknowledge that Jesus Christ is Lord, to the glory of God the Father' (Phil. 2:10–11).

d. Ben-Hadad and Ahab again (20:30b–34)

How different from verses 1–12 is the interaction now between Ben-Hadad and Ahab! With Ben-Hadad reduced to hiding (v. 30b) again his *officials* propose action (v. 31; see v. 23).Their argument is based on relationship: *kings of Israel are merciful.* The word ḥesed is a rich relational term, used widely in contexts of covenant relationships, including that between Yahweh and Israel. While often having a sense of 'faithfulness' and 'loyalty' that goes beyond strict requirements, ḥesed is also used of Yahweh's 'mercy' and 'kindness' when Israel breaks the covenant requirements and turns in repentance, and so also of 'mercy' fellow-Israelites are to show one another.[19] The

---

[18] The term 'public theology' has become widespread as various institutions and individuals engage issues of faith and society.

[19] E.g., 2:7; 3:6; 8:23; Exod. 34:6–7. D. A. Baer and R. P. Gordon, 'ḥsd #2874', *NIDOTTE*, 2, pp. 211–218.

officials are drawing on past covenantal relationships between Aram and Israel, wearing signs of penitence to seek mercy and forgiveness for having attacked Israel. At this stage we do not know what Ben-Hadad thinks – that comes in verses 33–34 – but the officials go ahead. They use the words of a subservient vassal, *your servant Ben-Hadad*, a humiliating reversal of Ahab's 'my lord, the king' of the opening encounter (vv. 4, 9).

Ahab's reply is surprise that Ben-Hadad has survived the collapsed wall, but unexpectedly he refers to Ben-Hadad as *my brother* (v. 32), a term appropriate for kings in an equal relationship. Ahab is more generous than expected so the officials eagerly repeat the phrase. Were they wondering if it was a mistake, or a trick? The offered equality is endorsed: *when Ben-Hadad came out, Ahab had him come up into his chariot* (v. 33). Negotiations involve a return to old territorial boundaries (*the cities*) and Ben-Hadad's offering of commercial advantages to Israel (*market areas*), and so Ahab accepts the offer and *made a treaty* (v. 34).

The concluding *and let him go* could be read as a good ending to the conflict. After decisive victory Ahab looks to the future, seeing a way to guarantee future peaceful relationships, with commercial advantages. His actions can be viewed as truly magnanimous, surely commendable and a possible end to a cycle of attacks from Arameans. But the story does not end there. There is another perspective.

e. Prophetic judgment (20:35–43)

Twice it has been stated that the victories are Yahweh's action: *I will give [all this vast army] into your hand today and you will know I am the* LORD (vv. 13, 28). Yet apart from the prophet's words Yahweh's name is absent. It is as if Ahab simply takes advantage of the final victory: he is king, so the victory is his and he can do as he pleases. Yahweh however has not finished with Ahab. He gives a command (*by the word of the* LORD) to *one of the company of the prophets*[20] which leads first to the death of a disobedient *companion*, an enacted parable of the importance of obedience and consequences of disobedience (v. 36; cf. 13:24). The next person obeys and only then is the purpose of being struck with a weapon evident. Acting as a battle-wounded soldier the prophet tells the king a story of an order to keep watch on a captive, with penalty for failure specified. The king is merciless, agreeing with the

---

[20] This is an otherwise unspecified group, mentioned elsewhere in association with Elisha (2 Kgs 2:3, 5, 7, 15, etc.). There is little evidence that they were 'a school of prophets' (Hobbs, pp. 25–27).

penalty.[21] In a manner reminiscent of Nathan's 'You are the man!' spoken to David (2 Sam. 12:7), Ahab hears back the sentence he has given, *it is your life for his life, your people for his people* (v. 42). The prophet brings the message Ahab had neglected: the battle has been Yahweh's, not Ahab's, so all the spoils and captives belonged to Yahweh.[22] Just as Achan had taken 'devoted things' after the destruction of Jericho (Josh. 7:1) and Saul had kept 'Agag and the best of the sheep and cattle, the fat calves and lambs' (1 Sam. 15:9), so now it was not Ahab's prerogative to free Ben-Hadad, seeking personal advantage. Ahab had failed to learn from the past. For now, Ahab returns *sullen and angry* (v. 43), a victim of his own divided faith. He has been happy for Yahweh to give victory, but treats lightly his responsibilities as a king under Yahweh. He has enough knowledge of Yahweh to recognize Yahweh's prophet and not to ignore the message, but is unwilling to follow Yahweh's ways when they seem politically and nationally inexpedient. Like the prophet's assumed role, he has been *busy here and there* (v. 40) making his own decisions regarding the future while neglecting his key responsibility.

By any common criteria today Ahab would be judged as successful in standing up to an aggressor and yet being merciful in victory, as well as restoring national territory and improving commercial opportunities. 'Yet, this passage of Scripture warns against our tendency to place pragmatic considerations ahead of a right relationship with God.'[23] Ahab is an example of the seemingly autonomous individual who makes decisions on the basis of what 'looks good' without reference to divine requirements, a human characteristic since the garden of Eden (Gen. 3:6).

2. Naboth's vineyard: property acquisition and God (21:1–29)

'Land' is more than 'dirt, rocks, sand . . . , land is a social symbol with a range of meanings'.[24] To some it is 'my property', whether the location of settled residence or a source of livelihood and wealth. For many, land is a place of remembered events and relationships shaping 'who we are', often associated with the attitude that land is held in trust from the past for the future. At times clashes arise between con-

---

[21] 'The talent of silver was meant to be an impossible sum for a simple soldier to pay'; R. Westbrook, 'Law in Kings', in Lemaire and Halpern, p. 458.

[22] *A man I had determined should die* renders the Hebrew 'the man of my ḥerem', referring to 'banned goods' that have been dedicated solely to Yahweh.

[23] Seow, p. 153.

[24] N. C. Habel, *The Land is Mine: Six Biblical Land Ideologies* (Minneapolis: Fortress, 1995), p. 1.

flicting values and between individual rights and community concerns, exacerbated by any history of invasion, forced appropriation or diverse cultural backgrounds. What does it mean to possess or use land? What rights and responsibilities are involved? The questions are as ancient as human life, and it should not surprise that the Bible has much about land.[25] The incident of Naboth's vineyard provides a window, highlighting both values and matters of morality and power.

a. The exercise of power to possess (21:1–16)

The narrative starts straightforwardly but soon turns. A good deal is offered on a piece of productive land, the offer is rejected and the prospective buyer is unhappy (vv. 1–4). The buyer's wife reminds him that he is king (vv. 5–7) and takes action to provide legal justification for expropriation, depriving the owner of his ultimate right, his life and honour (vv. 8–16). Already a short summary illustrates how powerful people can use the processes of justice to get their own way. Issues become focused through closer exploration.

(i) Two views of land (vv. 2–4)

Ahab clearly regards land as a commodity to be bought and sold at will. *Naboth* has a different perspective, seen in his double reference to *the inheritance of my ancestors* (vv. 3–4) and his invoking Yahweh's name in expressing horror at the thought of selling. Basic to OT understanding is that land belongs to God who brought Israel into the land and allocated it to clans as an *inheritance*. Laws were put in place to protect family heritage and economic viability, especially from the hands of the more powerful, and land could not be sold in perpetuity.[26] Israelite and Canaanite practices were sharply different:

> Although admittedly an argument from silence, it is nevertheless an impressive fact that the whole Old Testament provides not a single case of an Israelite voluntarily selling land outside his family group . . . This silence of the text is matched by the absence as yet of any inscriptional evidence from Palestine of Israelite sale and purchase of land, though there is abundant evidence of such transactions from Canaanite and surrounding societies.[27]

Laws can be enforced only by people with authority. So, in the century after Ahab, prophets spoke publicly against neglect of

---

[25] In addition to Habel, see C. J. H. Wright, *God's People in God's Land* (Grand Rapids: Eerdmans, 1990).

[26] See especially Lev. 25:8–38; Deut. 15:1–11; Josh. 13:6–7.

[27] Wright, *God's People in God's Land*, p. 56.

property laws (Isa. 5:8; Mic. 2:1–2) and in the exile Ezekiel looked forward to a time when rulers would no longer oppress but rather 'allow the people of Israel to possess the land according to their tribes' (Ezek. 45:8). In the century after the beginning of return from exile, Nehemiah as governor corrected the situation where land was forfeited due to poverty and high interest rates (Neh. 5:1–13).

As a person with power, influenced by Canaanite attitudes, Ahab acts as if Naboth shares 'the rejection of Mosaic torah as the basis for Israelite social life'.[28] In Ahab's favour, he is not being despotic and simply taking the land (as have many rulers and governments through the centuries) but offers fair compensation. Naboth however sees that faith in Yahweh brings with it loyalty to his extended family, past and future. Ahab returns to Samaria *sullen and angry* (v. 4), petulantly *sulking*. Is there some residual awareness of Naboth's rights that he cannot override? He is caught between conflicting attitudes to land and, as in 20:41, there is a suggestion of resentment against Yahweh and his demands.

(ii) Power corrupts and destroys community (21:5–16)

Jezebel now takes control. She assumes that to *act as king* is to 'have your own way' (vv. 5–7). To her, as to many since, the question is, 'Who's in charge? You or Naboth?', without any submission to a higher authority (contrast the kingship laws in Deuteronomy 17:14–20). Even though a foreigner, she utilises Israelite law to remove Naboth (vv. 8–14). Tragically, use of power and wealth to manipulate legal processes continues to be not uncommon, whether through intimidation, bribery, paying for the best lawyers or engaging in a process, even 'legal', that the innocent poor cannot afford.

She manipulates the very people who are bound to Naboth by community, *the elders and nobles who lived in Naboth's city with him* (v. 8; the repetition of the whole phrase in v. 11 emphasises its irony). She uses a religious act, a *day of fasting*, as another cloak, adding an air of sanctity to the setting of legality. Ambrose, the fourth century bishop of Milan, saw ongoing parallels: 'How clearly the custom of the rich is portrayed! . . . You fast, not that the cost of your banquet may profit the needy, but that you may obtain spoil from those in want', quoting at length the words on 'true fasting' from Isaiah 58.[29]

Precise repetition of details highlights how the community leaders do exactly as she says (compare vv. 9–10 and 11–13). There is no attempt to question or modify, let alone protest or warn Naboth.

---

[28] Sweeney, p. 249.
[29] Quoted in Conti, p. 129.

Were they more interested in their own security? Did they consider it dangerous to go against her plan, knowing her ruthlessness (18:4; 19:1)? Is this another case of 'it is better for you that one man die for the people than that the whole nation perish' (spoken by one who is part of the nation to be saved)?[30] Whatever the reason, the city leaders, the very people responsible for ensuring community well-being, take an active part in destroying a community member, so destroying community itself.

Ahab's non-involvement is significant. There is no mention of Jezebel telling him her scheme, and when she gives the news (v. 15), Ahab does not ask for details: his distancing himself from the act is another pattern all too often followed. One's hands are clean because others have done the dirty work! Why then is he regarded as culpable (v. 19)? The order in Jezebel's words is significant; *Get up and take possession ... Naboth ... is no longer alive but dead* (v. 15).

> The seeming redundancy of the [final] phrase hides a legalism ... a person found guilty of a capital offence was regarded in law as dead; the effect of a pardon [a king's prerogative] was thus to bring him back to life again ... Jezebel reverses the proper order of events:... expropriation, summary execution, guilty verdict ... Without saying anything explicit, Jezebel has made clear to the king that Naboth's fate was sealed before the trial began ... From this point on, therefore, Ahab cannot plead ignorance. He has become an accessory after the fact.[31]

Centuries later Jesus commented on the command, 'You shall not murder': 'Anyone who is angry with a brother or sister will be subject to judgment!' (Matt. 5:21–22). It was Ahab's early response of being *sullen and angry* that precipitated Jezebel's plot.

Power can be exercised to protect the poor and build a 'community of brothers and sisters' (to cite the Deuteronomic model), or it can foment division, forcing people to take sides, setting one against another. The narrating of this incident provides a mirror on manipulation of the legal system and use of a religious veneer, together with a certain distancing from the actual deed, all leading ultimately to community breakdown. Talk of 'community' is becoming common, at least in Western countries. As this incident illustrates, personal economic gain (or gain for 'our group' or even 'our country') tragically can have priority over creating community that embraces all.

---

[30] The words of Caiaphas the high priest regarding Jesus, John 11:50.
[31] Westbrook, 'Law in Kings', in Lemaire and Halpern, pp. 456–457.

b. Judgment by a greater power (21:17–24)

Ahab, or rather Jezebel, appears to be in control: in verses 1–16 the only instance of 'Yahweh' is on the lips of Naboth (v. 3). *Then the word of the LORD came to Elijah the Tishbite* (v. 17): of the thirteen verses, 17–29, nine report Yahweh's words. Neither Ahab nor Jezebel nor any of the elders is in charge. Humans may scheme and manipulate, others may feel helpless and suffer — ultimate results are in the hand of God.

Elijah is commissioned to confront Ahab in the very act of taking *possession* (v. 18). The choice and repetition of the verb *yāraš* 'take possession' (four times in vv. 15–19)[32] highlight the extent of the crime. The verb is prolific throughout Genesis-Judges for Yahweh's giving of the land to Israel to 'possess' as an inheritance.[33] Ahab has no rights over the land and Yahweh will not allow the king to distance himself from responsibility. All pretence is shattered: *Have you not murdered a man and seized his property?* (v. 19). The word 'murder' is that used in the Ten Commandments (Exod. 20:13) and denotes all kinds of illegal killing (murder and manslaughter), but not capital punishment. Naboth's death has no legal justification and Ahab is responsible. In keeping with a pattern throughout the OT, Ahab's punishment matches the crime, with a violent and humiliating death for himself and Jezebel and end of the dynasty.

Elijah accuses Ahab, *you have sold yourself to do evil* (vv. 20, 25). The king has become a slave to his own evil purposes. The Pauline imagery of being a 'slave to sin' springs to mind: wrongdoing ends up dominating a person, and pays 'wages' (Rom. 6:15–23). Doing *evil* results in *disaster* (v. 21; the same Hebrew word),[34] again a matching of crime and punishment. Just as previous dynasties in Israel came to a gory end, so too will the dynasty of Omri, Ahab's father (v. 22).[35] Rulers may think they are in control, but they survive only as they are faithful to the covenant obligations, doing what is just and right. Ahab's reign illustrates the connection between departing from single-minded worship of Yahweh and perpetrating injustice and oppression. When kings fail to fulfil their responsibility

---

[32] In v. 19 NIV has *seized his property*.

[33] First in the promise of Gen. 15:7; Numbers has 13 instances, Deuteronomy 63 and Joshua-Judges 45.

[34] Hebrew *ra'*, like English 'bad' (and its opposite *ṭôb* 'good'), is not limited to moral contexts, e.g., we may speak of weather or food as 'bad'. One could have translated here, 'you have done what is bad so you will experience what is bad'. EVV commonly have 'evil, wicked' when reference is moral, and 'disaster, woe' otherwise (cf. use of both *ṭôb* and *ra'* in 22:18).

[35] For the earlier dynasties, see prophetic announcement of judgment in 14:10–11; 16:2–4.

of doing what is right and just, especially protecting the weak and powerless, Yahweh steps in, announcing his action through his prophets.

No country today is 'God's land' in the way ancient Israel and Judah were, yet it is still true that 'the earth is the LORD's' (Ps. 24:1; 1 Cor. 10:26). The interplay of attitudes to land, being in community and God's actions, with ongoing relevance, are well-expressed by Walter Brueggemann:

> The prominent model for property in the ancient world and in our own time we may designate as 'royal/urban' . . . Possession gives legitimacy . . . so that 'haves' may have and legitimately seek more . . . The right of the 'have-nots' is nil.

> The Bible articulates an alternative view [which] . . . may be designated 'covenantal/ prophetic'. It holds that the 'haves' and the 'have-nots' are bound in community to each other, that viable life depends upon the legitimate respect, care and maintenance of the 'have-nots', and of restraints upon the 'haves' so that the needs and rights of the disadvantaged take priority over the yearnings of the advantaged. Thus the stress is upon *respect* and *restraint* precisely in those areas of public life where the distribution of power makes respect and restraint unenforceable.[36]

c. Change is possible (21:25–29)

The sordid narrative ends surprisingly. After being told that Ahab has been the worst king ever (vv. 25–26; 16:30–33) comes dramatic reversal. Ahab shows deep grief and repentance (v. 27). We may be tempted to think this is superficial, but God treats it as genuine. Change is reinforced by repetition of earlier statements:

When Ahab heard (vv. 16, 27)

that Naboth was dead, he got up and went down to take possession of Naboth's vineyard. (v. 16)	*these words, he tore his clothes, put on sackcloth and fasted. He lay in sackcloth and went around meekly.* (v. 27)

Then the word of the LORD came to Elijah the Tishbite.
(vv. 17, 28)

---

[36] W. Brueggemann, 'Reflections on Biblical Understandings of Property', *International Review of Mission* 64 (No. 256) (1975), pp. 354–355.

Now Yahweh's message is that the disaster that could have come in Ahab's own day is to be delayed. There is mercy, even for wicked Ahab (vv. 28–29).

Throughout Kings of only two people is it said that he *humbled himself*, Ahab, the worst king of all, and Josiah, the best of all, and in both cases promised judgment is deferred (cf. v. 29 and 2 Kgs 22:19–20). God's forgiveness truly is 'by grace . . . not of works' (Eph. 2:8–9). There is no mention of Elijah communicating this message to Ahab.[37] If he was more comfortable in bringing a word of judgment than of mercy, he would be in the company of all who still have difficulty in accepting that God's grace is freely offered to the worst sinner. Mercy does not fit with human zeal, but it is God who has the final word.[38]

One meets here the complexity of life: Ahab is not punished, but his sons are. Is this a case of children being punished for the sins of their parents? Yes and no! The Bible recognizes that parental actions do have consequences for the lives of their children. Social workers and other professionals working with dysfunctional families are well aware of the lasting impact of family patterns upon future generations. A pattern of disbelief and disobedience is rarely limited to one generation, reaching to 'the third and fourth generation', but such is the kindness and love of God that faithful commitment has an influence to 'thousand generations'.[39] Concurrent is the possibility of change and each generation is accountable.[40] In a subsequent narrative involving Ahab's son, Ahijah, judgment is because of Ahijah's own sin (2 Kgs 1:3–4, 16–17), although one could say he was following his father's example. Ahab's other son, Joram (Jehoram),[41] distances himself from his father's actions, but is still influenced by Jeroboam, the first king of Israel (2 Kgs 3:3), and is eventually killed in Jehu's purge (2 Kgs 9:24–26).

The chapter thus ends on a double note: God's mercy even to a repentant Ahab, and the ongoing consequences of wrongdoing. It contrasts a faithful Naboth who loses his life and a faithless, scheming Ahab who is shown mercy and continues to live. Sinners are forgiven, but the consequences of their wrongdoing remain: the lives of Naboth and his sons have been murderously cut short and the elders live with

---

[37] Josephus fills in the text's silence with 'and so the prophet revealed these things to the king' (*Antiquities* 8.13.8 §362).

[38] P. Yancey, *What's So Amazing About Grace?* (Grand Rapids: Zondervan, 1997) has a major section on 'Breaking the Cycle of Ungrace'.

[39] Exod. 20:5–6. Recent translations correctly notice the contrasting parallel between the 'threes and fours' (i.e., third and fourth generations) and the 'thousands' (i.e., thousandth generation).

[40] See the various scenarios of Ezek. 18.

[41] For the alternative names see on 2 Kgs 3:1, p. 223, n. 1.

the consequences of their self-protecting lies. The telling of the story is part of righting wrongs: Naboth is remembered, his name lives on, with the hope that this example will deter others from following the behaviour of Ahab and Jezebel. The passage affirms that God is on the side of Naboth, and that wrongdoing brings judgment.

Some wrongs can be righted in this life, but the further revelation of Jesus Christ points to a coming eternal vindication.[42] The promise of eternity is the warrant of a lasting hope that right will triumph. C. S. Lewis contended: 'If you read history you will find that the Christians who did most for the present world were just those who thought most of the next.'[43] Here is encouragement to live justly in the present, following the ways of God who is concerned for the livelihood and property of all in community.

3. The end of Ahab's reign (22:1–40)

The initiation by Ahab of another battle with the Aramaeans (vv. 1–4) and his death in the conflict (vv. 29–36) form the frame of the final act in the drama of Ahab's reign. At the end are recorded the fulfilment of the prophecies of 20:42 and 21:19, 21 (vv. 37–38) and the standard formulaic summary (vv. 39–40), but the key dynamics are in the major central section on prophets, their messages and their reception (vv. 5–28), bringing to the fore continuing issues. Ahab's behaviour shows the 'humbling' of 19:29 has not lasted long.

a. Ahab prepares to attack the Arameans (22:1–4)

Ahab's treaty with Ben-Hadad (20:34) had brought a period of cessation of hostilities (v. 1); but despite Ben-Hadad's promise a key Israelite city in Transjordan was still in Aramean hands[44] *and we are doing nothing*. The visit of *Jehoshaphat, king of Judah*[45] provides an opportune time to act with joint forces. Relationships in the account point to Israel as the stronger partner in their alliance (see below on v. 44), and possibly Jehoshaphat *went down* at Ahab's request: Jehoshaphat expresses willing partnership (cf. Ahab's earlier words to Benhadad, 20:4), he addresses Ahab as 'the king' (v. 8) and later joins the battle, following Ahab's plans (vv. 29–30).

---

[42] E.g., Rev. 11:15–18; Hebrews 11:1 – 12:3.

[43] C. S. Lewis, *Mere Christianity* (London: Collins Fontana, 1955), p. 116.

[44] *Ramoth Gilead* ('Heights of Gilead') had been a major administrative centre in the time of Solomon (4:13) and was important in protecting trade. See also 2 Kgs 8:28; 9:14.

[45] The account of Jehoshaphat's reign as king of Judah follows the conclusion of Ahab's (vv. 41–51).

b. Prophetic conflict (22:5–28)

(i) Jehoshaphat insists on Yahweh's word (vv. 5–9)

Ahab had met only with his *officials* (v. 3), but Jehoshaphat faithfully followed Yahweh (v. 43) and is unwilling to go into battle until they *seek the counsel* [lit. 'word'] *of the LORD* (v. 5). Ahab's response and the prophets' word contain a number of uncertainties. The opening *the king of Israel brought together the prophets – about four hundred men* (v. 6) recalls how at Mount Carmel he 'brought together[46] the prophets'. On that occasion 'the prophets of Baal' are killed but there is no mention of the fate of the 'four hundred prophets of Asherah'. Hence there is an ominous note: the description is simply 'prophets' and when they speak they use the common word 'Lord' not Yahweh (v. 6).[47] Further, their word is ambiguous: *The Lord will give into the king's hand.* There is no object to the verb (most translations, including NIV, insert 'it', i.e., Ramoth Gilead), 'the king' is not named and it is not clear who 'the lord' is! A contrast is the prophetic word of 20:13, 28 which specified 'into *your* hand'. A parallel is the famous occasion when Croesus, the rich and powerful Lydian king, asked the oracle at Delphi whether he should attack Persia. The message was that if he attacked he would destroy a great kingdom. Too late he discovered that the 'great kingdom' he destroyed was his own.

Jehoshaphat is not satisfied: he wants to be sure that the word is from Yahweh. Ahab's response shows his lack of interest in hearing anything contradicting his plans. The first-time hearer or reader of Ahab's *still one prophet* would expect this to be Elijah, but at the end is named, *Micaiah son of Imlah* (v. 8). He is known only in this narrative but Ahab's remarks are a reminder that biblical narrative is selective, and that opposition to Ahab was wider than Elijah thought (18:22; 19:10, 14).[48] The narrator's concern is Yahweh's bringing about his judgment on Ahab; Micaiah is but a messenger. Despite Ahab's protest, Jehoshaphat insists – he will not waver in his commitment to Yahweh. The order is giving brusquely, 'Hurry! Micaiah son of Imlah!'

(ii) Setting the scene for Micaiah (vv. 10–14)

Before we meet Micaiah, other activity is taking place. In the open public space before the two kings *all the prophets* are *prophesying*

---

[46] In 18:20 NIV has 'assembled' for the same Hebrew.

[47] Signified in NIV by 'Lord', distinguishing from 'LORD'. NRSV's 'LORD', i.e., Yahweh, follows some later manuscripts, most likely harmonizing with v. 12.

[48] See further D. G. Firth, 'Backward Masking: Implicit Characterisation of Elijah in the Micaiah Narrative', *Old Testament Essays* 13, 2 (2000), pp. 174–185.

– another echo of Mount Carmel (18:29)![49] Unexpectedly one of the group, *Zedekiah son of Kenaanah*, in symbolic act and in word proclaims, *This is what the LORD says*, with an unambiguous message. The *iron horns* reinforce the word *gore*, echoing Moses' description in blessing the dominant northern tribes of Joseph (Ephraim and Manasseh; Deut. 33:17). The other prophets join in: this time their message is unambiguous, adding *be victorious* and using the name Yahweh (v. 12). Like Satan's use of Scripture in tempting Jesus, the mere quoting of Scripture does not guarantee correct application.

> Is it a coincidence that Zedekiah (whose name is explicitly Yahwistic: 'Yahweh is Righteousness') is the son of 'Chenaanah' (Hebrew, *kĕna'ănâ*), whose name sounds suspiciously like 'Canaanite' (Hebrew, *kĕna'ănî*)? The continuing problem during Ahab's reign has been the tendency to blur the distinction between Israelite Yahwism and Canaanite Baalism (including the worship of Asherah) . . . Are Ahab's prophets equally at the service of Yahweh and of Baal or Asherah, depending on which deity the king wishes to consult at any given moment?[50]

Meanwhile, Micaiah is being forewarned. *The messenger* assumes that prophets fit their prophecy to the hearer: Ahab expected 'good' messages (vv. 8, 13).[51] Micaiah is firm, using the name *the LORD* twice (v. 14), that is his sole authority. The scene is set for confrontation: Zedekiah has given what he claims to be Yahweh's message of success, but the earlier messages from 'the prophet', judging the treaty with Ben-Hadad (20:42), and from Elijah, judging the murder and dis-possession of Naboth (21:21–22), together with Ahab's own words (v. 8), lead us to expect a message through Micaiah of death.

(iii) Micaiah's message and reactions (vv. 15–28)

Micaiah surprisingly repeats the other prophets' words (compare vv. 12, 15). It is unlikely that he has taken to heart the messenger's advice! Possibly he is testing Ahab's sincerity, or speaks with a sarcastic tone. What we know is that Ahab insists he tell *nothing but the truth in the name of the LORD* (v. 16). Micaiah's response is clear: with *shepherd* a common picture for kingship, Israel is to lose her king. Ahab's reaction says much about his attitude: his strong charge to Micaiah had been solely to verify to Jehoshaphat that *he never prophesies anything good about me, but only bad* (v. 18; cf. v. 8)! He has no intention of taking notice.

[49] See p. 173, n. 35, for 'prophesying' as involving ecstatic activity.
[50] Walsh, p. 347, n. 5.
[51] NIV's *favourably* (v. 13) translates *ṭôb* 'good' (cf. v. 8).

Ahab is a forerunner of all leaders who say 'tell me the truth' but expect affirmation and reject criticism, leaders who surround themselves with likeminded people. If that is dangerous on the human level of leadership and management, how much more when it shuts out any 'word of God' that is uncomfortable, questioning present attitudes and actions. Wise are leaders who are open to well-founded criticism, and Christian leaders who are open to having their understanding of Scripture corrected. As the pastor of those boarding the *Mayflower* in 1720 in Leiden to sail to Plymouth, the puritan John Robinson said, 'The Lord has yet more light and truth to break forth out of his holy word.'[52]

Ahab's response suggests that he is happy with the word of the rest of the prophets (four hundred against one) – or at least that is what he is going to act on because it agrees with his own desires. Micaiah's continuation suggests as much. He sees *the LORD sitting on his throne with all the multitudes of heaven standing round him on his right and on his left* (v. 19), a pointed contrast to the human setting of the two kings (cf. v. 10). Here is a vivid reminder of the locus of true power and authority. Ahab thought the decision to attack Ramoth Gilead was his initiative, but Micaiah points to Yahweh's action, implementing judgment announced by previous prophets. What Ahab has been hearing from the others is *a deceiving spirit*, to *entice* Ahab (vv. 20–23). Unknowingly the prophets are agents of God's judgment on persistent, wilful rejection of his ways, giving the only message that Ahab is willing to hear, so *enticing* him into battle. Paradoxically, Micaiah's words reinforce Ahab's guilt, as even when he hears Yahweh's revelation he refuses to change. Yahweh through Micaiah strips from Ahab any pretense in claiming that to attack has been supported by a prophetic word from the majority.

The thought of God sending a *deceiving spirit* raises, for many, questions of God's morality. It is consistent however with his actions elsewhere in both Testaments towards those who persist in rejecting his clear word. We see it in the exodus narrative with the hardening of Pharaoh's heart,[53] and later with prophets in Ezekiel 14:7–10. Paul writes similarly regarding those who 'perish because they refused to love the truth and so be saved. For this reason God sends them a powerful delusion so that they will believe the lie and so that all will be condemned who have not believed the truth but have delighted in wickedness' (2 Thess. 2:10–12). Micaiah's words become a last opportunity for Ahab to change – even Jehoshaphat's early insistent

---

[52] The basis of the hymn by George Rawson (1807–89), 'We limit not the truth of God / To our poor reach of mind'.

[53] Exod. 7:3–5, 13–14, 22; 8:15, 19, 32 (MT 11, 15, 28); 9:12; etc. See W. A. Ford, *God, Pharaoh and Moses* (Milton Keynes: Paternoster, 2006).

requests (vv. 5, 7–8) have opened the way. We turn to Paul again for a description of opposing results of the one message: 'We are to God the pleasing aroma of Christ among those who are being saved and those who are perishing. To the one we are an aroma that brings death; to the other, an aroma that brings life' (2 Cor. 2:15–16). The account of Ahab is a salutary instance of the tragedy of consistent rejection, going one's own way despite regular warnings.

The drama continues: *Zedekiah* is angry that his message is classed as untrue. How is one to know whether Micaiah or Zedekiah is telling the truth? Around 150 years later in a similar confrontation between Jeremiah and Hananiah (Jer. 28), both claimed to give Yahweh's word. Questions of discerning God's will in specific situations continue today. One negative criterion is whether the prophet enjoins following 'other gods', even if there is a 'sign or wonder' (Deut. 13:1–3). This may be compared to the Johannine 'test the spirits' because there are 'many false prophets', the positive criterion being acknowledgment 'that Jesus Christ has come in the flesh' (1 John 4:1–3). It could well be argued that track record would support Micaiah, although both claim to be 'prophets of Yahweh'. As the narrative unfolds, the ultimate test is which word comes to pass, the test outlined in Deuteronomy 18:21–22. That is the answer of Micaiah (vv. 25, 28). Ahab however knows that Micaiah's oracle is probably true (v. 16), but brazenly expects to *return safely* (v. 27)! He is in control, or so he thinks.

c. Ahab's stratagem and death (vv. 29–40)

Ahab is a picture of delusion. He has already decided to take back Ramoth Gilead (vv. 2–4); at Jehoshaphat's behest he has obtained a positive message from prophets, reinforced by Zedekiah (vv. 11–12, 24), but he has also heard the word of Micaiah whom he has ordered to 'tell me nothing but the truth' (v. 16). So he devises a plan to *disguise* himself as an ordinary soldier, with Jehoshaphat wearing *the royal robes* of command. 'Though he has chosen to disregard the oracle, he is not able to ignore it.'[54]

The stratagem seems to work, as the Arameans attack *the king of Israel* only to find they have the wrong person (vv. 31–33). But God's purposes are sure: Ahab is struck, the text highlighting the unintentional randomness, humanly speaking. He was not even struck in face-to-face combat. Ahab gives orders to be taken from the battle for treatment as the wound is not immediately fatal (v. 34). Even here he is powerless. With the battle raging all around, he

---

[54] Konkel, p. 354.

remains *all day long . . . propped up in his chariot* until *that evening he died* (v. 35). If he had been in royal clothes this could be seen as brave and heroic leadership to the end, but instead he is disguised. The call for the soldiers to return home seems to be spread by a leaderless army (cf. v. 17). Ironically his death *disguised* (v. 30) as a common soldier had been first foretold by a prophet likewise 'disguised' (20:38).

With slow death the *blood from his wound* is pooled at the bottom of the chariot. The final ignominy comes as the chariot is washed: 'Thus the dogs lapped up his blood and the whores bathed [in it], in accordance with the word that the LORD had spoken' (v. 38 NJPSV).[55] Here is fulfilment of the words of Elijah (21:19).

The concluding summary of Ahab's reign (vv. 39–40) mentions luxurious *adorning* of the palace with inlaid *ivory* and *the cities he fortified*. Each has been illustrated through archaeological findings,[56] both being measures often used to determine the lasting significance of a reign. For the biblical writer they are incidental, a mere endnote. The opening summary (16:29–33) had set the most important, and sadly lasting, aspect of his reign as religious apostasy. We have read of his confrontation with Elijah: culminating in the unequivocal demonstration of Yahweh's uniqueness and power on Mount Carmel; his confrontation with prophets in leniency towards Ben-Hadad, and with Elijah again over Naboth's vineyard; and his final futile and deluded attempt to avoid Yahweh's word of judgment. Throughout we meet an Ahab whose compromises show a person seeking to control events, and whose relationship with Yahweh is syncretistic and weak. He seeks to be a Canaanite king who himself determines the law, while he has vestiges of recognition of Yahweh as the God of Israel. He follows Yahweh's word only insofar as it accords with his own plans.

His importance in Israelite history, and for the ongoing biblical revelation of God, is that his reign provides the most extensive confrontation between a royal view of life and history – 'that may be understood as ordinary, commonsense establishment thinking'[57] – and a prophetic-covenantal perspective that refuses to equate God's will with state policy. On one hand Ahab's behaviour was characteristic of the nation of Israel as a whole (2 Kgs 17:7–17), his death

---

[55] NJPSV follows Hebrew word order and structure. 'Whores' may allude to prostitutes that were part of the fertility cult (14:24; 15:12) (Provan, p. 164). The alternative translation, 'weapons', in NIV footnote, is based on emending *zônôt* 'prostitutes' to *zĕyānôt* 'armour' as in Aramaic and Syriac versions.

[56] Walton, Matthews and Chavalas, p. 384; Sweeney, pp. 261–262; cf. Amos 3:15; Ps. 45:8.

[57] Brueggemann, p. 278.

foreshadowing the violent death of the nation. On the other hand, against all that is wrong, God sent prophets with his word. There was still the call to choose (18:21) and the opportunity to repent (cf. 21:28–29). Further, events demonstrate the fulfilment of God's word.[58] When religiously and morally all is at the lowest, God continues to speak and perform his word. He even delivers his people from an oppressive enemy – so 'then you may know I am the LORD' (20:13, 28). It is God's word, made known by the prophets, that determines the course of history.

The early Christians were a small minority living under the regime of Rome that saw itself as all-powerful, controlling a large empire with military and economic might. They sought the well-being of the community and prayed for 'kings and all those in authority',[59] but gave final allegiance to 'God, the blessed and only Ruler, the King of kings and Lord of lords'.[60] There were cultural and religious pressures to conform to societal norms as determined by the majority powers, including ritual practices binding the empire together in worship of emperors and other gods. The book of Revelation responds with vivid portrayal of the heavenly throne and the ultimate triumph of Christ. Over against the titles given to emperors of 'Lord and Saviour' Christians proclaimed Christ as the one 'Lord and Saviour'. It was he who had 'all authority' over 'all nations', transcending and relativizing political and imperial values and perspectives.[61]

The way the prophets confronted has continuing relevance. The authority was not theirs, as if it were prophet *versus* king, with the prophet seeking the king's submission, but rather Yahweh *versus* king, with the prophets' role being God's messengers in specific situations. King and people were accountable for their actions, bearing the consequences. Elijah was to anoint future rulers (19:15–16), but rulers were the ones who acted. This can throw light on later issues of 'church and state' and the responsibility to 'proclaim' and to exemplify 'the ways of God', no matter what the results. Rulers are accountable to God, not to the church. We see this pattern in the life of Christ and of the early Christians in relation to Jewish and Roman authorities. Our task is to know and proclaim the Scriptures, open to the Spirit who continues to guide and empower.

Another characteristic of the prophets' role is often overlooked. The prophetic words were addressed to God's own people, those in covenant relationship who in some way claim Yahweh as 'our

---

[58] 17:24; 18:1; 20:13, 28, 42; 21:19; 22:17, 38.
[59] Matt. 22:17–22; Rom. 13:1–6 (both passages are in contexts of taxes); 1 Tim. 2:2.
[60] 1 Tim. 6:15.
[61] Luke 2:10–11; Matt. 28:18–20; Rev. 17:14; 19:16.

God'.[62] This is relevant in seeking to hear and bring a 'prophetic-covenantal' word in a world enamoured of a 'royal view of life and history'. There is a mutuality as we 'spur one another on toward love and good deeds' (Heb. 10:24). God's word continues and what happens will be *as the word of the* LORD *had declared* (v. 38).

4. Jehoshaphat king of Judah - Ahab's ally is different (22:41–50)

In turning back to Judah, it comes as a relief to read of a king who *did what was right in the eyes of the* LORD, as had his father, *Asa* (v. 43; 15:9–24). As with similar reigns in Judah there is a qualification due to the continuance of *high places*, although positively Jehoshaphat continued Asa's work of removing the *male shrine prostitutes* (v. 46; 15:12).[63]

Ending years of conflict between Judah and Israel[64] Jehoshaphat *made peace*[65] *with the king of Israel* (v. 44 NRSV), sealing the alliance with a marriage of Ahab's daughter to his son Jehoram[66] (2 Kgs 8:18; 2 Chr. 18:1). The alliance gave security on the north and so he could extend Judahite influence to the south, abortively seeking a renewal of Solomon's trading (v. 48; 9:26). By then he was powerful enough to refuse Israel's offer of partnership in the venture (v. 49).

His desire to know and do Yahweh's will, affirmed in the summary statements, has been evident in the previous narrative (vv. 5, 7–8), yet his alliance as the junior partner involved him in Ahab's attack on Ramoth Gilead and stratagem to avoid death in battle. Jehoshaphat is an example of positive actions in following Yahweh, while also illustrating the situation of many who have to make decisions within unequal relationships. It is common for Christians to be working in organizations or business or government and to be citizens of nations where actions are planned contrary to what is believed to be God's will. Personal decisions have to be made as to whether and how to speak, and whether and how to participate in the joint action. One approach is seen here. Jehoshaphat was prepared to challenge Ahab regarding seeking Yahweh's will. He could do this because of a nominal shared faith, since at least officially Ahab was under the same covenant with Yahweh, nevertheless when Ahab made his decision Jehoshaphat (reluctantly?) participated in joint action. In

---

[62] Thus, there is no word addressed directly to Jezebel or Ben-Hadad (although both come under God's judgment).

[63] See on Asa's reforms, 15:11–15, pp. 155–156.

[64] 14:30; 15:6–7, 16–22.

[65] The verb form suggests the initiative was his and he was likely the weaker partner of the alliance.

[66] For the name and its alternative Joram see p. 223, n. 1.

the event he himself survived and continued a positive reign for a further seven years and he was able subsequently to refuse partnership with Ahab's successor. There is no criticism of Jehoshaphat for his actions, but rather overall commendation.

1 Kings 22:51 – 2 Kings 1:18
10. Ahaziah king of Israel and Elijah

Ahaziah's brief reign is introduced like other northern kings with reference back to Jeroboam, but unusual is mention of both *his father and mother* (v. 52), reminding readers of Jezebel's pernicious influence. Previous kings *aroused the anger of the* LORD, *the God of Israel* (v. 53),[1] but Ahab had been the first who explicitly *served and worshipped Baal* (v. 53; 1 Kgs 16:31), the example followed by Ahaziah (contrary to his name, 'Yahweh has grasped/sustained'). Possibly this combined indictment led scribes of Greek manuscripts to divide Kings here (and hence EVV), so providing a concluding summary to the narrative thus far.[2]

Two complementary statements, external and internal, open the narrative. That *Moab rebelled against Israel* (Moab next appears in 3:4)[3] contrasts with the Judahite Jehoshaphat's gaining control of Edom and refusing Ahaziah's assistance in trade (1 Kgs 22:47–49). Ahaziah injures himself in a fall and, fearing for his death, strikingly demonstrates his worship of Baal (1 Kgs 22:53) by sending *messengers* to *consult* a Philistine god *Baal-Zebub*,[4] *the*

---

[1] Cf. 14:9; 15:30; 16:7, 13, 26.

[2] In Hebrew manuscripts until around the fifteenth and sixteenth centuries, Kings is a single book. Marginal notes specify 1 Kgs 22:6 as the 'middle verse' and 1 Kgs 22:51[MT 52] – 2 Kgs 1:2 is a single paragraph.

[3] Henceforth references specifying only chapter and verse refer to 2 Kings.

[4] The name Baal-Zebub, 'Lord of the Flies' (only here in OT) is matched by LXX 'Baal, fly god (of Ekron)'. Ancient literature records association of deities with flies or plagues, the link being healing or warding off danger. Several scholars see a contemptuous alteration of Baal Zebul, 'exalted lord', as *zbl b'l* is a frequent title of Baal in Ugaritic texts, where he is also presented as a healer. This is the likely origin of *Beelzeboul* as the name of 'the head of the demons' in NT (Matt. 10:25; 12:24, 27; Mark 3:22; Luke 11:15–19; the Latin Vulgate however has 'Beelzebub'). See W. Herrmann, 'Baal Zebub', in *Dictionary of Deities and Demons in the Bible,* edited by K. van der Toon, B. Becking and P. W. van der Horst (Leiden: Brill, 1995), coll. 293–296, and K. van der Toorn, 'Baal-zebub', *NIDB* vol. 1: pp. 373–374.

god of Ekron[5] (1:2). The might of the Omride dynasty is declining, parallelling Ahaziah's physical injury and religious apostasy. The account of decline, leading to death, is all we know of Ahaziah's brief reign.

Ahaziah's sending *messengers* introduces confrontation with its repeated use of

> 'sending' (*šālaḥ*, 6x: vv. 2, 6, 9, 11, 13, 16) and 'messengers' (*mal'ākîm*, 5x: vv. 2, 3, 5, 15, 16). The various sendings . . . emanate from two distinct 'sources', namely Ahaziah (vv. 2, 9, 11, 13) and Yahweh acting through his *mal'āk* (vv. 3, 15). These two 'sources' stand in sharpest opposition to each other in that Ahaziah had expressed contempt for Yahweh by turning to another god. Which source will then emerge triumphant in the opposing 'missions' sent out?[6]

As in previous meetings between Ahab and prophets the focus throughout is on Ahaziah and Yahweh. Elijah's role is simply to convey Yahweh's message of judgment (vv. 4, 16), its reason and content being unavoidable, with two threefold repetitions:

> *Is it because there is no God in Israel that you are going off [sending messengers] to consult Baal-Zebub, the god of Ekron?* (vv. 3, 6, 16)

> *You will not leave the bed you are lying on. You will certainly die!* (vv. 4, 6, 16)

Confrontation is set up as Elijah obeys Yahweh's word and intercepts *the messengers* (v. 3), who, when they *returned to the king*, repeated verbatim Elijah's message (vv. 3, 6). From the description,[7] and no doubt remembering his father's past confrontations, the king recognizes *Elijah the Tishbite* (v. 8). Ahaziah's reaction is typical of many who receive an unwelcome message: remove the messenger!

The narrative's middle section (vv. 9–15) has another threefold pattern as Ahaziah sends successive parties of *a captain with his company of fifty men* (vv. 9, 11, 13)[8] and Elijah responds. Ahaziah

---

[5] Northernmost of the five Philistine cities (1 Sam. 5:10; 17:52), identified with Tell Miqne, a major centre on the Israel border.

[6] C. T. Beggs, 'Unifying Factors in 2 Kings 1.2–17a', *Journal for the Study of the Old Testament* 32 (1985), p. 76. As elsewhere in the Bible EVV have 'angel', from the Greek *angelos*, 'messenger', for Yahweh's 'messenger'.

[7] The description *ba'al śē'ār* 'a lord/owner of hair' suggests most likely 'a hairy man' (so LXX, NRSV, NLT, NJPSV, NIV mg), but may be *he had a garment of hair* (NIV). Cf. John the Baptist (Matt. 3:4; Mark 1:6).

[8] Identical in each, literally 'a commander of fifty' and 'his fifty'; cf. Deut. 1:15.

is not politely inviting, but seeking to intimidate. The first captain summarily orders, *Come down!*, but Elijah as *a man of God* does not submit to the demands of a king. The contrast between two authorities is seen verbally as Elijah says, repeating the captain's verb, *may fire come down.* Yahweh authenticates as *the fire fell from heaven* (vv. 9–10). Ahaziah does not learn anything, but is more determined to have Elijah captured as the next group come and order, *Come down at once!* Elijah's response is identical, and *the fire of God fell from heaven and consumed* the *men* (vv. 11–12).

Parallels with the earlier confrontation on Mount Carmel are evident. Elijah is *sitting on the top of the hill* (v. 9; 'hill' is definite in Hebrew). The only 'hill' mentioned elsewhere in the Elijah narrative is Carmel, also a place where Elisha dwells (2:25; 4:25), and is likely to be the present location. There Elijah confronted a Baal-worshipping king and called down fire from heaven which 'burned up' (1 Kgs 18). There is still much at stake as to who is the God of Israel. At a crisis time in the nation's history Elijah is 'a larger-than-life character . . . who def[ies] our familiarity and our reason'.[9] Later when people were amazed at Jesus some thought he was Elijah returned (Matt. 16:14). Jesus too did not fit the familiar, but in contrast to Elijah, when accused of using the power of Beelzebub, his answer was not calling down of fire, but arguing that his casting out demons was attacking Satan's power (Matt. 12:22–28). On another occasion, remembering Elijah, the disciples wanted Jesus to 'call fire down from heaven to destroy' a Samaritan village that did not welcome them, but he 'rebuked them' (Luke 9:54). The contingent sent by the king to arrest Elijah may also be compared with the 'large crowd armed with swords and clubs, sent from the chief priests and the elders of the people' to arrest Jesus, another troublemaker who had to be removed (Matt. 26:47). Jesus went, obeying his Father's will (Matt. 26:39), the only miracle being restoring the high priest's servant's ear (Luke 22:51)!

Still Ahaziah persists. Like army commanders ordering 'send in more troops' in a process of attrition, he is determined to intimidate and arrest Elijah. This time however the captain submits to Elijah and begs *have respect for my life and the lives of these fifty men*, significantly adding, *your servants* (vv. 13–14). Elijah responds only when *the angel* (messenger) of Yahweh gives orders to *go down*, with the addition, *do not be afraid of him* (v. 15). We may wonder whether Elijah's previous response was partly due to fear, similar to after the Carmel event – Jezebel is still alive (1 Kgs 19:1). Now he

---

[9] Brueggemann, p. 290.

went down because of Yahweh's command, irrespective of any fear he may have had.[10]

The rest is direct repetition of the earlier judgment (v. 16; as in vv. 3–4, 6), with no response from Ahaziah, only the simple *so he died*. The important addition, *according to the word of the LORD that Elijah had spoken* (v. 17) speaks to all subsequent generations: God's word may be opposed, efforts made to silence the messenger or to avoid its implications, but God remains God and his will comes to pass. Around the globe today Christians face threats and intimidation, violence and imprisonment. It is as if silencing the messenger removes the message. Christians in Western countries face intimidation in more subtle ways: 'keep your faith to yourself', 'religious views have no place in politics', 'that may be truth for you but don't impose it on others'. It is easy to remain 'on the hill', even to 'fear' – and at times doing nothing for the present may be appropriate. We pray for wisdom as to how to best respond, but when the Lord says 'go down', there is great truth in the words,

> Fear him, ye saints, and you will then
> Have nothing else to fear;
> Make but His service your delight;
> Your want shall be His care.[11]

A previous prophecy to Ahab had been that the dynasty would end in bloodshed 'in the days of his son' (1 Kgs 21:21–22, 29). That did not happen with Ahaziah, but *Ahaziah had no son* and so his brother, *Joram* became king (v. 17; 3:1).[12] His end will be in Jehu's bloody coup (9:24–26). The pattern set by Ahab and Jezebel was the path to disaster.

Another passage has highlighted the reality of the sovereign power of Yahweh over against rulers who act as if they are autonomous and in control of the lives of their subjects. Again we see the alternative perspective of a prophet who hears and communicates Yahweh's word fearlessly, no matter the cost. He speaks against 'consulting Baal-Zebub' just as in successive later centuries Isaiah speaks against those who in times of uncertainty and turmoil 'consult mediums and

---

[10] Josephus provides different dynamics, omitting the angel's words. Elijah goes because he 'approved of his [the officer's] words and the courtesy of his manner' (*Antiquities* 9.2.1 §260).

[11] Nahum Tate and Nicolas Brady's paraphrase of Psalm 34:9 ('Through all the changing scenes of life'). See also Isa. 8:12–13, LXX version being adapted in 1 Pet. 3:14–15.

[12] See p. 223, n. 1, regarding the alternative forms Joram and Jehoram for kings of Israel and Judah and synchronization details.

spiritists, who whisper and mutter' (Isa. 8:19), and Jeremiah warns against 'your prophets, your diviners, your interpreters of dreams, your mediums or your sorcerers' who give a false message of peace (Jer. 27:9). Some current equivalents might be seen in tarot cards, horoscopes, channelling and the like, which either deny the reality of the living God and his revelation in Jesus Christ, or else see them as more immediate and relevant than the Scriptures. Leithart goes further and challenges regarding the role of 'experts' in current life. He rightly affirms that 'there are times for expertise' – and 'all truth is God's truth'[13] –

. . . but the post-Enlightenment reliance on experts is often a form of practical idolatry, a version of consulting Baal-zebub instead of Yahweh. Elijah could well challenge churches that rely on Freud for counselling, on Marx and Weber for their sociology and politics, on Madison Avenue for their evangelistic planning with the question, 'Is there no God in Israel?'[14]

There is wisdom and knowledge whose foundation and criterion are 'the fear of the LORD',[15] but ever since the garden of Eden people search for wisdom independent of such relationship (Gen. 3:6). The collector of Proverbs knew, as the end of Ahaziah demonstrates, 'There is a way that appears to be right, but in the end it leads to death' (Prov. 14:12; 16:25). Much is encapsulated in the simple, but not simplistic, claim of Christ, 'I am the way and the truth and the life' (John 14:6).

---

[13] The title of a book by Arthur Holmes (Leicester: Inter-Varsity Press, 1979).
[14] Leithart, p. 168, citing C. Gray, *The Way of the (Modern) World; or, Why It's Tempting to Live as if God Doesn't Exist* (Grand Rapids: Eerdmans, 1998).
[15] Job 28:28; Ps. 111:10; Prov. 1:7; 9:10; 15:33.

2 Kings 2:1–25
11. Elijah's ascension and the transition to Elisha

The narrative structure for the period of the divided kingdoms is interrupted by a record of extraordinary events. Between the end of one king's reign (1:17–18) and resumption of the royal narrative (3:1) comes an account highlighting both transition and continuity. The unique ascension of Elijah is followed by evidence that Elisha comes with the same divine power and authority that is not bound by royal history.

The account of Elijah's ascension is a stirring divine endorsement of his ministry. It is more explicit as to 'ascension' than the accounts of Enoch, who 'was no more, because God took him away' (Gen. 5:24), and Moses, of whom it is said 'to this day no one knows where his grave is' (Deut. 34:6). Events surrounding the handover authenticate Elisha's authority as a visionary prophet succeeding Elijah at a crucial juncture in Israel's history: in fulfilment of Yahweh's charge to Elijah and Elijah's prophecies the Omride dynasty, with its blatant worship of Baal, will come to a violent end in Jehu's coup and subsequent purge.[1] Much however is strange and unexpected to readers today; a foretaste of aspects of the life and ascension of Jesus.

1. Elijah's journey from Gilgal to ascension (2:1–11)

The language is straightforward, but the content is amazing. *When the LORD was about to take Elijah up to heaven in a whirlwind* sets the scene with the same verb used in the culminating event, *Elijah went up to heaven in a whirlwind* (vv. 1, 11).[2] Between these verses

[1] 1 Kgs 19:16; 21:19, 23–24, 29; with fulfilment in 2 Kgs 9 – 10.
[2] In vv. 1–18, only vv. 1, 11 have forms of *'lh,* 'go up', drawing attention to ascension itself.

214

is a threefold dialogue between Elijah and Elisha, and the threefold response of *compan[ies] of the prophets*, with repeated phrases. The continuation from the preceding chapter of threefold patterns encourages readers to compare the two series of encounters, to see a contrast between the apostate actions of Azariah and his captains and men and the faithful, committed attitudes of Elisha and the prophets.

Elijah is told by Yahweh to go from *Gilgal* to *Bethel* and then to *Jericho*,[3] continuing across the *Jordan*. On three occasions he tells Elisha, *Stay here, for*[4] *the* LORD *has sent me to* . . . and to each Elisha responds with a standard oath formula, *As surely as the* LORD *lives and as you live, I will not leave you* (vv. 2, 4, 6). At both Bethel and Jericho *the company of the prophets* ask Elisha, *Do you know that the* LORD *is going to take your master from you*[5] *today?* to which Elisha replies, *Yes, I know . . . so be quiet* (vv. 3, 5). For the third leg of the journey, from Jericho to Jordan, *fifty men from the company of the prophets* go with them *at a distance* (v. 7). This is another allusion to the previous chapter (1:9, 11, 13) inviting readers to compare the two journeys of Elijah: one where he 'went down' with the officer and men at Yahweh's command with a message of death, the other where he 'goes up to heaven', also at Yahweh's initiative, with Elisha continuing in a ministry that begins with life-giving (v. 21).

What is being said is clear, but already readers may wonder, what is going on? Is Elijah, even on this day, reluctant to hand over to Elisha (see further below), or is he testing Elisha's resolve? Elijah had after all been told to anoint Elisha as his successor and Elisha has been with him, although at the beginning Elijah seemed less than enthusiastic (see on 1 Kgs 19:16, 19–21). What is the writer's purpose in telling this story to subsequent generations? A component of suspense is always a feature of good story-telling, but ongoing

---

[3] While *Gilgal* is often equated with the first stopping point after Joshua's crossing of the Jordan (Josh. 4:19), that they *went down to Bethel* has led some to see a location 'in the central highlands north of Bethel' (Hobbs, p. 19). J. S. Burnett, '"Going Down" to Bethel: Elijah and Elisha in the Theological Geography of the Deuteronomistic History', *Journal of Biblical Literature* 129 (2010), pp. 281–297, argues for a theological meaning with a 'down-up' pattern throughout chs 1 – 2. To 'go up' is commonly used of worship and Bethel is significant as the ancient cult centre which Jeroboam made the royal sanctuary (Gen. 35:1; 1 Kgs 12:29), and so 'go down' without actually entering the city signifies non-participation by Elijah and Elisha (see below on vv. 23–24). *Jericho* provides another major association with Joshua. See also vv. 18, 23.

[4] The particle *kî* 'for' is not evident in NIV, but is appropriately included in NRSV, NLT, NJPSV.

[5] Literally 'take from above your head'. Elisha is to be no longer subservient to his 'master' Elijah. The repeated *lqḥ* 'take' in vv. 3, 5, 9, 10, is a word of separation so focusing on Elisha's new position (also used in connection with Elijah's cloak, vv. 8, 14).

significance is best seen in the presentation of Elisha's response. The decision to continue is always his (vv. 2, 4, 6); he is ready to face whatever is involved as Elijah is taken from him (vv. 3, 5). The repetition emphasizes that Elisha 'is determined to follow his master, refusing to compromise his vow, though repeatedly challenged'.[6] In this he foreshadows Christ, who faced the challenge of his calling: 'Jesus resolutely set out for Jerusalem' (Luke 9:51). The series of meetings with *compan[ies] of the prophets* has another result: they witness Elisha's determination, so preparing to accept his status.

Just as Moses used his rod to divide the waters of the Sea, so Elijah rolls *his cloak* like a rod and the two *crossed over on dry ground* (v. 8), the imagery and language recalling also the Jordan crossing under Joshua (Exod. 14:16, 21–22; Josh. 3:17; 4:22). Crossing to the east of the Jordan provides another parallel as the region where Moses transferred leadership to Joshua. As the time of ascension and transition arrives, Elijah again challenges Elisha as to what he wants. In response, Elisha asks to *inherit a double portion of your spirit* (v. 9). A 'double portion' is that due to the first-born son (Deuteronomy 21:17 has the same phrase), so Elisha is not seeking double what Elijah had but requesting recognition as legitimate successor in Elijah's role. He seeks an inheritance not of property (cf. 1 Kgs 19:21) but of *your spirit*, the same Spirit that has been upon Elijah.[7] Elijah's reply may seem to be another example of reluctance, but is more likely recognition that the Spirit is not his to give. The condition that Elisha must *see* 'indicates that Elisha must become a visionary prophet; if he is unable to have visions of YHWH, he can hardly function as Elijah's successor'.[8] Thus Elijah does not place his 'cloak'[9] on Elisha, rather it is there for Elisha to pick up after the ascension (v. 14).

What Elisha sees is unexpected: *a chariot*[10] *of fire and horses of fire* come between them, signifying that they are now in separate realms, and Elijah *went up to heaven in a whirlwind* (v. 11). 'Fire' and 'whirlwind' are often associated with theophanies,[11] with the image

---

[6] Konkel, p. 380.

[7] The Spirit of Yahweh is commonly associated with a prophetic role: Num. 11:24–30; 1 Sam. 10:5–13; 19:20–24; 1 Kgs 22:24; Ezek. 11:5; Joel 2:28; Zech. 7:12; Luke 1:67; Acts 2:17.

[8] Sweeney, p. 273. 'Seer' (one who 'sees') is an older term for a 'prophet' (1 Sam. 9:9, 11, 19; also 2 Sam. 15:27; 24:11; Amos 7:12). In Chronicles it is the standard title for a 'king's seer' (1 Chr. 21:9; 25:5; etc.).

[9] *'adderet* is not common: of the ten OT instances, five refer to Elijah's 'cloak' (1 Kgs 19:13, 19; 2 Kgs 2:8, 13, 14). It appears to designate a prominent person (*HALOT*).

[10] The noun is probably collective, 'chariots', as in the following verse (also 13:14; Exodus 14:23; Dan. 11:40). 'Elijah is taken up in the whirlwind, not in a chariot' (Seow, p. 176).

[11] For example, *'ēš* 'fire', Exod. 3:2; 13:21; 19:18; Ezek. 1:4, 5, 13, 27; *sĕʿārâ* 'whirlwind', Job 38:1; 40:6; Isa. 29:6; Jer. 23:19; Ezek. 1:4; Zech. 9:14.

here of a celestial army protecting *Israel*. 'Elijah has been the powerful guarantor and indomitable protector of Israel. A negative implication is that the military apparatus of monarchy plays no role in the real securing of Israel.'[12] Later Elisha and his servant will 'see' the 'horses and chariots of fire' that prevent the Aramean capture of Dothan (6:17), while King Jehoash will exclaim the same words in anguish at Elisha's approaching death (13:14).

2. Elisha returns to Jericho (2:12–18)

Elisha's return-crossing of the Jordan is evidence to him and to the watching *company of the prophets from Jericho* that Yahweh is not only *the God of Elijah*. Phrasing in verse 14 identical to verse 8 reinforces that in very truth *the spirit of Elijah is resting on Elisha* (vv. 14–15). The prophets still wonder where Elijah's body is. The idea of a 'wind/Spirit' (*rûaḥ* is equivalent to both) carrying a prophet away seems to have been current (1 Kgs 18:12; cf. Acts 8:39) and so their only interpretation is that the body has been *set . . . down on some mountain or in some valley* (v. 16). Elisha cannot dissuade them, for they did not see the unique event. Telling this cameo of a fruitless search (vv. 17–18) reinforces the unusual nature of Elijah's ascension.

If the prophets had difficulty in accepting Elisha's account, how much more readers today: 'while the report may trouble our rationality, the narrative clearly intends to place Elijah well outside our rationality'.[13] The resurrection and ascension of Jesus likewise challenge perceptions of possibilities. They too were seen as 'irrational': the authorities thought the body had been stolen and hidden (Matt. 28:11–15) and disciples themselves had difficulties (Matt. 28:17; Luke 24:31, 13–35, 36–39; John 20:24–29). With Elijah's ascension there is no thought that others might likewise ascend, simply a later prophecy of his return to earth (Mal. 4:5–6). With Jesus there is also an announcement of his return (Acts 1:10–11), but now with the new dimension of believers sharing with him in eternal life (e.g., John 14:1–3; Eph. 2:6). Christ is 'the firstfruits', the promise of more to come (1 Cor. 15:20, 23).

The story of Elijah has been one of contrasts: despite his self-perception he was not the only prophet loyal to Yahweh and there were ways of being faithful other than Elijah's confrontational approach, but his zeal for Yahweh is unquestioned. He could be bold on Carmel, yet discouraged at Horeb and even fearful, but when Yahweh commanded him to give a word he obeyed. Apart from the

---

[12] Brueggemann, p. 297.
[13] Ibid., p. 296.

early period with the widow at Zarephath (1 Kgs 17:7–24), his ministry was almost entirely confronting kings Ahab and Ahaziah. Later exilic readers would remember the awesome judgment on apostasy that came 'according to the word of Yahweh', but would also find hope as they hear of God's grace when people, no matter how wicked, turn to him. They would be encouraged to be faithful to Yahweh despite many cultural pressures. Elijah was not perfect, but he knew Yahweh's sending, provision, compassion and finally affirmation in his ascension.

Elijah strides not only across these chapters but has a major role also in later Jewish and Christian thought, beginning with Malachi 4:5 [MT 3:23]: 'See, I will send the prophet Elijah to you before that great and dreadful day of the LORD comes.' Thus the Gospels record questions as to whether John the Baptist or Jesus is Elijah.[14] The NT refers to only three incidents in Elijah's ministry: Jesus cites his being sent to the widow of Zarephath as an example of God's grace (Luke 4:26); Paul cites God's reply to Elijah's protest about Israel as evidence that 'God did not reject his people' (Rom. 11:2–4); and James encourages prayer, citing Elijah, 'a human being, even as we are', praying concerning drought and rain (Jas 5:16–18). Standing out is his appearance with Moses at Jesus' transfiguration (Matt. 17:3; Mark 9:4; Luke 9:30). Luke includes the topic of their conversation: Jesus' departure (*exodos*), which he was about to bring to fulfilment at Jerusalem (Luke 9:30). Here is heavenly assurance for Jesus as he moves to Jerusalem fulfilling God's purpose, from Moses, the human leader of the first exodus, and Elijah, the prophet 'zealous for the LORD' in a time of blatant syncretism and apostasy (1 Kgs 19:10, 14).[15]

The transition narrative may be read alongside later Christian experience. Jesus had conducted his ministry 'full of the Spirit', in 'the power of the Spirit', and promised the same Spirit to his disciples.[16] His ascension was followed by the Spirit empowering those who continued on earth, his followers. It is not only one person who is empowered but, in fulfilment of Joel 2:28–29, 'all people . . . your sons and daughters . . . your young men . . . your old men . . . my

[14] Matt. 11:14; 16:14; 17:10–12; Mark 6:15; 8:28; 9:11–13; Luke 1:17; 9:8, 19; John 1:21; also the words of bystanders at the cross that Elijah might come to save Jesus (Matt. 27:47–49; Mark 15:35–36). See D. L. Bock, 'Elijah and Elisha', *DJG*, pp. 203–206.

[15] See M. Zetterholm, 'The Books of Kings in the New Testament and the Apostolic Fathers', in Lemaire and Halpern, pp. 561–584; J. T. Walsh, 'Elijah. C. Elijah in Later Tradition', *ABD* 2, pp. 465–466.

[16] While present in all Gospels this is particularly so in Luke (3:22; 4:1, 14, 18; 10:21), including promise of the Spirit to his disciples (11:13; 12:12; 24:49). See L. Morris, *Luke*, Tyndale NT Commentaries (Leicester: Inter-Varsity Press, revised ed., 1988), pp. 48–50.

servants, both men and women' (Acts 2:17–18). Ministry continues after ascension. Elisha will be active in personal and family situations and in national conflicts: the Spirit at work in Elijah who faithfully proclaimed 'this is what the LORD says' continues in Elisha. The ministry of Jesus saw much confrontation, culminating in his crucifixion, and the early church faced its own controversies and opposition, to be followed by experiences of the church through the centuries: 'Both in the ministry of Jesus and the life of the early church the Spirit of God is at work.'[17] The church witnesses to the ends of the earth and the end of the age, looking forward to Christ's return. Robin Mark wrote of the background of his popular song, 'The Days of Elijah':

> The song came from watching a television 'Review of the Year' at the end of 1994. This was the year of the Rwandan civil war tragedy which claimed 1 million people's lives, and also when the first ceasefires in N[orthern] I[reland] were declared. . . . I found myself despairing about the state of the world and, in prayer, began asking God if He was really in control and what sort of days were we living in.
>
> I felt in my spirit that He replied to my prayer by saying that indeed He was very much in control and that the days we were living in were special times when He would require Christians to be filled with integrity and to stand up for Him just like Elijah did, particularly with the prophets of Baal. 'These are "Elijah" days.'[18]

3. Elisha's public ministry has diverse results (2:19–25)

'Elijah and Elisha': their rhyming names naturally come together in the ear, appropriately associating their ministries as major prophets at a critical time in the northern kingdom. The name Elijah, 'my God is Yah', points to his zeal for Yahweh in the face of royal support of the worship of Baal and Asherah and syncretistic popular religion, a feature we have noted above. Now as we turn to Elisha his name, '[my] God saves', highlights the variety of incidents in which Elisha will bring healing and deliverance.

Before the royal narrative resumes (3:1), two incidents exemplify contrasting features of Elisha's subsequent ministry. The first is a life-giving act (vv. 19–22), but the second is judgment on those who scorn his Yahweh-commissioned prophetic ministry (vv. 23–25).

---

[17] Morris, *Luke*, p. 50.
[18] <http://www.robinmark.com/song_story.php?lyricID=10> (accessed March 2011).

Elisha's circle of influence grows as *the people of the city* come with a problem of *water* that is *bad*, no doubt from a large spring supplying Jericho, and he brings healing. The request for *a new bowl*[19] and use of *salt* suggest a ritual act of cleansing and the incident follows Joshua's curse and the rebuilding of Jericho during Ahab's reign (Josh. 6:26; 1 Kgs 6:34), so now marking God's gracious blessing on continuing habitation. While readers today might like more information on 'how it happened',[20] the narrator is more concerned to tell us why. Elisha announces a word from Yahweh, *This is what the LORD says: I have healed this water. Never again will it cause death or make the land unproductive*, the narrator then ensuring we know that all happened *according to the word Elisha had spoken* (vv. 21–22).

Yahweh's bringing life at Jericho at the beginning is a powerful message in the midst of all that was wrong in the nation of Israel. Elijah's first message had been the judgment of drought, narrated immediately after the fulfilment of the curse on Jericho's builder (1 Kgs 16:34; 17:1). Elisha's is of life-giving water to the people of Jericho: there is life when people turn to Yahweh, acknowledging his word spoken by his prophet. Much of Elisha's subsequent ministry will be bringing wholeness (4:1 – 6:6; 8:1–6). Exilic readers who have experienced Yahweh's judgment see his desire to *heal*, taking away that which will *cause death*. The brief cameo provides a picture of the salvation freely offered through Christ, the 'water' of 'life' (John 4:14), with promise of eternal access to 'the spring of the water of life' (Rev. 21:6; 22:1, 17). At the same time Jericho's water crisis is a reminder that millions in the world still do not have access to clean drinking water. It is a godlike act to bring about such access along with the good news of Christ.

The response changes as Elisha moves into Israel's territory and passes the royal sanctuary town of Bethel. The incident disturbs modern sensibilities,[21] but it needs to be read in the larger literary and religious context. The jeers of *some boys*[22] are blatant. Elisha's

---

[19] *ṣĕlōḥît* occurs only here in OT and is used in later Hebrew of a small jar or bottle (*HALOT*).

[20] The 'healing' may be linked with a geological shift that removed contact with radioactive strata or alternatively a parasite (Gray, pp. 477–478; Wiseman, p. 197; Walton, Matthew and Chavalas, pp. 386–387).

[21] E.g., Gray, pp. 479–480; Jones, pp. 389–390.

[22] *naʿar* is used of ages from newborn (Exod. 2:6) to young armed men (1 Kgs 20:15), and servants (1 Kgs 18:43; 2 Kgs 4:12). The addition of *qāṭān* 'small' justifies the translation 'boys', but age is still indeterminate (cf. David, 1 Sam. 16:11; 17:31). The parallel *yĕlādîm* (v. 24, NIV *boys*) is used of Rehoboam's younger advisors in 1 Kgs 12:8, 10. Burnett, '"Going Down"', pp. 295–26, cites texts which suggest 'young men of the royal and perhaps priestly establishment at Bethel'. See also H. F. Fuhs, '*naʿar*', *TDOT* 9, pp. 474–485.

baldness contrasts with Elijah's hair (1:8) and so the taunt 'is to deny that he is a prophet, or at least deny that he is a prophet like Elijah'.[23] Given the parallels already noted above between chapters 1 and 2, the twofold 'Go up, baldy!' and the mauling by *two bears* may be compared to the 'twofold nature of the speech and divine punishment against other groups of young men . . . who gave Elijah the directive to "come down" . . . Those who find themselves cursed by Yahweh are those who call for the prophet to "go up" to Bethel, language that elsewhere refers to worship at the sanctuary site.'[24] The curse is not vindictive anger but outworking of judgment on a city that wilfully ridicules Yahweh's prophet, rejecting his word. Bethel stands under a curse. Again at the beginning of Elisha's ministry is a cameo pointing to the future, particularly in the end of the Omride dynasty. The specification of *forty-two* being killed may be put alongside Jehu's slaughter of 'forty-two' of the relatives of the Baalist Ahaziah, king of Judah (10:12–14; cf. 8:26–27): the royal rejection of life from Yahweh leads to the alternative of death.[25] It is often overlooked that the majority of Jesus' parables contain warnings of judgment on willful rejection.[26] As with Elisha, the gracious offer of life is first, but persistent refusal to acknowledge Christ as Lord has as its end death.

Elisha's introduction concludes with his travelling to Mount Carmel, which was perhaps a base for Elijah (see on 1:9), and finally to Samaria, the capital of the northern kingdom, ready for involvement at a national level.

The opening chapters of Kings enabled reflection on leadership transitions, from David to Solomon to Rehoboam. How different is the transition of prophetic leadership from Elijah to Elisha! Echoes of transition from Moses to Joshua encourage reflection on situations today. The royal transitions saw spiritual decline, while the prophetic transition led to expansion in ministry faithful to Yahweh's word. Standing out is Elisha's persistence in following through on his initial call. We see willing acceptance of Elijah's leadership, without any scheming or pushing from Elisha or others. This could be an example of the younger person itching to be free to exercise ministry and leadership as there is no evidence of Elijah encouraging the younger Elisha, their relationship being that of master-servant.[27] How

---

[23] Konkel, p. 382. On the basis of the prohibition in Deut. 14:1 it is unlikely that a shaven head may be a mark of being a prophet, as with later Christian monks (Hobbs, p. 24; but opposite, Provan, p. 177).

[24] Burnett, '"Going Down"', pp. 296–297.

[25] Gray, p. 480; Sweeney, p. 175; Hobbs, p. 24 however says 'coincidental'.

[26] E.g., Matt. 13: 30, 36–43, 49; 18:21–35; 22:1–46.

[27] 1 Kgs 19:21; 2 Kgs 2:3, 5; 3:11; cf. the relationship between Elisha and Gehazi, 5:20.

different were Jesus' actions in sending out 'the Twelve' (Matt. 10:1; Mark 6:7; Luke 9:1) and the 'seventy-two' (Luke 10:1), giving them freedom and the joy of seeing results. In the upper room discourse he describes the disciples' relationship to him as 'no longer . . . servants . . . instead . . . friends' (John 15:15; cf. Luke 12:4).

Elisha's willingness was not the main criterion: the test was whether God had appointed him – was the same Spirit who empowered Elijah also with Elisha? Thoughts may go to the risen Christ's promise of the Spirit in commissioning the disciples as 'witnesses' (Acts 1:8), a promise expanded to 'all whom the Lord our God will call' (Acts 2:38–39). When the early church appointed leaders to 'wait on tables' the first qualification was to be people 'known to be full of the Spirit and wisdom' (Acts 6:2–3), and the appointment of Barnabas and Saul as missionaries was the initiative of the Spirit (Acts 13:2). Further, in taking on his leadership role Elisha does not copy Elijah's *modus operandi*. In both we see a combination of compassion and judgment, but Elisha's ministry will prove to be more diverse, with miracles of compassion and often associated with a 'company of the prophets'. Change of leadership in churches as in organizations often brings different leadership styles and abilities that enable forward movement. It is the ascended Christ who distributes gifts as needed (Eph. 4:7–13).

D. Elisha and individuals, kings and revolution
2 Kings 3 – 13

2 Kings 3:1–26
12. Kings of Israel, Judah and Moab – and Elisha

The royal narrative resumes with the new king of Israel, *Joram*, another *son of Ahab* (v. 1; 1:17).[1] Readers may initially sense *déjà vu* as the opening narrative has many similarities to battle accounts involving Ahab, with prophetic messages and Yahweh's actions (1 Kgs 20, 22). The beginning however is positive: Joram *got rid of the sacred stone of Baal that his father had made* (v. 2). Ahab had built a temple for Baal with an altar and 'an Asherah pole' (1 Kgs 16:32–33) and later Jehu 'demolished the sacred stone of Baal and tore down the temple' (2 Kgs 10:26–27). Joram simply *got rid of* it,[2] but at least he is acting in the direction of his name's meaning, 'Yahweh is exalted'. Joram 'is presented, then, as tolerating the Baal cult while not himself participating in it'.[3] The reader may wonder how he will act differently to Ahab in the following conflict situation. At the same time, Joram continues some policies of previous generations: the statement that fits all kings of Israel, *he did evil in the eyes of the LORD*, is followed by two statements commencing *raq* ('except'; NIV, *but . . . nevertheless*), the first positive as already noted, the second being the

---

[1] Jehoram, sometimes shortened to Joram, is the name of concurrent kings of Israel and Judah (1:17; 8:16) who are brothers-in-law (8:18). While some EVV follow MT's variations, to assist readers NIV consistently has *Joram* for the king of Israel and *Jehoram* for the king of Judah, with footnotes where MT differs. A similar variation occurs later with Jehoash/Joash (11:1, 21). For ease of reading, NIV practice is adopted here. In 1:17 it is said that Joram began his reign 'in the second year of Jehoram son of Jehoshaphat king of Judah', while 3:1 has 'in the eighteenth year of Jehoshaphat king of Judah' (cf. 1 Kgs 22:50). A period of coregency between father and son is generally assumed.

[2] Konkel, p. 393. The causative form of *sûr* is the simple 'take away'. Wiseman suggests it was 'perhaps reinstated by Jezebel' (p. 199).

[3] Provan, p. 181. Cf. v. 13; 9:22; 10:18–28.

continuation of *the sins of Jeroboam son of Nebat.* That he *clung* highlights the seriousness of the latter, a stronger word than 'commit' or 'follow' used of previous Israelite kings. For these reasons we can expect the promised violent end of the Omride dynasty.

The king of Moab (east of the Dead Sea) saw Ahab's death as an opportunity to cease paying a substantial *tribute* (vv. 4–5; 1:1). As had his father when seeking to regain Ramoth Gilead to the northeast, Joram sought *the king of Judah's* cooperation to attack Moab (vv. 4–7a). *Jehoshaphat* responded as he had previously to Ahab (v. 7; cf. 1 Kgs 22:5) and in turn they were joined by the forces of Edom. This time there is no evident initial prophetic consultation before setting out and the outcome is disheartening (vv. 8–9; cf. 1 Kgs 22:5–28). Unexpected is Joram's reaction, *Has the LORD called us three kings together only to deliver is into the hands of Moab?* (v. 10). We hear an echo of the Israelites' grumbling in the wilderness (Exod. 16:3). The ill-planned strategy had been Joram's and this first mention of Yahweh is a word of blame! Sinful humanity readily blames God for one's own decisions and failures (cf. Gen. 3:12; Jas 1:13–15).

As previously, Jehoshaphat asks regarding any *prophet of the LORD* (v. 11; cf. 1 Kgs 22:7). *An officer of the king* suggests *Elisha*, remembering his being Elijah's servant. Joram has yet to recognize Elisha as a prophet, but Jehoshaphat has obviously heard reports and from his lips we hear first the affirmation, *The word of the LORD is with him* (v. 12).[4] Unlike Ahab's resistance toward seeking counsel from the prophet Micaiah (1 Kgs 22:8), Joram concurs in going to Elisha.

Elisha's independence from royal employ is evident first in that the kings *went down to him* (v. 12; location unspecified) and secondly in his challenging Joram: why is Joram not following the path of his father Ahab who had inquired of the court prophets compromised by syncretism (1 Kgs 22:6)? How much is he still influenced by both parents? Joram affirms commitment to Yahweh (v. 13; cf. v. 10) but Elisha is unconvinced, although he knows Jehoshaphat's commitment and so is willing to seek a word from Yahweh (v. 14).[5] Given the parallels with 1 Kings 22 we expect a prophecy of doom, but instead the kings hear one of provision and victory, as in 1 Kings 20. There has been no water in the region of Edom (v. 9) but the vision is explicit, with the *valley*[6] . . . *filled with water* and the addition of a complete 'striking' of Moab (vv. 16–19).[7] Sudden rushing of water

---

[4] The first person to affirm this of Elijah was the widow at Zarephath (1 Kgs 17:24).
[5] For the use of music cf. 1 Sam. 10:5.
[6] A *naḥal* is a wadi or 'torrent-valley' that generally has water only with winter rains.
[7] Despoliation of land and springs was a way to prevent repopulation by an enemy, but is contrary to Deut. 20:19. The description may be read not as a command but simply a statement of what the army will do.

in dry wadis due to rainfall on higher ground is a regional phenomenon and here indicates Yahweh's favour. Unlike Ahab's fatal attack
of Ramoth Gilead, but like the earlier defeat of the Arameans who
had besieged Samaria (1 Kgs 20:13), Yahweh will give victory in
unexpected ways: *This is an easy thing in the eyes of the LORD; he
will also deliver Moab into your hands* (v. 18). His actions in the
natural world (*water*) are matched with those in human interaction
(defeat of Moab): the Creator is sovereign in nature and history.

The next day saw the vision fulfilled, enabling coalition forces to
drink (v. 20). The Moabite forces looked from above with the sun on
the wet red sandstone[8] and imagined blood from internal fighting
within the coalition and thought all that remained was to *plunder*. To
their surprise they became the victims and their towns were despoiled.
The *king of Moab* was desperate, even sacrificing his *firstborn son*[9]
on the *wall* of Kir Hareseth, the Moabite capital[10] that was being
attacked (vv. 25, 27). The referent of *fury* is unclear: NIV's *fury against
Israel* points to either Yahweh or Moab being angry towards Israel
while NRSV's *great wrath came upon Israel* allows for an expression
of disgust, or even fear, by Israel at the king's child sacrifice.
Irrespective, Israel *withdrew* and so the city was not captured, despite
Yahweh's apparent promise through Elisha (v. 18). Moab retains
independence, no longer paying tribute: 'Israel/Jehoram [Joram] –
and not YHWH – would be responsible for the failure to achieve
[complete] victory over the Moabites.'[11] Israel's power continues
weakening. Nevertheless, a situation that had seemed hopeless (v. 9)
had turned to substantial victory. The king of Israel has seen for
himself what the king of Judah had said, *The word of the LORD is
with Elisha* (v. 12), although the end was unexpected.

Reading the narrative today raises issues. Positively one can be
reminded of Yahweh's involvement in human endeavours, but the
nature of that involvement must be nuanced. Joram twice invokes
Yahweh as the initiator of the battle (vv. 10, 13), the forerunner of
many leaders who invoke God on their side in battles they have
initiated for their own purposes: 'We are God's people and so he
must bless everything we do in his name.' Further, the battle was not
to defend Israel but to maintain economic benefits from hegemony
or one's 'sphere of influence' (how many battles have been fought

---

[8] The name Edom is related to the word for 'reddish(-brown)'; cf. Gen. 25:30 and
red lentils (*HALOT*).
[9] Probably a sacrifice to the Moabite god Chemosh. On the Mesha stele, the
Moabite king asserts that Israel's subjection of Moab was due to Chemosh's anger
(*ANET*, p. 320; COS 2.23, pp. 137–138; Provan, *ZIBBC*, p. 116).
[10] Isa. 16:7, 11; Jer. 48:31, 36.
[11] Sweeney, p. 284.

for similar reasons?). Yahweh in his grace comes into the dire situation they have brought about themselves and provides for them. Even though Joram has moved only partially towards undivided allegiance to Yahweh, Jehoshaphat is loyal (1 Kgs 22:43) and it is due to him that Elisha, and thence Yahweh, responds. The promised victory comes, but with a twist. The end is retreat. Is this a case of Elisha not being told the whole of Yahweh's plan?[12] Or is it a case of limited fulfilment due to lack of trust, as will be explicit later for Jehoash (13:14–19)? A possibility is deliberate ambiguity: the prophecy is true, but not as Joram expected. The prophecy opens with what Yahweh will do (vv. 16–18), but follows with actions of Israel (v. 19). In verse 19 Elisha uses the verb 'strike' (*nkh*) to describe what will be done to *every . . . city*. While often meaning 'destroy' (NIV 'overthrow', NRSV 'conquer'; cf. in v. 25 a different verb, *hrs* 'destroy'), it can also mean simply 'strike, hit' (cf. Exod. 21:15). In verse 25 *nkh* recurs, but describing how the *men armed with slings . . . attacked* [*nkh*] *it,* and stones would not be effective 'hitting' against walls![13] We can see an immediate result in Joram now being positive towards Elisha and Yahweh's word, but in the long term Yahweh's purpose to bring judgment in Israel is furthered.

There is mystery in God's purposes: 'The horse is made ready for the day of battle, but victory rests with the LORD' (Prov. 21:31). Even here, with a prophetic word from Yahweh, results are unexpected. There is always danger in interpreting God's word to fit our desires. 'This is not to suggest divine assistance is never deserved or that failures of faith disqualify one from petitioning God . . . Joram was spared disaster for his forces but incurred enormous losses for his country.'[14]

Further, the narrative raises questions concerning the conduct and results of war itself: the futility and cost of war are well demonstrated in the denuding of the landscape, rendering it unfit for agriculture or grazing, and the sacrifice of human lives, of sons. Moab was devastated – but Israel failed to restore its hegemony. Joram returns with the same end result as when he started, except that he has seen Yahweh's provision of water, saving human and animal lives and initially giving victory, and he now knows that Elisha is indeed successor to Elijah as one who speaks Yahweh's word.

---

[12] So Provan, pp. 183–184.

[13] R. Westbrook, 'Elisha's True Prophecy in 2 Kings 3', *Journal of Biblical Literature* 124 (2005), pp. 530–532; summarised with further comments by D. G. Firth, 'Ambiguity', in *Words and the Word: Explorations in Biblical Interpretation and Literary Theory*, edited by D. G. Firth and J. A. Grant (Downers Grove: IVP Academic; Leicester, Apollos, 2008), pp. 167–169.

[14] Konkel, p. 405; see also Brueggemann, pp. 317–318.

2 Kings 4:1 – 6:7
13. Elisha: agent of Yahweh's compassion

Elisha stands out amongst biblical prophets. Apart from the account of Elijah and the widow of Zarephath and her son (1 Kgs 17:7–24), of no other prophet are we told of miracles that are acts of compassion, responding to specific needs.[1] The first two, the widow's oil (4:1–7) and the Shunammite's son (4:8–36), have surface similarities to Elijah and the widow, while the others are quite different: neutralizing a poisonous stew (4:38–41), feeding a hundred (4:42–44), healing Naaman (5:1–27), and recovering an axehead (6:1–7). Each account has movement from problem to solution.

The diversity is instructive, with various social relationships to the fore. An economically impoverished widow is in danger of losing the protective support of her two sons and a well-to-do husband and wife have no son, while a powerful foreign general has a socially threatening skin disease but his captive slave girl is willing to speak. Groups of people are fed unexpectedly and a borrower is able to return an implement. God's provision is seen amongst people far from the royal court, the commonly perceived centre of power and importance. Kings is unique amongst contemporary ancient Near Eastern records in its stories about people on the fringe who would otherwise be forgotten.

The ministry of Elisha, even more so than Elijah's, foreshadows the compassionate ministry of Jesus. Here is evident the character of God who 'defends the cause of the fatherless and the widow, and loves the foreigner residing among you, giving them food and clothing' (Deut. 10:18).

---

[1] The accounts of 'fire from heaven' associated with Elijah (1 Kgs 18:38; 2 Kgs 1:10, 12) are in contexts of confrontation.

It is a short step from this ideal, exemplified in the actions of Elisha, to the later prophetic voice raised on behalf of the poor and oppressed and those victims of monarchical society. . . . The actions of Elisha find echo in the ministry of Jesus. Like Elisha, Jesus responded to the needs of unfortunate women (Mark 7:24–30; 5:24–34); like Elisha, Jesus raised the dead (Mark 5:21–24, 35–43; Luke 7:11–17); and like Elisha, Jesus fed the hungry (Mark 6:30–44).[2]

Like Jesus, Elisha's ministry is itinerant, rather than settling in one place for people to come to him. Chapter 4 alone mentions *Shunem*, at the eastern end of the Jezreel Valley, which he often visits (vv. 8–9), *Mount Carmel* on the coast, 18 miles (30 km) away (v. 25), *Gilgal*, near the Jordan river north of Jericho (v. 38), and *Baal Shalishah*, probably on the coastal plain of Sharon (v. 42). All over the country he is able to respond to people in need where they are. God is as involved in the micro-economics and well-being of individuals and families as he is in the political and military actions of rulers in centres of power.

1. Freeing a widow from economic bondage (4:1–7)

A widow's cry of distress is heard. A member of *the company of the prophets* known for his commitment to Yahweh, a faithful member of the group under Elisha, has died and his creditor does not want to lose out. He demands that the widow's *two boys* become *his slaves* in payment of the debt.[3] Later Jewish tradition (Josephus and the Targums) identified the man as Obadiah (1 Kgs 18:3–4), the debt resulting from borrowing money to feed the hidden prophets. 'Quite apart from th[is] traditon . . . followers of the covenant would have paid a high price for their commitment in the hostile environment of the official Baal cult.'[4]

People may owe money for various reasons. In the ancient world, as in several countries today, people turned to individuals for loans, not for business development or a more comfortable lifestyle, but simply to survive (due to drought, poor crops, sickness, injury or

[2] Hobbs, p. 55.
[3] On debt-slavery and the widow's plea, see Provan, *ZIBBC*, pp. 128–131. The word translated 'slave' is used for 'servant' in general (including 'ministers of the crown'). For discussion of the many OT laws with their concern for amelioration and 'human rights rather than property rights' in comparison to generally harsher ancient Near Eastern practices, see D. L. Baker, *Tight Fists or Open Hands? Wealth and Poverty in Old Testament Law* (Grand Rapids and Cambridge: Eerdmans, 2009), pp. 111–174.
[4] Konkel, p. 412.

other misfortune). High interest rates were and are still common. The laws of Israel were unusual in forbidding the charging of interest: it was not right that one member of God's family exploit and benefit financially from the misfortune of another. Rather the obligation was to be generous and to aid one another.[5] Readers today may reflect on situations experienced in their own country. Diverse government laws and regulations for consumer protection and limits on interest rates sit alongside financial institutions enticing and pressuring people to borrow more, generally for some form of immediate gratification and 'lifestyle enhancement'. Many later experience institutions exacting their dues, with statements such as: 'we are a business, not a welfare agency'; 'we're following the rules agreed to'. There is much to learn from the biblical focus on community.

In this instance we do not know if the widow was being charged interest, but a loan was outstanding. In such a situation, because of the importance of community, relevant laws protected the weak. One way to repay a loan was for the person to become a 'slave' of the creditor.[6] The laws however recognised that there was something wrong in one Israelite being the slave of another, for Yahweh had brought all his people out of slavery in Egypt and so clear provisions were specified for the financial treatment and the setting free of slaves. Theology shaped their economics and labour laws! The order of laws in Exodus 20 – 22 is significant: after the Ten Commandments (Exod. 20:1–17) and rules relating to idols and altars (20:22–26), the first detailed laws concern setting slaves free (21:1–11), coming before laws on personal injuries (21:12–36), which in turn precede laws on property protection (22:1–15). God's priority is to enable all people to enjoy a livelihood in freedom and safety, commencing with the people in the weakest position. People come before property. The role of a king was thus to do what was right and just, especially on behalf of the powerless (Ps. 72:1–7), but the Omride dynasty was marked by injustice (1 Kgs 22): 'oppressed widows are forced to turn to prophets rather than the king's court for justice.'[7]

There is another poignant dimension in the woman's plight. As a widow she would be unprotected without the presence of her sons, a reason for God being known as protector of 'the fatherless and widow'.[8] A woman in danger of losing all – possessions, family and security – calls out to the prophet, Yahweh's representative. His

---

[5] Baker, *Tight Fists or Open Hands?*, pp. 252–285.
[6] Assumed in the mitigating law of Lev. 25:39–43. Cf. Jesus' reference to those who 'devour widow's houses' (Mark 12:40; Luke 20:47).
[7] Leithart, p. 186.
[8] Deut. 10:18; Ps. 68:5; 146:9; hence human responsibility to be like God (Exod. 22:22–23; Deut. 24:17–20; Isa. 1:17; Jer. 7:6).

response is surprising as he questions and involves her. Desperately she explains how little she has. What are her thoughts when Elisha calls for action, apparently to build on the little, with the added kind words, *Don't ask for just a few!* (v. 3)? What we know is that she and her sons obey, and the neighbours help as they are asked. The provision not only enables payment of the debt, but is adequate for ongoing livelihood without requiring another loan which would have continued the debt cycle.

In this cameo of seven verses we see how the prophet 'elicits faith and action by questions, encouragement and word'.[9] His compassion foreshadows the approach of Jesus Christ and provides a continuing model for Christian response to human need. The prophet is neither imperious nor paternalistic. He does not produce gold from somewhere else, even if he could, but respects the widow's integrity and dignity. She may start with the smallest possible contribution, but she is an active participant in the solution and is not over-shadowed by Elisha. She owns the problem and the way forward. Elisha's brief words covering both immediate need and future liveli-hood (v. 7) thoughtfully bring together two aspects often separated in popular thinking. Catering for present and future, however, is the practice of many agencies involved in welfare and development work. Elisha follows a God who does not simply solve problems but cares for people.

2. Life and hope for the future (4:8–36)

The following incident is another reminiscent of Elijah (cf. 1 Kgs 17:7–24). Elisha enjoys the hospitality of *a well-to-do woman* who recognizes him as *a holy man of God* (vv. 8–10)[10] and he understand-ably wants to do something in return. He has contacts in high places, but she is content with the support and protection of her local network and asks for nothing (although later she will need help, 8:1–6).

Elisha's servant, Gehazi,[11] perhaps with hesitancy, draws attention to the obvious: *she has no son and her husband is old* (v. 14). Here is another biblical situation of childlessness, although only here is the husband's age the main reason given for future childlessness.[12] As only sons can carry on the family name and property, wealth cannot

---

[9] Wiseman, p. 202.

[10] Shunem is on a major trade route, 'listed in Egyptian itineraries' (Walton, Matthews and Chavalas, p. 389).

[11] Gehazi is active alongside Elisha, unlike the lack of mention of Elisha in the same role *vis-à-vis* Elijah (see also vv. 25–31, 36; 5:20–27; 8:4–5).

[12] Gen. 15:2–3; 25:21; 29:31; Judg. 13:2–3; 1 Sam. 1:2.

substitute for children (hence the values of Psalm 127). Elisha announces that birth will happen, the woman's response showing how she had given up hope. As a true prophet, Elisha's word comes to pass and a son is born (vv. 15–17).

Tragically the child dies. The narrator draws us in with dramatic dialogue building tension to the climax. The woman knows only one person can help and she wastes no time, giving explanations to neither her husband nor Gehazi (vv.18–26). Again Elisha shows sensitivity: Gehazi tries to protect Elisha, but like Jesus centuries later,[13] Elisha responds directly to a person in need. He is willing to be interrupted. Although a prophet, Elisha recognises that God does not make everything plain to him (v. 27). The woman has to express her need in her own words. She reminds Elisha that the child was his idea, not hers. The hopes that she had not wanted raised have now been dashed (v. 28; cf. v. 16).

We may compare instances where Jesus asks people to state their request in their own words (Matt. 20:21, 32). This points to the importance of our own prayers of petition and intercession. God responds to the verbalised prayers of his people: is this because he knows the way we are made? Counsellors are now recognizing the importance of the counsellee being active in verbalising in their own words the situation and their wishes.

Compassionately Elisha responds in person and the child is restored to life and returned to his mother (vv. 31–37). Like people in Jesus' day, the woman regards the prophet's physical presence as essential. Sometimes in Jesus' ministry the disciples' actions made no difference and served to highlight the power of Jesus (e.g., Matt. 17:14–20), as this story and following ones point to the difference between Gehazi and Elisha. Elsewhere Jesus affirms 'greater things' that his followers will do and he commends the quality of faith of the foreign centurion who regards just a word as being adequate.[14]

3. Life-giving food for the hungry (4:38–44)

During famine, when people are gathering anything that appears to be edible (vv. 38–39), it seems all will go hungry. Even good ingredients, probably painstakingly acquired, have been ruined (v. 40). Elisha's actions make the stew enjoyable and beneficial, accomplishing his desire from the beginning, that all be fed.

Elisha's compassion shines in the next incident (vv. 42–44). Food is brought to him but he takes the initiative to feed *the people*. The

---

[13] E.g., Matt. 12:46–50; 14:15–16; 19:13–15; Mark 5:25–34; Luke 18:35–43.
[14] John 14:12; Matt. 8:5–13.

practical Gehazi says it is impossible, but Elisha tells him to go ahead. Yahweh's purposes are that people be fed, with food left over — and Yahweh's word is what happens. An obvious comparison is when a lad brings some food to Jesus. The disciples' initial inactivity is followed by obedience which leads to five thousand being fed, with food left over (John 6:1–13). As earlier (vv. 1–7; cf. 1 Kgs 17:12–16), God is in the business of taking what seems inadequate and multiplying it, with excess.[15]

Gehazi and the disciples of Jesus (including ourselves?) see the needs of the crowds as too great to be met with limited resources, and so respond by doing nothing: 'Send them away, for our resources are barely enough for our own needs.' Elisha, and Jesus, extend the challenge: 'Begin to feed them with what you have, and you will find the resources supplied, for God chooses to feed the hungry through you.' Paul knew this truth in writing to the church at Corinth regarding their giving to the poor in Jerusalem: 'Now he who supplies seed to the sower and bread for food will also supply and increase your store of seed and will enlarge the harvest of your righteousness' (2 Cor. 9:10). The picture is of a storehouse that seems to have limited capacity: the more that is given away the greater is the amount that is replaced! Limits are placed not by God's provision but by our willingness to be generous.

4. Reflection: magic or miracles?

The scenes in this chapter all point to Yahweh's power through Elisha and authenticate him as Elijah's successor, but readers today, influenced by the Enlightenment, want to know how such 'wonder-ful' deeds were possible. The Bible does not give explanations – 'by their very nature miracles transcend explanation'[16] – but there are common features in miracles.

a. Acts of compassion, not displays of power

The use of the *staff* (v. 31) or *flour* (v. 41) might suggest to some the use of magic. Magic always draws attention to the magician with deeds that are 'wonders' in themselves, but all of Elisha's deeds are for the benefit of others in genuine, basic need. Elisha acts, not to prove he is a prophet, but because he is a prophet. Similarly Jesus

---

[15] Hospitality customs in many cultures require that guests be supplied with more food than they can eat.

[16] Konkel, p. 419. He includes discussion of relationship to stories of 'magic makers' in other cultures.

performed miracles (the usual word is 'signs'), not to prove he was the Son of God, but because he was.[17] For both Elisha and Jesus, miracles were an outworking of their character empowered by the Spirit, responding in compassion to basic needs.

b. A result of trust in the word spoken

All these miracles are an outworking of faith, not a means to faith. The woman and her sons have to trust Elisha's word by *going* and *collecting* the jars and *pouring* oil; the sorrowing mother *comes* to him in expectation that he can act; the company of prophets has to *get some flour*; and Gehazi has to *give* the bread to the people. The result comes as they act. Again, a parallel may be seen with 'the Synoptic image of Jesus [as] one who evoked faith before the performance of miracles (cf. Mark 5:36)'.[18]

c. Miracles at significant times

If these stories were simply an expression of a 'pre-scientific mind', one would expect miracles throughout the Bible. To the contrary, they are clustered at key periods: the exodus, the founding of the nation; the time of Elijah and Elisha, with religious conflict and apostasy in the north; the ministry of Jesus; and the early years of the formation of the church. They come at key times as sovereign acts of powerful compassion of the God who is present with his people. At other times God chooses to work in less spectacular ways, but with the same mighty grace.

The call is for God's people at all times to act compassionately in response to the needs of others, trusting God in his sovereignty to supply what is needed in his way.

5. 'Not one of them was cleansed—only Naaman the Syrian' (5:1–27)

The setting changes dramatically and exceptionally to the home of a foreign military commander who is benefiting from sorties into Israel. The story is popular – I heard it often as a child – and it is the only narrative involving Elisha alluded to in the New Testament.[19] Its familiarity may however dull us to many unexpected elements and twists of plot.

---

[17] A simple analogy is to say we breathe because we are alive, not to prove it, nevertheless breathing proves we are alive.

[18] Hobbs, p. 54. See also Matt. 8:5–13; 9:18–34; Mark 6:5–6; 8:22–30.

[19] Luke 4:27, quoted here as the section heading.

The central character is the first surprise. In the preceding long narrative from Joshua to this point, positive incidents initiated by non-Israelites or from outside the land of Israel have been rare.[20] With previous conflict between Israel and Aram, the opening statement that *Naaman was commander of the army of the king of Aram* arouses expectation of some trouble. The favourable description of an enemy, *a great man in the sight of his master and highly regarded*, would not be welcomed by the first Israelite hearers. Another surprise comes with *through him the* LORD *had given victory to Aram* (v. 1). Nations commonly ascribe victories to their gods, but the writer has seen that, if there is only one God, that God has been in charge not only in Israel but amongst all nations, including in their defeats of Israel.[21] We are unprepared for the final statement: *he had leprosy*. Leprosy through the ages has had associations with abhorrence and isolation. The Hebrew word however is used for a wide range of skin diseases and mildews on walls and clothing (Lev. 13 – 14) and is generally regarded as precluding the disfiguring Hansen's disease.[22] Under biblical law such a skin complaint would render a person ritually unclean and social ostracism was common. It could also be divine judgment.[23] On three counts Naaman is an 'outsider': a foreigner, an enemy general and a 'leper'.

The attention-grabbing opening verse is matched by the rest of the chapter, the whole story being told with art. It is full of drama and irony, with touches of humour and with role reversals and unexpected twists throughout.

- A young captive servant girl keeps her faith in a foreign land and provides the way forward for an experienced, dynamic general (vv. 2–3).
- A foreigner knows of a prophet in Israel who may help, and receives support from his king, including a considerable sum of money[24] (vv. 4–6).
- Foreigners believe, but the *king of Israel* does not know about Elisha and is more worried about himself (vv. 4–7).

[20] E.g., Rahab in Jericho (Josh. 2) and the widow at Zarephath (1 Kgs 17).

[21] Yahweh's sovereignty over all nations and his participation in their history is common in prophetic books, e.g., just as God brought Israel out of Egypt so he acted for the Philistines and Arameans (Amos 9:7), Assyria was God's agent (Isa. 7:17–20; 10:5–16) and the Persian Cyrus was 'my anointed' (Isa. 45:1).

[22] R. K. Harrison, 'ṣrʿ', *NIDOTTE* 3, pp. 846–847; D. P. Wright and R. N. Jones, 'Leprosy', *ABD* 4, pp. 277–284.

[23] Num. 12:10–15; 2 Kgs 5:27; 15:5.

[24] 'Equivalent to some 660 to 1,320 pounds of silver . . . some 110 to 220 pounds of gold' (Sweeney, p. 299).

- Somehow Elisha hears and says *Have the man come to me*,[25] but when the mighty general comes to Elisha's *door* in glory befitting his rank, Elisha simply sends *a messenger* with instructions (vv. 8–10).
- The instruction to complete a lowly task is met with anger and disdain (vv. 11–12).
- His *servants* (not Israelites) show the way forward as their astute diplomacy causes Naaman to calm down, reflect and act, and so be healed (vv. 13–14; as in ch. 4, trusting action brings about a miracle of compassion).
- Pagan Naaman comes to recognise what many in Israel did not, that there is only one God (vv. 15–18).
- Elisha accepts Naaman's request regarding participation with his master in worship of Rimmon[26] (v. 18).
- When we expect the story to end with its message of *go in peace*, another reversal describes grasping Gehazi, who is unhappy with his unselfish master and cloaks his greed in a bogus concern for others (vv. 19–23).
- Gehazi does not enjoy the spoils of his scheme: now he becomes *leprous*, as judgment (vv. 24–27); leprosy frames the story (vv. 1, 27).

Each twist opens windows into human behaviour, in person-to-person and person-to-God relationships. They illustrate strengths and foibles, and question attitudes to status and its rewards.

a. Seeing beyond his agents to God

Naaman is told of a prophet who can cure him (v. 3) and due to their own background he and *the king of Aram* expect a prophet to be associated with the royal court. One has to go through the right channels (vv. 4–6). He has no doubt the prophet can cure him by saying so (v. 11), but he comes to see beyond the prophet to Yahweh (v. 15). Why this change?

> The way the cure has been wrought, however, has made it clear to him that Elisha's god is not simply a convenient metaphor for unnatural prophetic powers but a living person. Healing has not come via a semi-magical wave of the prophetic hand (v. 11). It had been delivered by the living LORD, at a distance from the prophet

---

[25] The Hebrew leaves the initiative with Naaman, but does not mention his name or status.

[26] An alternative name of the storm god, Hadad.

... It was necessary to take him to the Jordan if he was to experience that directness [of God's action].[27]

The woman of Shunem relied upon Elisha and his presence (4:30); Naaman has gone further. The comparison is a reminder of how easy it is to associate God's power with a person, and for one's faith to depend on that person (or group) rather than on the living God.

b. God's gifts and human profit

The principle that a labourer is worthy of his hire is biblical,[28] and prophets relied upon the gifts of people.[29] In this case Elisha's refusal reinforces that it was God who healed, not Elisha. Like Paul much later,[30] his attitude is that claiming personal rights and material advantage is not as important as seeing people grow in faith in the life-giving God. Gehazi thinks otherwise. With the famines and travelling they experienced, one can assume the life of a prophet and his servant was fairly spartan, especially when Elisha was generous in sharing (cf. 4:42–44). Here is a chance to live more comfortably. Gehazi may well have justified his actions (as have many since), but the use of a lie and asking for only some of the gift 'is a classic model of graft'.[31] Elisha pinpoints not only Gehazi's deceit, but his self-seeking at a time of hardship for others (v. 26). 'Comprehensive catalogs of wealth and prosperity [as in v. 26] are a common feature . . . They are seen as a gift from God (Deut 8:8; Josh 24:13), a temptation to apostasy (Deut 6:11; Neh 9:25) or a sign of self-seeking greed (1 Sam 8:14–17).'[32]

The temptation is common to seek individual gain from God's actions, a reward for qualities and abilities that are actually God's gifts. From the early days of the church there have been those who 'peddle the word of God for profit' (2 Cor. 2:17). Paul deliberately uses the word *charismata* ('gifts') to highlight God's giving rather than human achievement: such gifts are not for personal benefit but 'for the common good', to be exercised in 'love'.[33] God's desire is to bring new life to those such as Naaman, and blessing to the whole community.

[27] Provan, p. 193.
[28] Matt. 10:10; Luke 10:7; 1 Tim. 5:17–18.
[29] 1 Sam. 9:8; 2 Kgs 4:42; Amos 7:12.
[30] 1 Thess. 2:9; 1 Cor. 9 argues for the right for support, which nevertheless Paul does not claim.
[31] Sweeney, p. 301.
[32] Hobbs, p. 68.
[33] 1 Cor. 12 – 13.

An interest in acquisition of material or social gain is often associated with a focus on self, affecting attitudes to God's purposes and other people:

Whereas the 'young maiden' (*na'arāh qĕtannā*) wanted to help Naaman, Gehazi, the 'young man' (*na'ar* [v. 20, NIV 'servant']) aims to exploit him. And while Naaman was concerned to support his lord with his 'hand' (*'al-yādî*, v. 18), it is from that very hand that Gehazi wants to steal: '. . . taking from his hand (*miyyādô*)' . . . With the derogatory epithet, 'this Aramean' [v. 20], Gehazi impugns the man who has declared his faith in YHWH and who is about to act on it.

The soliloquy, finally, serves to set Gehazi against Elisha. Whereas Gehazi swears an oath on YHWH's name to take (*wĕlāqahtî*) something from Naaman, Elisha has sworn by the same oath not to take (*'im-éqqah*, v. 16) from Naaman . . . The immoral and secret intentions of Gehazi thus stand in opposition to the righteous and open refusal of Elisha.[34]

The story that started with the positive results of a lowly, captive girl's witness ends not with the account of her master's healing but with the judgment on a person who was not open to God's free compassion to an outsider, even an enemy (*this Aramean*, v. 20). In a similar way, Jesus' 'eating with tax-collectors and sinners' was a contributing human factor towards his crucifixion. The story of Acts points to struggles and tensions as Gentiles became Christians, while Revelation is a message of warning and hope to Christians in danger of succumbing to cultural pressures, with much on wealth. How much human rivalry and conflict is associated with derogatory labelling ('this Aramean') that places the other in a different and lower category of human and excuses showing love to another who is also made in the image of God?[35]

c. An outsider restored and clean

Jesus came preaching 'good news to the poor . . . the year of the Lord's favour'. People 'were amazed at the gracious words' but when he cites Naaman's healing, noting the absence of healing of lepers in Israel, the hearers were 'furious' and wanted to 'throw him off the cliff' (Luke 4:17–30). God's grace is not always popular! 'For Elisha to assist an Aramean general is like a colonial pastor assisting a British

---

[34] Cohn, p. 40.
[35] Cf. Prov. 14:31; 17:5; Job 31:13–15.

general during the American War of Independence and also analogous to Jesus' ministry to Roman centurions.'[36] God can be generous to people 'like us' (in categories of race, social grouping or theology), but the thought that others might be more blessed is unwelcome! Such reactions show how easily God's grace is distorted into something we deserve because of our faith, or faithfulness, or good character, or similar. The fact remains, God did show favour to an outsider, and the hearers' theology has to adapt (as did Peter's when the Holy Spirit came upon the Gentile Cornelius [Acts 10]).

The healing of Naaman, reinforced by Jesus' words and example, continues to expose and challenge situations of

> competition and conflicts among people of different cultural identities [that] have been with us since the dawn of history. . . [W]hat is new today is . . . their global manifestation . . . [and] 'ethno-nationalism', according to Walker Connor . . . The strong ethnic character involved in the breakup of the former Soviet Union and former Yugoslavia, the ethno-racial tensions in the US and most of Europe, the ongoing interethnic clashes in various parts of Africa, and the ethnoreligious tensions in many parts of Asia, and between Middle Eastern Muslims and Western white Christians in most European and North American countries, and the ongoing ethnic conflicts in many parts of Asia all lend support to Connor's point.[37]

Lalsangkima Pachuau, a leading missiologist, originally from Mizoram, India, now in the US, proceeds to argue for 'a theology of identity formation based on the faith in God's reconciling work in Christ'. Further, 'how the other is perceived by the self . . . produces "what kind of self" one becomes', associated with 'the capacity to see and recognize the "*imago dei*" in others'. He then turns to the 'other-centred mission of God' that has been so often lacking in the life of Israel and of the church.[38] The actions of a servant girl and Elisha and the consequent healing of Naaman stand out as a beacon in the midst of the darkness of the life of Israel in the Omride period. To the leader of the enemy army Elisha says a word of 'peace' (v. 19), not simply cessation of conflict but restoration to full enjoyment of community life in relationship with God.

[36] Leithart, p. 196.

[37] L. Pachuau, 'Ethnic Identity and the Gospel of Reconciliation', *Mission Studies* 26 (2009), p. 52, citing W. Connor, *Ethnonationalism: The Quest for Understanding* (Princeton: Princeton University Press, 1994).

[38] Ibid., pp. 54, 55, 61. See also E. Glanville, 'Missiological reflections on difference: foundations in the Gospel of Luke', *Mission Studies* 26 (2009), pp. 64–79.

The king of Israel sees only an occasion for a 'quarrel' (v. 7), but Elisha sees opportunity to bring restoration. A true peacemaker who seeks not his own benefit but the well-being of the enemy, he exemplifies 'love your enemies' (Matt. 5:44).

The story of Naaman evokes other echoes from the NT, for example:

- Naaman is only healed as he humbles himself and no longer seeks special treatment because of status;[39]
- he must do things God's way, and not the way he prefers God to act;[40]
- he is both physically and socially restored, healed (given new life) and made clean, with faith in the one living God;[41]
- the washing clean in the river can be associated with baptism, also a sign of change of status, and open to Jew and Gentile.[42]

Jews in exile in Babylon or in the time of Christ under Roman rule and Christians 'enslaved' by a majority community or oppressive government are here given the example of a *young girl* whose compassion to her captor led to his being healed and acknowledging God. Alongside is the warning against the contrasting attitude of Gehazi. With a number of examples of God's compassion through Elisha to people on the fringe, at the end the person who was closest to Elisha in all of these incidents was the person who missed the message.

6. Recovering a lost borrowed axe-head (6:1–7)

The concluding act in the series involving individuals is again at the Jordan, so associating with Elisha's earlier crossing (2:13–14) and Naaman's healing (5:10). The river is a place where Elisha's power has been evident. The barest of details are given concerning the meeting place being *too small*, its location unspecified. Elisha joins in the work and thereby saves one of the group from the difficulty of paying for a lost, expensive *iron axehead*.[43] There may have even been potential of debt-slavery. The situation was not trivial to this man – nor to Elisha. Recovery is described briefly, with the man himself lifting it out at Elisha's word. Coming between two longer

[39] Matt. 18:1–4; Luke 18:9–30.
[40] Matt. 7:24–27; 21:28–32; 1 Cor. 1:18–31.
[41] Rom. 6:1–4; Col. 2:11–15; Titus 3:3–7; 1 John 1:9.
[42] Gal. 3:26–29; Titus 3:5; 1 Pet. 3:21; see discussion in Leithart, pp. 192–195.
[43] Although the Iron Age commenced around 1200 BC, 'implements of iron remain expensive and valuable' (Walton, Matthews and Chavalas, p. 392).

narratives concerning Aramaeans, this cameo illustrates again God's compassion through Elisha reaching to individuals in common activities.

As we journey with Elisha we see vivid portrayals of God's concern for all people, without qualification. The situations cross boundaries of gender, social status and ethnic background, whether past relationships have been friendly or hostile and whether the immediate need is the result of carelessness or not. They are an encouragement to trust God's gracious provision and to be open to receive from him a spirit of compassion towards all, not only those 'like us'. The grace of God is practical in its outworking.

2 Kings 6:8 – 8:15
14. Elisha and Arameans

The healing of Naaman, despite his having been involved in raids against Israel, raises expectations of a changed relationship between the two nations. At least it shows God's openness to the well-being of Arameans. At the same time we still wait for fulfilment of prophecies of judgment on Joram, son of Ahab. The next incidents (chronology is indeterminate) return again to war between Aram and Israel – and in both, due to action by Yahweh and his prophet Elisha, unexpected reversal sees the Aramean army leave without being destroyed. Here are non-violent solutions in times of conflict, both despite wishes of the Israelite king – and in the second incident it is an unbelieving Israelite leader who is killed. We see Yahweh's compassion for ordinary people, beginning with outcast lepers, despite the religious practices and uncaring rule of their king. Significantly these incidents occur before Jehu's violent coup, with its massacres, and will provide some counter-images for evaluating that revolution (see later discussion).

1. Elisha thwarts Aramean plans (6:8–23)

Of the three key players in the drama – *the king of Aram . . . the king of Israel* and *the man of God* – only one name is given, *Elisha.* The story's focus is that true power belongs not with kings but with the one who is serving God. He is the one who knows where the Arameans are camped. The interaction is told entertainingly (vv. 8–12). The king of Aram thinks he has a traitor or spy in their midst, but *one of his officers* simply states that it is Elisha – further details as to how Elisha knew are irrelevant to the narrative. We are also not told why Elisha is telling the king of Israel, given past relationships (3:14; 5:7; cf. 6:31) and the judgment to come. Is his interest (and Yahweh's) more with the Arameans and perhaps the common people of Israel, avoiding bloodshed and the devastation of warfare? That certainly fits the outcome.

The interplay leads to the Aramean king sending a substantial force in a farcical attempt to capture one man! We might see a reprise of Ahaziah's earlier futile repeated sending of 'a captain and company of fifty' to intimidate Elijah who was also 'on the hill' (1:9, 11, 13).[1] *Dothan* is strategically located around 12 miles (19 km) north of Samaria, where the Dothan Valley opens into the Jezreel Valley, a region of agriculture and trade routes.[2] The key dramatic feature focuses on 'seeing': Gehazi sees what one would expect, what is observed physically, and so is fearful, but Elisha responds with a standard oracular word, *Don't be afraid* (v. 16), always in a context of facing danger or new and daunting tasks.[3] Elisha speaks first a reason and then prays for Gehazi's *eyes* to be *open*. It is only *the* LORD who can open eyes to see the greater reality, leading to peace. Elisha had said, *Those who are with us are more than those who are with them* (v. 16); now Gehazi *sees* the hill *full of horses and chariots of fire all around Elisha* (v. 17; cf. 2:11–12).

A hundred years later, when Jerusalem was being attacked by the Assyrians, king Hezekiah encouraged his officers and people with the words, 'There is a greater power with us than with him. With him is only the arm of flesh, but with us is the LORD our God to help us and to fight our battles' (2 Chr. 32:7–8), while to Christians John wrote, 'You, dear children, are from God and have overcome them, because the one who is in you is greater than the one who is in the world' (1 John 4:4). Similar affirmations of the greatness of God over against all gods are seen in worship (e.g., Exod. 18:11; Ps. 135:5). The challenge is that it can be easy to sing and affirm such words within the confines of church walls surrounded by like-minded people but harder to live out in the battles of the everyday world where other people or powers (such as 'market forces', or 'what life is like' or *Realpolitik*) seek to bully and control.

As the enemy came down toward him, again *Elisha prayed to the* LORD (v. 18) and Yahweh *struck them with blindness* (v. 18).[4]

---

[1] In v. 17, 'the hill' is singular (*hāhār*) as in AV/KJV, NRSV, NLT; NIV and NJPSV treat the noun as collective, 'hills'.

[2] W. G. Dever, 'Dothan', *ABD* 2, pp. 226–227; elsewhere mentioned in written sources only in Gen. 37:15–36 and the later Judith 3:9; 4:6; 7:3–18.

[3] The phrase, *'al-tîrā'* occurs forty times in OT, the first being spoken to Abraham, Gen 15:1. The two other instances in Kings are to Elijah (2 Kgs 1:15) and Hezekiah (2 Kgs 19:6). The first NT instance of the equivalent Greek is spoken to Joseph (Matt. 1:20).

[4] This is not the usual word for 'blindness' and appears elsewhere only in Gen.19:11, but cf. Akkadian 'make radiant' (Provan, ZIBBC, p. 137), so 'dazzling' (*HALOT*; cf. Hobbs, p. 78).

The two prayers [vv. 17–18] and Yahweh's two powerful responses to the prayers are perfectly symmetrical. The servant, who was blind to the allies now sees; the Syrians who discerned according to their power can now see nothing. The prophet has, by prayer, completely inverted the military realities of the situation.[5]

Last century Stalin said dismissively, 'How many divisions does the Pope have?'[6] – decades later the Soviet empire collapsed without battles. In 2001, while in what was formerly East Berlin, I was struck by the testimony of the two verses in gold across the front of the Berlin Cathedral: 'See, I am with you always to the end of the world' and 'Our faith is the victory that has conquered the world.'[7] It is through faith that we are enabled to see (Heb. 11:1), and in this light we pray with confidence. In response to comments that 'answers to prayer' are just coincidences, a friend of mine comments, 'All I know is that when I pray coincidences are more frequent!'

Elisha leads the Arameans into Samaria where, again in answer to prayer, *the* LORD *opened their eyes* (v. 20). Now *the king of Israel* sees an opportunity, his eagerness shown by repetition – did he remember his father's failure to kill Benhadad (1 Kgs 20:42), and why else would Elisha have led the men to him? Elisha's reply surprises him (and us): he would not treat prisoners of war that way,[8] and besides they had not been *captured with* his *own sword or bow* (v. 22). Amazingly Elisha orders *a great feast* before sending them home. The result is cessation of hostilities.

In a context of ongoing hostility, and in contradistinction to current practice, Elisha exemplifies Proverbs 25: 21–22: 'If your enemy is hungry, give him food to eat; if he is thirsty, give him water to drink. In doing this, you will heap burning coals on his head, and the LORD will reward you.' These words are cited by Paul to support his exhortation to 'not repay anyone evil for evil. . . . as far as it depends on you, live at peace with everyone . . . overcome evil with good' (Rom. 12:17–21). The stories of Naaman and the freeing of the Aramean forces belong together as examples of not conforming 'to the pattern of this world, but [being] transformed by the renewing of your mind', informed by 'God's mercy' (Rom. 12:1–2).

---

[5] Brueggemann, p. 347.

[6] At the Yalta Conference (1945) when Winston Churchill asked him to respect religious freedom in Eastern Europe and asked what the Pope would say about his dictates; M. Król, 'The Pope's New Divisions', <http://www.project-syndicate.org/commentary/kro10/English> (posted 10 Dec 1998).

[7] *Siehe, ich bin bei euch alle Tage bis an der Welt Ende* (Matt. 28:20) and *Unser Glaube ist der Sieg, der die Welt ueberwunden hat* (1 John 5:4).

[8] Hobbs, p. 78, details general practices.

2. Besieged Samaria (6:24 – 7:20)

The next incident is vastly different. This time *Ben-Hadad, king of Aram,*[9] has *mobilized his entire army* (contrast v. 14) and *laid siege to Samaria* (v. 24; cf., 1 Kgs 20:1). Changes of scene are introduced in Hebrew by 'and' followed by a noun: 6:32,[10] 'and Elisha'; 7:3, 'and four men'; 7:17, 'and the king'.[11] They outline the story in a chiastic fashion:

6:24–31		Extreme famine and the king of Israel's failure
	6:32 – 7:2	Elisha's response: deliverance and judgment
	7:3–16	Four lepers lead in seeing God's deliverance and provision
7:17–20		The king sees the unbelieving officer's judgment

The story demonstrates the king's failure: he persists in defence and is powerless to provide for the people of the city; he blames Yahweh while failing to show any sign of trust in him; and unlike four desperate lepers he fails to see Yahweh's deliverance. Here is a continuation of the contrast between the faith of the foreigner Naaman and the self-centred king (ch. 5). In the event, the siege is lifted without any loss of Aramean lives and the common people of the city share the spoils. God's judgment on the whole dynasty is nearing, while his compassion for the poor who suffer is made evident, as is the reliability of the word he speaks through his prophet.

a. Extreme famine in the city (6:24–31)

The king has persisted so long in resisting the siege that there was *a great famine,*[12] dire circumstances shown vividly by the exorbitant price[13] of *a donkey's head*, the least desirable flesh, and *dove's dung*[14] (v. 25, NIV mg, NRSV). Action begins *as the king of Israel was passing by on the wall* (v. 26), surveying the defences and observing the

---

[9] While the name Ben-Hadad is shared by a number of Aramean kings, it leads readers to associate the earlier siege and Ahab's failure to kill that Ben-Hadad (1 Kgs 20). See Hobbs, pp. 78–79; Walton, Matthews and Chavalas, p. 393.

[10] Usual narrative syntax is 'and' followed by verb then subject.

[11] Sweeney, p. 310.

[12] The only OT instance of a 'famine' described as 'great'.

[13] 'The standard wage was only about one shekel per month' (Walton, Matthews and Chavalas, p. 393).

[14] This LXX interpretation is followed by many English versions. Gray, p. 518, notes a plant known in Arabic as 'dove's dung'; also Cogan and Tadmor, p. 79, Konkel, p. 450. NJPSV notes: 'Apparently a popular term for "carob pods," as in Akkadian'; cf. NIV *seed pods*.

besieging army – that is where he is focused. He is interrupted by a woman crying, *Help me*, a form of the common word for 'save, deliver' that elsewhere is a cry to Yahweh.[15] Taking up Psalm 118:25 and its 'hosanna' is the joyous acclamation of Palm Sunday (Matt. 21:9 and parallels). The king's role is to care for his people but he is failing. His first reaction – even before hearing her need – is effectively to blame *the LORD* for the situation. Desperation is seen in her concern for her own survival, with eating of her child, the actuality of the horrendous situation described as the result of covenant-breaking (Deut. 28:53–5).[16] The contrast with the situation of the two prostitutes who came to Solomon and between Solomon's wise solution and Joram's failure to accept responsibility are a measure of the 'topsy-turvy'[17] decline in the kingdom, the result of turning away from Yahweh and his ways (cf. 1 Kgs 3:16–28).

The king has been wearing *sackcloth*: this could be sincere mourning, seeing the siege as judgment and so an act of humbling before Yahweh as had done his father Ahab (1 Kgs 21:27), or might be no more than an expression of grief and public mourning (cf. 5:7).[18] Absent is any indication of seeking Yahweh, leading the people in prayer for deliverance (contrast Hezekiah in 19:1–2) or going to Elisha for a word from Yahweh, and, again like his father, he blames Elisha (cf. 1 Kgs 18:17). Did he see Elisha as 'a traitor who failed to employ his powers to intercede with YHWH'?[19] Evident is the desperation and anger of someone who has relied on his own position and abilities and not on following Yahweh but who now finds the situation outside his control and so seeks to deflect blame. Tragically he is an example of those who are quick to say God is responsible (vv. 27, 33) but have no sense of their own accountability.

b. Elisha's response (6:32 – 7:2)

The scene switches to Elisha's *house*, probably in the city, where *the elders were sitting with him*, perhaps seeking an oracle (cf. Ezek. 8:1). Just as he was aware of Aramean movements (vv. 10, 12) so he knows the king's plans. He significantly refers to him not as 'the

[15] Ps. 12:1; 20:9; 28:9; 60:5; 108:6.

[16] Cf. Lam. 2:20; 4:10; Ezek. 5:10; and descriptions of the Assyrian Ashurbanipal's attack on Babylon (*ANET*, p. 298).

[17] S. Lasine, 'Jehoram and the Cannibal Mothers (2 Kings 6:24–33): Solomon's Judgment in an Inverted World', *Journal for Study of the Old Testament* 50 (1991), pp. 27–53.

[18] Wiseman, p. 211, and Provan, p. 200, see the former, while Seow, p. 204, 208, aptly notes his inactivity.

[19] Sweeney, p. 311.

king' but as 'this son of a murderer', a combination which enables reference both to his character in the present action (NIV, NRSV, *this murderer*)[20] and to his being like his mother Jezebel who killed prophets (1 Kgs 18:4) and his father Ahab who 'murdered' Naboth (1 Kgs 21:19). The king's view is clear: Yahweh has brought about the siege and he can have no hope that Yahweh will deliver (v. 33).

Surprisingly Elisha is given a positive oracle: a dramatic reversal of supplies will see the very next day prices back to normal *at the gate of Samaria*, the usual market area (7:1). Readers may well ask, 'Why wait until the desperate situation of cannibalism of children?' The narration suggests that the oracle of deliverance had to wait until the king came to Elisha. It was to be unmistakable to all that Joram was to blame for the dire circumstances, not Yahweh, and that 'YHWH, working through Elisha, is the true power capable of defeating the Arameans even when they play a key, albeit secondary, role in overthrowing the house of Omri'.[21] The king's adjutant[22] sees the reversal as impossible: even with rain (although that is not the issue here) it would still take time for growth to take place. His scepticism reflects the official view (see also 7:12–13), which will result in his seeing but not eating.

The scene is set: as often in life a word of God has been spoken which seems impossible and unrealistic. Faith and practicality come into contradiction. Elisha's final word defines the alternative results: it will happen (*you will see it*) but blatant disbelief leads to failure to enjoy blessing (*you will not eat any of it*).

c. Four lepers and unexpected reversal (7:3–16)

Elisha has announced a miracle that will happen *tomorrow . . . at the gate of Samaria* (v. 1), but as the scene moves 'today' to the *entrance of the city gate* attention is amazingly turned to *four men with leprosy*,[23] forced to live outside the city until declared clean of their skin complaint (Lev. 13:45–46; their later communication with others is by shouting, v. 10). They may be at the other end of the social spectrum from the king and his officer, but they will be the first see *the good news* (v. 9).

[20] Hebrew 'son of . . .' may refer to 'one characterized by, possessing the characteristics of'; 'one of a group of', e.g., 'son of worthlessness' (1 Sam. 25:17), 'son of valour' (Deut. 3:18), 'sons of prophets' (2 Kgs 2:3) (*DCH*).

[21] Sweeney, p. 307.

[22] For background of *the officer on whose arm the king was leaning* (7:2), see Hobbs, pp. 89–90, Walton, Matthews and Chavalas, p. 394. Cf. Naaman, 5:18.

[23] See on 5:1, p. 234.

The lepers reason that their situation is so bad they have nothing to lose by going to the Aramean camp; at least then they might *live* (vv. 3–4). Going *at dusk* to conceal their movements they find the Aramean camp empty! Again *the Lord* has been present with his *chariots and horses* (cf. 2:12; 6:17), this time as a *sound of . . . a great army* heard at dusk by the Arameans. The rumour spread quickly through the camp that mercenaries had come to help the king of Israel,[24] leading to great disarray, the army fleeing in such haste that everything was left behind.[25] The story 'now borders on the comic. The Syrians flee out the back door as the four harmless lepers arrive at the front!'[26] The lepers enjoy their unexpected bounty: they not only *ate and drank* but also twice hid for themselves *silver, gold and clothes* (v. 8).

They come to a realization that has been applied often to proclaiming the gospel of Jesus Christ: *What we're doing is not right. This is a day of good news and we are keeping it to ourselves* (v. 9). The Hebrew *bśr* is widely used for bringing 'news, a message', generally good and joyful and often of victory, and so occurring in contexts of Yahweh's deeds of deliverance.[27] Since it flows from Yahweh's covenantal relationship, his mercy and faithfulness, deliverance is at core spiritual but contexts relate to the diversity of human situations from which deliverance is necessary.

The fact is that sin and evil constitute bad news in every area of life on this planet. The redemptive work of God through the cross of Christ is good news for every area of life on earth that has been touched by sin, which means every area of life. Bluntly, we need a holistic gospel because the world is in a holistic mess.[28]

That here lepers are first to experience the 'good news' may be compared to the oft-quoted statement of the Sri Lankan Christian leader, D. T. Niles, 'Evangelism is one beggar telling another beggar where he found bread.' The 'bread' is to be shared. Brueggemann appositely notes that 'the ruse of Yahweh's sounds would be incomplete without the reporting lepers. But the lepers by themselves

---

[24] The hiring of such forces fits current practices (Hobbs, pp. 90–91). Cf. Yahweh's 'hired razor' of Assyria (Isa. 7:20). Provan (pp. 200–201) sees a possible wordplay between *měṣōrā'îm* 'lepers' and *miṣrayim* 'Egypt'.

[25] Compare other interventions by Yahweh against the Arameans (1 Kgs 20:13–21, 28–30) and Moab (2 Kgs 3:20–25).

[26] Hobbs, p. 91.

[27] As here, 2 Sam. 18:19–20, 25–26; Ps. 68:11; Isa. 52:7; Nahum 1:15 [MT 2:1]. LXX often has a form related to *euangelizō*, whence the English 'evangel'. See O. Schilling, '*bśr*', *TDOT* 2, pp. 313–316.

[28] C. J. H. Wright, *The Mission of God* (Nottingham: Inter-Varsity Press, 2006), p. 315.

would have had nothing to report.'[29] They may have been partly motivated by self-interest (*if we wait until daylight, punishment will overtake us*), but also they know that they belong to a group larger than themselves who need to share in the bounty. In a similar way Christ commissions his followers to share the Good News so that others may 'share in the inheritance of his holy people in the kingdom of light' (Col. 1:12).

The lepers shout out to *the city gatekeepers* the news of the Aramean camp, empty of people but full of goods, and that news is shouted to others in the middle of the night, finally reaching *the palace* (vv. 10–11). Five times the verb 'tell' is used as various groups hear.[30] In the event it appears that everyone believes except the king and his adjutant. The unbelieving king has another interpretation: what had been Yahweh's ruse to scare away the Arameans becomes the Arameans' ruse to capture the city (v. 12)! As elsewhere it is *one of his officers* who comes up with a solution (cf. 3:11; 5:15; 6:12); he at least, like the lepers, views the desperate situation (illustrated by the sending of just *two chariots*) and is open to the possibility of good news. The scouts soon discover how desperate the Aramean flight has been. After they returned and *reported this to the royal palace*, it is *the people* who *went out and plundered the camp*. Yahweh's good news announced by Elisha concerning the availability of food has been fulfilled (vv. 15–16).

d. The king sees the unbelieving officer's judgment (7:17–20)

Attention returns to *the king* who throughout has been ineffective and faithless, demonstrating the failure of the Omride dynasty. We quickly see how the king's *officer* (as in v. 2) knew about Yahweh's amazing provision but was *trampled* in the people's rush. One can only wonder if he was trying to stop the people. The narrative could have ended with verse 17 and its fulfilment comment, but to highlight the fulfilment's twofold nature details of verses 1–2 are reprised. We are reminded of Elisha's words to the king, the officer's unbelieving response and Elisha's word of doom. The conclusion reinforces *that is exactly what happened to him* (v. 20).

Media reports provide today instant pictures of disasters and violence around the globe. People are suffering, crying out like the woman to anyone who will listen, 'Help me!' Alongside is often the question, 'Where is God? Why doesn't he do something?' Like Joram there can be a rejection of God or a belief that he is distant

---

[29] Brueggemann, p. 363.
[30] Verses 9, 10, 11, 12, 15 (NIV 'report' and 'tell').

and unconcerned. The instant relief that God brought to Samaria, with good news shared by lepers, was unique in its content, but in a variety of ways God continues to bring deliverance, especially through his people. As in Samaria, where the dire situation was the result of the king's leadership, Wright pointedly comments that, while lives are lost through 'natural disasters', many thousands more lives are lost, including in locations of such disasters, through human injustice, oppression and selfishness.[31] It is precisely in such situations that, like Elisha, Christians continue to be known for their acts of mercy. The Canadian foreign correspondent, Brian Stewart, 'in over forty years . . . from the "ringside" seat of a reporter found there is no movement closer to the raw truth of war, famines, or crisis and the vast human predicament than organized Christianity in action'. Wherever he went, no matter how horrendous the situation, he found 'Christians already in the thick of it . . . countless acts of human love and charity, total respect for the most forsaken'.[32] The incarnation, crucifixion and resurrection of Christ is *par excellence* the evidence of the saving presence of God when all seems lost, and the presence of Christ by his Spirit in the lives of his followers continues to be active in the world. God's word of love and mercy is still more than words – they come to pass.

3. Land restored (8:1–6)

News broadcasts often include an individual 'human interest story' in the midst of bulletins that otherwise report international events, national politics and major disasters. So here (as in 4:1 – 6:7) comes a cameo of care and justice for an individual woman, surrounded by events at the national level involving both international and internal conflict, with dramatic intervention by Elisha.

The chronological relationship to other events and various details are uncertain. It is unclear when *the famine that will last seven years* happened: a famine is mentioned earlier (4:38, immediately after the account of Elisha and the woman of Shunem), possibly a factor in Elisha's feeding of a hundred (4:42–44) and in the siege of Samaria. The anonymous *king* is probably Joram, who is here unusually favourable to Elisha but seeks more information *about all the great things Elisha has done* (v. 4) – perhaps this followed the relief of the siege in the preceding chapter. He is in conversation with Gehazi,

---

[31] C. J. H. Wright, *The God I Don't Understand* (Grand Rapids: Zondervan, 2008), pp. 30–32.
[32] Konkel, pp. 464, 466, following a summary (pp. 462–464) of Stewart's experiences as recounted in a convocation address at Knox College, University of Toronto, 12 May 2004.

the servant of the man of God (it is unstated whether this was before 5:27 or Gehazi has been restored to the role). Joram also acts justly, his only commendable action apart from partial religious reform (3:2)!

Just as during famine God had provided outside the boundaries of Israel for Elijah (1 Kgs 17), so he provides for the woman from Shunem and her family. Elisha's kind action however has had unforeseen negative effects. Now the woman seeks redress from the king, from whom on the basis of past accounts we would not expect a positive outcome. The sentence structure highlights that the woman came *just as Gehazi was telling the king* about Elisha and her son. The reason for the loss of land tenure is unstated,[33] although the king's subsequent action (v. 8) suggests it may have been appropriated by the crown. The story ends with full restoration. She asked for *her house and land* (v. 5) and receives also past income in full (v. 6).

After several interventions which are readily labelled 'miraculous', here is an 'ordinary' occurrence whose 'extra-ordinary' nature is seen in the timing and result. Similar situations are part of life experiences today and may be either described as 'mere coincidence' and 'luck' or else seen through the eyes of faith as evidence of God's gracious hand. Here is no 'god-of-the gaps' who is invoked only when other explanations fail. Further, it is a situation in which Elisha's good and kind action leads to unforeseen difficulties, in which his sole contribution to rectification is reports of his reputation. It is the king, whom Elisha has opposed in the past, who acts justly and compassionately. Many know the experience of good deeds that have unforeseen negative outcomes, with solutions coming from unexpected sources:

> God moves in a mysterious way,
> His wonders to perform . . .
> His purposes will ripen fast,
> Unfolding every hour;
> The bud may have a bitter taste,
> But sweet will be the flower.[34]

4. Elisha and Hazael (8:7–15)

There remains a much larger matter regarding God's 'mysterious ways'. Due to religious apostasy and consequent injustice Elijah had announced the death of Jezebel and the complete annihilation of all

---

[33] For possibilities see Konkel, p. 453.
[34] William Cowper (1731–1800).

the males of Ahab's family, although delayed until after Ahab's death following the fact that he 'humbled himself' (1 Kgs 21:21–22, 28–29). Twelve years have passed since Ahab's death and his family has not been obliterated, Jezebel is still alive, and the family's influence is expanding into Judah. With a key theme of Kings being fulfilment of Yahweh's word spoken by his prophets, readers may wonder what is happening. Even with prophetic words it is not easy to read God's activity in history. The hall of fame in Hebrews 11 describes countless people for whom 'faith' meant living in an uncertain present in the light of God's promised future.

Fulfilment is near but it will not be without pain. Elisha knows both that God's judgment on the house of Omri is sure, and that this will bring much distress throughout the nation. Years previously Elijah had been commissioned to 'go to the Desert of Damascus . . . there, anoint Hazael king over Aram' (1 Kgs 19:15). It is now that *Elisha went to Damascus*, the Aramean centre a hundred miles (160 km) north of Samaria (v. 7). His reputation is known, not least through the healing of Naaman (ch. 5) as well as the battles, and so the ill *Ben-Hadad king of Aram* sends *Hazael* to Elisha, the large gift and *your son*[35] showing regard and respect. Hazael loyally asks for an oracle (vv. 7–9). A king of Israel in whose name was Yah(weh) had asked the same 'will [I] recover?' of a Philistine god (1:2); in contrast a foreign king of Aram in whose name is Hadad (storm god) now seeks to *consult* Yahweh. Jesus too highlighted unexpected 'outsiders' who showed faith: a centurion (Matt. 8:10) and a Canaanite woman (Matt. 15:22–28).[36]

Elisha's reply, *Go and say to him, 'You will certainly recover.' Nevertheless, the* LORD *has revealed to me that he will in fact die* (v. 10), may seem to involve Elisha in a deliberate lie.[37] While the first part may give Ben-Hadad hope, hiding his imminent fate at Hazael's hands (v. 14), the contrast expresses the truth, 'The king may recover from illness but he will die anyway.'[38] The means or time of death are not specified, being up to Hazael. The message is terse and the two look at each other[39] until Elisha *began to weep*. He realizes that

---

[35] Cf. 'my father' in the address to Elisha by Joram (6:21) and later Jehoash (13:14).

[36] In Matthew these two had 'great faith' while the disciples show 'little faith' (6:30; 8:26; 14:31; 16:8; 17:20).

[37] MT is written 'say you will *not* [lō'] live' but read as 'say to him [lô] you will live', the latter being also LXX understanding. See NIV note; also Gray, pp. 530–531, Provan, pp. 207–208 and Seow, p. 212.

[38] Brueggemann, p. 372.

[39] The subjects of verbs in the first half of the sentence are undefined, the first specification being in the phrase, *the man of God began to weep*. 'Hazael' is inserted by NIV before *was embarrassed*, so making Elisha the subject of *stared*, while NJPSV sees Elisha as subject throughout (as he is the preceding defined subject, v. 10).

Hazael will kill Ben-Hadad, so becoming king, but that he will then attack Israel, resulting in all the atrocities and rampant violence against the population that accompany warfare. This is the *weeping* answer given to Hazael (vv. 12–13). Hazael returns to Ben-Hadad, communicates part of Elisha's words and the next day treacherously kills his king. The short time frame suggests that Hazael had been planning revolt for some time but was encouraged to act by Elisha's words. The result was, *Then Hazael succeeded him as king* (v. 15).[40]

Embedded in the story is Yahweh's powerful presence and activity outside of Israel, and his recognition by non-Israelites. He works through human actions, whether Elijah's failure to go to Damascus or Elisha's later going at a time when Ben-Hadad was ill. The appointment of Hazael as king is not endorsement of his rebellious actions[41] but rather affirms that God is behind the later Aramean incursions led by Hazael[42] as part of his judgment on Israel. Elisha's *weeping* foreshadows Christ's weeping over Jerusalem: judgment was to come on the city, with devastation and death, but there was 'weeping' at what could have been avoided through 'recogniz[ing] the time of God's coming to you' (Luke 19:41–44). Later Paul was to write 'with tears' as he thought of those who 'live as enemies of the cross of Christ' (Phil. 3:18). Judgment is real, but the message is not a denial of compassion. It is one's fellow human beings who are to suffer.

---

[40] On a basalt statue the Assyrian king Shalmaneser III tells how 'Hazael, a commoner (lit.: son of nobody), seized the throne', *ANET*, p. 280; *COS* 2.113G, p. 270.

[41] See discussion on Baasha (1 Kgs 16:1–7, pp. 158–159).

[42] 9:14–15; 12:17–18; 13:3–7.

2 Kings 8:16 – 13:25
15. Revolution and reform in Israel and Judah

Hazael's usurping the Aramean throne and Elisha's words prepare the reader for turmoil. Not only Israel but also Judah will be embroiled in bloodshed and violence for Judah too has been infected with the same idolatrous practices. The central activity in following chapters will be Jehu's coup (chs 9 – 10), but the narrator first returns to Judah's kings and events preceding the coup in the north.

1. Kings of Judah entwined with Israel (8:16–29)

a. Jehoram[1] king of Judah (8:16–24)

Jehoram has been co-regent with his father *Jehoshaphat,* but here begins his sole reign.[2] Although Jehoram's grandfather and father received positive assessments,[3] the alliance between Judah and Israel[4] was sealed by Jehoram's marriage to *a daughter of Ahab* (v. 18; 2 Chr. 18:1). No details are given as to how Jehoram *followed the ways of the kings of Israel, as the house of Ahab had done* (v. 18), although later reforms will include tearing down 'the temple of Baal' and smashing 'the altars and idols to pieces' (11:18). Like Ahab in his capital of Samaria (1 Kgs 16:32) Jehoram built a temple of Baal in Jerusalem. *Nevertheless,* as with the previous major turning from Yahweh in the reign of Abijah, there is a counter

---

[1] See on 3:1 (p. 223, n. 1) regarding the variant forms, Jehoram and Joram. Here Jehoram will be used consistently for the Judahite king.
[2] Mentioned briefly in 1 Kgs 22:50; 2 Kgs 1:17; see note on 2 Kgs 3:1 regarding co-regency, p. 223, n. 1.
[3] 1 Kgs 15:11–15; 22:43.
[4] See on 1 Kgs 22:4, 44; 2 Kgs 3:7, pp. 200, 207, 224.

statement of Yahweh's commitment to Judah because of promises to David.[5]

There is one setback: the Davidic dynasty may continue unbroken but territory is lost in Edom's rebellion, which Jehoram disastrously failed to suppress (vv. 20–21).[6] Future relations continue to be tumultuous as *to this day Edom has been in rebellion* (v. 22; cf. 14:7; 16:6), culminating in Edom's rejoicing over the destruction of Jerusalem in 597 BC and consequent prophetic judgment.[7] Judah's weakening power is seen further in a revolt in the south west by *Libnah*, a traditional Levitical city towards the coast.[8]

b. Ahaziah king of Judah (8:25–29)

The account of Ahaziah's short reign commences in the standard manner, his mother being identified as *Athaliah*. She is here *daughter of king Omri of Israel* (v. 26, NJPSV),[9] reminding readers of the dynastic link. After Ahaziah's death, Athaliah will appear as key player in an attempt to overthrow the house of David, effectively ruling for six years before she too was killed (11:1–16). The syncretising marriage association is made explicit, as for his father (v. 27; cf. v. 18), a pointer to what is to follow: Ahaziah and Athaliah will join with Joram of Israel as victims in Jehu's coup, an outworking of God's judgment on the house of Omri.

The close relationship of Ahaziah and Joram – to be matched in death – is introduced as Ahaziah joins in Joram's battle against the Arameans at Ramoth Gilead, just as Jehoshaphat had joined with Ahab at the same location (1 Kgs 22:1–38). Like his father Ahab, Joram is wounded, but unlike Ahab not fatally, and he returns to Jezreel where Ahaziah also comes.[10] We have been told already that Ahaziah reigned *one year* (which probably means only a few

---

[5] See on 1 Kgs 15:4–5, pp. 154–155.

[6] David subjugated Edom (2 Sam. 8:13–14); during Solomon's reign Hadad, an Edomite leader, was unsuccessful in revolt and fled to Egypt (1 Kgs 11:14–22); during Jehoshaphat's reign Edom's status meant a 'deputy' ruled rather than 'king' (1 Kgs 22:47); and 'the king of Edom' joined with Israel and Judah in fighting against Moab (2 Kgs 3:9).

[7] E.g., Ps. 137:7; Jer. 49:7–22; Ezek. 25:12–14. See J. A. Thompson, 'Edom, Edomites', *NBD*, pp. 290–292.

[8] Josh. 21:13: near Lachish, Josh. 10:29–39; 2 Kgs 19:8.

[9] As she was previously described as 'daughter of Ahab' (v. 18), NRSV and NIV here have 'granddaughter of Omri'. Like *bēn* 'son', *bat* 'daughter' is used of a direct female descendant.

[10] Jezreel was 20 miles (32 km) north of the capital, Samaria, on a strategic summit. It was likely Israel's military centre, including a royal residence (also 1 Kgs 18:45; 21:1; 2 Kgs 9:30); D. Ussishkin, 'Jezreel – where Jezebel was thrown to the dogs', *Biblical Archaeology Review* 36, 4 (Jul/Aug 2010), pp. 32–42, 75.

months), commencing *in the twelfth year of Joram son of Ahab king of Israel* – and Joram reigned for 'twelve years'(3:1). We expect dramatic ends: the stage is set for Jehu's coup, to be initiated by Elisha's action.

Judean readers in exile are again reminded that they cannot point the finger at Israel's sins, for Judah too has been closely aligned, sharing in the same practices. Their hope for the future is not in their 'being better' but in God's faithfulness to his promises to David (v. 19). Paul was to widen the scope when he affirmed that 'Jews and Gentiles alike are all under the power of sin . . . for all have sinned and fall short of the glory of God'; we can see ourselves in the syncretising, compromising story of Judah and Israel. Paul did not end there, continuing: 'all are justified freely by his grace through the redemption that came by Christ Jesus' (Rom. 3:9, 23–24), the one who 'was a descendant of David' (Rom. 1:3).

2. Jehu's bloody purge (9:1 – 10:36)

a. Preparing to read the account

Violence, coups, revolution, slaughter, if not experienced directly are brought instantly into view through international media. Violence as entertainment is rampant in blockbuster movies and popular video games. Former generations fought the Crusades, the War of the Roses, the Hundred Years War, American, French, Russian and Chinese Revolutions and the US Civil War, while the twentieth century saw two World Wars, brutal overthrow of governments and regional wars, many continuing – yet alongside were revolutions with no or limited bloodshed.[11] Conflict is heightened in the partisan language and distortions of political rhetoric. The saga of human conflict, of naked grasp for power and overthrow of governments, of ethnic and communal tensions, is constant, often with 'religion' invoked as justification. Responding to claims that 'religion' has been the *major* cause of much intolerant violence and

---

[11] Some examples: the influence of Gandhi in independence for India and Pakistan; the end of the Marcos era in the Philippines; the breakdown of the Soviet Union and changes in Eastern Europe; and collapse of apartheid in South Africa. Maria J. Stephan (US State Department) and Erica Chenoweth (Wesleyan University) compared the outcomes of hundreds of violent insurgencies with those of major nonviolent resistance campaigns from 1900 to 2006. They found that 53 percent of the nonviolent movements succeeded, compared with 26 percent of the violent insurgencies; 'Why Civil Resistance Works', *International Security* 33, 1 (2008), pp. 7–44, http://www. mitpressjournals.org/doi/pdf/10.1162/isec.2008.33.1.7 (accessed 15 March 2011); see also 'Give Peaceful Resistance a Chance', *New York Times*, 10 March 2011, p. A31 of NY edition.

bloodshed,[12] Alister McGrath highlighted the 'distressing paradox' that 'the greatest intolerance and violence of [the twentieth] century were practised by those who believed that religions caused intolerance and violence'.[13] Causes are diverse and comments of the historian Latourette regarding the European Thirty Years War (1618–48) are relevant to many other conflicts:

> The religious conflict was only one factor. Rivalries between ambitious monarchs, generals, and adventurers, reinforced by burgeoning national loyalties, entered and may have been more important. Had the religious element not been present, they alone may have produced the war.[14]

Implicit repeatedly is the attitude, 'We are right. If only we could get rid of "them" or force "them" to become like us, life would be peaceful.' Sometimes is added, 'God is on our side'.

With violence embedded in the human story, it is not surprising to see such incidents in the biblical narrative. Names and places may change, but Jehu's revolution and its aftermath fit easily into the world as we know it. The account could be read as just another of many similar incidents in history and evaluated accordingly, except that the violence is linked with prophecies from God and we yearn for something different. How often are a 'God of love' in the NT and a 'God of vengeance and violence' in the OT simplistically but erroneously contrasted.[15] I remember Old Testament battle stories in Sunday School (Joshua and Jericho, Samson and the Philistines, David and Goliath), but rarely heard them in the adult world of church services. Were they told because they were exciting and full of action, but difficult in sermons? The words of Jesus about forgiving enemies and 'turning the other cheek' (Matt. 5:14–48) are often cited – but put aside when our nation is being attacked or our lifestyle threatened, or when we live in a violent society. What does it mean to 'be subject to the governing authorities' (Rom. 13:1) when authorities are clearly promoting wickedness and injustice? Christians have grappled with the issues for centuries, with diverse

[12] E.g., C. Hitchens, *God is Not Great: How Religion Poisons Everything* (New York: Hachette, 2007).

[13] *The Twilight of Atheism* (Oxford: Oxford University Press, 2004), p. 230.

[14] K. S. Latourette, *A History of Christianity* (London: Eyre and Spottiswoode, 1954), p. 884.

[15] J. Goldingay, 'Old Testament Theology and the Canon', *Tyndale Bulletin* 59, 1 (2008), p. 23, summarizes where one sees 'the footsteps of the crucified God' in the OT, and how when 'God does from time to time act in wrath in relation to the world and to Israel, these acts appear in the context of a story that begins and continues only because God acts in love'.

responses. Countless words have been spoken and written; but more tragically, millions of lives have ended violently, either because it has been 'Christian' to fight (from childhood I saw war memorials with the words 'for God and country'), or because 'following Christ' has meant non-violent action resulting in imprisonment or martyrdom.

2 Kings 9 –10 is difficult for readers who see mirrored the horrors of ongoing civil wars and state-authorised terrorism and oppression. The narrative vividly describes a military *coup d'état* with deliberate and thorough brutal removal of all opposition. It portrays one person's zealous actions to remove evil from society. Further, the action was initiated by a word of Yahweh (9:6–10) and at the end all is stated to be according to Yahweh's word and commended by him as 'accomplishing what is right in my eyes and you have done to the house of Ahab all I had in mind to do' (10:10, 30). 'These chapters carry us deep into the paradox created by divine and human violence as it intersects with God's will for peace.'[16]

This vivid narrative is not all the Bible has to say about violence and the removal of evil, but it is part of the whole picture. Reading may help us both to recognise some of our own attitudes and to reflect on God's character and involvement in the defeat of wickedness.

b. Elisha sparks a coup d'état (9:1–13)

The prophet Elisha says it is time to anoint Jehu (cf. 1 Kgs 19:15–16)[17] and summons *a man from the company of the prophets.*[18] As earlier for Naaman when 'a messenger' was sent (5:10), it is Yahweh's word that is effective, not Elisha's powerful presence. Instructions show the dangers: Jehu, from outside the royal family, is to be secretly anointed *king over Israel* in the very place where the current king had been injured in battle against the Arameans (vv. 1–3; cf. 8:28–29). That is all Elisha says as he disappears from the narrative until his dying days forty years later (13:14).

The actual anointing is told with drama. The messenger includes explicit instructions *to destroy the house of Ahab* (v. 7),[19] its seriousness underlined by *your master.* Central is Yahweh's involvement:

---

[16] Nelson, p. 197.

[17] The double patronymic *son of Jehoshaphat, the son of Nimshi* avoids equating his father with king Jehoshaphat of Judah.

[18] The group is associated with Elisha in 4:1; 6:1.

[19] These words may have been added by the messenger, seeing in the anointing (which was all Elisha mentioned) the occasion for implementing Yahweh's previously prophesied judgment.

Jehu is reminded that the Yahweh is *the God of Israel*[20] and that the nation over which he is to rule is *the LORD's people Israel* (v. 6). Jehu is simply God's agent to *avenge the blood of my servants the prophets and the blood of all the LORD's servants shed by Jezebel* (v. 7). Apposite are the words of Paul, 'Do not take revenge, my dear friends, but leave room for God's wrath, for it is written: "It is mine to avenge; I will repay," says the Lord' (Rom. 12:19, quoting Deut. 32:35).[21] We will return to this key element in final evaluation of his reign.

After David had been anointed king during Saul's reign he initiated no action to remove Saul, simply biding his time.[22] In contrast, Jehu acts immediately. His initial response to his fellow officers is a way of testing them as he seems to agree that the man who came is a *maniac*! They persist and so for the third time we read that *the LORD says: I anoint* Jehu *king over Israel* (v. 12; cf. vv. 3, 6). Immediately the army officers agree – it is likely that there had already been rumbling and discussions of possibilities. The anointing lit the fuse of the explosives already prepared. In a small ceremony, with a carpet of their cloaks, they shout, *Jehu is king!* With the trumpet and shouting the act of treason against Joram, instigated by Elisha, is no longer secret. 'God's quiet ways are, for the moment, at an end. Earthquake is the order of the day.'[23]

How is one to interpret dramatic social upheaval? In Chinese tradition, a rebellion against an emperor could be attempted, the result alone telling whether the 'mandate of heaven' had been transferred because 'the rulers did not treat the people well'. No other reason or argument can be used, since 'heaven' is impersonal.[24] For many today, transitions of power are simply the result of human forces and chance. In the Judaeo-Christian tradition however all authority ultimately flows from a personal God. He may give, and one can ask for, reasons for his actions. The biblical presentation

---

[20] The first instances in 2 Kings of the combination 'the LORD, the God of Israel' frame the Jehu account. Despite the opening reminder (9:6), the conclusion is, 'Jehu was not careful to keep the law of the LORD, the God of Israel, with all his heart' (10:31).

[21] D. G. Firth, *Surrendering Retribution in the Psalms: Responses to Violence in Individual Complaints* (Paternoster Biblical Monographs; Carlisle: Paternoster, 2005), demonstrates that many psalms have cries that hand to God the treatment of the petitioner's enemies. His research was undertaken in South Africa during the apartheid period as a resource for grappling with responses to that regime's violence.

[22] E.g., 1 Sam. 24; 26, and his separating himself from any involvement in Saul's end, 2 Sam. 1.

[23] Provan, p. 209.

[24] First propounded by the Duke of Chou around 1100 BC; H. G. Creel, *Chinese Thought from Confucius to Mao Tse-tung* (New York: New American Library, 1953), pp. 20–24.

here is unambiguous: the coup is not just another example of a military takeover by an ambitious and popular officer, although army commanders in council endorsed Jehu as king (vv. 5, 11–13); it is an act of divine justice.

c. No peace with wickedness (9:14–37)

Other coups in Israel have been described briefly: those by Baasha and Zimri included massacre of the king's family, according to prophetic words (1 Kgs 15:27–29; 16:9–13) while Omri's was due to division in the nation (1 Kgs 16:15–22). The end of the disastrous Omride dynasty is told in much more detail, and its extent is much wider than the immediate royal family. The narrator uses literary artistry including suspense to involve hearers and bring to the fore key issues.

Action is temporarily halted to recall the setting. There are three kings: *Hazael king of Aram* is still threatening Ramoth Gilead, while injured *King Joram* is 40 miles (60 km) away back in Jezreel, accompanied by *Ahaziah king of Judah*. None will play a central role! Hazael does not appear again until 10:32, while Joram proves to be powerless and is killed (vv. 23–24) as is Ahaziah (v 27). The narrative focuses on how Jehu *conspired*, soon turning to his decisive, dramatic actions.

The allegiance of the officers who have made Jehu king is tested with the order to ensure no one escapes to warn Joram, while Jehu himself goes in *his chariot*. His driving is like his rebellion, as we later read of his reputation for speed (v. 20)! With increasing suspense his motivation is made obvious as, on three occasions, once with repetition, Jehu is asked, *Is it peace?* (vv. 17, 18, 19, 22 NRSV).[25] On Joram's lips the simple phrase initially refers to news from the battlefield, as what is seen is 'a crowd'.[26] By the end, with messengers not returning and realization it is Jehu coming, there may be the nuance of NIV's *Have you come in peace?*[27] although his actions, accompanied by Ahaziah, show he does not suspect betrayal (see v. 23).

The narrator sets up a contrast with Jehu's repeated response to the messengers, *What do you have to do with peace? Fall in behind me* (vv. 18, 19), but its import is only clear when Joram and Ahaziah come personally, ominously *at the plot of ground that had belonged to Naboth the Jezreelite* (v. 21). Elijah's announcements of judgment

---

[25] Cf. NJPSV, 'Is all well?' In v. 11 NIV translates 'Is everything all right?' (cf. 4:26, three times, and 5:21).

[26] *šipʿâ* (NIV 'some troops') is 'crowd, heaving mass' (*HALOT*).

[27] So NIV throughout vv. 17–22; also in v. 31.

on Ahab and his house come to mind (cf. 1 Kgs 21:1, 19–22; 22:38). Jehu bluntly declares two irreconcilable situations: *How can there be peace . . . as long as all the idolatry and witchcraft of your mother Jezebel abound?* (v. 22). Joram sees only a matter of military victory but Jehu cuts to the core of the problem. NIV's 'idolatry' translates the common word for 'acts of prostitution' (NRSV, 'whoredoms; NJPSV, 'harlotries'), a common description of fertility religion in Hosea,[28] with 'witchcraft' or 'sorcery' often associated (cf. Deut. 18:9–14; Mic. 5:12).[29] Jezebel's practices (she is still alive; v. 30) have permeated the life of Israel and Judah, supported by both kings. From Jehu's perspective there can be no peace between a loyal follower of Yahweh and those who actively promote pagan practices – Ahab's family.

There follow explicit accounts of the deaths of Joram (vv. 23–26), Ahaziah (vv. 27–29) and Jezebel (vv. 30–37). Joram quickly realizes Jehu's intention, warning Ahaziah as well with the cry, *Treachery*, but to no avail as Joram is killed by Jehu's *arrow*. Jehu's words to *his chariot officer* are significant: Remember Yahweh's oracle we both heard given to Ahab (vv. 25–26). That was more than twelve years previously! Had Jehu kept this alive in his thinking? Had the seed for a coup been sown then, or, at least, did he see himself as being the person to fulfil the oracle? Had it grown in his mind, since his details expand what we have heard earlier with *I will surely make you pay for it* (cf. 1 Kgs 21:19)? In any case, he now makes sure the oracle is fulfilled literally. He shows a zeal for Yahweh (as he himself says in 10:16). Again comes the phrase, *in accordance with the word of the* LORD (v. 26).

Ahaziah[30] is *chased* and *wounded*, and although he *escaped to Megiddo*,[31] he *died there* but, as for other Davidic kings, is buried in Jerusalem. There is no mention here of 'according to the word of the LORD' so this could be one instance of Jehu's excessive zeal that is behind the criticism in Hosea 1:4 ('the massacre at Jezreel').[32] Ahaziah is a descendant of Ahab through his mother and shares the pagan worship, so to Jehu the whole household must be removed. Ahaziah reigned one year.

[28] Hos. 1:2; 2:2; 4:12; 5:4. Cf. Deut. 31:16.

[29] Another sexual metaphor is translated 'adultery', expressing unfaithfulness within the covenant relationship, also in Hosea (1:2, 2:2, 4; etc.) and elsewhere, including the NT (e.g., Jas. 4:4; Rev. 2:22; 19:2).

[30] His wife, Athaliah, a daughter of Ahab, will play a key role in ch. 11; see on 8:25, p. 254.

[31] For locations and significance of the route, see Walton, Matthews and Chavalas, p. 397.

[32] E.g., Wiseman, p. 223. House, p. 290, lists other proposals as to Jehu's motivation.

Jezebel remains defiant to the end, acting as a proud queen mother. She taunts Jehu by recalling *Zimri*'s rebellion that lasted just seven days before the commencement of her father's dynasty (1 Kgs 16:15–19). She is betrayed however by *two or three eunuchs*[33] who obey Jehu's order to *throw her down!* (vv. 30–33). Jehu contemptuously shows his authority as he entered her palace and *ate and drank* (v. 34). The circumstances of her death and savaging of the corpse are again in accord with Elijah's word, on the very ground that had belonged to Naboth (cf. 1 Kgs 21:23).

What are the criteria for 'peace'?[34] For Joram, as for many throughout history, it was negatively cessation of war, living without threats. In contrast Jehu knew that lasting peace, with a harmonious community, comes with walking in a right relationship with the one God.

The theme of peace that can flow only from God, with the corollary of the ultimate futility of seeking peace in other ways, runs throughout Scripture. Two hundred years later, in a context of worship of other gods and violent and unjust behaviour in Jerusalem, Jeremiah brought God's word against prophets who 'dress the wound of my people as though it were not serious. "Peace, peace," they say, when there is no peace' (Jer. 8:11; cf. Jer. 7:9–11). Jeremiah brought a word of 'no peace', the coming destruction and exile – but beyond was forgiveness and restoration in a new relationship (e.g., Jer. 33:6). Centuries later Jesus was to weep over Jerusalem, 'If you, even you, had only known on this day what would bring you peace – but now it is hidden from your eyes' (Luke 19:42). The leaders in Jerusalem had rejected his rule, defending their own position and fragile relationship with Rome that they saw giving 'peace' – but less than forty years later the temple and city would be destroyed. The contrast with human quests is well expressed in Jesus' words to his disciples, 'My peace I give you. I do not give to you as the world gives' (John 14:27). Paul quoted Isaiah 59:8, followed by Psalm 36:1, in describing the parlous situation of both Jews and Gentiles 'under the power of sin': 'the way of peace they do not know . . . There is no fear of God before their eyes' (Rom. 3: 9, 17–18); but he went on to proclaim joyfully, 'since we have been justified through faith, we have peace with God through our Lord Jesus Christ' (Rom. 5:1), a 'peace' that was lived out in human relationships (Rom. 12:18; 14:19). How is that peace to be accomplished, and how are we to react towards those who threaten and oppose such peace? We will return to this question after Jehu's death, but

---

[33] Provan aptly comments that they 'are least able to benefit from the cult she has introduced' (p. 211).

[34] 'Peace', *šālôm*, occurs nine times in ch. 9, the most of any chapter in OT.

for now note that Jehu's answer is an approach of many through the centuries: the removal of all who actively encourage a policy of worshipping other gods.

d. Removing opposition, political and religious (10:1–27)

As so common in revolutions, violence escalates. In four separate massacres Jehu removes potential opposition, continuing to act with speed, backed by deliberate thought.

Joram may be dead but in the capital of Samaria are *seventy sons of the house of Ahab* (family members and associates), each having more right to the throne than Jehu. Jehu lays down a challenge: writing *letters* to relevant people with authority he dares them to *choose the best and most worthy of your master's sons and set him on his father's throne* (v. 3). Reminding them of the military force at their disposal (minimal since Jehu has been leading the forces resisting Hazael), he throws down the gauntlet, *then fight for your master's house* (dynasty). The response of the officials is immediate: *they were terrified* (lit., 'they were very very afraid'), and promise full allegiance. The extent of the support is highlighted by repeating, with expansion, the list of different officials (cf. vv. 1, 5), which also serves to isolate the 'sons'. Jehu writes what appears to be a deliberately ambiguous letter: *Take the heads of your master's sons* (v. 6) could mean 'count the numbers' or 'take the leaders of the sons', but it is taken literally as decapitation (vv. 7–8)! Jehu can then point to the *seventy . . . heads* as not the result of his own action but evidence that Yahweh is behind it all (vv. 9–10). The summary (v. 11) is comprehensive: there is no one left who 'would be honor-bound to avenge the death of the previous king'.[35]

On his way to Samaria Jehu meets and slaughters an unsuspecting group of forty-two of Ahaziah's relatives who are clearly aligned with the Omrides (vv. 12–14). A similar fate awaits remnants of *Ahab's family* in Samaria (vv. 17). Does the fact that 'such annihilation of ruling families was common practice'[36] and that it was *according to the word of the LORD spoken to Elijah* (v. 17) justify the action? The question remains.

In between the latter groups comes different treatment afforded *Jehonadab son of Rekab* (vv. 15–16). Balancing phrases show Jehu recognizes him favourably: 'Is your heart right, just as my heart is with your heart?' Jehonadab enthusiastically responds, 'It is' (literal

---

[35] Walton, Matthews and Chavalas, p. 398.
[36] Ibid.

translations). Soon Jehonadab will be with Jehu in the purging of the Baal temple (v. 23). We learn more of Jehonadab in Jeremiah 35:6–16: as leader of the Rekabites he enjoined an ascetic nomadic lifestyle, an expression of loyalty to Yahweh (possibly reflecting rejection of the temptations of urban life) still practiced two hundred years later. His loyalty to Jehu is expressed in a *hand* up into *the chariot*,[37] mirroring Ahab's earlier positive acceptance of Ben-Hadad (1 Kgs 20:33). For Ahab the action was a faithless treaty with Ben-Hadad (cf. 1 Kgs 20:34, 42) but for Jehu and Jehonadab it was partnership in *zeal for the LORD* (v. 16).

The final large group who experience Jehu's cunning are those who identify themselves as *the prophets of Baal, all his servants* [NRSV, NLT, NJPSV, 'worshippers'] *and all his priests* (v. 19), with careful exclusion of any who *serve the LORD* (v. 23.)[38] Jehu gives the impression of being single-mindedly on the side of Baal (vv. 18–24a), a ruse to bring complete destruction of *all* Baal worshippers (vv. 19d, 24b–25). There is a 'clever play on words' in that the 'great sacrifice (*zbḥ*) for Baal' (v. 19) uses a word that also describes 'slaughter' of apostates (cf. 1 Kgs 13:2; 2 Kgs 23:20).[39] The temple built by Ahab (1 Kgs 16:32) and its sacred objects are destroyed and, in the ultimate insult to Baal, the temple becomes a latrine (vv. 26–27). If previous killings had removed potential political opposition, here is a pointedly thorough religious purge.

e. Evaluation: God, Jehu and violence (10:28–36)

Jehu reigned *in Samaria . . . twenty-eight years* (v. 36), but the whole period is covered briefly in summary statements, each opening positively but then qualified. On the surface all looks well for the future of a nation committed solely to Yahweh. It appears that this could be the turning point that will mark the end of Israel's downward spiral that began with the reign of the first king Jeroboam. Commendation is in the narrator's words (v. 28) and then, unusually, in the words *the LORD said to Jehu* (v. 30). He has *destroyed Baal worship* and annihilated *the house of Ahab*. Twice however the qualification is that he continued the very worship that brought about the downfall of the first dynasty of Israel, that of Jeroboam I (vv. 29, 31). Further, as Yahweh's doing (*the LORD began to reduce*), the nation loses its territory across the Jordan at

---

[37] Wiseman, pp. 226–227. Hobbs, pp. 128–129, and Konkel, p. 481, discuss the possibility that Jehonadab is associated with chariotry (*rkb*).

[38] In v. 23 NIV's 'servants (of Baal)' and 'who serve (the LORD)' translate *'ābādîm* 'servants', commonly used also of 'worshippers'.

[39] Hobbs, p. 129.

the hands of Hazael and the Arameans (vv. 32–33).[40] For Jewish readers that in itself shows that in some way Yahweh is not pleased. Yahweh's words to Jehu (v. 30) contain a further clue that all is not well. Jehu has *done to the house of Ahab all I had in mind to do*: someone had to be God's instrument of judgment. The result however is *your descendants will sit on the throne of Israel to the fourth generation*, a phrase with negative associations! While Jehu's dynasty was to last the longest of any in the northern kingdom, in the Ten Commandments God's remembering of sin is to the 'third and fourth generation', while of faithfulness to 'a thousand generations'.[41] Mention of Jehu still worshipping *the golden calves* (v. 29) suggests a contributing factor: here is the only explicit reference to 'golden calves' in Kings apart from Jeroboam's making them (1 Kgs 12:28) and to *the law of the LORD* and *with all his heart* in connection with a king of Israel.[42] Another factor is seen in the prophecy of Hosea only decades after Jehu, with Yahweh saying, 'I will soon punish the house of Jehu for the massacre at Jezreel' (Hos. 1:4).[43] 'Zeal' that removes idolaters, even as an agent of God's judgment, is no substitute for obedience to God's law.

Throughout the narrative are specific references to fulfilment of prophecy. The first three are spoken by Jehu and he acts to ensure literal fulfilment (9:25–26, 36–37; 10:10), while the narrator is more restrained (10:17, 30). There is, however, no prophecy requiring the massacre of Ahab's supporters and the prophets, worshippers and priests of Baal. As is all too common in revolutions, violence escalates without mercy, with attempts to remove all potential opposition.

The narrator also gives clues that all is not right in that we first meet Jehu in a gathering with fellow military officers who readily join him (9:5, 13), that he justifies killing Joram of Israel by reminding his officer of a prophecy (9:25–26), and that having 'zeal for Yahweh' is his self-description (10:16). (Compare Elijah in 1 Kings 19:10, 14 – he likewise ordered mass slaughter of Baal prophets without an explicit word of God.) Jehu's undivided loyalty to Yahweh in terms of worship is clear, but has there been a subtle shift? The French

---

[40] Not mentioned is his bringing tribute at the beginning of his reign (841 BC) to the Assyrian Shalmaneser III. On the Black Obelisk of Shalmaneser, Jehu is shown prostrate (see http://www.britishmuseum.org and Provan, *ZIBBC*, p. 149, for picture, description and translation). Shortly afterwards Assyrian power weakened for several decades, enabling the Arameans to expand their territory.

[41] Exod. 20:5–6; Deut. 5:9–10.

[42] Cf. 1 Kgs 2:3, 'law', and 1 Kgs 2:4; 11:9, 'heart' in promises to Solomon and his successors.

[43] Cf. judgment on Baasha for destroying 'the house of Jeroboam', although the destruction was 'according to the word of the LORD' (1 Kgs 15:29; 16:7). See on 1 Kgs 16:7 and comparison with Acts 2:22–23, p. 159.

sociologist, Jacques Ellul, argues that, instead of being 'under God's Word', Jehu in fact

> commandeers the prophecy (9:25–26) in order to fulfil it . . . Undoubtedly Jehu is the man who executes what God has previously announced . . . But in the last resort he does it for his own interests . . . Jehu uses prophecy in the interest of politics while pretending to use politics in the interest of prophecy.[44]

The narrative helps us reflect on the interplay of religious zeal, personal ambition, even justified as 'the good of the nation' (or my group), and violent actions. Three people are specifically commended in the OT for their 'zeal' against those who served other gods, Phinehas (Num 25:11–13), Elijah (1 Kgs 19:10, 14) and Jehu. All were involved in the killing of opponents.[45] Paul likewise speaks of his former 'zeal, persecuting the church' (Phil. 3:6). Different is the action of Jesus, whose clearing of the temple courts is linked with the psalmist's 'Zeal for your house will consume me,' a reference to resulting antagonism (John 2:17; Ps. 69:9). In Christ and in his death we see God's 'zeal' against all wrongdoing (see further below).[46]

(i) God's judgment

> To read the Bible seriously and to open one's eyes to the chronicle of history is to be awed and terrified. God has declared himself the Judge of sinners and his judgments crowd the pages of the Bible and shout at us in every segment of human life . . . We are given no hope of reprieve so long as we persist in our rebellion against God.[47]

The most terrifying descriptions of God's judgment are not in the OT but in the NT, in the parables of Jesus and the Book of Revelation.[48] These speak of eternal dimensions, but judgment is often experienced in this life. God's people, in both the OT and NT, came to know, through seeing such judgment, both his abhorrence of all that is wrong and unjust, and his grace and mercy, for he is willing to forgive

---

[44] J. Ellul, *The Politics of God and the Politics of Man* (Grand Rapids: Eerdmans, 1972), pp. 100–101, 115.

[45] Saul is criticized for acting in 'zeal for Israel and Judah' in killing Gibeonites (2 Sam. 21:1–2).

[46] For God's 'zeal' for his glory and name, in both judgment and restorative deliverance, see Num. 25:11; Deut. 29:18–20; 2 Kgs 19:31; Isa. 9:7; 59:17; Ezek. 39:25.

[47] J. W. Wenham, *The Enigma of Evil: Can We Believe in the Goodness of God?*, second edition (London: Inter-Varsity, 1985), p. 174.

[48] E.g., Matt. 13:24–30, 36–43, 49–50; 18:21–35; Rev. 16 – 19.

all who turn to him (including even Ahab himself, 1 Kgs 21:28–29). Judgment of Ahab's family is deserved, but what kind of God does Jehu's actions portray? Ellul comments that 'by his actual choice of means Jehu is not a witness to the God who shows mercy to a thousand generations, but rather to the God who exterminates and chastises without pity'.[49] In the following chapters we will read of different actions in Judah by Jehosheba, Jehoiada and Joash which may show another way of being agents of God's judgment, of pointing to a different kind of God. A parallel is the earlier contrast between the means of Elijah and those of Obadiah.[50] Yet again, God works through both.

Prophecies of judgment bear out the general statement enunciated by Jesus, 'All who draw the sword will die by the sword' (Matt. 26:52). Violence begets violence. There is cause and effect in a sinful world. Jehu's dynasty itself came to an end with assassination (15:10–12). A pattern through the whole OT is how 'the punishment matches the crime'. God's just rule of his world is sometimes expressed in allowing the outworking of persistent human wickedness, although usually with a delay to allow for repentance.[51] Of necessity he works in a sinful world through human agents, who may not always act in ways that reflect both his justice and compassion.

(ii) Does violence bring peace?

Was Jehu's revolution effective? Can the wicked be removed? The coup removed the active encouragement of Baal worship by the royal family, along with priests and worshippers, but, other than Jehu's purge and the people acknowledging him as king, there is no mention of spiritual renewal. It was 'the guards and officers' who participated in the massacre of the Baalists. Life may have been easier for true followers of Yahweh, but nothing is said as to who and where they were. Different will be the southern reforms of Jehoiada and Joash with 'a covenant between the LORD and the king and people that they would be the LORD's people' and it was 'all the people of the land' (probably rural leaders) who destroyed the Baal temple (11:17–18).

The violence of Jehu's coup removed the royal house of Ahab (as earlier coups had brought an end to the dynasties of Jeroboam and Baasha), but there is little evidence of lasting religious or moral change. Shortly after Jehu's reign the prophecies of Amos and Hosea decry social injustice and religious syncretism by rulers

---

[49] Ellul, *Politics*, p. 118.
[50] See on 1 Kgs 18:1–15, pp. 170–171.
[51] Cf. Paul's review of human society, Rom. 1:18–32, soon followed by a statement on 'the riches of God's kindness, forbearance and patience' (2:4).

and people. The readers knew that a hundred years later, in 722 BC, the northern kingdom would be destroyed by the Assyrians (17:3–6). In presenting reasons for the fall, the narrator presents a sad catalogue of how the Israelites as a whole 'worshipped other gods and followed the practices of other nations the LORD had driven out before them, as well as the practices the kings of Israel introduced' (17:7–23). 'If revolution leads only to a change of rulers within the same power system and to an increase in violence, it cannot be the solution.'[52]

It is easy to see the wickedness in other people and to blame them for the ills of society (or even of the church). Jehu saw the imported religion of Jezebel, but was blind to the insidious effects of the worship introduced by Jeroboam. It is far easier to see others' compromises and sins than one's own. Sometimes it is only in the process of recognising others' motivations that we honestly face the complexity of our own personalities. This is one value of being drawn into the dramatic telling of Jehu's revolution and its ramifications. A moving review of a book on the Holocaust ends by quoting from *Black Dog,* by British novelist Ian McEwan:

> The evil lies in us all. It takes hold in an individual, in private lives, within a family . . . and then, when the conditions are right . . . a terrible cruelty, a viciousness against life erupts, and everyone is surprised by the depth of hatred within himself. Then it sinks back and waits. It's in our hearts.[53]

Jehu had said that there could be no 'peace' while Ahab's dynasty continued with its practices. Something had to be done to restore the harmony between God and the people. The Hebrew word used by Jehu in his quoting of a prophecy, 'make you pay for it' (9:26, recognition of the need for some restitution), is related to *shalom,* normally translated 'peace', but always with a connotation of good relationships, well-being and harmony.

> Yet even in this narrative, the outcome is not complete and perfect shalom between God and Israel, as the final evaluation of Jehu makes clear. Even a violence as brutal and widespread as Jehu's could not reform Israel. Even more radical violence would have to be employed by God, defeat at the hands of Hazael, then the Assyrians, and finally the Babylonians . . .

[52] U. Duchrow, 'God or Mammon: Economies in Conflict', *Mission Studies* 25/26 (1996), p. 45.
[53] B. Oakley, 'The Evil Within', *The Australian Magazine*, September 25–26, 1993, p. 62.

There is a paradox here that goes deep into the nature of the biblical God and into what a terrible, violent price that God must pay in order to restore peace and harmony with a sinful people. The New Testament will raise this paradox to an even higher order of magnitude and focus it on the cross (Rom 4:25; 5:8; 8:32; II Cor 5:19).[54]

The cross focuses both violence and peace. There Christ submitted to violent death and absorbed the violence of the world, bringing peace. The road through various acts of judgment in Israel's history leads to Calvary. 'Whereas *at the conquest* [and elsewhere], *God poured out his judgment on a wicked society who deserved it, at the cross, God bore on himself the judgment of God on human wickedness, through the person of his own sinless Son – who deserved it not one bit.*'[55] In the cross a new pattern is given for Christian behaviour (1 Pet. 2:21–25). Paul, in the light of 'God's mercies', reaffirms the OT statement that '"It is mine to avenge; I will repay", says the Lord' while enjoining 'live at peace with everyone', not taking 'revenge' (Rom. 12:18–19). God brings vindication and peace in his time, in his way, answering the cry of suffering people (Rev. 6:10). Only God can rightly use violence to bring peace and so human acts of judgment, a role of the state, or of revolution against an unjust state, must be evaluated with humility at the foot of the cross.[56] The Jehu narrative is one God-given resource shining light on and exposing the mixture of motivations, both good and self-centred, that inform decisions and illustrating results.

3. A queen, a priest and a young royal son (11:1–20)

With the killing of king Ahaziah and several relatives (9:27–28; 10:12–14) the coup in Israel has obvious ramifications for Judah. What takes place will be confrontation, but eventually will illustrate another way forward in change that is religious, political and cultural.

These are turbulent times. After the formulaic ending of Jehu's reign (10:36), instead of the usual orderly introduction to the next king of Israel or Judah, we read dramatically, *When Athaliah the mother of Ahaziah saw that her son was dead, she proceeded to*

[54] Nelson, p. 206.

[55] C. J. H. Wright, *The God I Don't Understand* (Grand Rapids: Zondervan, 2008), p. 107 (emphasis his), in concluding two chapters on 'What about the Canaanites?'.

[56] A. F. Holmes, ed., *War and Christian Ethics: Classic and Contemporary Readings on the Morality of War*, Second Edition (Grand Rapids: Baker, 2005) is a stimulating compendium of Christian arguments and attitudes through the centuries.

destroy the whole royal family (v. 1). Its matter-of-fact statement enhances the stark reality! While Ahaziah was king Athaliah had a significant position, likely the prime sponsor of Baal worship.[57] Now as a daughter of Ahab, and granddaughter of Omri, she either is fiercely angry and revengeful or sees her own life at risk (or both) and like Jehu she acts decisively and brutally. We can only guess the factions within the palace and level of support for her policies, but her plot to kill all potential claimants to the throne would wipe out the Davidic line – where then would be God's promise? In the event one nursling royal prince, *Joash*,[58] and his wet-nurse are stealthily saved in the temple by *Jehosheba*, a sister of his father.[59] It is likely that Joash's mother Zibiah (12:1) was killed at that time – she, as other mothers of princes, would be a rival to Athaliah as queen mother. Joash is hidden for *six years* in the temple complex which Athaliah, as a foreigner, was unable to enter. The priority of worship to Yahweh over against Baal is seen in the full phrase, *the temple of the LORD*, which will resound like a drumbeat in this and the following chapter.[60] 'The house of Yahweh' represents true power and authority over against the 'house of the king' (*royal palace*, vv. 5, 16) and the 'house of Baal' (v. 18).

In the event Athaliah *ruled* for *six years* (v. 3), the illegitimate hiatus in Davidic kingship highlighted by the absence of the standard introductory and closing formulae. Nothing more is told of her reign apart from her death (vv. 13–16), but as mother of Ahaziah she is an ancestress of all future kings of Judah. We are reminded of the association when king Manasseh is likened to Ahab (21:3), but Manasseh was not alone as a king actively sponsoring pagan worship (e.g., Ahaz, 16:2–4, 10–18). Syncretistic practices from the time of Solomon continued. Regicide that destabilized Israel was now to be seen in Judah, Joash (12:20–21, after forty years reign), and Amaziah (14:19, after fifteen years), but without change of dynasty. More importantly, the taint of worship of other gods and syncretistic practices associated with Baalism continues in the south.

[57] See on 1 Kgs 15:13 for queen mother's position, pp. 155–156.

[58] The Judahite king's name occurs in MT as both Joash and Jehoash. The concurrent king of Israel's name has similar variation, followed by NRSV and NJPSV. Context always indicates which king is intended, but to assist readers NIV and NLT consistently have *Joash* for the Judahite king and *Jehoash* for the king of Israel.

[59] Jehosheba disappears from the narrative, the key role being taken by Jehoiada. 2 Chr. 22:11 and later Josephus (*Antiquities* ix. 141) identify Jehosheba as wife of Jehoiada, which would explain her action.

[60] 11:3, 4 (twice), 7, 10, 13, 15, 18, 19; 12:4 (twice), 9 (twice), 10, 11 (twice), 12, 13 (twice), 14, 16, 18. Each instance is translated fully in NRSV (NIV occasionally omits 'of the LORD'). This represents the greatest concentration of 'the house of Yahweh' in the OT, 22 in the block, matched by 18 instances in the parallel 2 Chr. 23 – 24.

For some unstated reason the priest *Jehoiada* made a decisive risky move *in the seventh year* (v. 4).[61] With expected opposition from those loyal to Athaliah, Jehoiada plans meticulously to have the child Joash crowned as king. The process leading to coronation (v. 12) is narrated in detail, with many steps taken to ensure security of the young Joash. Jehoiada binds the leaders of the temple guard[62] by *oath* before what must have been a dramatic scene as *he showed them the king's son*. As the priest of the temple of Yahweh he 'plays the key role in legitimizing the Davidic monarchs by identifying them as YHWH's choice to rule the state'.[63] His designated time for action is at the end of the Sabbath when changing of the guard means a double number of soldiers on duty and so ready. His intention is explicit as he speaks of guarding *the king* (vv. 7–8; not simply 'king's son'), with others ensuring there is neither escape from the temple (to warn) nor opposition entering as the coronation takes place by the pillar at the temple entrance (cf. v. 14; 23:3). The narrator reinforces legitimacy with specific reference to weaponry *that had belonged to King David and that were in the temple of the LORD* (v. 10).

Central in the coronation ceremony is presentation of *a copy of the covenant* (v. 12). The phrase translates *'ēdût* ('testimony, witness'), which may refer either to some insignia or 'more precisely ... a written charter delineating both the prerogatives and requirements of power', which may be compared with Deuteronomy 17:14–20.[64] In the context of Kings and Davidic succession there is clear association with the Sinaitic covenant to which kings are also bound (1 Kgs 2:3; 2 Kgs 17:15; 23:3).[65] After six years of Athaliah's Baalist and non-Davidic reign, affirmation of both allegiance to the covenant with Yahweh and the Davidic succession is a major statement of renewed direction.

Two responses follow from the coronation. As expected, Athaliah cries *Treason!* – the same word used of Jehu's plot against Joram and her relatives in Israel (9:14) – but to Jehoiada she is the interloper.

---

[61] 'He is the first significant priest to appear in 1 – 2 Kings since Solomon's accession and plays a creative role normally reserved for prophets' (Leithart, p. 225).

[62] The *Carites* may be a group of mercenaries linking with Kerethites in 2 Sam. 20:23, and 'foreigners uncircumcised in heart and flesh' in Ezek. 44:7, but this interpretation is disputed and the term may refer to a class of soldiers. LXX interprets as the name of one of the commanders, Chorri. See Wiseman, p. 231, Hobbs, p. 139, Sweeney, p. 345.

[63] Sweeney, p. 345. Cf. 1 Kgs 1:32, 38–39.

[64] Brueggemann, p. 409; Cogan and Tadmor, p. 128; NJPSV, 'insignia'; *DCH*, 'royal protocol'.

[65] The only instances of *'ēdût* in Kings, matching its use for the tangible 'testimony' of the Ten Commandments (e.g., Exod. 25:16, 21, etc.; Deut. 4:45; 6:17, 20).

Her death ensues, Jehoiada making sure it is not in the temple precincts (vv. 15–16). The other response is that of *the people* who join the *guards* in welcoming the coronation (vv. 12–14). *The people of the land* (v. 14) are civic leaders whose 'presence is required to confirm the accession . . . ; they represent the residents of the land'.[66] Repeatedly we read of universal support (*all*, vv. 14, 18, 19, 20), a distinction from Jehu's coup in the north where only military support is mentioned.

The process is not yet completed. Coronation is greater than simply a matter between king and people, for more important is that all be *the LORD's people* (v. 17). So Jehoiada makes *a covenant* binding Yahweh, king and people. Some see here renewal, after the interregnum, of the Davidic covenant between Yahweh and king (cf. 2 Sam. 7:1–16), the Sinai covenant between Yahweh and people (cf. Deut. 27; Josh. 24) and a covenant between king and people (cf. 2 Sam. 5:3).[67] The NIV[68] sees two covenants, combining the first two (cf. 23:3) as suggested by MT word order. Others, noting that *covenant* occurs only once in Hebrew and has the definite article, 'the covenant', see rather a single covenant with threefold aspect, similar to the perspective of Deuteronomy which binds Yahweh, people and king together in mutual relationships. The three relationships may be distinguished but not separated.[69] There is no place for despotism or a future palace coup as the involvement of 'the people of the land' marks a return to the mutuality evident in David's rule (2 Sam. 2:4; 5:1–5). Further, a covenant with Yahweh leaves no place for *the temple of Baal* (built by Athaliah?) and so *all the people of the land* destroy the temple and kill its priest.

One final installation act remains, the king sitting on the throne in the palace. No doubt wondering whether there will be retaliation by any in the palace, the military guard takes the boy king to the throne. We expect as conclusion that *all the people of the land rejoiced;* unexpected is the striking addition that *the city was calm,* a term used in Joshua and Judges of the land having 'rest'.[70] Each instance there is after the people have returned to Yahweh following deliverance from enemies, with a 'leader/judge' acting appropriately. This is society with Yahweh at the centre.

[66] 'Their activity at time of dynastic crisis is regularly noted (21:23–24; 23:30), and they are listed with other civic leaders (Jer. 1:18; 34:19; 37:2)' (Konkel, p. 500).

[67] Gray, pp. 579–580; Jones, pp. 485–486; House, pp. 299–300.

[68] Followed by Provan, p. 220.

[69] Cf. NJPSV: 'And Jehoiada solemnized the covenant between the LORD, on the one hand, and the king and the people, on the other – as well as between the king and the people – that they should be the people of the LORD'; Hobbs, p. 143; Konkel, p. 501; Brueggemann, pp. 411–412.

[70] Josh. 11:23; Judg.3:11, 30; 5:31; 8:28.

How different was the change in Judah from that in Israel following Jehu's coup.[71] Both include overthrow of a ruler and removal of Baal worship, but in Judah there is much popular support and involvement. Further, there are only two deaths, Athaliah and Mattan, the priest of the Baal temple in Jerusalem, and the city is 'calm'. The Davidic line and Yahweh worship continue as a result of quiet, thoughtful and deliberate action. As elsewhere in the Bible, with Moses (Exod. 2:1–10) and Jesus (Matt. 2:1–23), hope for the future is in a young child who is protected and delivered from a threatening, ruthless ruler.

> To be sure, God is silent in this story of the deliverance [and enthronement] of the infant Joash . . . However there can be little doubt that the reader is to understand that God is working behind the scenes . . . God does not have to act or speak . . . In history there will always be agents, witting or unwitting, who will bring about the divine will.[72]

Jehosheba and Jehoiada are examples of people willing to take risks, not for the sake of their own future but selflessly for the future of God's people and their witness among the nations, especially when the very existence of God's people in that location is severely threatened by ruthless rulers and groups. 'The strength of the church is not violent political resistance but a willingness to obey God rather than human beings even to the point of death.'[73] For Jehoiada, and we may assume Jehosheba, actions flow from trust in God's promises and the continuation of the covenant relationship including the Davidic dynasty. There is no personal power-play using religion for one's own purposes. They are unable to predict the results, but action must be taken, done thoughtfully. There is violence, but it is minimized; there is leadership, but it is sensitive to the wider population and embraces their support. Their faith, attitudes and actions provide a mirror for reflecting on what leads to 'calm' for communities, cities and nations.

The destruction of the Baal temples and their altars and idols in both kingdoms (10:26–27; 11:18), similar to the injunction of

---

[71] Several literary parallels, including secluded enthronement (camp, 9:6, 13; temple, 11:12), two key women (Jezebel and Athaliah), a contrast between two houses (of Baal and Yahweh) and their named priests (Mattan and Jehoiada), and a purge of Baal worship, show that the two are to be compared. See N. Na'aman, 'Royal Inscriptions and the Histories of Joash and Ahaz, Kings of Judah', *Vetus Testamentum* 48 (1998), p. 342.

[72] Seow, p. 233.

[73] Konkel, pp. 506–507.

Deuteronomy 12:2–3 to completely destroy any aspect of Canaanite worship, has been an example followed by others at different stages in history. Whether the iconoclastic ('image breaking') controversies in the Byzantine Church (726–843 AD), the burning of Jewish and Islamic books in Spain by Cardinal Ximenes in the 1490s or the destruction of statuary by Oliver Cromwell in England in the seventeenth century, biblical precedents are cited. Similar attitudes are in the Taliban destruction in 2001 of ancient Buddhist statuary in Afghanistan and debates continue over government policies regarding the building of mosques in Christian countries and the prohibition of Christian building in some Islamic countries. The nations of Israel and Judah were theocracies, expressed here in the covenant making (11:17). Since the emperor Constantine became a Christian, debates and struggles concerning state-church relationships, and hence allowance of alternative practices, have been a feature of European history (paralleled in Islamic countries). With the rise of religious freedom and tolerance of a variety of religious practices, debates now often use the language of 'cultural values and cohesion'. What is to be said about the relevance today of the destruction of Baal temples and idols?

In ninth century BC Israel and Judah, Baal temples and idols represented syncretism and a denial of the sole lordship of Yahweh over king and people. They were powerful visual symbols that constantly presented an alternative value system and lifestyle to the people. NT writers lived in a culture with its powerful symbols including temples and statuary, associated in particular with the might and wealth of Rome. Religious ceremonies demonstrated loyalty and provided social networking, but apart from issues of allegiance to Rome there was religious tolerance. When speaking to worshippers of idols, Paul commends their religiosity but points to the Creator and the resurrected Christ (Acts 17:16–31), while all messages addressed to Christians condemn Christian participation in idol worship (for example, the contrast in 1 Corinthians 5:9–11; and one of a number of acts to avoid in Galatians 5:19–21). Striking is the Pauline statement that 'greed is idolatry' (Col. 3:5), with 'greed' embracing generally 'unchecked hunger for physical pleasure . . . [which] places at the centre of one's attention and devotion that which is not God'.[74]

Jehoiada 'seeks to break the social power of a certain oppressive kind by an assault upon ideological symbols'.[75] Today the most prevalent visual symbols that promise 'life' with happiness, security,

---

[74] N. T. Wright, *Colossians and Philemon*, Tyndale NT Commentaries (Leicester: Inter-Varsity Press, 1986), p. 134.
[75] Brueggemann, p. 417.

status, well-being and belonging are not associated with traditional religions but are presented in television commercials, reinforced by omnipresent logos, and in lifestyle programmes. In some countries the symbols are of blatant nationalism, often including shows of military might. When such symbols also appear in church buildings the question must be asked as to their influence on worshippers. The actions of Jehu and Jehoiada can focus for us the destructive power of physical symbols portraying a lifestyle that is at root idolatrous or syncretistic. There is need to expose (de-construct) their emptiness through turning to Christ and the cross (e.g., Phil. 3:12–21). With clear purpose, the final book of Scripture is the vision given to John: the book of Revelation presents a vision of the glory of God and the triumph of his purposes that challenges and ultimately destroys the wealth and power images of Rome.[76]

4. Reform and loss in Judah under Joash (11:21 – 12:21)[77]

The account of Joash's reign is demarcated by the opening and closing formulaic statements (11:21; 12:1–3, 19–21),[78] the specific elements alone illustrating the mixed aspects of the reign and its end. The two longer narratives describe the slowness of temple renovations (12:4–16) and costly submission to the attacking Arameans (12:17–21). We see commendation, alongside evidence of decline. All is still not well in Judah. Here is a foreshadowing of a later boy king, Josiah,[79] whose temple renovations two hundred years later led to major reforms. That reign also ended in untimely death, and shortly afterwards the southern kingdom came to an end (chs 22 – 24). Readers today may reflect on continuing intertwining of good intentions and human failings, of positive reform and entrenched influence of past patterns.

Jehoiada's influence on Joash is significant as he *instructed him* in what was *right in the eyes of the LORD* (12:2).[80] Uniquely in Kings we read of a priest fulfilling the God-given task of teaching the law

---

[76] See, e.g., J. N. Kraybill, *Imperial Cult and Commerce in John's Apocalypse* (Sheffield: Sheffield Academic Press, 1996); R. M. Royalty, *The Streets of Heaven: The Ideology of Wealth in the Apocalypse of John* (Macon, Georgia: Mercer University Press, 1998).

[77] 12:1–22 in MT.

[78] After the end of the northern kingdom the opening details of all Judahite kings include, as here, accession age.

[79] Josiah was eight years old at the beginning of his reign (22:1).

[80] The duration of Joash's obedience is most naturally read according to MT phrasing as 'all *his* days, because Jehoiada the priest taught him' (cf. NRSV, NLT, NJPSV). NIV follows LXX interpretation, probably influenced by the shorter 2 Chr. 24:2 ('all the days of *Jehoiada the priest*').

(Lev. 10:11; Deut. 10:10–11; 33:10). Here is an echo of Solomon's prayer at the dedication of the temple, suggesting the expectation of blessing. Then there was a plea for forgiveness and for God to 'teach [your people] the right way to live' and to renew the land through rain (1 Kgs 8:36).[81] It is not Joash's enthronement and Athaliah's death that ensure the future, but learning and doing God's revealed will.

a. Repairing the temple (12:4–16)

Prior to Joash's being hidden in the temple (11:3), the last mention of the temple has been Asa's depletion of the temple treasury (1 Kgs 15:18). 'After this long hiatus in the story of the temple, the narrator makes it a major theme in the closing half of 2 Kings.'[82] From the forty-year reign of Joash the narrator has chosen two matters, both involving the temple. The main subject is Joash's directions to repair the temple, the positive action that accompanies rejection of past worship of Baal (vv. 4–16). He orders collection of moneys due to the temple, whether *collected in the census* (cf. Exod. 30:11–16)[83] or in fulfilment of *vows* (Lev. 27:1–13) or *brought voluntarily*. There may have been a general appeal to the populace, echoing the generous voluntary gifts for the building of the tabernacle (Exod. 35:20–29).

Nothing however has been done by *the twenty-third year* of his reign, suggesting lack of attention by Joash, although the year of the initial command is unspecified.[84] Certainly Jehoiada and the priests have been tardy so the king takes away their responsibility to collect and use the money (vv. 6–8). Renovation is handed to those experienced, the workers and their supervisors. Instructions are quite specific: money was to be collected publicly and counted and distributed jointly by *the royal secretary and the high priest*, used solely for the actual repairs, with the supervisors being trusted as *they acted*

---

[81] While no doubt priests instructed other kings, the explicit mention stands out. Apart from here and in Solomon's prayer the only instance of 'teaching' (*yrh*, hif'il) in Kings is when the king of Assyria appoints captive priests from Samaria to 'teach the people what the god of the land requires' (2 Kgs 17:27–28). Cf. Judg. 13:8; 1 Sam. 12:23.

[82] Leithart, p. 229. After the reign of Joash, 14:14; 15:35; 16:8–18; 19:1, 14–19; 20:5, 8; 21:4–8; 22:3–7; 23:1–12; 24:13; 25:9, 13–17.

[83] The unusual *ksp 'br* 'money of crossing' occurs in both Exodus and Kings. At least from the post-exilic period the collection was annual (Neh. 10:32), the 'temple-tax' mentioned in Matt. 17:24–27. See J. R. Wagner, 'Piety, Jewish. 2.3. Financial Support of the Temple', *DNTB*, p. 799.

[84] Cf. the indefinite 'some time later' in 2 Chr. 24:4. In comparison, after the disastrous reigns of Manasseh and Amon, Josiah began purging places of Baal and Asherah worship in his eighth year (2 Chr. 34:3), turning to temple repair in his eighteenth year (2 Kgs 22:3; 2 Chr. 34:8).

with complete honesty (vv. 9–15). Josiah implemented similar arrangements (22:3–7). As with the tabernacle building, listing honours the variety of artisans: *the carpenters and builders, the masons and stone-cutters*. Two further comments note that no money was used for the various *articles of gold or silver* (v. 13) and, as specified in the law, the priests retained their share of *the guilt offerings and sin offerings* (v. 16; cf. Lev. 5:16; Num. 5:5–9).[85]

The narrative is told simply, but readers are left with questions as to varying dynamics suggested by Joash's arrangements. No reason is stated for the tardiness of Jehoiada and the priests and, while the honesty of the workers' supervisors is affirmed, there is no suggestion of priestly misappropriation. The transparent collection and distribution process set in place by Joash is however a model with contemporary relevance. It forestalls any possible accusation of misappropriation or favouritism. It seems likely that the priests' priorities for use of the money were different. Possibly Jehoiada, used to instructing the young Joash, still saw him as young and inexperienced and so took responsibility for deciding priorities. He would not be the first leader who has had difficulty handing over genuine leadership to someone younger – Paul's words to Timothy are apposite, 'Don't let anyone look down on you because you are young' (1 Tim. 4:12). Given the neglect of temple worship by Athaliah, Jehoiada, as both older and involved at the coalface, no doubt saw daily the need of resources, including the justifiable livelihood of priests and other temple personnel. Nor would this be the first time that people have resisted major changes in budgetary allocations between areas of an enterprise, feeling that 'we can't do our work with less resources' or 'what we do is fundamental and we are under-resourced, so we need increases first'. That no money was to be used for objects other than the building suggests limited finances. Did the priests feel humiliated in losing responsibility? How did the artisans feel being trusted? Why did Joash delay in acting? Did he lack enthusiasm? Each reader will bring personal experiences in answering.

More likely is a matter of expertise, a perennial issue:

The story also points to the potential and limitations of human beings who strive to serve God. Jehoiada, who so valiantly and efficiently orchestrated the restoration of the heir to the throne of David, does not seem to have the ability to manage the finances of the Temple efficiently enough to carry out the needed repairs. By the same token, King Joash had initiated the fund-raising

---

[85] I. Eph'al-Jaruzelska, 'Officialdom and Society in the Book of Kings', in Lemaire and Halpern, pp. 494–497, discusses the various terms and arrangements, including comparison with ancient Near Eastern sources.

campaign to repair the Temple, but he seemed so out of touch with the project that it took him more than two decades to realize the repairs had not been done.[86]

Paul's letters list varieties of gifts which are 'for the common good'.[87] In Ephesians 5:18–21 one of the results of the filling of the Spirit is submitting 'to one another out of reverence for Christ', allowing and encouraging others in the exercise of their gifts, working together. Since I live in a country where sport is prominent, a sporting analogy comes to mind in reflecting on leadership and teamwork. A good coach knows, develops and maximizes the gifts of all players and helps them play together for the good of the whole, and the attaining of goals! A good team is where each player majors on their strengths in cooperation with others. As Joash implemented a plan delineating for the good of the temple the differing gifts and responsibilities of priests and artisans, so now Christ is building his living temple with a variety of stones (1 Pet. 2:4–10). Sometimes a Jehoiada needs to recognize the leadership of a younger Joash whom he has nurtured and a Joash is needed to help 'priests' be aware of their limitations and to trust others to whom Christ has given different gifts. Through various gifts working together 'the whole body . . . grows and builds itself in love', the goal being 'the fullness of Christ' (Eph. 4:13, 16).

b. Loss of temple wealth and life (12:17–21)

Following Joash's orders, there is no mention of repairs being completed.[88] Instead, the narrative shifts the scene to *Hazael king of Aram's* attack. With Assyrian power weakened, the Arameans extended their territory, recovering parts of Israel east of the Jordan in Jehu's time (10:32–33), although later, under Jehoahaz and Jehoash, Israel regained some territory (13:3–5, 22–25). With Jehoahaz now king of Israel,[89] the Aramean attack on the weaker Philistine territory and Jerusalem was likely an effort to contain Israel. As the earlier marriage of Athaliah to Jehoram had been associated with alliance between the weaker Judah and stronger Israel, Joash's ready submission to the Arameans may have been in part an attempt to move

---

[86] Seow, p. 233.
[87] Rom. 12: 3–8; 1 Cor. 12; Eph. 4:11–16; cf. 1 Pet. 4:10.
[88] Na'aman, 'Royal Inscriptions', pp. 337–340, notes that mention of a date ('twenty-third year') is unusual and there are 'some expressions [in vv. 5–9] not found elsewhere in the Bible which may have been taken from an original inscription' on the building (p. 337).
[89] Cf. 12:6; 13:1.

Judah away from Israel's influence, as also will be attempted by Joash's successor, Amaziah.[90] Whatever the motivation, the narrator's interest is the extent of the giving of *all the sacred objects* that previous kings had accumulated. The last king who had so done was Asa (1 Kgs 15:18–19), again to an Aramean king and making a treaty, and now (v. 18) are listed all the subsequent kings through to Joash. In addition he gave *all the gold* in *the treasuries* of both *temple* and *palace*.[91] The temple may have been repaired but the resources are completely depleted. As previously with Asa, there is neither any prophetic message nor mention of trusting in Yahweh – those will feature in the later narrative of Hezekiah when the Assyrians attack (chs 18–19).

Was the ready submission to the Arameans with depletion of the treasury, and what that symbolized, the reason for Joash being assassinated by two of *his officials* (vv. 20–21)? The narrator's juxtaposition hints at such but he has chosen to focus in the story of Joash upon temple renovations and depletion of its resources. The writer of Chronicles however gives a more detailed account of the latter years of Joash's reign, reporting a major desertion from the temple and Yahweh worship that persisted despite prophetic warnings. The Chronicler gives as reason for the assassination the king's ordering of the stoning of Zechariah, son of Jehoiada the priest (2 Chr. 24:17–27).

In a pale reflection of Solomon, Joash is an example of someone who started with great promise and with much God-honouring support, who initiated with wisdom a major temple repair, but whose life ended in loss and untimely death. Here is a microcosm of the story of Judah: one of decline that has its periods of reformation but which leads ultimately to complete loss of the temple and its contents. Nevertheless the telling of the story is itself an expression of hope, a remembering that God continues with his imperfect people, working in the midst of the turmoil and decisions of history. While being warned by actions that lead to loss and death, God's people can learn from Yahweh-honouring acts, being 'instructed' in 'what was right in the eyes of the LORD'.

5. Jehoahaz king of Israel (13:1–9)

In the year Joash of Judah took determined action regarding temple building (v. 1; cf. 12:6) *Jehoahaz* succeeded his father Jehu as king of Israel. He receives the standard formulaic condemnation of all kings

---

[90] 14:8–14; cf. earlier relationship, 1 Kgs 22:4; 2 Kgs 3:7; 8:18, 28; 10:12. See Sweeney, p. 353.

[91] Hebrew: 'the house of Yahweh and the house of the king'.

of Israel (v. 2):[92] *the LORD's anger* is the reason for Israel's being dominated by Aramean kings, *Hazael* then *Ben-Hadad*, not simply their superior forces.

This block[93] provides the only instance in Kings of the language and form of the cycle in Judges: the people 'forsook' Yahweh and served other gods, and so Yahweh 'became angry' and the people were handed over to foreign oppression (vv. 2–3; Judg. 2:11–15, 19–21; 3:7–8; 10:6–9).[94] Yahweh's grace is seen in the cycle's continuation: when the people were in 'great distress' (Judg. 2:15; 10:9) and 'cried out to the LORD' (Judg. 3:9; 10:10),[95] he 'raised up for them judges who delivered them/a deliverer' (Judg. 2: 16; 3:9).[96] So here *Jehoahaz sought the LORD's favour.* There is no mention of repentance (the opposite is stated in v. 6), rather *the LORD listened* because *he saw how severely the king of Aram was oppressing Israel*[97] (v. 4), repeating exactly the form of Exodus 3:9: 'I have seen the way the Egyptians are oppressing them.' God is moved to compassionate action as people experience oppression, even when their situation is an outworking of his anger! This juxtaposition of compassion and judgment is expressed with great pathos in the dramatic confrontation and promise of Hosea 11, addressed to rebellious Israel, and comes together most powerfully on the cross where love and justice meet.

As in Judges *the LORD provided a deliverer* (v. 5), but no details are given other than the Israelites *escaped from the power of Aram* and could live *in their own homes*; that is, the men were no longer needed for fighting.[98] Commentators suggest various candidates as to the 'deliverer'. Campaigns of the Assyrian Adad-Nirari III distracted the Arameans,[99] and this would not be the only time God

---

[92] Despite his revolution Jehu continued those practices (10:29) and we now learn he did not destroy the *Asherah pole* in Samaria (v. 6). It is not only that 'Jehu's reformation was short-lived' (Wiseman, p. 239; similarly Hobbs, p. 166) but that it was incomplete.

[93] I have examined several features of ch. 13 and 14:23–29 in more detail in '2 Kings 13: A Cluster of Hope in God', *Journal for the Study of the Old Testament* (forthcoming).

[94] Also language of covenant curses, Deut. 6:14–15; 7:4; 11:16–17; 29:26–27.

[95] Cf. the exodus when God hears the people 'crying out' under oppression (Exod. 3:7, 9; Deut. 26:7).

[96] EVV translate forms of *yš'* as both 'deliver/deliverer' and 'save/saviour', and the related nouns, 'salvation/deliverance/victory'. Like the Greek *sōzō*, *yš'* occurs in various contexts.

[97] The 'excesses of Hazael and Ben Hadad' are alluded to in the imagery of Amos 1:3–5 (Hobbs, p. 166).

[98] Cf. Josh. 22:4, 6–8; Judg. 7:8; 20:8; 1 Sam. 13:2, etc. The translation 'homes' (so most EVV) understands *'ohŏlēhem* 'their tents' as a stock phrase.

[99] E.g., Wiseman, p. 240; Walton, Matthews and Chavalas, p. 399.

used a pagan ruler as deliverer (cf. the Persian Cyrus in Isa. 44:24 – 45:7). Subsequent kings, Jehoash (13:25) and Jeroboam II (14:25–27), are also spoken of as having 'delivered' Israel in times of distress.[100] Alternatively, the language of the block points to a Moses/prophetic figure and immediately following is interaction with Elisha after a gap of around forty years: his name means 'My God delivered' and he is spoken of as *the chariots and horsemen of Israel* (v. 14).[101] While all are feasible, anonymity draws attention away from a specific individual. Ultimately neither prophet nor king can deliver; Yahweh is the one who 'delivers' (as in 14:27; 19:19, 34).[102]

In Judges, return to Canaanite practices was usually a generation after the deliverance, but here the narrator moves quickly to show that 'God's gracious intervention makes no difference to Israel's religious outlook (v. 6)'.[103] The fertility cult was still being practiced as we read again of the *Asherah pole*, the cult object introduced by Ahab (1 Kgs 16:33).[104] Further, despite the (temporary) removal of Aramean threat, the army of Jehoahaz was sadly depleted, woefully inadequate for defending the country (v. 7). The enumeration prepares us for the next passage: the only way Israel can be protected is by Yahweh.

The narrative of Jehoahaz's seventeen-year reign is a sad one of religious compromise, foreign oppression and resulting military powerlessness. Exilic and later readers will recognize that this was not merely the result of the ebb and flow of national fortunes as larger nations waxed and waned. It continues the cycle of sin-judgment-cry-deliverance-return-to-sin known from the period of judges. At the same time, it is a reminder of the grace of God, who has compassion on his people in their oppression, sending a deliverer. This will be their hope in exile: beyond anger there can be gracious deliverance. But how long can the cycle continue? Is there any limit? Jesus provides an answer in response to Peter's question, 'Lord, how many times shall I forgive my brother or sister who sins against me? Up to seven times?' God's own character is revealed: 'I tell you, not seven times, but seventy-seven times' (Matt. 18:21–22). Readers in the Christian era can read this account of Jehoahaz and again be amazed at the patient grace of God.

---

[100] Sweeney, p. 355; Cogan and Tadmor, p. 143; although the phrase for Jeroboam is 'the LORD . . . saved them by the hand of Jeroboam'.

[101] Gray, pp. 594–596; Hobbs, pp. 167–168; Konkel, p. 525.

[102] Cf. Seow, p. 236. Only from here on in Kings do forms of $y\check{s}^{\prime}$ occur in a positive sense relating to Israel.

[103] Provan, p. 228.

[104] The only previous mention of the object.

6. Jehoash king of Israel and the death of Elisha, yet hope (13:10–25)

Towards the end of Joash's reign in Judah, *Jehoash* became king of Israel.[105] His sixteen year reign is passed over with the standard introductory and concluding statements juxtaposed (vv. 10–13). The simple statement of *his war against Amaziah king of Judah* has no editorial comment, details being included later in the narrative of Amaziah's reign, so focusing on its significance for Judah (14:8–14). The structure draws attention to the following account of Elisha and Yahweh's grace and compassion.

a. Elisha and Jehoash (13:14–19)

Elisha was last mentioned when he sent one from the company of the prophets to anoint Jehu (9:1). Now in the reign of Jehu's grandson, as Elisha nears death Jehoash goes to meet him. What transpired suggests previous relationships between the two have been positive, with the king's worship of Yahweh being genuine (within the limitations of continuing policies, v. 11). His cry, *My father! My father! . . . The chariots and horsemen of Israel!* (v. 14) echoes Elisha's at Elijah's ascension (2:12), but more desperate in light of the recently-mentioned reduction of Israel's forces to *fifty horsemen, ten chariots* (v. 7). Affirmation of the centrality of the prophet in Israel's defence recognizes that ultimately victory depends on Yahweh. The question is, who is to succeed Elisha? We expect a prophet, but surprisingly Elisha calls for response from the king.

In an acted prophecy with a bow and arrow, Elisha identifies himself, and so Yahweh, with Jehoash as he *put his hands on the king's hands*. In turn, Jehoash would have understood the powerful combination of his actions and Elisha's words. The exact conformity of the king's actions (vv. 15–18) is shown in Hebrew by exact repetition ('"Take a bow and arrows"; so he took a bow and arrows . . . "Put your hand[106] on the bow"; and he put his hand', etc.). Prophetic enactment announces to Jehoash *the LORD's arrow of victory*[107] . . . *over Aram* (v. 17). Further, *Aphek* is a reminder of Ahab's victory at the same location. Then however Ahab did not *completely* destroy the Arameans, so disregarding that it was 'the LORD's victory' (see

---

[105] For these two kings' names, see on 11:2, p. 269, n. 58.

[106] NRSV's 'draw' is unwarranted, wrongly leading to questions over the 'drawing' of the bow before opening the window. Reference may be to stringing the bow, sometimes requiring two people; see W. B. Barrick, 'Elisha and the Magic Bow: A Note on 2 Kings xiii 15–17', *Vetus Testamentum* 35 (1985), pp. 355–363.

[107] See n. 96; the noun *těšû'â* is elsewhere variously translated 'deliverance, salvation'.

on 1 Kgs 20:26–43, pp. 189–191). Lasting victory is not ensured by a prophet but by obeying the words prophets have spoken.

The orders continue, and again are obeyed, except that on the order, *strike the ground*, Jehoash *struck it three times and stopped* (v. 18). Elisha's *angry* reaction surprises the modern reader but the vocabulary provides the answer. Jehoash has been told 'you will completely *destroy* [*nkh*] Aram'[108] and is then told to 'strike [*nkh*][109] the ground [*'ereṣ*, also 'country, land']', i.e., the acted order is also 'destroy the land [of Aram]'. His response is thus half-hearted; Aram will not be 'completely destroyed'. The *three times* comes to pass in v. 25, but Aramean influence continues in the story of both Israel and Judah (15:37; 16:5–7; 24:2). Jehoash's failure has been explained variously: 'humouring the dying man rather than sharing his convictions',[110] 'limited faith and resolve',[111] or 'tendency to think small'.[112] The intertextual echo of Ahab's action at Aphek with its prophetic denunciation, reinforced by use of *man of God* rather than 'Elisha' (v. 19; cf. 1 Kgs 20:28), points to a matching situation: 'the issue here is not the insufficiency of Jehoash's enthusiasm, but his flagrant disregard for the will of God in holy war'.[113] He has some faith in Yahweh, evidenced by coming to Elisha, but he still sees life and its challenges with human eyes. Elisha's last word, instead of *completely*, is now limited to *three times*. Failure to obey God wholeheartedly always has consequences. Paul writes of 'the wages of sin', and they will become evident in Israel and Judah, but is there still 'the gift of God' that is 'life' (Rom. 6:23)?

b. Life beyond death (13:20–25)

The next paragraph[114] is a striking answer! Beginning simply *Elisha died and was buried* (v. 20), it ends with a dead man who *touched Elisha's bones* and *came to life* (v. 21). The mention of *Moabite raiders*[115] sets the scene for confused mourners throwing *the man's body* (lit. 'the man') into Elisha's grave.[116] Elisha's ministry resulted

---

[108] As is common, Hebrew has the name of the nation or country with English translations varying between 'Aram' and 'Arameans', even in the same verse.

[109] NIV's 'defeated' for the same verb in vv. 19 (second and third instances), 25 misses the repetition.

[110] Gray, p. 599.

[111] Konkel, p. 529.

[112] Hobbs, p. 170.

[113] Seow, p. 238.

[114] Verses 20–21 are a single paragraph in MT.

[115] Moab was last mentioned in 3:26 and will not reappear until 24:2. *Spring* (lit. 'the coming of the year') is ideal after winter rains and during harvest (cf. 2 Sam. 11:1).

[116] Mention of *bones* points to some time after Elisha's death.

in several life-giving events[117] and 'the power of life that has been operative in Israel through this enigmatic figure is at work yet'.[118] Even in times of attack, confusion and death there is life through the prophet. The event may be unique, but readers in exile may see a pointer to life after death for a people who have been attacked and 'thrown' away.[119]

The message of hope comes differently in the following paragraph (vv. 22–25). Framing verses narrate the fulfilment of the *three times* victory of Jehoash, reversing the earlier defeat of Jehoahaz (vv. 22, 24–25; cf. vv. 4–5, 19), but standing out, prominently placed in the middle (v. 23), is a most unexpected theological statement, unique to Kings. The language is redolent of the traditions of the people of God:

(a) *The Lord was gracious to them and had compassion*: the words 'be gracious' (*ḥnn*) and 'have compassion' (*rḥm*) were previously joined together only in the opening of Yahweh's self-revelation (Exod. 33:19; 34:6), which comes after the golden calf incident.[120] That incident is pertinent because 'the sins of Jeroboam son of Nebat', for which every king of Israel (including Jehoash) are condemned, begin with the making of 'golden calves' (see on 1 Kgs 12:28, pp. 135–136). God is willing to show grace and compassion to rebels who cry to him in their distress. Indeed, he *showed concern for them* ['he faced them'], which continues, *he has been unwilling to destroy them or banish* [same verb as 'throw', v. 21] *them from his presence* ['his face'].

(b) The reason given goes back behind Exodus and Sinai, to *his covenant with Abraham, Isaac and Jacob*. Here is the only naming of the patriarchs in all of Judges-Kings, apart from Elijah's prayer on Mount Carmel to 'the Lord, the God of Abraham, Isaac and Israel' (1 Kgs 18:36). In the narrative of 'God's dealings with Judah' there has been

a tension . . . precisely because at one level there seems to be an unconditionality . . . (David will always reign over Judah; cf. 1 Kgs. 11:36; 15:4; 2 Kgs. 8:19), while at another there is undeniable conditionality (David's sons must obey or face dire consequences;

---

[117] 2:19–22; 4:1–7, 38–41, 42–33; 5:14; 6:1–7; 7:1–16.

[118] Brueggemann, p. 433.

[119] The same Hebrew verb is used in v. 23 ('banish') and 17:20 ('thrust').

[120] See also 2 Chr. 30:9; Neh. 9:17; Ps. 86:15; 103:8; 111:4; 112:4; 145:8; Joel 2:13; Jon. 4:2; and the balancing of Isa. 27:11 and 30:18. Influenced by Judaism and Christianity these characteristics are prominent in the fundamental Islamic description, 'Allah, the Merciful, the Compassionate One', though separated from the historical narrative and without the covenantal relationship of promise.

cf. 1 Kgs. 2:4; 8:25; 9:4–9). . . . Second Kings 13:23 now presents
the Abraham promise as analogous to the David promise and
introduces a tension between law and grace . . . . God was *unwilling
to destroy* Israel because of Abraham and was 'unwilling to
destroy' Judah because of David (cf. Hb. *lō' 'ābâ hašhît* in both
2 Kgs. 8:19 and 13:23). The two kingdoms are ultimately being
treated by God in the same way.[121]

The focus is on *Israel*, not only the king. 'It is as though the tradition
continues to advocate for a single, unified Israel that Yhwh will
protect and save.'[122] Right when it seems there is little lasting hope,
we have a story about life given to a corpse and the assertion of
Yahweh's longstanding covenant. But how long is this to last? His
'unwillingness' is *until now* (v. 23, NRSV),[123] but what time is that?
With the subsequent destruction of Samaria it is said that 'the LORD
. . . thrust them from his presence' (17:20). Is that final, the limit of
'unwillingness'? What are Jewish readers in exile to hear? And what
of the northern exiles? This is where the corpse who is given life has
particular relevance. In 'touching' the prophet, the conveyor of
Yahweh's life-giving word, there is hope of '*life*' *after* being 'thrown'.
A close equivalence is in Deuteronomy 4:31: in a context announcing
the judgment of exile comes God's openness to their return 'for the
LORD your God is a merciful [*rahûm*] God; he will not abandon or
destroy[124] you or forget the covenant with your ancestors, which
he confirmed to them by oath.' In the midst of death is the promise
of life.

The words of Yahweh's mercy and compassion resound in the
petitions and praise of the Psalms.[125] Psalm 145 is replete with 'all'
or 'every' (seventeen times). Yahweh's self-description is taken up,
'The LORD is gracious and compassionate, slow to anger and rich in
love' (v. 8; cf. Exod. 34:6). This has been the faith and experience
of Israel,

> but verse 9 [of Ps. 145] immediately universalizes it: "The Lord is
> good *to all*; / he has compassion *on all* he has made." This is then
> repeated with variations at verses 13 and 17 . . . The only exception

---

[121] Provan, pp. 229–230.

[122] W. Brueggemann, 'Stereotype and Nuance: The Dynasty of Jehu', *Catholic
Biblical Quarterly* 70 (2008), p. 24.

[123] NIV's *until this day* equates the phrase here ('*ad 'attâ* as in Gen 32:5; Deut. 12:9;
2 Sam. 19:8) with a more common phrase ('*ad hayyôm hazzeh*) referring to the time
of the writer or editor (as in Gen. 26:33; 32:32; etc.; and in 2 Kings: 2:22; 8:22; 10:27).

[124] The verb *hišhît* as in 2 Kgs 8:19; 13:23.

[125] See above on v. 23.

in this litany to the universality of God's love are the wicked who choose, in their wickedness, to refuse it . . . (Ps. 145:20b).[126]

The NT message of God's grace and compassion to 'all nations' is strikingly foreshadowed in the tragic, often depressing, account of the decline of the nation of Israel. In the midst of disobedient kings, idolatrous people, foreign attackers and raiders – as in the confusion and turmoil of the twenty-first century – there shines the gracious and compassionate God's life-giving covenantal promise to 'Abraham, Isaac and Jacob', a promise of blessing to 'all peoples on earth' (Gen. 12:3). He is unwilling to 'banish . . . from his presence' but is willing for all to turn to him and find life out of death.

[126] C. J. H. Wright, *The Mission of God* (Nottingham: Inter-Varsity Press, 2006), p. 235.

E. To the end of Israel
2 Kings 14 – 17

2 Kings 14:1 – 17:6
16. Kings of Judah and Israel

Kings is like no other national history with its story of failure, but pointing to God and a way forward in hope. These four chapters are a depressing but necessary telling of the northern kingdom's final decline into chaos and death, yet in the midst is an instance of God's gracious deliverance (14:25–27). The contemporaneous story of Judah is mixed, but standing out is the blatant apostasy of king Ahaz (ch. 16). After Elisha's death no prophet plays a key role in the narrative until after the fall of the nation of Israel around seventy years later.[1] While towards the end of the period the prophets Amos and Hosea were active in the north and Micah and Isaiah in the south, they do not appear in these chapters[2] except in the general reference to 'my/his servants the prophets' whose warnings went unheeded (17:13, 23). The story has to be listened to as it leads into sermonic analysis of reasons for Israel's demise and a description of the new mixed population in Samaria (17:7–41). What happened to Israel becomes a forceful warning to Judah – and to subsequent readers.

What is the impact of one generation on the next? In the north, Jehu's reign had ended with commendation for his destruction of the house of Ahab but hesitation regarding his wholehearted commitment to 'the law of the LORD' (10:30–31). As with all northern kings, he continued Jeroboam's religious practices. None of Jehu's promised four dynastic successors (10:30) receives any commendation, although Jeroboam II will be an agent of Yahweh's deliverance. Jehu's example seems to have been solely religious zeal, leading to violent removal of foreign (Phoenician) influence. Quite different was the pattern in Judah, beginning with the less violent coup that

---

[1] Jonah is cited briefly (14:25).
[2] Isaiah is actively involved in the later reign of Hezekiah (chs 19 – 20).

brought Joash to the throne and resulted in temple renovations (chs 11 – 12). His three successors each *did what was right in the eyes of the* LORD, doing everything *his father* (name) did, although the pattern handed down was *not* that of *David*, but initially of *Joash* (14:3), the difference relating to *the high places* (there is no mention of foreign gods).[3]

1. Amaziah king of Judah (14:1–22)

Internal struggle followed Joash's assassination (12:20–21) before *the kingdom was firmly in* Amaziah's *grasp* and the assassins *executed* (v. 5) — and Amaziah himself will be assassinated (v. 19). The narrator however is less interested in explaining tensions than in describing how the king responded to his father's assassination *in accordance with what is written in the Book of the Law of Moses where the* LORD *commanded* (v. 6). David instructed Solomon to 'walk in' the LORD's ways, 'as written in the Law of Moses' (1 Kgs 2:3), but only of Amaziah and later Josiah (23:2) is it explicitly said that they obeyed 'the Law of Moses'. As these are the only instances of 'the law of Moses' in all of Judges-Kings,[4] mention here points to importance for readers. Added emphasis and implied ongoing relevance are seen in full quoting of the law (v. 6b; Deut. 24:16). The principle is cited extensively by Ezekiel, teasing out all variations, in answer to the complaint that the exiles were suffering because of the sins of their ancestors (Ezek. 18; cf. Jer. 31:29–30). Amaziah obeys a law that exemplifies God's own practice. Its citation here is a general message to readers, both to themselves as sinners and in their treatment of others: *each will die for their own sin*.[5]

Examples abound in life of how what one generation does affects the next 'to the third and fourth generation' (Exod. 20:5) but the assertion here is that no one can avoid personal accountability by saying 'I am/we are being punished for the sins of our ancestors' (compare the view of Jesus' disciples, John 9:1–2). Such evasion is a common human trait, ever since Adam blamed 'the woman you put here with me' (Gen. 3:12) – a blaming of one's environment or the givenness of heredity and birth situations. A corollary is that we are to follow God's pattern in treating others. While recognizing

---

[3] See on 1 Kgs 3:2 (pp. 59–60); 14:22–24 (pp. 152–153). Some practices had been removed by Asa, of whom alone is it said that he 'did what was right in the eyes of the LORD, *as his father David had done*' (1 Kgs 15:11–15).

[4] Rare also in Joshua, 8:31, 32; 23:6.

[5] See further on 24:3–4 (p. 361), which seems to say the exilic generation is being punished for the sins of the generation ruled by Manasseh, a possible background of Ezek. 18:2.

situations of group complicity in actions – Kings abounds in instances, especially of worship of other gods – human response to wrongdoing can too readily punish whole families, including children, for the actions of parents, or communities for the actions of individuals, particularly when such groups are of a different social or ethnic background. Feuds can continue for generations. No language of 'collateral damage' or 'teaching a lesson' or 'protecting our way of life' can evade the issue. The challenge is to live in the confidence of receiving God's mercy and so living out his justice and mercy to others.

Amaziah *reigned . . . twenty-nine years* (v. 2) but the only other incidents that interest the narrator involve military action and the king's own violent death. Although there is no editorial evaluation or mention of Yahweh, the defeat of Edomites to the south east (v. 7) could be read as indicating divine favour. Hitherto 'when the king has been generally faithful, Edom has been a vassal of Judah (so in the reign of Jehoshaphat, 1 Kgs 22:47; 2 Kgs 3:8). When the king has been unfaithful, however, Judah has lost control of its neighbor (so in the reign of Joram, 8:20).'[6]

The next venture, that against Israel, is portrayed however as *arrogant* and foolhardy (v. 10). Emboldened by his defeat of Edom, and probably incited by some border warfare,[7] Amaziah seeks confrontation with Jehoash of Israel (v. 8). Hitherto Judah has been the weaker partner in relationship with Israel, but Amaziah now sees himself as strong and so demanding.[8] Jehoash's response shows 'judicious patience'[9] as he uses a recognized literary form of parable,[10] where clearly Amaziah is the *thistle* (or 'thornbush') and Jehoash the *cedar*. The *wild beast* could be either Aram or Assyria – the implication may be that Judah can only survive under the protection of Israel. In the event, Amaziah's self-importance leads to Jehoash strategically attacking *Beth Shemesh*, on Judah's southwestern border. Judah is routed, Amaziah's troops desert him and he himself is captured. Humiliation continues as Jehoash marches on Jerusalem, breaks down a large section of *the wall*, empties *the temple* coffers – previous kings of Judah had at least 'given' such resources as tribute to ensure peace and protection[11] – and takes *hostages* (vv. 11–14). Judah is very much under Israel's control. The

---

[6] Seow, p. 241.

[7] 2 Chr. 25:5–10, 13.

[8] The Edomite force Amaziah defeated was 'ten thousand', the same figure given for Jehoahaz's reduced army (v. 7; cf. 13:7).

[9] Sweeney, p. 365.

[10] Cf. Judg. 9:7–15; Ezek. 17:1–10; 'The Dispute between the Tamarisk and the Date Palm', *ANET*, pp. 592–593; 'The Heron and the Turtle', *COS* 1.178, p. 571–573.

[11] 1 Kgs 14:25–28; 15:17–19; 2 Kgs 12:18–19; and later 2 Kgs 16:7–9; 18:13–16; 24:10–13.

unusually lengthy *Amaziah king of Judah, the son of Joash, the son of Ahaziah* (v. 13) may be an implicit theological evaluation, a suggestion that Amaziah is now following not the ways of Joash (v. 3) but of Ahaziah (8:27). 2 Chronicles 25:14–20 is explicit regarding Amaziah's idolatry following the Edom campaign.

The following passage may appear disjointed, but a flow can be seen. First we are reminded that Jehoash died before Amaziah (vv. 15–16 repeat 13:12–13) and Amaziah *lived* a further *fifteen years* (v. 17), but the narrator moves straight to the manner of his death. He faced solid opposition from people in Jerusalem, as even fleeing about 25 miles (40 km) south-west to the 'sort of second capital'[12] at *Lachish* did not prevent his death (vv. 19–20). The chronology of kings of Judah and Israel at this time is uncertain, with co-regencies likely.[13] A probable scenario is that *Azariah* (v. 21) was Amaziah's co-regent, and hence effective ruler for at least part of the fifteen years, and that with the Jerusalem leaders he pursued peaceful relationships with Jeroboam II of Israel. It is also probable that Amaziah remained a prisoner in Samaria for part of that period (suggested by *lived* rather than 'reigned', v. 17). His return to Jerusalem may have threatened the alliance with Israel, people remembering the previous disastrous years. The text is silent on reasons for the antagonism. Another apparent dislocation is the reference to *Azariah* as the one who *rebuilt Elath and restored it to Judah* (v. 22), a statement one might have expected in the later account of his reign (15:1–7). Its position here is understandable with a literal translation of the rest of v. 22: 'after the king rested with his fathers'. While 'the king' is sometimes seen as Amaziah (so NIV; cf. 2 Chr. 26:2), 'rested with his fathers' is used only of kings who die peacefully, as in this chapter for Jehoash of Israel (v. 16; contrast v. 20).[14] Assuming 'the king' is Jehoash (most likely), it was during the period of co-regency, with Jeroboam II concurrently king of Israel, that Azariah was able to consolidate Amaziah's victory over the Edomites and so control the southern port city of Elath.[15]

Where is God at work during Amaziah's reign? That the story is narrated, even without mentioning God's name, is a reminder that God works out his purposes in the midst of human decisions,

---

[12] Sweeney, p. 366.

[13] Konkel, pp. 677–678; Hobbs, pp. 184–185.

[14] Used for all kings except Nadab, Elah, Zimri, Ahaziah and Joram of Israel, and in Judah Ahaziah, Joash and Amaziah.

[15] See further N. Na'aman, 'Azariah of Judah and Jeroboam II of Israel', *Vetus Testamentum* 43 (1993), pp. 227–234; also Provan, pp. 236–237; Cogan and Tadmor, p. 158.

whether good or bad. The narrator can commend good acts of a king, doing justice in accord with God's law, an example for others to follow, while also showing the consequences of foolish arrogance. We see an example of 'war as folly', the going to war without 'counting the cost' (Luke 14:28–32), against all advice and data. Amaziah received warning but brashly swept that aside: 'My mind's made up; don't confuse me with facts.' Proverbs has much about the 'fool', the term referring not to the naïve, immature or simple (who are to be taught) but to the wilfully obstinate, rejecting all discipline and advice. Amaziah's challenge to Jehoash can be an example of 'war as hobby', 'an endless temptation to government leaders who feel strong, need to flex their muscles, and imagine that such posturing makes them important and/or secure in office'.[16] Amaziah becomes a warning to all who have an inflated view of their own strength and who vaunt this before others, like a 'thistle' before a 'cedar'.

While the narrative is of kings and nations, dangers are present in all human relationships. Amaziah, like other preceding kings, is a warning that beginning well in relationship with God is to be followed by continuing obedience and trust, having a right estimate of oneself in that relationship. Success can lead to a false sense of one's status and resources (compare Deuteronomy 8:10–20). Amaziah's arrogance followed his turning from a devout relationship with God. Paul's advice stands: 'For by the grace given me I say to every one of you: Do not think of yourself more highly than you ought, but rather think of yourself with sober judgment, in accordance with the faith God has distributed to each of you' (Rom. 12:3).[17] Paul's exhortation proceeds, speaking of each being a 'member' of a 'body', having a function in relationship to others, each being 'in Christ': we can only have a right view of ourselves as we continue in relationship to Christ and to one another.

2. Jeroboam II, king of Israel (14:23–29)

In moving from the Amaziah account to that of Jeroboam there is 'an unusual tension . . . The life of the pious southern king ends in calamity, and the fortunes of the impious northern kings go from strength to strength.'[18] Jeroboam has no commendation (v. 24) and yet his reign was the longest of any king of Israel and Israel's territory

---

[16] Brueggemann, p. 447 (pp. 446–447 explore 'war as folly' and 'war as hobby').

[17] 'Faith' may refer to 'stewardship' (what is entrusted); see J. C. Poirier, 'The Measure of Stewardship: *Pistis* in Romans 12:3', *Tyndale Bulletin* 59, 1 (2008), pp. 145–152.

[18] Hobbs, pp. 177–178.

became as extensive as under Solomon.[19] Further, such expansion has been affirmed in a prophetic word, although exceptionally there is a fulfilment formula, *in accordance with the word of the* LORD, *the God of Israel* (v. 25), but no record of the prophecy. The focus will shift from the prophecy *per se* to Yahweh's rationale (vv. 26–27), enough being said to ensure that readers see the expansion as due not to Jeroboam's military superiority (as in verse 28) but Yahweh's work announced beforehand. He is still *the God of Israel.*

The naming of *Jonah son of Amittai, the prophet from Gath Hepher,* but with no other involvement, can now be read in association with the book of Jonah. As noted on 13:23, a statement combining Yahweh's 'grace' and 'compassion' is not common in the OT but is a key affirmation in Jonah 4:2. Jonah is 'angry' that Yahweh shows mercy to repentant Assyrians but 'can proclaim prosperity to wicked Israel. . . . Mercy to unrepentant Israel is his mission, at least as stated in the only historical note he receives in the Deuteronomistic History (2 Kings 14:25).'[20]

God's mercy is expressed more emphatically than in 13:4. The opening of verse 26 is clear: *the* LORD *had seen* the *suffering* of Israel, with *'ŏnî* used of the 'oppression' in Egypt[21] but only here in Kings. Further the combination, *whether slave or free*, was seen hitherto only in announcement of complete destruction of northern dynasties,[22] but now is in a context of deliverance, matching the only other instance in MT, the promise of restoration in Deuteronomy 32:36: 'The LORD will vindicate his people and relent concerning his servants when he sees their strength is gone and no one is left, slave or free.' EVV and most commentators follow LXX in seeing the 'suffering' as being very bitter (v. 26).[23] The only preceding use of 'bitter' for corporate suffering is again relating to Egyptian oppression of the Israelites, the significance of the 'bitter herbs' of the Passover (Exod. 12:8; Num. 9:11).

Another unusual element is the phrase *there was no one to help them. 'zr* ('help') is rare in Judges to Kings. The first instance, significantly, is when Samuel commemorates Yahweh's defeat of the

---

[19] Cf. 1 Kgs 8:65. *Lebo Hamath* is the ideal northern boundary (Num. 13:21), while 'the sea of the Arabah' is equated with *the Dead Sea* (Josh. 3:16; 12:3); Wiseman, pp. 248–249. Cf. the judgment in Amos 6:14.

[20] Konkel, p. 538.

[21] Exod. 3:7, 17; 4:31; Deut. 26:7.

[22] 1 Kgs 14:10; 21:21; 2 Kgs 9:8.

[23] Reading *mārāh* or *hammar*; MT *mōreh* gives 'very rebellious', describing Israel. The motif of 'rebellion' is seen especially in Deut. 9:7, 24; 31:27, and the root *mrh* is elsewhere in Kings only in 1 Kgs 13:21, 26, the disobedient 'man of God' directing attention to Jeroboam I. MT thus associates the 'suffering' and Israel's 'very rebellious' actions, but nevertheless Yahweh 'delivers' – his compassion is thus heightened.

Philistines by erecting a stone named Ebenezer ('stone of help'), saying 'Thus far the LORD has helped us' (1 Sam. 7:12), a key statement prior to the institution of monarchy. The only other instances in Samuel-Kings either are instances of human 'help' that was unsuccessful (2 Sam. 8:5; 1 Kgs 1:7; 20:16) or tell of David's inactivity as he either 'helps' by remaining in the city instead of fighting (2 Sam. 18:3) or is 'helped' by another who prevented David from being killed (2 Sam. 21:17). It is thus likely that the phrase in verse 14 is an echo of 1 Samuel 7: Yahweh is still the one who 'helps' by delivering from attackers, independent of the existence of kingship. Psalm 107:10–14 celebrates Yahweh's actions as a 'helper' who 'delivers',[24] the context similar to the cycle in Judges, including 'rebellion':

> Some sat in darkness, in utter darkness,
>   prisoners suffering in iron chains,
> because they had rebelled against God's commands
>   and despised the plans of the Most High.
> So he subjected them to bitter labour;
>   they stumbled, and there was no one to help.
> Then they cried to the LORD in their trouble,
>   and he saved them from their distress.
> He brought them out of darkness, the utter darkness,
>   and broke away their chains.

In Kings, as in Exodus, it is *the LORD* who *saved them*, with Jeroboam simply an agent. The reason for such unexpected action is not that the people have 'turned to' him, or even 'cried out',[25] but that *the LORD had not said he would blot out the name of Israel from under heaven* (v. 27). The argument from silence (what he had not said) is significant. Once, following the rebellion of the golden calf, he did say he would 'blot out' them (Exod. 32:32–33 = Deut. 9:14). On that occasion, while some died with a plague, God continued with the people of Israel, not just Moses. In the similar warning of Deuteronomy 29:20, while individuals may be judged, the continuation of Israel is obvious. Once again, the experience of the exodus and Sinai provides current hope for the future. 'For all the predictable, formulaic condemnation of the North, these are still Yahweh's people. The theological implication . . . substantiates Yahweh's lingering graciousness toward a people already in principle rejected, but not yet "fated" for "blotting out".'[26]

---

[24] Yahweh is 'helper' in Gen. 49:25; Exod. 18:4; Deut. 33:7, 26, 29; 1 Sam. 7:12; Ps. 10:14; 20:2; 28:7; etc.

[25] See on 13:4, p. 279.

[26] Brueggemann, p. 448.

The Jeroboam account ends with another statement of territorial expansion (v. 28). Control of trade routes from the north and through Moab led to much prosperity – for those in a position to benefit – but Amos was to preach during Jeroboam's reign against the rising social injustice and to warn that territorial expansion was temporary (Amos 6:13–14). God's deliverance did not lead to a lifestyle pleasing to him.

As a whole, Kings reinforces the broad message of Deuteronomy that obedience brings blessing and life but disobedience leads to destruction and death. Israel is urged to 'choose life' (Deut. 30:19), but the story of Kings is leading to death. Nevertheless, particularly in chapters 13 – 14, Yahweh's delivering grace and compassion are to the fore. He continues with the people descended from Abraham, the people he delivered from bitter oppression in Egypt, the people he continued to deliver even when their suffering was a result of his 'anger'. God acts on the basis of his covenantal faithfulness, with mercy. The writer, by placing these notes of hope in the narrative of the northern kingdom, affirms hope for all God's people, Israel and Judah.

How do we respond to the tensions mentioned at the beginning of this block concerning the 'success' of Jeroboam and 'failure' of Amaziah? Mark Galli reflects on

> how hard it is to exorcize the quid pro quo god. *Quid pro quo* is a Latin phrase meaning 'something for something'. The quid pro quo god is one who does something for us if we do something for him, and the one who refuses to do something for us, or even punishes us, if we fail to do something for him. Put this way, it seems impossible that anyone in their right mind would believe in such a god. The rub, of course, is that none of us are in our right mind—that's one of the effects of sin. And one reason we're attracted to the quid pro quo god is that he's a god we can get our minds around. He makes sense. He seems reasonable and fair.[27]

He describes various ways in which as Christians we may live out such a belief in thought and deed, while saying we don't believe in such a god.[28] He continues:

> This is also not to deny that God does indeed discipline those whom he loves (Heb. 12)—but he does so not as a quid pro quo god does but only as a Father. That is, the discipline has nothing

[27] M. Galli, 'Love of Unimaginable Proportions', *Christianity Today* 4 March 2010 <http://www.christianitytoday.com/ct/2010/marchweb-only/19-41.0.html>.

[28] See also P. Yancey, *What's So Amazing About Grace?* (Grand Rapids: Zondervan, 1997).

to do with something we've done or failed to do, but only with the person he wants us to become. It has no relation to our sin, but only a relation to the grace of the One in whose image we are being created, Jesus Christ.

The writer of Kings already knows something of that grace – and our response to the narrative of these two chapters may help us reflect on our image of God and rejoice in his grace. The story of Kings opens our eyes to God's dealings with humanity:

> So the persistent love of God for Israel, carrying them from one generation to another for all the centuries of their ingratitude, rejection, and disobedience concentrates in one story the much larger story of the love of God for the human race for all the generations of their rebellious ways. And it was that love of God for the world that would ultimately lead him to the cross.[29]

3. Azariah (Uzziah) king of Judah (15:1–7)

The narrator's evaluation of any continuing relevance of Azariah's[30] very long reign is evident in the very little detail given! Apart from the standard introductory and concluding formulaic details (vv. 1–4, 6–7), with the same qualified commendation as for previous kings (see p. 288), there is little else. Beyond the previous mention of his restoring Elath (14:22), we read only of his *leprosy* and consequent isolation[31] and death (v. 5). Being ritually unclean (Lev. 13:44–46) restricted his leadership in administrative and judicial matters and in temple ritual, hence the role of his son, *Jotham*. That *the* LORD *afflicted the king with leprosy* may point to punishment, but no reason is given (cf. Gehazi, 5:26–27). Quite different is the long Chronicles account which describes his military ventures, with a strengthened army, and building of fortifications and other structures (2 Chr. 26:6–15) – 'as long as he sought the LORD, God gave him success' (v. 5) – but then he usurped the priestly function of burning incense and was struck with leprosy (vv. 16–20). The focus of the writer of Kings made Azariah's leprosy 'indeed a defining

---

[29] C. J. H. Wright, *The God I Don't Understand* (Grand Rapids: Zondervan, 2008), p. 115.

[30] Azariah ('Yah has helped') is also named Uzziah ('Yah is my strength'), both names being used in Kings, but generally Uzziah in Chronicles (except 1 Chr. 3:12) and Isaiah.

[31] The exact significance of the Hebrew translated *a separate house* is unclear, apart from some isolation; see Wiseman, p. 251; Konkel, p. 548.

mark of his long rule ... that made his rule a deep shadow in the history of kingship'.[32]

The long reigns of Jeroboam II in Israel and Azariah in Judah were times of peace and geographical expansion through military ventures, leading to economic prosperity. Such are the kinds of success that national historians generally praise, the goal of many nations still today. These were, however, also times of social injustice, great disparity between rich and poor, internal oppression and religious formality. Just as Amos challenged the Northern Kingdom so Isaiah began his ministry in the time of Azariah. The 'leprosy' evaluation of the writer of Kings is supported by the words of Isaiah:

> Their land is full of silver and gold;
>   there is no end to their treasures.
> Their land is full of horses;
>   there is no end to their chariots.
> Their land is full of idols ...
> So people will be brought low
>   and everyone humbled –
>   do not forgive them. ...
> The LORD enters into judgment
>   against the elders and leaders of his people:
> 'It is you who have ruined my vineyard;
>   the plunder from the poor is in your houses.
> What do you mean by crushing my people
>   and grinding the faces of the poor?'
>   declares the Lord, the LORD Almighty. (Isa. 2:7–9; 3:14–15)

Azariah is another example in Kings that starting well does not necessarily mean finishing well. 'These things happened to them as examples and were written down as warnings for us, on whom the culmination of the ages has come. So, if you think you are standing firm, be careful that you don't fall!' (1 Cor. 10:11–12). Throughout history, examples abound where public failure overshadows and reinterprets previous achievements. What would have been our evaluation of Judas Iscariot if the narrative had stopped at the Last Supper, if all we knew was his being with Jesus and having responsibility as treasurer? Not that failure need be final: reflect on how we might have evaluated Peter at the time of his confession of Christ and then at the trial of Jesus – but Jesus re-commissions him and we move on to Pentecost and beyond. Repentance and restoration then reinterpret past failures!

---

[32] Brueggemann, p. 453.

4. In Israel, five kings and four coups (15:8–31)

> All of them are hot as an oven;
> they devour their rulers.
> All their kings fall,
> and none of them calls on me. (Hos. 7:7)

After the stability, peace and prosperity – with injustice – of the long reign of Jeroboam II in Israel, the following years bring chaotic political turmoil with internal violence and the threatening resurgence of Assyrian power. The reigns of successive kings are *six months* (v. 8), *one month* (v. 13), *ten years* (v. 17), less than *two years* (v. 23), *twenty years* (v. 27), four of the five kings coming to a violent end with a palace coup (vv. 10. 14, 25, 30). The standard regnal introductions and conclusions take up much of the block. Additional information is almost entirely details of the assassinations, sometimes involving wider violence (vv. 16,[33] 25[34]), and the attacks of the Assyrian *Pul*, i.e., *Tiglath-Pileser*[35] (vv. 19–20, 29). Tensions arising from Assyrian expansion could have triggered the coups.[36] The cost for the nation of Israel in terms of tribute and loss of territory were high, and by the end of Pekah's reign the fall of the north is only a decade away.

How does the turmoil relate to Yahweh's previous compassion in 'saving' the people during the reign of Jeroboam II (14:26–27)? As he saw the worship of Baal and Asherah and the blatant violence and injustice in society, Hosea expressed Yahweh's anguish vividly in the marriage language of chapters 1 – 3 and the emotion of chapter 11. There is judgment on persistent rebellion, but beyond is hope in Yahweh's compassion. Later, facing the destruction of Jerusalem and exile, Jeremiah and Ezekiel come to see that, despite countless warnings and God's acts of deliverance, judgment is inevitable, but through the judgment God will restore and renew. Paul likewise, especially in Romans, grapples with ways in which God allows human sin to work its way to destruction yet amazingly, beyond that, puts us right with himself in Christ. The pattern can be repeated in individual lives and personal relationships. A key passage where

---

[33] An Israelite behaves as cruelly as Arameans (8:12) and Ammonites (Amos 1:13).

[34] *Argob and Arieh* are interpreted as people in NIV, NRSV, and place names in NJPSV. See Wiseman, p. 255; Hobbs, pp. 200–201; Sweeney, p. 374.

[35] *Pul* is a short form or nickname for *Tiglath-Pileser* III; see Cogan and Tadmor, pp. 171–172.

[36] The turmoil of the period, relationship of biblical statements to Assyrian records, chronology and translation of some phrases are discussed particularly in Hobbs, pp. 196–205.

Christ speaks of relationships within a congregation deals with discipline of persistent sin: the person is to be 'treated as a pagan or tax collector' (Matt. 18:15–17). The person is excluded from Christian fellowship, but compassion continues: as with 'pagans or tax-collectors' those who (re)turn to Christ are welcome.[37]

Jehu's dynasty that started with assassinations – but with promise of renewal of Yahwism – ends in the assassination of Zechariah after only six-months reign (v. 8). Included in the horrific tale is a strong reminder of Yahweh's sovereignty: 'This was the word of Yahweh which he promised to Jehu, "Four generations of your descendants will sit on the throne of Israel" – and it was so' (v. 12; literal translation following MT order). One certainty through the turmoil and tragedies of history, then and now, is that God keeps his word and is working out his purposes.

5. Jotham king of Judah (15:32–38)

At least in Judah the reign of Jotham shines a glimmer of light. He is able to improve defences, the *Upper Gate* (v. 35) being on the relatively flat and open part of the city and so the direction from which most attacks came.[38] A parenthesis (v. 37) introduces the attack on Judah by an alliance between Aram and Israel. The Syro-Ephraimite[39] war (735–732 BC) was an attempt to force Judah to join an alliance against the Assyrian threat and it is evident that Jotham died in the early days, leaving his successor Ahaz to handle the crisis.

6. Ahaz king of Judah, Assyria and apostasy (16:1–20)

After decades of peace and prosperity *Ahaz* became *king of Judah* at a time of uncertainty. Assyrian influence was resurging under Tiglath-Pileser III (745–727 BC), with fearsome military might soon enforcing control over nations of the Levant. Emperors exacted regular tribute from loyal vassals, but turned the realms of rebel kings into Assyrian provinces (as was to happen to Israel). Assyrian dominance continued for more than a century until decline from 626 to 612 BC (fall of Nineveh) in face of Babylon's increasing power. Final defeat was in 605 BC at Carchemish (on the Euphrates

---

[37] Cf. 1 Cor. 5:1–5, a specific instance of excommunication with a view to being 'saved'.

[38] 2 Chr. 27 describes other building activity strengthening defences and a successful campaign against the Ammonites.

[39] Syria is the later Greek name of Aram, while Ephraim was the dominant tribe in Israel.

in northern Syria).[40] As mentioned above (15:17), *Rezin king of Aram* and *Pekah . . . king of Israel* had formed an alliance to resist Assyria and sought to force Judah to join. Ahaz's response and his consequent actions are the subject matter of the Kings narrative and the background of Isaiah 7:1 – 9:7.

The standard opening (vv. 2–4) is damning in its detailed theological evaluation. Unlike his predecessors there is not even qualified commendation,[41] only severe condemnation. Threefold apostasy is described as *he followed the ways of the kings of Israel*[42] and *the detestable practices* of the Canaanite nations, and himself participated in the fertility cult worship of the people outside Jerusalem. To be identified with *the kings of Israel* at the very time when Israel is racing towards doom raises questions as to the basis for Judah continuing if there is no difference. The description of forbidden Canaanite practices[43] which led to *the Lord* having *driven* them *out before the Israelites* is a reminder of Yahweh's promised judgment on his own people should they do the same.[44] In the reign of Rehoboam, Solomon's son, the people 'set up for themselves *high places*, sacred stones and Asherah poles on every *high hill and under every spreading tree*' (1 Kgs 14:23, emphasis added), contrary to the Deuteronomic prohibition (Deut. 12:2), but now the king himself participates in these practices whereby people seek safety and well-being. Here is another portent of disaster for Judah, as for Israel (17:10–11). Ahaz's failure to show loyalty and trust in Yahweh is the lens through which we are to read his leadership decisions. Faith cannot be separated from public life and decision-making.

Only the 'bare bones'[45] are given of the attack by *Rezin* and *Pekah* (vv. 5–6), a contrast to the detail in *Ahaz's* consequent actions (in verses 7–18 he is the subject of all verbs except in verse 9, the Assyrian king, and verses 11, 16, where Uriah the priest obeys the king's orders). The narrator's evaluation is clear: the attack merely sets the scene for the king's disastrous actions. The opening verse (v. 5) mirrors

---

[40] A. K. Grayson, 'Assyria, Assyrians' and B. E. Kelle and B. A. Strawn, 'History of Israel 5: Assyrian Period', *DOTHB*, pp. 97–105, 458–478. Excellent maps are in T. Dowley, ed., *The Baker Atlas of Christian History* (Grand Rapids: Baker, 1997), pp. 43–46, and Y. Aharoni *et al.*, ed., *The Macmillan Bible Atlas*, third edn. (New York: Macmillan, 1993), pp. 110–116.

[41] Cf. 12:2–3; 14:3–4; 15:3–4, 34–35.

[42] The only other Judahite king of whom this is said is Jehoram, who was married to a daughter of Ahab (8:18).

[43] Whether 'made his son pass through the fire' (v. 3, nrsv) always involved actual 'sacrifice' (niv) is much debated; cf. Deut. 18:10; 2 Kgs 17:17; 21:6; 23:10; Jer. 7:31; 19:5; 32:35; Ezek. 16:20–21; 23:39. See Wiseman, pp. 260–61; Cogan and Tadmor, pp. 266–267; Hobbs, p. 213.

[44] Deut. 8:19–20; 18:9–12; 28:36.

[45] Hobbs, p. 209.

Isa. 7:1, there introducing an account of Isaiah's message to a fearfully trembling Ahaz and his court. The Isaianic message has three components: (1) Rezin and Pekah are nothing but 'two smouldering stubs of fire-wood' (Isa. 7:4); (2) a warning that 'if you do not stand firm in your faith, you will not stand at all' (Isa. 7:9b);[46] and (3) Assyria will prove to be a ravaging destroyer of the nation (7:18–25). Isaiah's message 'must have seemed ludicrous, insofar as it did not come with a relief column',[47] but Ahaz's response, failing to trust in Yahweh, shows panic and short-sightedness. Fear affects what we see! Isaiah is realistic concerning the short-term threat: the attacking forces 'could ill afford to waste much time in a protracted siege while Aram's borders with Assyria lay open to assault'[48] and Jerusalem could easily withstand a short siege. Further, the appeal to Assyria, initiated by Ahaz, brought Judah under Assyria's demanding suzerainty. Pointedly the final words in the Kings account of Ahaz, preceding the standard death notice, are *in deference to the king of Assyria* (v. 18).

Ahaz seeks help from *Tiglath-Pileser, king of Assyria*, humbly describing himself as *your servant and your son* (v. 7 NRSV).[49] For the first time a king of Judah comes as supplicant and brings in Assyrian influence.[50] The narrator's language exposes Ahaz's faithlessness and folly: it is Yahweh alone to whom kings and people are to cry *save me*;[51] there is a mirroring of the recent action of the northern Menahem, where the results were loss of territory and deportation of Israelites (15:19–20, 29–30); what Ahaz sends is the same as had been taken when Israel defeated Judah during Amaziah's reign (14:14); and the *gift* sent uses not the normal word for tribute (*minḥâ*, as in 17:3, 4) but *šōḥad*, 'bribe'. Such is meant to be an incentive for favourable action, but the receiving of 'bribes' is prohibited in the Pentateuch,[52] and the language shows that 'the writer took exception to this appropriation of temple property'.[53]

In an ironic echo of times when Yahweh 'listened to' the cry of people (13:4), *the king of Assyria complied* ('listened to him'; v. 9),

---

[46] Hebrew has a rhyming play on words *'im lō' ta'ămînû kî lō' tē'āmēnû*.

[47] Sweeney, p. 380.

[48] Ibid.

[49] NIV interprets 'son' as *vassal*. Whether historically Ahaz was already a vassal, and so appealing to his suzerain for help, or whether this initiates the relationship, is unclear due to incomplete Assyrian records. Whether 'son' is a term used by a vassal is also debatable. See Hobbs, p. 214; Cogan and Tadmor, pp. 187, 191.

[50] Israel has already been a vassal: Jehu of Israel is portrayed on the earlier Black Obelisk of Shalmaneser (see on 10:32–33, pp. 263–264, n. 40), and a stela of Adad Nirari V indicates Jehoash of Israel as a tributary (Sweeney, p. 380).

[51] See on 13:5, p. 280.

[52] Deut. 10:17; 16:19; 27:25; cf. 1 Sam. 8:3.

[53] Cogan and Tadmor, p. 188.

capturing Damascus, deporting Arameans to their original homeland (cf. Amos 9:7) and killing the Aramean king. This may have instigated the assassination of Pekah of Israel as Hoshea became a vassal (15:30; 17:3).

If using temple treasures as a 'bribe' is criticized, a new altar receives even more narrative attention. What was Ahaz doing when *he saw an altar in Damascus* and what was the motivation in his sending *to Uriah the priest a sketch of the altar, with detailed plans for its construction* (v. 10)? Elsewhere in the OT there is 'a close connection between "seeing" and "acting" which often carries with it the sense of misdeed or sin'.[54] Although some have interpreted the altar as being Assyrian, adopted by Ahaz as an act of subservience,[55] Assyrian policy did not require vassals to worship Assyrian gods and Assyrian ritual did not include whole burnt offerings or sprinkling of blood (the later 2 Chronicles 28:23 refers to 'the gods of Damascus'). The appeal may well have been the impressive aesthetics, with size one factor (v. 15), the existing Jerusalem temple *bronze altar* being small (1 Kgs 8:64).[56] The ready implementation by *Uriah the priest* (vv. 11, 16; associated with Isaiah as 'a reliable witness', Isa. 8:2) suggests that he himself saw no conflict with Yahweh worship, and the sacrifices listed in detail (v. 15) are unexceptional. While the smaller *bronze altar* is moved, Ahaz uses it personally.[57] Thus, on the surface, one might see a positive act by Ahaz, enhancing the temple grandeur with a new altar for sacrifices to Yahweh.

There are however features that raise questions. The theological evaluation of Ahaz (vv. 3–4; matched by Isaiah) denies his commitment to Yahweh alone (2 Chr. 28:23 describes him as explicitly offering to 'the gods of Damascus'). Second is the way in which his actions as *king* dominate: while the simple 'Ahaz' is seen in verses 7–8, in verses 10–18 it is always *King Ahaz* or *the king*, heightened in the key, drawn-out verse 12: 'And the king returned from Damascus and the king saw the altar and the king approached the altar and ascended it' (literal translation).[58] Thirdly, the Hebrew word

[54] Hobbs, p. 215, listing Gen. 3:6; 6:2; 12:15; 34:2; 38:2; 2 Sam. 11:2. See also v. 12.

[55] E.g., Gray, p. 635.

[56] For discussion of Assyrian policy and practices and of possible background of the altar, see Hobbs, pp. 215–218; Cogan and Tadmor, pp. 192–193.

[57] The exact content of 'to seek, look for' is unclear: NIV *use . . . for seeking guidance*; NRSV 'to inquire'; NLT 'for my personal use'; NJPSV 'I will decide about'. The word is used of general prayer or worship in Ps. 27:4; cf. the similar *drš* in Deut. 12:5. Provan, *ZIBBC*, pp. 175–177, argues for divination.

[58] The final *wayya'al* can be either 'and he went up' (NRSV, NJPSV, NIV mg; Hobbs; Cogan and Tadmor) or 'he caused to go up (=offer)', hence NIV *presented offerings* (also Sweeney), although usually what is 'offered' is specified. Details of offerings follow in the next verse, each with its own verb.

order in verse 14, followed in NIV and NRSV, interrupts the narrative flow and draws attention to *the bronze altar that stood before the LORD*, suggesting demotion in the king's actions. We see mirrored Jeroboam's innovations as king of Israel (1 Kgs 12:26–33). Finally, his actions continue uninterrupted with other changes (vv. 17–18) until the final dénouement, *in deference to the king of Assyria*, an *inclusio* with verse 10.[59]

Ahaz may well have thought he had succeeded: he had survived the attack by Aram and Israel, shown he would be a loyal vassal to the new superpower Assyria, and modernized the temple in terms of 'current international fashions', a process of 'acculturation to the practices of the Assyrian empire . . . which would reach new heights in the mid-seventh century in the days of King Manasseh'.[60] The financial cost was worth it – or was it? The biblical writer says otherwise: this was not *right in the eyes of the LORD* (v. 2). Ahaz was more concerned to be well thought of by *the king of Assyria* (v. 18) than by Yahweh: the new altar, modelled in detail on that seen in Damascus when he went to meet Tiglath-Pileser, showed that 'YHWH would be subservient to Assur'.[61]

While Hebrews 11 has its list of people of faith, of those who have 'confidence in what we hope for and assurance of what we do not see', Ahaz is a prime exemplar of those who do not trust (Isa. 7:9) but rely on a distorted, short-term tunnel vision. He represents all who see solutions using political strategy and economic resources as means of self-protection and success. In contrast, Ahaz's son Hezekiah will grapple positively with what is involved in 'trust' in the face of Assyrian might (chs 18 – 20).

While Ahaz declined a sign from Isaiah, he was given the sign of 'Immanuel', God-with-us (Isa. 7:13–14). As Ahaz was challenged whether to trust in God's presence or to experience that presence in judgment, so the coming of Christ, even at his birth, became a challenge either to trust and worship or to endeavour to protect one's own (precarious) status and social-wellbeing: Joseph, Mary and the foreign magi trusted, while Herod and the religious leaders of the day sought to protect their own small worlds (Matt. 1:18 – 2:23). To trust in God is not to retreat from hard decisions, nor to withdraw into passive isolation, but to live in the real world of power-struggles and turmoil, whether Pekah, Rezin and Tiglath-Pileser, or Herod and Archelaus, or any power in the world today, be it military, political, economic or religious. The sign of Immanuel continues to require response.

[59] As Assyrians did not interfere in the worship of vassals, this was a voluntary act, possibly linked with the metal needed for tribute.

[60] Cogan and Tadmor, p. 193.

[61] Sweeney, p. 384.

The historical context of Ahaz is of a nation that is the people of Yahweh, and so 'trust' relates to national decisions in the light of Yahweh's covenantal promises. How might this be worked out when churches and individual believers are being attacked? As citizens of a country it is right to look to governmental involvement and protection within the laws of the land and responsibility for justice. At the same time, this narrative may help reflection on prior allegiance, God or 'my country', the glory of God among the nations or personal status and security.

Ahaz's building of a new altar can be a mirror to look at cultural forms of worship. Just as Solomon had made use of contemporary Phoenician patterns in temple design and ornamentation, so now an international cultural pattern is being copied, ostensibly for the worship of Yahweh – and is not a more magnificent altar God-honouring? The history of God's people provides many examples of ways in which faith, life and worship have adopted or adapted, or resisted, widespread cultural forms – and of ensuing debates. Hellenistic culture brought its challenges and opportunities to Jews (after 333 BC with Alexander the Great's final defeat of the Persians), with many conflicts especially in Jerusalem as evident in writings from the Maccabean period; the early church struggled with relationships between Jewish and Gentile believers; Greek philosophy brought its thought forms and language; and the Constantinian era saw major changes in worship and practice. The story could continue, right through to 'music in worship' in recent decades, and active global debates over 'contextualization' and 'inculturation'. Debate shows many factors are involved, and it is always easier to see ways in which others may have become captive to a dominant culture.[62] This chapter becomes a mirror focusing light on the centrality of motivation. Are changes a matter of acceptance, adopting cultural norms that are contrary to the way of Christ, lessening 'the offence of the cross' (Gal. 5:11)? Or is the drive missiological (1 Cor. 9:19–23), an outworking of the work of the Spirit who speaks to all 'in our native language' (Acts 2:8)? Is the action seeking to please 'the LORD' or 'the king of Assyria'?

[62] See papers from the Lausanne Movement 'Contextualization Revisited' Consultation, Haslev, Denmark, 1997, <http://www.lausanne.org/haslev-1997/overview.html>; C. Ott, S. J. Strauss, *Encountering Theology for Mission* (Grand Rapids: Baker, 2010), pp. 265–291, on 'Contextualization and Mission'. S.-C. Rah, *The Next Evangelicalism: Releasing the Church from Western Cultural Captivity* (Downers Grove: InterVarsity Press, 2009) is a challenge to practices in Western churches.

7. Hoshea, last king of Israel (17:1–6)

Hoshea's introduction tantalizes: he is the only Israelite king of whom it is said *but not like the kings of Israel who preceded him* (v. 2), but the text is silent as to how and whether he changed the longstanding religious policies of the north. All we are told concerns his relationship with Assyria. Initially a vassal under Tiglath-Pileser III's successor *Shalmaneser* V (726–722 BC), he may have sensed some Assyrian weakness and sought independence through plotting with Egypt (v. 4). As a result he is *seized* and *put . . . in prison* and is heard of no more. Heavily fortified *Samaria* is besieged for three years, until it finally succumbs and the population is *deported . . . to Assyria*, dispersed over a wide area (v. 6; 18:11). The Assyrians may have been the first empire to use deportation as a method of preventing subsequent local rebellion (cf. 16:9), dispersion being also a means to lessen ethnic identity.[63] The northern kingdom of Israel, the nation of 'ten tribes' (1 Kgs 11:31), has come to an end. That dramatic point is where the writer pauses the narrative for lengthy sermonic analysis.

[63] After the death of Shalmaneser V, Sargon II finally captured Samaria and deported the Israelites (see 15:29 for earlier deportations). Using Assyrian documents, K. L. Younger, Jr., 'The Deportation of the Israelites', *Journal of Biblical Literature* 117 (1998), pp. 201–227, discusses the different policies and their impact on Israel. Brief comments are in Walton, Matthews and Chavalas, p. 403, and Hobbs, pp. 230–231. For identification of the places named here, see Sweeney, pp. 393–394, and Cogan and Tadmor, p. 197.

2 Kings 17:7–41
17. Understanding change to Israel and in Israel

The dramatic end of the nation of Israel is a time for reassessment. How is one to understand God and his purposes in the light of this disaster, and what of the future? What does this imply for Judah? As at other major transitions in the narrative of Deuteronomy to Kings there is lengthy sermonic commentary.[1] It is 'saturated with the most poignantly insistent phrasing of the book of Deuteronomy that is the norm and interpretive standard',[2] some terms appearing in Kings only here. After reflection on the fate of Israel (vv. 7–23) come description and reflection on changes in population of the northern region (vv. 24–41). Although Judah is mentioned explicitly only in verses 13, 18–19, hints throughout show that the sermon is addressed to the southern nation: it is *about* Israel *to* Judah. There are warnings if Judah acts like Israel, and the judgment of verse 20 includes Judah (see below).

Just as Paul and the writer to Hebrews use OT passages as warnings,[3] so this sermon continues to speak across the generations to God's covenant people. Here is a stern reminder of God's grace in deliverance and his patient and persistent warning of the consequences of deliberately and continually choosing to live outside the covenantal relationship. If read in narrative time, i.e., following the storyline of Kings, the sermon is a warning to Judah at a time soon after the fall of Samaria and its subsequent resettlement. The readers of Kings however are exiles in Babylon (see below on verses 19–20) – as well as all subsequent generations to the present. The sermon affirms that

[1] The structure of Deuteronomy as sermons of Moses before entry into the land; and Josh. 1; 23; Judg. 2:10–23; 1 Sam. 12:6–25; 2 Sam. 7; and 1 Kgs 8:22–53.
[2] Brueggemann, p. 477.
[3] E.g., 1 Cor. 10:1–13; Heb. 12:18–29; cf. Rom. 15:4.

persistent idolatry leads to destruction, a result of not accidents of history but an act of God. That in itself becomes a pointer to ways forward. God has made a *covenant . . . with their ancestors* (vv. 15, 38) and he still calls for people to worship him alone (with the consequences of not doing so being clear). The God who *brought them up out . . . from under the power* ['hand'] *of Pharaoh* (v. 7), but who now *gave them into the hands of plunderers* (v. 20), is still *he who will deliver you from the hand of all your enemies* (v. 39). That may be but a glimmer of hope for exiles, but centuries later Zechariah, father of John the Baptist, 'prophesied' using similar phrases:

> He has raised up a horn of salvation for us
> in the house of his servant David
> (as he said through his holy prophets of long ago),
> salvation from our enemies
> and from the hand of all who hate us –
> to show mercy to our ancestors
> and to remember his holy covenant,
> the oath he swore to our father Abraham:
> to rescue us from the hand of our enemies,
> and to enable him to serve him without fear
> in holiness and righteousness before him all our days.
> (Luke 1:69–75)

As Paul could affirm, 'no matter how many promises God has made, they are "Yes" in Christ. And so through him the "Amen" is spoken by us to the glory of God' (2 Cor. 1:20).

1. Learning from the fall of the nation of Israel (17:7–23)

'Balance and form' are seen with each of two parts beginning 'with a general statement (vv. 7–9a, 14), which is followed by a specific catalog of misdeeds (vv. 9b–12, 15–18), which is followed by a warning. In the first case the prophets had warned Israel (v. 13), and in the second, Israel stands as a warning to Judah (v. 19).'[4] The conclusion (vv. 20–23) recapitulates. The opening focuses immediately on *the Israelites* (v. 7) and *they* remain the centre of attention throughout, with *kings* (v. 8) and *Jeroboam* (vv. 21–22) mentioned only in asides to explain what the people did. While the preceding narrative may have routinely condemned royal religious policies of Jeroboam and his successors, the people are responsible for their own actions, with a history predating the monarchy.

---

[4] Hobbs, p. 227.

In words resembling the prologue and first of the Ten Commandments we read of *the* LORD *their God, who had brought them up out of Egypt from under the power of Pharaoh king of Egypt,* but contrary to the commandment *they worshipped other gods* (v. 7; cf. Exod. 20:2–3). The verb *yr'*, often translated 'worship' throughout the chapter[5] (so NIV, NRSV, NJPSV), occurs in Kings with Yahweh or gods as object only in this chapter, but it is a key word in Deuteronomy where EVV generally translate 'fear' or 'revere'.[6] In Deuteronomy 'fear of Yahweh' is predominantly linked with keeping the commandments, with other instances of the verb exhorting to not 'be afraid' of enemies or obstacles in entering the land. While to an English reader 'worship' might suggest only religious activity (and in some circles narrowed even to singing!), in biblical usage 'fear the LORD' embraces undivided allegiance, expressed in worship that is inseparably associated with trust in God in all areas of life, obeying his instructions.[7] The people's failure to 'fear' Yahweh alone reverberates throughout this chapter.

While contemporary prophecies of Amos and Hosea in the north and Micah and Isaiah in the south often mention social injustice, violence and oppression of the poor, such are not explicit here, although implicit in phrases such as *the practices of the nations* (v. 8) and failure to obey *the entire Law that I commanded your ancestors* (v. 13). The contrast between two ways is even sharper in Hebrew: *decrees* (*ḥuqqôt/ḥuqqîm*) that are part of Yahweh's covenant (as in verses 13, 15, 34),[8] appears only in this chapter in Kings for the *practices* of the nations also.[9] The people have chosen one over the other, focused explicitly in religious practice, the setting up of other objects, places and forms of worship (vv. 9b–12; 15b; 16b–17).

Not only the northern kingdom is indicted, for the combination *sacred stones and Asherah poles on every high hill and under every spreading tree* (v. 10) has previously been mentioned only in the reigns of kings of Judah, Rehoboam and Ahaz, the first and the latest after Solomon (1 Kgs 14:23; 2 Kgs 16:4). As often in Kings, the term *Israelites* ('children of Israel', vv. 7, 8,[10] 9) can signify the people of both kingdoms: they are the ones whom God *brought . . . up out of*

---

[5] With object either Yahweh (vv. 25, 28, 36, 39) or 'other gods' (vv. 7, 35, 37, 38).

[6] Deut. 4:10; 5:29[26]; 6:2, 13, 24; 8:6; 10:12, 20; 13:4; 14:23; 17:19; 28:58; 31:12, 13; in Samuel only in another transitional sermon, Samuel's address to the people after the anointing of Saul as king, 1 Sam. 12:14, 18, 24.

[7] Hence 'the fear of Yahweh is [the beginning/principle of] wisdom' (Job 28:28; Ps. 111:10; Prov. 1:7; 9:10; 15:33; Mic. 6:9). See H. F. Fuhs, '*yārē*', *TDOT* 6, pp. 290–315; M. V. Van Pelt and W. C. Kaiser, Jr., '*yr*' I', *NIDOTTE* 2, pp. 527–533.

[8] 29 times in Deuteronomy.

[9] Cf. *ḥuqqôt* for both the prohibited 'practices, customs' of the nations and Yahweh's 'statutes, laws' in Lev. 18:3–4; 20:22–23.

[10] NIV *them*; cf. NRSV, 'the people of Israel'.

Egypt and before whom he *had driven out [the nations]* – and they are the ones now worshipping other gods. They may have thought they were worshipping Yahweh, but cultic embellishments were 'practices unauthorized by YHWH, yet attributed by them to divine command' (v. 9).[11] The word translated *idols* (*gillulîm*; v. 12) is also in accounts of both kingdoms. Its only preceding instances in Kings relate to Asa of Judah removing 'idols his ancestors had made' and Ahab of Israel 'going after idols, like the Amorites the LORD drove out before the Israelites' (1 Kgs 15:12; 21:26). Subsequently we read of the worship of Manasseh and his son Amon and the removal of 'idols' by Josiah (2 Kgs 21:11, 21; 23:24). The practice was endemic at the time of Jerusalem's destruction, with 'idols' prominent in Ezekiel (39 times).

The horror of persistent idolatrous behaviour is portrayed not only over against the exodus and entry in the land, along with giving of the law, and not only by contrasting the *practices* of *the nations* and *the decrees* of Yahweh, but also in repeated exhortation to the whole people through *my servants the prophets* to *turn* (v. 13). 'Turn' is a single word summary of the message, a theme 'in almost all the important passages which enable us to recognize [the editor's] intention . . . A return will reverse the judgment, though it might already have been decreed [cf. 23:25].'[12] Tragically, *they would not listen and were as stiff-necked as their ancestors* (v. 14), the sole instance of 'stiff-necked' in Joshua-Kings. Here is another word that recalls the exodus: it was after the golden-calf incident that Yahweh forgives and makes his covenant with the people who are 'stiff-necked'.[13] 'Stiff-necked' then becomes a motif in Deuteronomy in exhortation before entering the land.[14] *Trust* (v. 14; *'mn* hif.) is a key word in the Isaiah account of Ahaz and the Syro-Ephraimite war (see above on 16:5–9, p. 300) and will come to the fore in the immediately following narrative of Hezekiah (chs 18 – 20; although there a different Hebrew word).

Idolatry is a failure to rely on God, instead relying on what is in fact *worthless* (v. 15). *Hebel* is widely used in the OT, its meaning seen by associated words:[15] it is a 'vapour, (transitory) breath' (Ps.

---

[11] Cogan and Tadmor, p. 205. The verb *ḥph* occurs only here and earlier commentators linked it with another verb meaning 'hide, cover' hence NIV and NRSV, *secretly did* (cf. *DCH*). Similar to Cogan and Tadmor, Provan suggests 'overlaid' (p. 251; cf. *HALOT*, 'ascribe, impute'), while Konkel (p. 577) notes the early understanding of LXX 'clothed themselves (with words)' (*NETS*).

[12] H. W. Wolff, 'The Kerygma of the Deuteronomistic Historical Work', pp. 90–91 (McConville and Knoppers, pp. 69–70).

[13] Exod. 32:9; 33:3, 5; 34:9.

[14] Deut. 9:6, 13; 10:16; 31:27.

[15] *DCH* lists associated words; see also K. Seybold, '*Hebel*', *TDOT* 3, pp. 313–320.

62:9; 144:4; Isa. 57:13);[16] 'fleeting, insubstantial' (Ps. 39:6; 78:33; 94:11); 'empty, useless' (Isa. 30:7; 49:4). It is the key motif running through Ecclesiastes, and a feature of polemic against idols, seen earlier in condemnation of Israel in the reigns of Elah and Omri (1 Kgs 16:13, 26).[17] Sadly, worshippers who create a god according to their own desires end up like their god, they *themselves became worthless* (or 'insubstantial'; also Jer. 2:5).[18] The tragedy is that God's people, who were to be his 'treasured possession . . . a kingdom of priests . . . a holy nation' bringing blessing to the nations by being different (Exod. 19:5–6; cf. Deut. 4:5–8), have simply *imitated the nations around them* (v. 15; cf. Exod. 23:24; Lev. 18:3).

The indictment continues (vv. 16–17), again covering both Israel and Judah. The *two idols cast in the shape of calves* (v. 16a) recalls Jeroboam's innovations, although *cast* ('molten') echoes the golden calf at Sinai.[19] The first mention of worshipping *starry hosts* will be Manasseh,[20] who also *practised divination and sought omens*,[21] while previously Ahaz 'passed his son through fire' (16:3).[22] In narrative time, it can be said that *the LORD was very angry with Israel and removed them from his presence. Only the tribe of Judah was left* (v. 18), but by the time of writing *Judah . . . followed*. The result was that *the LORD rejected all the people* ['seed'] *of Israel* (v. 20; cf. 23:27). The people have *rejected his decrees and the covenant* (v. 15), so he *rejected* them as finally *he thrust them from his presence*.

Is this the absolute end? Once more, phrasing occurs only here in Kings with echoes of earlier times. Now is the sending of *plunderers* (v. 20), an echo of Judges 2:14,[23] but then he sent 'judges, who saved them' (Judg. 2:16; cf. 1 Sam. 14:48). Surrounded by 'rejection' and 'thrusting from his presence' (cf. 13:23) is the surprising phrase 'the

---

[16] Possibly the sense in the name known in English as Abel.

[17] See also Deut. 32:21; Jer. 2:5; 8:19; 10:3, 8, 15; 14:22; 16:19; 51:18; Jon. 2:8. In D. C. Fredericks and D. J. Estes, *Ecclesiastes and the Song of Songs* (Apollos Old Testament Commentary [Nottingham: Apollos; Downers Grove: InterVarsity Press, 2010], pp. 23–31, 46–54), Fredericks argues persuasively for the basic meaning of 'temporary' as applying in Ecclesiastes, but comments regarding passages elsewhere on false religion that 'not only is breath momentary; it is weightless, or insubstantial' (p. 27).

[18] See also G. Beale, *We Become What We Worship: A Biblical Theology of Idolatry* (Nottingham: Apollos; Downers Grove: InterVarsity Press, 2008).

[19] Exod. 32:4, 8; Deut. 9:12, 16; cf. Hos. 13:2.

[20] 21:3, 5; cf. Deut. 4:19; 17:3.

[21] 21:6; cf. Jer. 14:14; 29:8, and the prohibition of Deut. 18:10, 14. The verb 'seek and give omens' (*nḥš*) describes those who advised the Aramean Ben-Hadad (1 Kgs 20:33: 'took this as a good sign'), an example of the 'practices of the nations around' which Israel followed.

[22] Literal translation. See comment on 16:3, p. 299, n. 43.

[23] 'Plunder' will similarly describe exile in 21:14.

seed [people] of Israel' (v. 20). Other than in worship (1 Chr. 16:13; Ps. 22:23) and a post-exilic instance (Neh. 9:2), the phrase is only in prophecies of continuation beyond the exile of Israel as a people, based on God's covenantal relationship (Isa. 45:25; Jer. 31:36–37).[24] More directly, 'your seed' occurs prolifically in the covenantal promises to the fathers, Abraham, Isaac and Jacob/Israel[25] (compare the mention in verse 15 of the *covenant he made with their ancestors*). Previously the continuity of Judah had been because of the covenant with David,[26] but in the midst of the sombre reality of rejection and thrusting away there is interposed a contrasting word of trust and hope based on the Abrahamic covenantal relationship.[27] There is a clinging to the possibility that through the 'seed' of Abraham, Isaac and Israel there can still be blessing not only for Israel but for all the peoples of the earth. The use throughout of language recalling the golden calf incident or the time of judges is also a reminder of occasions of renewal of relationship beyond judgment: God is compassionate. There is hope.

The NT repeatedly affirms that the promise of blessing to and through Abraham's 'seed' is dramatically made real in Christ, whether in the song of Zechariah (Luke 1:55), the preaching of the apostles (Acts 3:25), Paul's writing on the relationship with God through faith (Rom. 4:13, 16, 18; 9:7–8; 11:1; Gal. 3:6, 19, 29) or the vision of John (Rev. 12:17). What the writer of Kings could barely see beyond the judgment of exile, and what the disciples on Easter Saturday could not imagine possible, has become a worldwide community of God's people who see in the cross of Christ both judgment on mankind's endemic sinfulness and the wonder of God's blessing in restored relationship.

Nevertheless, the example of the people's idolatry, following *the practices of the nations*, remains a warning to be heard. The writer returns to the narrated present in recalling how it was Yahweh who *tore Israel away from the house of David* (v. 21; cf. 1 Kgs 11:11, 30–31), but the people sinned *a great sin*, the description of the golden calf apostasy (Exod. 32:21, 30–31), repeated in syncretistic worship under royal patronage. There is judgment: the people *were taken from their homeland into exile in Assyria*. Any hope is unrealized: *they are still there* (v. 23).

Martin Luther saw the importance of the first commandment, for 'where the heart is right with God and this commandment is kept,

---

[24] NIV has variously 'people of Israel, descendants of Israel, Israelite descent, Israel'.
[25] 32 times in Genesis (beginning 12:7); reaffirmed at the time of the golden calf incident at Sinai (Exod. 32:13; 33:1). NIV has 'offspring, descendants'.
[26] 1 Kgs 11:12–13, 32, 34, 36; 15:4; 2 Kgs 8:19; and subsequently 2 Kgs 19:34; 20:6.
[27] See above on ch. 13 and 14:26–27, pages 283–284 and 294.

fulfilment of all the others will follow of its own accord'.[28] The corollary has been expressed in this century:

> We never break the other commandments without breaking the first. Why do we ever fail to love or keep promises or live unselfishly? . . . The specific answer in any actual circumstance is that there is something you feel you *must* have to be happy, that is more important to your heart than God himself – [for example] human approval, reputation, power over others, financial advantage.[29]

Idols are a human creation, often making absolute some good feature of God's creation and of the mind God has given us. In Genesis 3:6 'the woman saw that the fruit of the tree was good for food and pleasing to the eye, and also desirable for gaining wisdom', all commendable in themselves, but none being the absolute good of living in obedient trust in God. Idols and related worship express the values and aspirations of a culture and individuals, and so shape that culture by exalting those aspects, validating and commending a lifestyle. Associated will be power structures and wealth distribution, so that challenging the idols threatens those who benefit from the worship (e.g., Paul at Ephesus, Acts 19). Martin Luther gave as his prime example:

> Many a person thinks he has God and everything he needs when he has money and property; in them he trusts and of them he boasts so stubbornly and securely that he cares for no one. Surely such a man also has a god – mammon by name, that is, money and possessions – on which he fixes his whole heart. It is the most common idol on earth. He who has money and property feels secure, happy, fearless, as if he were sitting in the midst of paradise. On the other hand, he who has nothing doubts and despairs as if he had never heard of God. Very few there are who are cheerful, who do not fret and complain, if they do not have mammon. This desire for wealth clings and cleaves to our nature all the way to the grave.[30]

As I write governments, businesses and ordinary citizens are still uncertain whether the global financial crisis is over as several nations

---

[28] From 'The Large Catechism' (1529), English translation, in *The Book of Concord: The Confessions of the Evangelical Lutheran Church*, edited and translated by T. G. Tappert (Philadelphia: Fortress, 1959), p. 371.

[29] T. Keller, 'How to Find Your Rival Gods', <http://www.christianitytoday.com/ct/2009/octoberweb-only/142-21.0.html>, adapted from his *Counterfeit Gods* (New York: Dutton, 2009).

[30] 'The Large Catechism'; *Book of Concord*, p. 365–66.

grapple with excessive sovereign debt and unpopular governmental solutions. The 'worthless, insubstantial' nature of such a god, failing to deliver but demanding more, is illustrated in the oft-quoted observation of the nineteenth-century philosopher Arthur Schopenhauer, 'Wealth is like sea water, the more we drink, the thirstier we become; and the same is true of fame.'[31] Areas of idolatry can be extended: *high places, sacred stones* and *Asherah poles* (vv. 9–10), 'all markers of other religious options . . . are not narrowly "religious," but have wide and deep dimensions . . . signify[ing] alternative forms of sexuality, economics and well-being that compromise the single demand of Yahwism'.[32] In Ezekiel, with many references to idols, LXX translators in a later Hellenistic cultural context commonly used words that drew readers' attention to human thinking, reasoning or imagination, and consequent actions,[33] and every NT instance of the related *enthymēsis* ('thought, design') is in a context of being contrary to God.[34] This broadens the anti-idol polemic of Isaiah and Jeremiah which mocks human making of idols.[35] Human constructions are good – including economic, financial, political, business and educational systems devised for the well-functioning of local and global society, scientific systems that aid understanding of creation, systems of philosophy and theology, ecclesiastical structures – but when they are relied on for security, status and well-being, to control 'forces beyond the human',[36] when any is made ultimate, there is a god to whom its worshippers *sold themselves* (v. 17; cf. Deut. 28:68). The worship of 'created [and human-made] things rather than the Creator' (Rom. 1:25; Acts 17:29) is the path to ultimate failure and judgment, for worshippers become like their objects of worship: 'insubstantial' (v. 15) or 'vile' (Hos. 9:10) or literally 'sense-less', unable to succeed (Ps. 115:4–8).

2. Changes in Samaria (17:24–41)

Deportation does not mean the end of the people of God, although it is common to speak loosely of 'the lost tribes of Israel'. We noted in chapter 13 a cluster of words of hope beyond death. Outside Kings

---

[31] *Parerga and Paralipomena* (1851), 1, p. 347, cited by B. Magee, *The Philosophy of Schopenhauer*, rev. ed. (Oxford University Press, 1997), p. 255.

[32] Brueggemann, p. 378.

[33] E.g., *dianoēma* 'thought', *dianoia* 'thinking', *enthymēma* 'imagination', *epitēdeuma* 'pursuit'. See Olley, *Ezekiel* (Septuagint Commentary Series; Leiden: Brill, 2009), pp. 25, 27, 311–313.

[34] Matt. 9:4; 12:25; Acts 17:29; Heb. 4:12. Philo, a contemporaneous Jewish philosopher, however uses *enthymēma* in positive or neutral contexts.

[35] Isa. 40:18–20; 41:5–7; 44:9–20; 46:1–2, 6–7; Jer. 10:1–9; cf. Rev. 9:20.

[36] Hobbs, p. 235, commenting on v. 17.

the prophets look forward to a restored 'Israel and Judah' (e.g., Jer. 3; 31; Ezek. 37:15–28; 48:1–35), and writings after the return from the later Babylonian exile not only provide genealogical lists from the whole people (1 Chr. 1 – 9), but relate how, between the end of the nation Israel and the fall of Jerusalem, people from the north were welcomed in worship at Jerusalem (2 Chr. 30:1–12). How God brings all to pass continues to be expressed variously in the NT, whether the 'twelve apostles' of Christ (cf. Rev. 21:14), or Christ's gathering of 'one flock and one shepherd' (John 10:16; an echo of Ezekiel), or Paul's 'all Israel' (Rom. 11:26). We await the fulfilment.

Into the mix of God's gathering are changes in the territory of the former kingdom of Israel, which becomes for the next century an Assyrian province. The simple statement that *the king of Assyria brought people from Babylon, Kuthah, Avva, Hamath and Sepharvaim and settled them in the towns of Samaria to replace the Israelites* (v. 24) summarizes waves of settlement over the next years, each *national group* continuing to worship *its own gods*, which the text pointedly says they *made* and *set . . . up in the shrines* where the Israelites had worshipped (vv. 29–31).[37] Are they somehow to experience God's promise to 'bless . . . all peoples on earth' (Gen. 12:3; 26:4; 28:14)?

Importantly for the writer Yahweh is still asserting his sovereignty, evidenced in *he sent lions*, emphasized by repetition in the reporting (vv. 25–26; cf. 1 Kgs 13:24; 20:36). The Assyrians have a view of territorial gods,[38] and so arranged for an Israelite priest to return and *live in Bethel* where he *taught them how to worship* ['fear'] *the LORD* (v. 28). This looks positive, except that he is a priest of the place with syncretistic religious practices that had been condemned. Ironically parallel to Jeroboam's actions (1 Kgs 12:31) the new settlers *also appointed all sorts of their own people to officiate for them as priests in the shrines at the high places* (v. 32). Syncretism continues as the people both *worshipped* ['feared'] *the LORD* as the priest taught them and *served their own gods in accordance with the customs of the nations* (v. 33). Here again is a contrast with the Deuteronomic requirement to 'fear [Yahweh], serve him only' (Deut. 6:13; 10:12, 20).

Another dimension to the narrative is easily overlooked: foreigners are given the opportunity to 'fear Yahweh', the implication being that

---

[37] For Assyrian records on the resettlement see Younger, 'The Deportation of the Israelites', Hobbs, pp. 236–237, and Cogan and Tadmor, p. 209, and for identification of the various gods, Hobbs, pp. 238–239. See also Sweeney, pp. 395–396; Walton, Matthews and Chavalas, pp. 404–405.

[38] Brueggemann, p. 483, compares the Peace of Augsburg, 1555, with its principle of *cuius regio, eius religio,* 'who rules determines the religion'.

they are welcome to join the covenant family, to share in the blessings. Assyrian emperors may be making what to them are astute political decisions, but in this God is at work to bring blessing to 'the nations'. (One might compare the impact of migration in the movement of peoples who come into contact with Christian churches.) The hilly region of the province of Samaria and the adjacent province from the valley of Jezreel north, the region of Galilee, experienced much turmoil over the next 750 years. A melting pot of peoples, with their cultures and religions, resulted from trade, battles and rule by successive powers, Babylonian, Persian, Hellenistic and Roman, together with the impact of the Hasmomean rule in Judah from the middle of the second century BC. By the time of Christ, in Galilee there were Jewish synagogues and in the region of Samaria a people with allegiance to Yahweh, but based around the old covenantal centre of Shechem and a temple on Mount Gerizim, and having as their sacred text a form of the Pentateuch (so regarding the move of the tabernacle to Shiloh and later Jerusalem as a corruption of faith).[39] It is from culturally diverse Galilee that Jesus called his early disciples and it was in that region that people flocked to him, while the Gospels and Acts tell of the response of Samaritans – none more surprising, but typical of God's working, than the woman at the well who led many others to faith in Christ (John 4:39–42).[40] God's blessing is for all who will fear him.

The concluding summary (vv. 34–41) is a 'comparison of what obtained in the north after the exile [vv. 34, 40–41] and what should have existed in Israel before the exile [vv. 35–39]', it is 'brimming with typically deuteronomic vocabulary'.[41] It could be read as simply a narrating of the past that continues *to this day*, a justification and affirming of Yahweh's judgment. Its deuteronomic sermonic style, however, points to its being an exhortation to the hearers/readers. Here is the way forward: face the reality of your futile double standard, remember who you are and what Yahweh has done for you. You are *the descendants of Jacob, whom he named Israel,* with whom *the LORD made a covenant* (vv. 34–35); *the LORD . . . brought you up out of Egypt* (v. 36) – and again, *do not forget the covenant I have made with you* (v. 38). So obey his instructions for living in the relationship (vv. 35b, 36b–37), summarized in *do not worship* ['fear'] *other gods . . . rather, worship* ['fear'] *the LORD your God* (vv.

---

[39] Direct link between practices of the resettled population in Samaria (v. 24) and the 'Samaritans' of the NT is tenuous; see H. G. M. Williamson and C. A. Evans, 'Samaritans', *DNTB*, pp. 1056–1061; J. F. Strange, 'Galilee', *DNTB*, pp. 391–398.

[40] Luke 17:6; Acts 8:25. The conversation with the woman relating to place of worship (John 4:19–24) provides a response to the opposition seen in Luke 9:52–53.

[41] Hobbs, p. 227.

38b–39a). The exhortation could have ended there, and the hearers/ readers could have responded, 'What's the point? We're exiles, delivered into the hands of plunderers' (cf. v. 20) – but it continues, *it is he who will deliver you from the hand of all your enemies* (v. 39).[42] How amazing is the grace of God.

The sermon continues to confront all readers with the reality, but futility, of idolatry, whether ancient, modern or post-modern! 'It is a homily to those of us for whom there is still opportunity to do what is right. It is a homily about what happens when we violate the first commandment and betray God.'[43] Like the people of Israel and Judah we remain living in a world which, like Athens, is 'full of idols' (Acts 17:16), and the warning remains current, 'Dear children, keep yourselves from idols' (1 John 5:21). We hear something of God's heart, of his anger against persistent rejection of his word and of his compassionate plea to return, to serve him alone. He still delivers from enemies that enslave and oppress, even when our present situation is a result of our own sinfulness. Still today there is joy and deliverance as people turn 'to God from idols to serve the living and true God' (1 Thess. 1:9).

---

[42] Hebrew emphasizes 'he', hence NIV's 'it is he who . . .'
[43] Seow, p. 257.

F. From trust to exile – to the end of Judah
2 Kings 18 – 25

2 Kings 18:1 – 20:21
18. Hezekiah and trust

The account of Hezekiah, king of Judah, is a burst of light after the darkness of the decline and ultimate demise of the northern nation of Israel. The narrative stands out in speaking of 'having confidence in', 'trusting', 'depending on', 'relying on' (words vary in EVV). The relevant Hebrew words (forms of *bṭḥ*) occur ten times in chapters 18 – 19, but with meaning 'trust' only three other times in the whole narrative of Genesis to Kings.[1] In all OT narrative, only of Hezekiah is it explicitly said that he *trusted [bāṭaḥ] in the LORD* (18:5). While no doubt others believed or trusted in God,[2] the clustering of *bṭḥ* catches readers' attention. An audience today that often hears reference to 'believing in God' may be challenged by a sermon that speaks of 'depending on/having confidence in God'.

Confidence, trust and reliance are part of all human relationships, but the object and quality of trust are most evident in times of difficulty. The situation faced by Hezekiah and his responses can be a mirror to examine a wide range of current behaviour, both personal and corporate. The narrative teases out trust or reliance in trying circumstances, along with other possibilities as to who or what to rely on, and the consequences. With 'trust in Yahweh' common in Psalms,[3] the Hezekiah narrative helps us relate the worship-context exhortation of psalms to practical decisions – taking Sunday affirmations into Monday.

---

[1] 18:5, 19 (twice), 20, 21 (twice), 22, 24, 30; 19:10; also Deut. 28:52, Judg. 9:26; 20:36. NIV has 'trust' when the phrase is 'trust in the LORD' (18:5, 30), but otherwise 'depend' (18: 20–24) or, for the noun-verb combination in 18:19, 'On what are you basing this confidence of yours?' (lit., 'what is this trust you are trusting?').

[2] As for instance, with a form of *'mn*, Abraham (Gen. 15:6); see Isa. 7:9 and discussion above on Ahaz (16:5, p. 300).

[3] Psalms has 48 instances of the verb, 62:8–10; 115:8–11; 118:8–9; 146:3 being examples of contrast between 'trust in Yahweh' and trust placed otherwise.

The Hezekiah narrative is also unique in being the only Kings narrative involving a prophet whose messages are included in the Latter Prophets. There is also a parallel version in Isaiah 36 – 39. Thus at times we will look at the book of Isaiah.[4]

1. Hezekiah, a good king (18:1–12)

Good kings may have bad sons, the narrative thus far giving examples.[5] Now a bad king, Ahaz, has a good son, Hezekiah (vv. 1–3). Who or what had shaped his attitudes, growing up in the palace in Jerusalem – his mother, the priests,[6] prophets, teachers, observing what was happening in Israel? We are not told. There are many influences on children, then and now. Research is highlighting the key role of parental modelling and values, while recognizing that the shaping of individual lives and the factors in personal response to that shaping are complex.

The formulaic introduction to Hezekiah's reign has the longest summary evaluation of any king, with three components: reforms, trust, and success. His religious reforms (v. 4) are a reminder (still needed today) that even something good from the past can become an object of worship in itself and hinder present obedience. The *bronze snake*[7] *Moses had made* had been a sign both of judgment on impatient speaking 'against the LORD and against . . . Moses' and of healing and life (Num. 21:4–9). The story has resonated through the centuries, with the first century BC Wisdom of Solomon expounding,

> Their short-lived trouble was sent them as a lesson, and they were given a symbol of salvation to remind them of the requirements of your law. Anyone turning towards it was saved, not by what he looked at but by you, the saviour of all. (Wisdom 16:6–7 REB)

Here is foreshadowed Christ's being 'lifting up' that brought 'eternal life' (John 3:14–15; cf. 12:32). More widely, copper and bronze serpents are found around the ancient Near East and appear as cultic

---

[4] For detailed discussions see my '"Trust in the Lord": Hezekiah, Kings and Isaiah', *Tyndale Bulletin* 50.1 (1999), pp. 59–77; B. Webb, *The Message of Isaiah*, The Bible Speaks Today (Leicester: Inter-Varsity Press, 1996), pp. 147–159; and D. Bostock, *A Portrayal of Trust: The Theme of Faith in the Hezekiah Narratives* (Milton Keynes: Paternoster, 2006).

[5] From David to Solomon (mixed) then Rehoboam; Jehoshaphat (1 Kgs 22:41–50) to Jehoram (2 Kgs 8:36–24); Jotham (15:32–38) to Ahaz (16:1–20).

[6] Cf. the raising of Joash, chs 11 – 12.

[7] 'The term *nḥštn* Nehushtan "The Brass Thing" is a clever combination of the similar words *nḥš* "snake" and *nḥšt* "bronze", and outside this passage the word does not exist' (Hobbs, p. 252).

images for a god of healing, and so by Hezekiah's time the bronze serpent had become associated with Canaanite worship, along with other symbols he destroyed.[8]

The Kings writer is not however primarily interested in Hezekiah's reforms, giving only this one-verse summary. (Quite different is the later Chronicles with three chapters, 2 Chronicles 29 – 31, on the reforms.) Of greater import is that *in the LORD, the God of Israel, he trusted* (v. 5, following the emphatic Hebrew word order). Three kings have a statement of incomparability, being unlike any king before or after: 'Solomon is lauded for unparalleled wisdom and wealth, Hezekiah for unparalleled trust, and Josiah for unparalleled reforms.'[9] Unlike Solomon who 'held fast . . . in love' to many foreign women (1 Kgs 11:1–2), Hezekiah *held fast* [NJPSV, 'clung'] *to the LORD* (v. 6), a peculiarly Deuteronomic phrase.[10] What was important from the time of Moses was not 'the bronze snake', but keeping *the commands the LORD had given Moses.* Hezekiah fulfils God's intention for his people.

Being *successful* in overcoming oppression by Assyria and the Philistines comes after trust and obedience in all areas of life: *the LORD was with him* (v. 7). This is reinforced by repetition of the report of the defeat of the northern kingdom (vv. 9–11; compare 17:3–6). At the human level one might say Israel's defeat was because she broke the treaty (covenant)[11] with Assyria and suffered the consequences (17:2–4). The narrator is quite definite: the reason was Israel *violated [the LORD's] covenant* (v. 12). A contrast between Israel and Judah is set up, presenting an issue to be resolved in what follows:

	Israel	Judah (Hezekiah)
Covenant/treaty with Yahweh	Violated covenant; disobeyed commands	Kept covenant; obeyed commands
Treaty with Assyria	Rebelled	Rebelled
Result	Israel destroyed	? Yet to be seen

[8] Walton, Matthews and Chavalas, p. 405; cf. Deut. 4:15–18.

[9] G. N. Knoppers, '"There Was None Like Him": Incomparability in the Books of Kings', *Catholic Biblical Quarterly* 54 (1992), p. 413; see 1 Kgs 3:12; 2 Kgs 18:5; 23:25.

[10] Deut. 10:20; 11:22; 13:4; 30:20, with the similar Josh. 22:5; 23:8; Jer. 13:11; elsewhere only in Ps. 63:8. The verb also describes how Joram, son of Ahab, 'clung to the sins of Jeroboam' (2 Kgs 3:3).

[11] *běrît* 'covenant' (17:15, 35, 38; 18:12) is also a 'treaty' between kings or nations (e.g., 1 Kgs 5:12; 15:19; 20:34).

2. Who or what to rely on? (18:13–35)

After the introduction (vv. 1–12) we might have expected that Hezekiah and Judah would be protected on the basis of their *trust in the LORD* and obedience of his commands. What eventuates (v. 13) comes as a surprise: several cities are captured by the Assyrians under *Sennacherib*, including the major royal centre of *Lachish*, 25 miles (40 km) south-west of Jerusalem.[12] Like earlier kings, from Rehoboam on, Hezekiah seeks peace with an aggrieved foreign ruler by paying tribute of *all the silver that was found in the temple of the LORD and in the treasuries of the royal palace* (v. 15), along with stripping off *gold* (vv. 14b–16). A narrative conflict is set up: how can Hezekiah's standard apology to Sennacherib, backed by tribute (vv. 14–15), be reconciled with the introduction that makes Hezekiah's rebellion evidence of 'success' because 'the LORD was with him'?

In the event, the tribute does not satisfy *the king of Assyria* and he lays siege on Jerusalem with *a large army* (v. 17). Hezekiah has sought peace, but it has not to come through traditional political means. Sennacherib, backed by the awesome Assyrian military machine, can dictate terms. In Sennacherib's own words, 'As to Hezekiah, the Judean, . . . he himself, I locked up within Jerusalem, his royal city, like a bird in a cage. I surrounded him with earthworks, and made it unthinkable for him to exit by the city gate.'[13]

The scene is set as *the king of Assyria* sends *his supreme commander, his chief officer and his field commander*[14] to Jerusalem. The location of *the aqueduct of the Upper Pool, on the road to the Washerman's Field* is uncertain, but just outside the city wall (cf. v. 26). Here Isaiah had earlier confronted Ahaz when he was seeking Assyrian aid (Isa. 7:3; cf. 36:2), one of several literary links in Isaiah between Ahaz's

---

[12] A baked clay prism now in the University of Chicago Oriental Institute records Sennacherib's account of eight campaigns, including his third campaign against Judah in 701 BC (translation: *ANET*, pp. 287–288, *COS* 2.119B, pp. 302–303). The capture of Lachish was pictured in expansive stone reliefs on his palace walls, now on display in the British Museum, London <http://www.britishmuseum.org/explore/galleries/middle_east/room_10b_assyria_siege_of_la.aspx> (accessed 24 Mar 2010).

[13] *COS* 2.119B, p. 303; also *ANET*, p. 288. Significantly, there is no following account of conquering Jerusalem and his palace reliefs are of Lachish. See A. K. Grayson, 'Assyria, Assyrians', *DOTHB*, pp. 101–102; B. T. Arnold, 'Hezekiah', *DOTHB*, pp. 411–412.

[14] NRSV transliterates the titles: *Tartan* (also in Isa. 20:1) is the highest official under the king, *Rabsaris*, lit. 'chief eunuch', is often in texts as head of Assyrian forces, while the *Rabshakeh*, 'chief butler', has a role mainly linked with king and court, and so probably not 'field commander' (Wiseman, p. 276; *pace* NIV), although possibly 'provincial governor' (Walton, Matthews and Chavalas, p. 405). See also Hobbs, p. 256; Cogan and Tadmor, pp. 229–230; Sweeney, p. 414.

unbelieving response and Hezekiah's trust.[15] On the side of Judah, top officials are also named. As common in Hebrew narrative, the story is now told through the dynamics of dialogue. Throughout verses 17–37 and 19:9–13 Sennacherib, through officers and messengers, exudes the confidence of one who thinks he is in control, and so he taunts Hezekiah. In the *field commander's* speech, perceptions of relative power and status are clear: *Hezekiah* is referred to by name, but never as 'king' (vv. 22, 29–32), while Sennacherib is never named but is *the great king* (vv. 19, 28) or *the king of Assyria* (vv. 19, 23, 28, 30, 31, 33) – in contrast the writer's own words are *King Hezekiah* (v. 17; 19:1, 5). Point by point Sennacherib seeks to demolish all on which Hezekiah (and nations through history) may be *basing this confidence of yours* (v. 19).[16]

a. Political strategy and military preparedness (18:20)

The opening critique is brief, but can be interpreted variously. The Hebrew, 'You say only word of lips (is) counsel and strength for war', has the sense of either 'Do you think that mere words are strategy and power for war?' (NRSV; similarly REB, NLT, NJPSV), or *You say you have the counsel and might for war – but you speak only empty words* (NIV). The former, and dominant, interpretation[17] suggests diplomatic negotiations and alliance with Egypt, which fits the following question, *On whom are you depending [bṭḥ], that you rebel against me?*, joined with verse 21. A reader of Kings, having been told however that Hezekiah is the superb example of one who 'trusted in the LORD' (v. 5), may see his 'rebellion' (vv. 7, 20) as a consequence of such trust (cf. v. 30) – and so the 'word' of v. 20 is that of Yahweh through his prophet.[18] This is an alternative object of 'dependence' raised by the field commander (vv. 22, 29–30).

The NIV translation is supported by what is known of earlier diplomatic attempts and Hezekiah's strengthening of the fortifications. Information from the concluding regnal summary statement (20:20), the book of Isaiah and archaeology shows how Hezekiah changed the water supply and extended the city walls because of the Assyrian threat. Sennacherib then says these preparations are 'mere words'; they can do nothing. This is not only Sennacherib's interpretation: in Isaiah, the prophet brings Yahweh's word of judgment

---

[15] P. R. Ackroyd, 'Isaiah 36–39: Structure and Function', in his *Studies in the Religious Tradition of the Old Testament* (London: SCM, 1987), pp. 105–120.

[16] See introduction to the Hezekiah account for translations of forms of *bṭḥ* (p. 317).

[17] See also Hobbs, p. 243; Cogan and Tadmor, pp. 223, 231; Sweeney, pp. 405, 407.

[18] So Provan, pp. 260–261, comparing 19:6, 20–21.

because the city of Jerusalem was relying on military preparation rather than on turning to God (Isa. 22:8–11).

b. Military alliances (18:21, 23–24)

Being located on the bridge between Asia and Africa made small Judah the meat in the sandwich between the great powers, Assyria and Egypt. It seemed wise, if one were to rebel against Assyria, to seek protection from Egypt, *depending* [*bṭḥ*] on her (vv. 21, 24). With vivid imagery of *a splintered reed* (appropriate for Egypt on the Nile) that *pierces the hand of anyone who leans on it* Sennacherib rightly points to dubious benefit: Egypt will be friendly only while it suits her. In any case, the Assyrian army is much stronger (vv. 23–24). Again we see similarity with God's warning in Isaiah: to trust in Egypt is folly (Isa. 30:1–7; 31:1–3). Isaiah's rationale however differs from Sennacherib's: reliance on Egypt is a sign of failure to rely on Yahweh. It is mere human decision-making, without taking God's will into account. There are several biblical passages, particularly in Isaiah and Psalms, stating the folly of trusting in military strength ('horses', 'mere humans', 'alliances') instead of remaining faithful to Yahweh, obeying his commands.[19]

How ironic that both Sennacherib and Isaiah should point to false confidence. Sennacherib does so because he himself relies on his bigger war machine and past successes. Can *he* really succeed in the long run? How different is the biblical critique. While there is no specific prohibition against military preparedness (other than the purchase of horses), the dominant biblical thrust is Yahweh giving victory to small numbers and in surprising ways. The best method of defence is to obey Yahweh, to do what is right and just.

Despite such scriptural warnings and examples, readers, ancient and modern, seem to regard Sennacherib's method as the way to achieve true security. Human history sadly illustrates the choice of military might, with its high social cost, the accumulation of weapons having priority over deeper social needs. Hezekiah's wall-building that involved destroying homes (Isa. 22:10) is one illustration of misplaced human priorities.

Ellul observes how Sennacherib through his envoy

> unwittingly pronounces a divine judgment on Hezekiah. It is often thus. In the word it speaks to the church, in its judgments and criticisms, the world often speaks at two levels. In explicit content, and according to its own express intention, what it says is of little

---

[19] E.g., Ps. 20:7; 33:16–22; 147:10–11; Isa. 31:1.

worth and simply expresses secular mediocrity. Thus Rabshakeh tells Hezekiah he would have done better to rely on the stronger power of Assyria.

But behind this word . . . there is a profound truth which faith can apprehend because it descries God's intention. Hezekiah knows that he is reproved for having trusted in Egypt, but that he would have been guilty of the same error if he had trusted in Assyria. The reproach of Rabshakeh is true even if wrongly motivated . . .

It is at this level and within these limits that the church should be infinitely attentive to the criticisms and attacks of unbelievers or enemies. It should not accept their advice or motivation but should look behind this to the judgment which God pronounces on it, and which may be the very opposite of what the world has in view.[20]

c. 'God!' (18:22, 25)

Sennacherib's confidence rises in its arrogance. He knows of Hezekiah's reforms (cf. v. 4), but to him they are negatives. Has not Hezekiah destroyed places of Yahweh worship? Has not Hezekiah's centralization of worship been a grab for power, focusing everything in Jerusalem? At last the hearers can see Sennacherib's folly; they know Hezekiah's actions are pleasing to God.[21]

Next Sennacherib surprisingly claims that *the LORD himself told me to march against this country and destroy it* (v. 25)! He has support from an unexpected source: some thirty years earlier Isaiah had prophesied that Assyria would be 'the rod of [God's] anger', the agent of God's judgment upon a disobedient, faithless Israel and Judah, although in turn Assyria would be judged for her own arrogance (Isa. 10:5–19; see further below). Whatever the reason for making his statement, Sennacherib is right – he has been sent by Yahweh. But that is only part of the story.

d. Sennacherib's ultimatum: 'choose life and not death!' (18:26–35)

While Hezekiah may be the fore in these chapters, the dialogue regarding language – Aramaic was the diplomatic language for

---

[20] J. Ellul, *The Politics of God and the Politics of Man* (Grand Rapids: Eerdmans, 1972), pp. 148–149.

[21] Centralization in Jerusalem is a criterion for condemnation of Jeroboam and his successors in Israel, and for repeated negative reference to continuing 'high places' in Judah.

centuries in the ancient Near East – ensures that readers know that
'trust' is a matter not only for the king but for *the people on
the wall* (vv. 26–27), the Judean soldiers who will be at the fore-
front of any Assyrian attack and who share the desperation of
famine. Ordinary people are called to *choose* as Sennacherib offers
life and not death (v. 32). *The commander* passes on Sennacherib's
arrogant message, a contrast of two kings' words, the first being
Sennacherib's, *Hezekiah . . . cannot deliver you from my hand,*
and the other Hezekiah's, *The LORD will surely deliver us: this
city will not be given into the hand of the king of Assyria* (vv.
29–30).

Sennacherib offers the people *life*, in another land, as opposed to
death, in their own (vv. 31–32). They can have life by surrendering
to his greater power. The stark human situation makes this seem the
only realistic way with any future. To anyone familiar with the
covenant address of Deuteronomy, however, Sennacherib's offer of
life or death with the plea to *choose life* is ironic. These very words
are the key conclusion to the covenant appeal (Deut. 30:15–20) where
the alternatives are 'life' (blessing in the land Yahweh is giving them)
or 'death' (destruction and removal from the land). Two offers of
blessing in two different lands: Sennacherib's and Yahweh's. Who is
to be relied on? Sennacherib's offer requires submission to his
authority; Yahweh's demands submission to his! How is Hezekiah
to respond? How can he 'trust in the LORD'? Is it realistic to have
'confidence' in Yahweh?

Sennacherib increases his level of arrogance: with a recital of the
nations he has already defeated, he asserts *Has the god of any nation
ever delivered his land from the hand of the king of Assyria?* He
continues to speak of the gods' inability to 'deliver',[22] with the final
How then can the LORD deliver Jerusalem from my hand? He boasts,
No god, not even Yahweh, can *deliver* its land from *me* (vv. 32–35).
The true battle lines are now explicit: it is not Sennacherib versus
Hezekiah, but Sennacherib versus *Yahweh*. That is where the battle
always is. With dramatic heightening of tension, Sennacherib's
arrogance reflects other situations where God's people feel besieged,
at the mercy of a greater power.

In everyday human relationships and in places of employment,
politics and commerce, situations arise where it seems the only way
to enjoy 'life' is to follow the orders of the powerful or the way of
the system ('that's the way of business/politics/ . . . '). Faith
seems irrelevant, if not a hindrance; an idealistic path to failure.

---

[22] For the same verb, *hiṣṣîl*, NIV stylistically changes to 'rescue' in v. 34 and 'save' in
v. 35a.

One may turn to a picture of the apparently powerless Christ standing before Pilate, representative of the might of Rome and supported by powerful religious leaders. It may be difficult to see how to follow God's way of justice and compassion. This narrative exposes the short-sighted arrogance of those who claim their way to be superior. It demonstrates how the conflict is between human self-sufficiency and power-plays (another name for arrogance), and how God's way as made known above all in Christ.

3. The response: people, king, prophet and Yahweh (18:36 – 19:37)

The people remained silent, following the *command* of Hezekiah – they at least are willing to follow the lead of their *king* (v. 36). So the king's representatives (v. 37; cf. v. 18) pass on the message to Hezekiah. How will he respond?

a. Seeking help from Yahweh through Isaiah (19:1–7)

Hezekiah's response is to act in humility. As had Joram, king of Israel, when Samaria was besieged (6:30), he *tore his clothes and put on sackcloth,* but the addition shows the difference: he *went into the temple of the LORD* (v. 1), seeking Yahweh's answer through *the prophet Isaiah* (v. 2). Previously he had gone to the temple to obtain wealth to appease Sennacherib (18:15), but now (also v. 14) he turns to Yahweh. His statement reflects impotence and *disgrace* (v. 3). The quoting of what may have been a proverb concerning failed birth finds a parallel in Hosea (13:13) describing the end of the nation of Israel – is this the end of Judah as well? Hezekiah clings on in hope (*it may be*): surely God *will hear* the words that *ridicule*[23] *the living God* (v. 4). 'The one who scoffs at another seeks to denigrate the latter in significance, worth and ability; he makes clear that he scorns and despises the other.'[24] It is one matter to ridicule dead non-gods, but Yahweh alone is *the living God.* Sennacherib may have arrogantly brought *rebuke* to Hezekiah (v. 3), but that has included Yahweh, who surely will *rebuke* Sennacherib *for the words the LORD your God has heard* (v. 4). Sennacherib cannot have the last word: hope for *the remnant that still survives* is based on God's honour among the nations (see v. 19).

---

[23] NRSV, 'mock'; NJPSV, 'blaspheme'; the word features prominently in the David-Goliath narrative (1 Sam. 17:10, 25, 26, 36, 45).

[24] E. Kutsch, '*ḥrp* II', *TDOT* 5, p. 211.

Isaiah's response is brief: *Do not be afraid*.[25] It is God who has been *blasphemed* and he will respond and *put a spirit in* Sennacherib (v. 7, NRSV, translating literally): the king will hear *a certain report* (*šāmaʿ šĕmûʿâ*) that will lead to his *return* [*šûb*] *to his own country* and ultimately his death. A comparison is the enticing spirit that led to Ahab's death in battle (1 Kgs 22:20–23), or the sounds heard by the Syrians besieging Samaria (2 Kgs 7:6).[26]

b. Sennacherib's arrogance in crescendo (19:8–13)

Isaiah's words had been specific, but as so often in Scripture and in common experience, God's timetable does not conform to our expectations, nor is the path to fulfilment always direct. The drama in the ensuing narrative is heightened by repetition of the words in Isaiah's message, *šāmaʿ* ('hear') and *šûb* ('turn, return').[27] First the *field commander heard* (*šāmaʿ*) and so he *withdrew* (*šûb*). Sennacherib however was not withdrawing but rather *fighting against Libnah*, a smaller city not far from Lachish and strategic in tightening the noose around Jerusalem.[28] There however he *received a report* (*šāmaʿ šĕmûʿâ*): a combined group of Nubian (Cushite) and Egyptian forces under *Tirhakah*[29] is marching against him. Sennacherib 'returned' (*šûb*), not to 'his own country' but to Jerusalem as he *sent messengers to Hezekiah!*[30] He reinforces his defiance: before it was Hezekiah who was 'misleading' the people (18:32); now it is Hezekiah's god, *the god you depend on* [*bṭḥ*] who is *deceiv[ing] you* (v. 10). With a catalogue to justify his arrogance, he boastfully lists gods that have been powerless against the whole line of Assyrian rulers (vv. 11–13). It is unmistakably a confrontation between the awesome military machine of Assyria with its powerful king and Yahweh.

What has happened to the prophecy of vv. 6–7? The denouement will not come until verses 35–37. Sennacherib's enhanced defiance

---

[25] 'Do not fear' is a common opening to oracles, especially in times of conflict; E. W. Conrad, *Fear Not Warrior: A Study of 'al tîrā' Pericopes in the Hebrew Scriptures* (Chico, CA: Scholars Press, 1985).

[26] Hence NJPSV's 'I will delude him'; NIV: 'I will make him want to'.

[27] As is common EVV have a variety of translations.

[28] For possible locations, see Hobbs, p. 246; Walton, Matthews and Chavalas, p. 406.

[29] Assyrian and Egyptian sources shows Tirhakah to be commander-in-chief for the army of his brother, then king of Egypt. Soon after he became *king of Cush* (the region of classical 'Ethiopia'), the title used here, and in 690 BC 'king of Egypt'. See Wiseman, pp. 279–80; Hobbs, p. 276; Walton, Matthews and Chavalas, p. 406.

[30] The verb *šûb* is often in contexts where English speakers would say 'again' (hence NIV, NRSV and others in v. 9), but here it adds to the drama of the narrative in light of the prophetic word.

is first to be answered with a passionate prayer by Hezekiah and a lengthy oracle of deliverance through Isaiah.[31]

c. Hezekiah prays (19:14–19)

A new dimension is introduced: rather than a verbal message conveyed by the 'field commander' who has left the scene (v. 8) or even by anonymous 'messengers' (v. 9) a *letter* is written (v. 14). Sennacherib's attitude is unmistakable. Hezekiah responds as before by going up *to the temple of the LORD*, this time praying personally, trusting in Isaiah's earlier words. In a symbolic act he *spread* the letter *out before the LORD*;[32] this is a matter for God alone to handle. As he prays confidently, he focuses not on his own safety, but on Yahweh's reputation amongst *all the kingdoms of the earth* (vv. 15, 19).[33]

Hezekiah's prayer (vv. 15–19) has a simple structure seen elsewhere in Scripture, particularly in psalms of lament or complaint, with invocation (v. 15), lament or description of the situation (vv. 16–18) and supplication (v. 19). Prominent is the extended address to Yahweh. Being *the God of Israel* does not limit his power to Israel (as Sennacherib derisively thought), nor does his being *enthroned between the cherubim* on the ark[34] mean that his reign is threatened along with Jerusalem; rather, *you alone are God over all the kingdoms of the earth* – and that includes Assyria and the nations whose 'gods' were powerless before Assyrian power; and *you have made heaven and earth*. The basis for appeal is the universal reign of God, 'the Maker of heaven and earth', an ascription seen only here in Joshua-Kings.[35]

---

[31] Hebrew manuscripts have a break in the middle of v. 9 and due to similarities between vv. 9b–37 and 18:17 – 19:9a, many older commentators saw parallel accounts (e.g., Gray, p. 668; Jones, pp. 568–569). It is now more common to see a unity with developing tension (e.g., Hobbs, pp. 268–274; Sweeney, pp. 413–414), although it is possible to see a literary technique of a brief narrative followed by a more expansive account; see R. S. Hess, 'Hezekiah and Sennacherib in 2 Kings 18–20', in *Zion, City of Our God*, edited by R. S. Hess and G. J. Wenham (Grand Rapids and Cambridge: Eerdmans, 1999), pp. 36–41.

[32] Wiseman, p. 281, cites parallels with Mesopotamian practice.

[33] Cf. David's response to Goliath's challenge (1 Sam. 17:46); see D. G. Firth, '"That the World May Know". Narrative Poetics in 1 Samuel 16 – 17', in *Text and Task: Scripture and Mission*, edited by M. Parsons (Milton Keynes: Paternoster, 2005), pp. 20–32.

[34] Cf. 1 Sam. 4:4; 2 Sam. 6:2; Ps. 80:1; 99:1.

[35] Elsewhere in Exodus-Kings description of God as the Maker of heavens and earth is only in the Sabbath command (Exod. 20:11; 31:17). It is common in later psalms (Ps. 115:15; 121:2; 124:8; 134:3; 146:6), Isaiah 40 – 66 (e.g., 40:12–26; 44:24; 45:12, 18) and Jeremiah (e.g., 32:17; 33:2).

As previously (v. 4) the central issue is that Sennacherib has *ridicule[d] the living God*, but now the contrast with the gods of the nations who are *not gods* is explicit (v. 18).[36] The prayer ends with *so that*: the opening divine characteristics (v. 15) are turned to a plea that through the deliverance of Jerusalem *all the kingdoms of the earth* (over whom is God) *may know that you alone, LORD, are God* (v. 19). In the midst of distress, when it seems that Judah is at its weakest, the concern is God's honour throughout the entire world he has made.

> God alone is uncreated, self-existent, noncontingent . . . Idolatry dethrones God . . . [and] exalts things within the created order . . . The mission of God is ultimately to restore his whole creation to what it was intended to be—*God's* creation, ruled over by redeemed *humanity*, giving glory and praise to its Creator.[37]

Hezekiah joins that mission in a bold prayer of faith, a foreshadowing of our praying the prayer Christ has given, 'Our Father in heaven, hallowed be your name, your kingdom come.' His prayer likewise provides another example of the simple, yet powerful, pattern:[38]

- address to God, with his characteristics described (relevant to the petition);
- the petition;
- the intended result ('so that').

Explicitly dwelling on characteristics of the God to whom we pray strengthens faith while *so that* (v. 19) makes explicit the motive: why do I want God to answer my prayer? Prayer, then, is not self-centred but outward-looking. We join Hezekiah in a long tradition of intercession and supplication that flows from God choosing to make himself known to the nations through his people. God links his own reputation with the life and fortunes of his people and so prayer for personal or local group deliverance has cosmic consequences.

d. Isaiah brings Yahweh's word of deliverance (19:20–34)

Hezekiah's *prayer* is *heard* (*šāmaʿ*) and Isaiah is given a stirring word of judgment upon Sennacherib's arrogance. The message first addresses Sennacherib (vv. 21–28): 'Sennacherib's word is now

---

[36] Cf. Ps. 115:4–8; 135:15–18; Isa. 40:18–20; 41:6–7; 44:9–20; Jer. 10:3–5, 8–9, 14–15.
[37] C. J. H. Wright, *The Mission of God* (Nottingham: Inter-Varsity Press, 2006), pp. 163–165; see the whole chapter, 'The Living God Confronts Idolatry' (pp. 136–188).
[38] Cf. Elijah's prayer on Carmel, 1 Kgs 18:36–37.

opposed by the word of Yahweh'.[39] As Hezekiah hears these words (the message is given to his ears) the literary form makes him the trusting bystander as Yahweh confronts Sennacherib directly. As in other oracles against nations and foreign rulers, judgment is on self-vaunting arrogance, which, along with injustice, flows from an understanding of and attitude to God.

The opening words could not describe a greater contrast to existing circumstances. Words spoken in the present dynamically describe what will be: a complete reversal as the *Virgin Daughter Zion despises you and mocks you* (v. 21) – she will not be violated. *The Holy One of Israel*[40] cannot be *ridiculed* (v. 22). Sennacherib may boast of what '*I*' have done: the pronoun is emphasized at the beginning of descriptions of victory in even the highest mountains (vv. 23b) and defeat of Egypt (v. 24), and the repeated first person verbs show 'the braggadocio of the empire',[41] an attitude that reverberates on the lips of others through history to the present. Further, his 'images draw upon the classical Assyrian portrayal of the god Assur ... and Mesopotamian mythologies',[42] highlighting his blasphemy. In abrogating to himself divine power he has failed to *hear* (*šāmaʿ*, v. 25) the reality of God's sovereignty in history: Yahweh is accomplishing what *I planned* (vv. 25–26) for Assyria was 'the rod of my anger' (Isa. 10:5–11). The Assyrian practice of humiliating captured rulers by pulling them with ropes attached by rings through lips and jaws[43] is mocked as Yahweh announces the same treatment of Sennacherib, that is the way *I will make you return* (v. 28; a form of *šûb*). In the announced defeat and humiliation of the then most powerful ruler in the world we might see foreshadowed the time when God, 'having disarmed the powers and authorities, made a public spectacle of them, triumphing over them by the cross' (Col. 2:15).

With Sennacherib shamed, the message addresses Hezekiah. Agricultural land has been devastated by the Assyrians, but there will be lasting peace and harvests will return (v. 29), a picture also of the renewal of a *remnant* (cf. v. 4) and growth of the nation of Judah from its centre in Jerusalem (vv. 30–31). 'In the distance, Isaiah looks

[39] Hobbs, p. 279. This is the only extended poetic oracle in Kings, almost identical to Isa. 37:22–35.

[40] 'The Holy One of Israel' is a common divine title throughout Isaiah, occurring twenty-five times here, but only six times elsewhere (here, Ps. 71:22; 78:41; 89:18; Jer. 50:29; 51:5). 'The God who is transcendent in holiness has brought himself into close relationship with a specified people whereby they may claim he is theirs and he that they are his' (J. A. Motyer, *The Prophecy of Isaiah* [Leicester: Inter-Varsity Press, 1993], p. 18).

[41] Brueggemann, p. 509.

[42] Sweeney, p. 418.

[43] Walton, Matthews and Chavalas, p. 406; Wiseman, p. 283.

forward to the restoration of the surviving remnant of Judah and Israel, who would return and flourish in the land after exile.'[44] All of this will happen because of *the zeal of the LORD Almighty*,[45] a phrase seen elsewhere in Isaiah affirming Yahweh's 'passionate commitment' (so NLT) that will bring about the birth of a child, for whom 'of the greatness of his government and peace there will be no end' and who will 'reign on David's throne . . . with justice and righteousness . . . forever' (Isa. 9:7).

The third component of the oracle answers Sennacherib's threatening boasts with a series of five 'nots', for *I will defend this city and save it* (v. 34), answering Hezekiah's plea (v. 19).[46] The reason given is *for my* [Yahweh's] *sake* (again cf. v. 19), and *for the sake of David my servant*, the twofold reason repeated in the next chapter (20:6).[47] This is the first mention in the whole narrative of Davidic kingship: deliverance is due neither to Hezekiah's faithfulness nor to any commitment of Yahweh to Zion, but based on Yahweh's covenant faithfulness.

e. Deliverance and Sennacherib's assassination (19:35–36)

The chapter ends concisely: the siege ends, Sennacherib *returned* (*šûb*) to his capital, *Nineveh*, and twenty years later is there assassinated (19:35–37).[48] The final irony is that *his god* (v. 37) could not protect him. In time all of Yahweh's word on which Hezekiah has relied has come to pass. Jerusalem is delivered; Yahweh, the God of Israel, is trustworthy.

In reviewing the narrative of chapters 18 – 19, evident throughout are features seen also in other passages where 'trust' (*bṭḥ*) occurs.[49]

a) 'Trust in Yahweh' is evidenced by worship of the one living God and a life of doing what is just and right, following his ways. When these are present there is protection and security.

[44] Leithart, p. 259. See Isa. 7:3; 10:21–22; 11:11, 16; 28:5; 49:21.

[45] 'Yahweh of hosts' has a military connotation (Exod. 12:41; 1 Sam. 15:2; 17:45), associated with the ark (1 Sam. 4:4; 2 Sam. 6:2), and is a common title in the prophets (56 times in Isaiah 1 – 39). 'He is the God who has numberless hosts to do his bidding in any affair at any moment (2 K[gs] 6:15–18)' (J. N. Oswalt, *The Book of Isaiah Chapters 1–39*, New International Commentary on the Old Testament [Grand Rapids: Eerdmans, 1986], p. 92).

[46] NIV's 'deliver' (v. 19) and 'save' (v. 34) translate the same verb.

[47] In the parallel Isaiah account the double phrase is in Isa. 37:5, but not in 38:6. 'For the sake of David (my/ his servant)' is a feature of Kings (see Introduction, pp. 29–30).

[48] The siege was in 701 BC and Sennacherib's death 681 BC.

[49] 17 times elsewhere in Isaiah, 52 in Psalms, 18 in Proverbs, 23 in Jeremiah, 13 in Ezekiel and 9 in the Twelve. See Olley, '"Trust in the LORD": Hezekiah, Kings and Isaiah', *Tyndale Bulletin* 50.1 (1999), pp. 66–73.

2 KINGS 18:1 – 20:21

b) It is pointless to 'trust' instead in military might or wealth or status or anything else which seems to give protection and security. Where such 'trust' is condemned there is concurrently worship of other gods and/or practice of injustice and oppression.

c) Yahweh acts when the honour of his name is at stake, when an opposing power arrogantly claims self-sufficiency and/or belittles Yahweh.

d) Linked with (c), in some contexts it is explicitly affirmed that Yahweh is 'king' of all the earth.

As people in exile hear this narrative the focus on Hezekiah's 'trust', rather than religious reforms, becomes pertinent. They have lost king and temple and know Babylon's scorn (portrayed in Isaiah 47), but they can still look to Yahweh, who alone is 'God over all the kingdoms of the earth' and who has 'made heaven and earth' (v. 15), they can still have 'confidence' and pray that 'all kingdoms on earth may know that you alone, LORD, are God' (v. 19).[50]

What does it mean today for a people to trust God? At a national level, for instance, the preamble of the Constitution of the Commonwealth of Australia has the participating states 'humbly relying on the blessing of Almighty God'. The United States of America Declaration of Independence of 1776 proclaims 'a firm reliance on the protection of Divine Providence' and much of that nation's currency has the words inscribed, 'In God We Trust'. How does a nation trust in or rely on God, when 'God' is meant to embrace more than Christian beliefs? There is a warning in the arrogance of Sennacherib. Yet, with no modern nation being God's people, the question may be better focused for the Christian church: just as Judah was called to trust in Yahweh when surrounded by Assyria, what does it mean for the church, a 'holy nation' (1 Pet. 2:9), to trust in God in the midst of a diverse population and amongst the world of nations?

The Hezekiah narrative encourages the church – whether small or large congregations, national bodies or international organizations – to show dependence upon God by following his ways. This is the pattern of Christ, relying on his, at times surprising, provision rather than on its own strength – the pragmatic strategies leading to 'success' and political alliances or government

---

[50] Yahweh's uniqueness as Creator and as Sovereign over nations is dominant in Isaiah 40 – 55 (e.g., Motyer, *The Prophecy of Isaiah*, pp. 302–311), while the nations knowing 'that I am Yahweh' is a feature of Ezekiel (e.g., C. J. H. Wright, *The Message of Ezekiel* [Leicester: Inter-Varsity Press, 2001], pp. 35–38).

support.[51] It is to make our priority the prayer, 'Hallowed be your name' (and not our short-term well-being). The mirror of the narrative shines light on our willingness to rely on God, personally and as congregations. It is in tackling the issue of the church trusting God in the face of threatening situations that examples are given whereby a modern nation, which is not God's people, can 'trust or rely on God'.

4. Healing of king and nation is not permanent (20:1–21)

'Trust' at the time of the Assyrian siege has been the fore, now two other incidents *in those days* (v. 1) and *at that time* (v. 12) follow, the literary arrangement providing further insights as to the future of the nation and the basis of hope for exiles. Twice the setting of the scene is followed by a word from Yahweh announcing delay: a word of healing from life-threatening illness, linked with a promise of deliverance of the city, delays Hezekiah's death (vv. 1–11), while a word of judgment following a visit of Babylonian envoys announces despoliation and exile, again with delay (vv. 12–19).

a. Hezekiah's healing (20:1–11)

In those days, the time of Assyrian threat, associates Hezekiah's personal situation with that of the city and nation (cf. v. 6). That *Hezekiah became ill and was at the point of death* is reinforced by Isaiah bringing Yahweh's word. The situation is desperate. That *Hezekiah turned his face to the wall* recalls Ahab's 'sulking' (1 Kgs 21:4) but with the difference of bitter tears as Hezekiah *prayed to the Lord* (vv. 2–3). Unlike the prayer of 19:15–19, which focused on God and his honour, his plea is based purely on his own piety.[52] The correlation between human behaviour and well-being runs deep throughout the scriptures, whether in accounts of blessing and judgment or the instructions of wisdom, but there are also the questions and anguish of many psalms and the book of Job.[53] In

---

[51] The lasting influence of the period of Christendom is much debated; see, e.g., A. Kreider, *The Change of Conversion and the Origin of Christendom* (Christian Mission and Modern Culture; Harrisburg, Pennsylvania: Trinity Press International, 1999).

[52] To 'walk before God' elsewhere describes Noah and Abraham (Gen. 6:9; 24:40; 48:15), while to show 'wholehearted devotion' is Jehoshaphat's charge to religious leaders (2 Chr. 19:9).

[53] J. Goldingay, *Old Testament Theology, Volume 2: Israel's Faith* (Milton Keynes: Paternoster; Downers Grove: IVP Academic, 2006), pp. 615–631 ('How Life Does Not Work'), is a good overview.

particular, such psalms show how, in extreme suffering, cries of 'why?' often express social isolation.[54] The speed of Yahweh's response is vividly illustrated by Isaiah's having barely left Hezekiah, and the wording is freighted with meaning (vv. 5–6). The answer's frame shows Yahweh's concern is not only for Hezekiah as an individual – although that is part. The covenant relationship with *my people* over whom Hezekiah is *ruler* (*nāgîd*) under Yahweh as 'king'[55] means that not only does Hezekiah need deliverance from his illness but both *you and this city* need deliverance from the Assyrians (v. 6). The basis of the response is not Hezekiah's piety (although that is not questioned) but Yahweh's covenant promise to David: the opening *the LORD, the God of your father David*, is striking, reinforced by the concluding *for my sake and for the sake of my servant David*. In Yahweh's *I have heard your prayer and seen your tears* is another example of his response to his people's distress. Both king and people are 'delivered' by grace, with Hezekiah's life to be extended by *fifteen years*.[56]

Hezekiah's sickness mirrors Jerusalem's sickness—his faithful prayer postpones a sentence of judgment spoken by the prophet Isaiah ([v.1]). The key verse in this regard ([v. 6]) links Hezekiah's recovery to the recovery of the city, even though this upsets the narrative depiction of chaps. [18 – 19], where the deliverance of the city had already been concluded ([19:36–37]).[57]

Two further components are included in the narrative. First comes a known ancient medical treatment, the applying of a *poultice of figs*[58] to *the boil* (v. 7). This is the only clue to the nature of Hezekiah's illness[59] – only recent decades have seen the impact of antibiotics in dramatically reducing the number of deaths from infection of sores and wounds. In this cameo we see the interplay of God's sovereignty, prayer and medical treatment: 'divine sovereignty does not render prayer in sickness inappropriate'.[60]

---

[54] E.g., Ps. 31:9–13; 73; 102:1–11.

[55] See on 1 Kgs 1:35, pp. 46–47; also used of Jeroboam and Baasha in 1 Kgs 14:7 and 16:2.

[56] Sennacherib's siege is in 'the fourteenth year' of Hezekiah's reign (18:13) and Hezekiah reigned 'twenty nine years' (18:2).

[57] C. R. Seitz, 'Isaiah, Book of', *ABD* 3, p. 481.

[58] Walton, Matthews and Chavalas, p. 407; D. P. O'Mathúna, 'Sickness and Disease', *DOTHB*, pp. 895–899.

[59] A serious skin complaint, e.g. ulcer, inflammation; *šĕḥîn* describes serious disease in Exod. 9:9–11; Lev. 13:18–20, 23; Deut. 28:27, 35; Job 2:7. See *HALOT*.

[60] Wiseman, p. 286: cf. 1 Tim. 5:23; James 5:14–18; also O'Mathúna, 'Sickness and Disease', p. 899.

Hezekiah's request for a *sign* (v. 8) 'elaborate[s] with a different emphasis'.[61] Again the king speaks only of personal need. Many still know, whether from personal pain or pastoral care, that 'one of the characteristics of acute suffering is its tendency to obliterate all other experience'.[62] A sign is to be given that *the LORD will do what he has promised* (v. 9), the wording pointing to 'the complete prophetic word [vv. 5–6] . . . almost a rebuke for Hezekiah's self-centeredness'.[63] Rather than moving ahead, the shadow go[*ing*] *back ten steps* signifies 'a return to life and health instead of approaching death. Shadows naturally lengthen, just as people naturally grow old'.[64] Fulfilment provides assurance, a reminder too that Yahweh 'made heaven and earth' (19:15) and is sovereign in human life and history. Unlike Azariah who was prevented from entering the temple due to a skin complaint (15:5), Hezekiah is healed and able again to *go up to the temple of the LORD* (v. 8). Isolation is taken away.

b. Babylon enters the scene (20:12–19)

A question lingers: lengthening the king's life can be regarded as merely delaying death, so will the city's deliverance also be temporary? Readers in exile already know the answer which is now announced. The visit of *envoys* of *Marduk-Baladan . . . king of Babylon* was no doubt associated with seeking Hezekiah's help against the Assyrians, as the Chaldean leader was a key instigator of Babylonian independence from Assyrian rule.[65] For the first time in Kings we read of Babylonian activity, and while Hezekiah sees no threat, readers are aware of what followed a hundred years later. Clearly Hezekiah was willing to join any alliance, showing the full range of resources he could contribute. The narrator makes sure that hearers do not miss Hezekiah's action, adding after the inventory *there was nothing in his palace or in all his kingdom that Hezekiah did not show them* (v. 13). Is there in the repetitive *his* (five times in

[61] Hess, 'Hezekiah and Sennacherib', p. 40. Cf. NIV's *had asked*. In Isaiah, the equivalent of vv. 7–8 is at the end of the narrative (Isa. 38:21–22).

[62] C. Newsom, 'The Book of Job', *New Interpreter's Bible*, vol. 4 (Nashville: Abingdon, 1996), p. 520.

[63] Hobbs, p. 287.

[64] Konkel, p. 604, citing the interpretation of Josephus (*Ant.* 10.28). In v. 9 MT (followed by NRSV) has, rather than two alternatives, a statement and question, 'the shadow has now advanced ten intervals; shall it retreat ten intervals?' 'The contrast in v. 10 is between what is natural and has already happened (cf. v. 11), and what is unnatural and still to happen' (Provan, p. 265).

[65] Marduk-apla-iddinna (Marduk was the chief god of Babylon) is known in Assyrian and Babylonian sources as king of Babylon 721–710 BC and again in 703 BC. It is uncertain whether the visit is to be located prior to the 703 revolt or a subsequent attempt. See Walton, Matthews and Chavalas, p. 407.

v. 13) a suggestion of Solomon-like self-vaunting? Absent is any mention of seeking a word from Yahweh.[66]

Isaiah comes (uninvited?) with questions (vv. 14–15). At first they appear to be simple curiosity, but the narrative soon shows that, like Nathan's approach to David after his adultery with Bathsheba and the death of Uriah (2 Sam. 12), they lead to Hezekiah's self-condemnation. Hezekiah's *from a distant land* is ominous. The Babylonian king had heard of Hezekiah's *illness* (v. 12; *ḥālāh*) but amongst the covenant curses Deuteronomy 29:22 warned that 'foreigners who come *from distant lands* will see the calamities that have fallen on the land and the diseases with which the LORD has afflicted (*ḥillāh*) it' and elsewhere 'distant lands' refers to places to which people may be exiled or from which exiles will return.[67] As in verse 6, Hezekiah's personal situation parallels that of the city. Yahweh's word is that *the time will surely come when everything in your palace* (cf. vv. 13, 15) . . . *will be carried off to Babylon* (v. 17). The message is repeated: *Nothing will be left*. Not only physical wealth, but, with another emphatic doubling, *some of your descendants, your own flesh and blood who will be born to you, will be taken away*. Instead of enjoying the palace in Jerusalem *they will become eunuchs in the palace of the king of Babylon* (v. 18). Of note is the repeated 'show, see' (*rā'āh*, five times in vv. 13–20) and 'all, everything' (*kol*, six times), with 'seeing' becoming a 'taking away' by Babylon. 'Before Yahweh delivers he sees (v. 5) and Babylon's "seeing" the complete stock of treasures and kingdom prefigures the opposite.'[68] Exile is no historical accident but the operation of divine will. The first group 'taken away' was to be in 605 BC (Dan. 1:1–7), followed by a larger group in 597 BC (24:12–16), before final destruction in 587/6 BC (ch. 25).

Hezekiah's response, *The word of the LORD you have spoken is good*, followed by the comment that *he thought, Will there not be peace and security in my lifetime?* (v. 19), has 'from the earliest tradition . . . been interpreted as a very impious response'.[69] More can be said. The acceptance of God's word as *good* invites comparison with Eli's response when Samuel told him of judgment on his family (1 Sam. 3:18), an acknowledgment that the word is true. In

---

[66] Cf. 2 Chr. 32:24, 31.

[67] E.g., 1 Kgs 8:46 (// 2 Chr. 6:36); Isa. 43:6; Jer. 46:27; 51:50; Zech. 6:15. See P. R. Ackroyd, 'An Interpretation of the Babylonian Exile: A Study of II Kings 20, Isaiah 38 – 39', *Scottish Journal of Theology* 27 (1974), pp. 338–339; Hobbs, p. 295; Konkel, p. 611.

[68] Hobbs, p. 288.

[69] Ibid., p. 295. 'There was apparently some discomfort with this verse in the LXX (also Peshitta) which omits Hezekiah's question' (Sweeney, p. 423).

Hezekiah's situation there is no indication that the coming judgment is due to his actions, but the announcement can be seen as a relenting, a promise of delay – as with Ahab (1 Kgs 21:28–29) and later Josiah (2 Kgs 22:18–20). A hundred years later 'elders of the land' will recall how Hezekiah took note of a warning through Micah and so 'the LORD relent[ed]' (Jer. 26:17–19). In the parallel account in Isaiah, following his recovery Hezekiah writes a poem which breathes life and hope (Isa. 38:10–20). While having an element of self-interest (*in my lifetime*), 'the response of Hezekiah is to be regarded as acceptance of the divine will and, with the final phrase, emphasizes the divine grace extended during the lifetime of the faithful king.'[70] God is willing to delay judgment; there is opportunity to change (cf. 2 Pet. 3:9). Faithful response to Yahweh's word may not bring permanent change but there is influence for good that brings peace and wellbeing – and opportunity for further turning to God.

c. Concluding comments (20:20–21)

The standard conclusion notes briefly the major construction of the tunnel which remains to this day.[71] While a human characteristic is to focus on major infrastructure the biblical account has once again included a mere endnote, the dominant attention given to 'trust in the LORD'. The concluding two cameos have shown that, whether in personal life (illness) or ongoing national prosperity and security (the envoys' visit), there is to be faithful reliance on the grace of God. The Hezekiah account opened affirming his unparalleled trust (18:5) but has ended with his turning to alliance with Babylon (20:12–13).

It is only after Hezekiah, reduced to helplessness by the Assyrians, pays tribute (18, 14b), that an oracle of deliverance for Judah comes, 20, 6b . . . It is the sequel to the oracle that is most surprising, however, for in the context of Hezekiah's preoccupation with his personal health and safety, and his incaution with regard to the Babylonian embassy, the promise of deliverance is quickly transmuted into a prediction of downfall at the hands of that power . . . The narrative does not want us to miss the contrasts it sets forth . . . between the formal report on Hezekiah's life and his actual bearing under pressure, and the sharp reverse that occurs between the oracle of deliverance and the oracle that promises

[70] Konkel, p. 612.
[71] More detail in 2 Chr. 32:2–4, 30. The Siloam inscription, discovered in 1880, describes how two parties of excavators met in the centre (R. B. Coote, 'Siloam Inscription', *ABD* 6, pp. 23–24).

demise. The question whether any king in Jerusalem can usher in permanent salvation is by this stage very urgent.[72]

The ending of the Hezekiah narrative remains to this day a reminder that even good leaders may prove to be unreliable. Nevertheless, Hezekiah is presented as an exemplar for what it means to 'trust in the LORD', the variety of responses being both encouragement and warning to readers. The narrative above all points to God, the Maker of heaven and earth, who alone can be trusted, who delivers and who in grace delays judgment.

---

[72] J. G. McConville, 'Narrative and Meaning in the Books of Kings', *Biblica* 70 (1989), p. 43.

2 Kings 21:1–26
19. Apostasy of Manasseh and Amon

In stark contrast to Hezekiah's 'trust' in Yahweh, the Kings account of the long reign of his son Manasseh is of unmitigated *evil in the eyes of the LORD* (v. 2), to be matched completely by his son Amon (v. 20). The period so embeds behaviour in the whole nation that even Josiah's reforms (chs 22 – 23) only delay the inevitable destruction of Jerusalem and exile of its citizens.[1] While 'children are not to be put to death for their parents: each will die for their own sin' (14:6), dominant societal practices and attitudes have a powerful influence through generations.

1. Manasseh (21:1–18)

Manasseh reigned the longest of any king of Judah or Israel, and yet the only details in Kings concern his blatant apostasy, followed by the people. Between the normal introductory and concluding statements (vv. 1, 17–18) comes not the usual narrating of some incident (or incidents) but 'one extended speech of judgment',[2] with three references to acting contrary to what *the LORD had said* (vv. 4, 7, 10). Such is the emphasis on Manasseh's apostasy that there is no mention of the resurgence of Assyrian might early in his reign, with Esarhaddon conquering Egypt by 671 BC.[3] Manasseh is mentioned twice in Assyrian inscriptions as a loyal vassal, including providing troops,[4] and Ekron on the coastal plain west of Jerusalem became

---

[1] 22:15–20; 23:26–27; 24:3–4.

[2] Brueggemann, p. 531.

[3] The first ten years were likely co-regency with Hezekiah, his sole reign being 687–642 BC.

[4] L.-S. Tiemeyer, 'Manasseh', *DOTHB*, pp. 674–675.

the wealthy producer of olive oil for the whole Assyrian empire.[5] After the previous devastation by Sennacherib during Hezekiah's reign, Judah under Assyrian overlordship experienced steady recovery and growth in trade. Elsewhere Manasseh might have been praised for a rule that saw extended peace and stability, but of such the narrative is conspicuously silent. His policies are seen as confirming the coming disaster; peace would be short-lived.

The account in 2 Chronicles 33 starts similarly (vv. 1–9) but then (vv. 10–20) describes his being taken as a prisoner by the king of Assyria and subsequent turning to God[6] and some reforms. While some have seen a contradiction, the two accounts can be seen as complementary, addressing different audiences:

> Kings underlines for its audience the awful consequences of idolatry . . . [and] a summons to repentance is a more immediate concern. Chronicles, on the other hand, addresses a much later time and audience, and therefore draws a different (but complementary) lesson from the life of Manasseh, in emphasizing God's grace to a notorious sinner.[7]

The indictment of verses 2–11 is framed by mention of *the detestable practices of the nations the* LORD *had driven out before the Israelites* (v. 2) and *these detestable* things *more evil than the Amorites who preceded him* (v. 11). With these phrases from Deuteronomy – there describing as 'detestable' the worship of idols and heavenly objects, occult practices and use of dishonest weights[8] – the die is cast. Manasseh has deliberately chosen to make Judah no different from the nations whose practices had led to their being dispossessed of the land. His actions are compared to those of *Ahab* (v. 3), the worst king of Israel, and so Judah will face the same judgment (v. 13). *Arousing [the* LORD*'s] anger* (v. 6) was first mentioned in Kings right at the beginning of the divided kingdoms, in response to Jeroboam I's making of idols, and repeated for other kings of Israel and the people.[9] While Judah also 'stirred up his jealous anger',[10] the first specific mention relating to a king of Judah is Manasseh, to be repeated for

---

[5] C. S. Ehrlich, 'Ekron', *NIDB* 2, pp. 227–228.

[6] Inspiring a later apocryphal devotional psalm, the penitential Prayer of Manasseh.

[7] B. Kelly, 'Manasseh in the Books of Kings and Chronicles (2 Kings 21:1–18; 2 Chron 33:1–20)' in *Windows into Old Testament History*, edited by V. P. Long *et al.* (Grand Rapids and Cambridge: Eerdmans, 2002), p. 140.

[8] Deut. 7:25–26; 12:31; 13:14[15]; 17:4; 18:9–12; 25:13–16; 32:16. 'Detestable practices of the nations Yahweh had driven out before the Israelites' also occurs in 1 Kgs 14:24 (Judah) and 2 Kgs 16:3 (Ahaz, king of Judah).

[9] 1 Kgs 14:9; 15:30; 16:2, 7, 13, 26; 21:22; 22:53.

[10] See on 1 Kgs 14:22 (different vocabulary), pp. 152–153.

the people (v. 15; 22:17).[11] In following the practices of the nations, and acting against Yahweh's promised presence in the temple (v. 4), with the promise to David and Solomon concerning the city (vv. 7–8), 'Manasseh lives now before the time of that promise, and hence beyond it'.[12]

Not only has Manasseh followed the ways of Ahab, but he innovates in worship of *the starry hosts* (vv. 3, 5; 'host of heaven', NRSV, NJPSV). The mention of such in the general summary of 17:16, which covered both Israel and Judah,[13] foreshadowed these actions of Manasseh and the people (23:4–5). Forbidden in Deuteronomy since these bodies have been 'apportioned to all the nations under heaven' (Deut. 4:19; cf. Deut. 17:3), worship of the heavenly bodies, with the belief that in some way they determine events on earth, was common throughout Syro-Palestine and Mesopotamia.[14] In Mesopotamia this developed into astrology, whose allure continues around the globe in diverse cultures. The present distinction between astrology and astronomy developed only gradually with modern science.[15] In contrast to Micaiah's vision of Yahweh 'sitting on his throne with *all the multitudes of heaven* standing round him on his right and on his left' (1 Kgs 22:19, emphasis added), 'the LORD of hosts has thus become merely a god *among* hosts, ... open to manipulation by occult means.'[16]

The sun, moon and stars are God's creation: Genesis 1:14–19 describes them polemically not as powers but unnamed 'lights' to mark 'sacred times, and days and years' and 'to give light on the earth'. As God's 'host' (Isa. 40:26) they are not to be worshipped and God's people are not to 'be terrified by signs in the heavens' (Jer. 10:2). Babylonian astrologers 'who make predictions month by month' are impotent (Isa. 47:13). The first century BC Wisdom of Solomon speaks of people 'ignorant of God (being) foolish by nature: ... they supposed that ... the circle of the stars ... or the luminaries of heaven were the gods that rule the world' (Wisdom 13:1–2, NRSV). Such a statement is still relevant in the world today: whether at the popular level of daily horoscopes in print and electronic media, or national leaders in many countries, East and West, North and South, seeking 'auspicious' times for key events or for

---

[11] See on 23:19, 26, pp. 353, 354–355.

[12] Hobbs, p. 311.

[13] See on 17:16–17, p. 309; also 23:5, p. 352.

[14] Walton, Matthews and Chavalas, p. 456.

[15] See, e.g., A. Koestler, *The Sleepwalkers: A History of Man's Changing View of the Universe* (Harmondsworth: Penguin, 1964), pp. 114–115 (medieval Europe and the influence of Aristotle), 244–248 (Kepler), 291–294 (Tycho).

[16] Provan, p. 267.

help in decision-making. When people turn from trust in the living God who has created all, and in his revealed word, there is substitution of other powers. There is much to cause wonder in looking to the heavens, a factor in the ingrained allure; but there is dangerous folly in worshipping and serving 'created things rather than the Creator' (Rom. 1:25).[17]

In his practices Manasseh followed not only Ahab (v. 3) but also his grandfather Ahaz (v. 6; cf. 16:3–4), going even further. He not only *made a [carved] Asherah pole* (v. 3) but *put it in the temple* (v. 7), giving state endorsement to worship of Asherah as Yahweh's consort.[18] That action goes against the conditions of the promise of remaining in the land (v. 8). *The land I gave their ancestors* significantly recalls the only other instances of the phrase in Kings: in Solomon's temple dedicatory prayer, that God would show favour and bring captives back to the land (1 Kgs 8:34, 40, 48), and the warning of judgment to Jeroboam I and Israel due to the making of Asherah poles (1 Kgs 14:15). Tragically not only Manasseh but also *the people did not listen* (v. 9). 'The verb "listen" (*shemaʿ*) is, of course, defining for the covenantal theology of Deuteronomy. "Listening" is the acknowledgement that one receives life in address from another who has the authority to call into existence by utterance. Failure to listen is an attempt at autonomy.'[19] The link between 'hear/listen' and 'act on the basis of what is said' is a feature of many languages and is seen in Jesus' frequent exhortations to 'hear'.[20] To disobey is to act as if the words have not been spoken, they have not been 'heard'.

Manasseh's apostasy is made more blatant by Yahweh's warnings given by *his servants the prophets* (v. 10).[21] Phrases and vocabulary evoke links back to the beginning of monarchy and to the place of the temple in Israelite life. Judgment is inevitable and public: *I am going to bring such disaster on Jerusalem and Judah that the ears of everyone who hears of it will tingle* (v. 12). The final phrase is seen elsewhere only in the announcement of judgment on the house of Eli, which was to be associated with the capture of the ark and the first destruction of a national sanctuary, that at Shiloh (1 Sam. 3:11). In this and other ways, judgment frames the whole period of

---

[17] R. Clifford and P. Johnson, *Jesus and the Gods of the New Age* (Oxford: Lion Publishing, 2001), pp. 66–79, interact with current practices.

[18] A. H. W. Curtis, 'Canaanite Gods and Religion: 4.3 Asherah', *DOTHB*, pp. 140–141.

[19] Brueggemann, p. 533.

[20] E.g., Matt. 11:15; 13:9, 43.

[21] This generic description is also in 9:7; 17:13, 23; 24:2 and Jer. 7:25; 25:4; 26:5; 29:19; 35:15; 44:4; Dan. 9:6, 10; Ezra 9:11, all in contexts of rejected messages.

monarchy.[22] Its justice is illustrated by the imagery of *measuring line* and *plumb line*[23] and its thoroughness by the *[wiping] out*[24] . . . *as one wipes a dish,* both sides (v. 13). The severity is freighted with significance through further phrasing that is rare in Kings: the people as Yahweh's *inheritance,* and *forsake* (v. 14), are elsewhere only in Solomon's temple prayer (1 Kgs 8:51, 53, 57), and *remnant* only in the Isaianic words to Hezekiah (19:31), while *looted* and *plundered*[25] occur only here. The people's wrongdoing is not only recent but *from the day their ancestors came out of Egypt until this day* (v. 15). The same indictment is made at the initiation of kingship (1 Sam. 8:8), while 'from Egypt to this day' is seen elsewhere only in God's words that deny his need of a temple (2 Sam. 7:6). The three instances of the phrase, along with the other phrases and words noted, provide a sad trajectory from beginning to end of monarchy, together with a relativizing of the temple.

The indictment resumes with Manasseh's shedding *so much innocent blood* (v. 16). Josephus records that Manasseh slaughtered prophets daily[26] and Justin Martyr and Tertullian both mention a tradition that Isaiah was sawn in half under Manasseh (probably alluded to in Hebrews 11:37).[27] Here is a brutal reminder that when rulers do not recognize accountability to a God who requires justice towards all, the way is open to institutional violence of many forms, often directed to people of certain ethnicity, political or religious views, or social status. When God is removed from public life the way is open to justify actions on the grounds of 'the good of the country' (as interpreted by those in power or the majority group) or even to despotic individual rule where 'might is right'. While the twentieth century provided several illustrations of widespread killings and imprisonments, sadly instances multiply into the third millennium, resulting in a continuing flood of refugees and asylum seekers. Brutal oppression can be expressed in various ways. Not long after Manasseh's reign, Jeremiah spoke against those who relied

[22] A. T. Ohm, 'Manasseh and the Punishment Narrative', *Tyndale Bulletin* 61, 2 (2010), pp. 237–254. See also above on 20:19.

[23] In Isa. 28:17 the 'measuring line' is 'justice' and 'righteousness the plumb line'. The similar Amos 7:7–8 has a different word.

[24] As NIV aptly translates, this is more thorough than a simple 'wiping'; *māḥāh* is elsewhere 'blot out, obliterate' (cf. Gen. 6:7; 7:4; Exod. 17:14; 32:32, etc.).

[25] MT has nouns; similarly the verb, 'plunder', occurs only in 17:20, an echo of Judg. 2:14.

[26] *Antiquities* 10.38.

[27] A later work, parts dating variously from second century BC to fourth century AD, is 'The Martydom and Ascension of Isaiah'. A translation and introduction by M. A. Knibb is in *The Old Testament Pseudepigrapha*, vol. 2, ed. J. H. Charlesworth (Garden City, NY: Doubleday, 1985), pp. 143–176.

on the existence of the temple for peace and security, and warned that continued life 'in this place' could only be 'if you do not oppress the foreigner, the fatherless or the widow and do not shed innocent blood in this place, and if you do not follow other gods to your own harm' (Jer. 7:6), while the book of Revelation describes in detail the material prosperity of Babylon (Rome) that comes at the cost of 'human beings' (Rev. 18:13). Ezekiel looked forward to the new temple where 'my princes will no longer oppress my people' (Ezek. 45:8).

No reasons are given for Manasseh's apostasy. While the worship of heavenly bodies was prevalent in Assyria, Assyrian rulers did not impose their religious practices on vassals.[28] A clue may be the repeated *practices of the nations* (vv. 2, 9). Did Manasseh believe that following, and as ruler encouraging, such religious practice was the way to gain favour and standing in the eyes of both people and neighbouring nations, including Assyria? Did he see this as the way to both buttress his own reign and build up the nation? Did he feel that the stance of his father, while saving Jerusalem, had caused devastation of the rest of Judah? Was he swayed by the resurgence of Assyria? Did he believe that he was not rejecting worship of Yahweh, simply adding others for security? Were reasons like this also in the minds of the people? Certainly such pragmatic factors, with their immediate appeal, continue through the ages in diverse cultures, heightened now by the immediacy of global media with its visual images.

The period of Manasseh provides a challenge for Christians living in countries that are sometimes described as 'Christian'. Judah, with the temple and its continuing worship in Jerusalem, could pride itself as 'the people of Yahweh' but its lifestyle had copied and absorbed 'the detestable practices of the nations'. A lifestyle that is indistinguishable from the wider community, apart from participation in religious activities, despite current prosperity is doomed. It also fails to be a means of bringing God's blessing to the nations.

In the time of Hezekiah, the Assyrian king had presented a vision of 'life' in submission to him outside the land (18:31–32), but Hezekiah chose to have confidence in Yahweh alone and Jerusalem was saved. Now Manasseh, continuing the Davidic line, appeared to be enjoying life in the land while serving many gods – but the word of Yahweh's judgment is a warning to all readers not to follow that path. Fifty years later the city and nation were devastated. Seven hundred years later Satan offered Jesus power and wealth in

---

[28] See on 16:10–18, pp. 301–302.

submission to him, but the Son of David replied, 'Worship the Lord your God, and serve him *only*' (Matt. 4:10, emphasis added).

2. Amon (21:19–26)

Amon's reign is brief, less than two years. The formulaic introduction leaves no doubt as to his wrongdoing. With balancing Hebrew phrases we read (vv. 20–22):

> he walked in all the way his father walked
>> and he served the idols his father served
>>> and he bowed down to them
>> and he forsook Yahweh the God of his ancestors
> and did not walk in the way of Yahweh.

The alternatives are clear: *the ways of his father* or Yahweh's way, *the idols* of *his father* or *the God of his ancestors*. The language echoes Judges 2:12: 'They *forsook Yahweh, the God of their ancestors*, who had brought them out of Egypt, and they *walked* after other gods from the gods of the peoples around them and *bowed down to them*' (my translation and emphasis). Amon is repeating a longstanding pattern, despite the ongoing grace of God.

No reason is given for his assassination. As with Joash *officials* were involved, and subsequently *killed* (cf. 12:20–21; 14:5), and again *the people of the land* (elders of key families, cf. 11:14) appoint the successor, the young Josiah. Unlike reforms upon the accession of Joash (11:17–18) however, there is no hint of disenchantment with existing royal practices.

How could Judah – a people delivered from Egypt and brought into the land, given laws that are the way of life, blessed by the presence of God now centred in the temple, with a promised continuity of kingship, and with ongoing words through his prophets – deteriorate to become such an apostate, oppressive nation? This is the mystery of human sin that begins with decisions in the plenteous beauty of Eden, and that is behind the warnings in Deuteronomy 4 of apostasy while enjoying God's blessing in the land. Alongside is the wonder of God's continuing gracious perseverance with his people and the world he has made.

> Humanity seems utterly incapable of sustaining anything good. . . . Doom is inevitable because human beings are bent on their destructive course, turning away from the way of God. Yet . . . even as one hears the word of judgment, one hears a message of God's persistent grace . . . Judgment comes not so much because of

isolated acts of disobedience, but because of a people's history of willful rejection of grace.[29]

It is this that leads to the anguish of Christ as 'he wept over [the city]' of Jerusalem (Luke 19:41). It is the reality that Paul grapples with, especially in Romans, proclaiming the wonders of God's grace and the enabling of the Spirit who shares in the 'groaning' as we look forward to the time when 'the creation itself will be liberated from its bondage to decay and brought into the freedom and glory of the children of God' (Rom. 8:21). Then 'there will be no more death or mourning or crying or pain' (Rev. 21:4).

[29] Seow, pp. 277–278.

2 Kings 22:1 – 23:30
20. Josiah and whole-hearted turning to God

'Hear, O Israel: The LORD our God, the LORD is one. Love the LORD your God with all your heart and with all your soul and with all your strength. These commandments that I give you today are to be upon your hearts' (Deut. 6:4–6). Here is a clarion call to full-orbed, undivided love of God with all one is and all one has.[1] The *Shema'*, named from the first word, has echoed through the centuries on the lips of Jewish people morning and evening.[2] Jesus affirmed the heart of the covenantal relationship as the greatest commandment, reminding his hearers that the call to love God, to serve him alone, cannot be separated from loving one's neighbour.[3]

The story of Kings has led, however, to severe judgment on Manasseh and the people: they 'did not listen' (21:9). Amon's brief reign has been no better but destruction has not yet come. Into such a bleak, apostate and threatening setting shines the account of Josiah, the only person throughout Joshua to Kings of whom it is said that he 'turned to the LORD . . . with all his heart and with all his soul and with all his strength, in accordance with all the Law of Moses' (23:25).[4]

Sometimes it seems easier to love God when the general community ethos is sympathetic, when a God-honouring tone and a concern for

---

[1] 'Strength' translates *mĕ'ōd*, generally the common adverb, 'very, muchly', but seen as a noun only in Deut. 6:5 and 2 Kgs 23:25. Qumran and later Jewish writings interpret as 'property, wealth'; M. Weinfeld, *Deuteronomy 1–11* (Anchor Bible; New York: Doubleday, 1991), pp. 339–340.

[2] The complete *Shema'* is Deut. 6:4–9; 11:13–21; Num. 15:37–41 (Reform synagogues recite only Deut. 6:4–9; Num. 15:40–41).

[3] Matt. 22:35–40, and parallel passages.

[4] 1 Kgs 14:8 affirms that David followed Yahweh 'with all his heart'.

morality prevail. A person born into a devout family has a good example to follow. Josiah did not have such advantages, although Manasseh's repentance (as in Chronicles) may have influenced some of his advisors and associates. Although Amon had 'followed completely the ways of his father [Manasseh]' (21:20–21), Josiah *did what was right in the eyes of the LORD and followed completely the ways of his father David*, exemplifying the Deuteronomic law of the king in *not turning aside to the right or to the left* (v. 2; cf. Deut. 17:20).[5] Josiah is presented as the model king *par excellence*, his life illustrating the exhortation of the writer of Proverbs:

> My son, pay attention to what I say;
> turn your ear to my words.
> Do not let them out of your sight,
> keep them within your heart;
> for they are life to those who find them
> and health to one's whole body. . . .
> Let your eyes look straight ahead;
> fix your gaze directly before you.
> Give careful thought to the paths for your feet
> and be steadfast in all your ways.
> Do not turn to the right or the left;
> keep your foot from evil. (Prov. 4:20–22, 25–27)

The social environment was harsh and the previous half-century marked by apostasy, corruption and violence, but Josiah's behaviour shows how it is still possible to obey God. That path was open also for his successors, but they did not follow. Although history will show that his actions only delay judgment until after his death (22:19–20), the narrative is an encouragement that the command is not unrealistic; obedience does make a difference. The presence of heavy darkness is no excuse for failing to shine a bright light.

Josiah takes the initiative throughout. His actions, with repeated vocabulary[6] and involving a widening circle of other people, provide a useful structure for the narrative:[7]

- He 'sent' Shaphan the secretary to Hilkiah the high priest, resulting in discovery of the book of the law (22:3–11).
- He 'commanded' Hilkiah, Shaphan and three others to make inquiries about the book and implications of its contents, and they go to the prophet Huldah (22:12–20).

[5] Said also to the people (Deut. 28:14; Josh. 23:6) and Joshua (Josh. 1:7).
[6] Varying translations in EVV.
[7] Partly based on Nelson, p. 254.

- He 'sent' and all the elders of Judah and Jerusalem gathered before him, along with all the people, for a public reading of the book leading to reaffirmation of their covenant allegiance (23:1–3).
- He 'commanded ... burned ... put an end to ... ' (several actions of which he is the subject, in Jerusalem, Bethel and other places), accomplishing reforms that flowed from the book (23:4–20).
- He 'commanded all the people' to join in celebration of the Passover 'as written in the book' (23:21–23).
- Finally he 'got rid of ... ', showing complete obedience to the book (23:24–25).

1. Repair and discovery of the book (22:3–11)

The narrative begins with clear echoes of temple renovations ordered one hundred and fifty years earlier by Joash, who also began his reign as a child (vv. 3–7; cf. 12:1–16), but attention soon shifts to what will be central to Josiah's actions, *the Book of the Law/Covenant.*[8] For the writer of Kings, the finding of the book *in the eighteenth year of his reign* (v. 3; also 23:23) is the defining event and so is brought to the fore. It has ongoing relevance, even to people in exile, for, as in the earlier Solomon narrative, concern for the temple building is shown to be secondary to obeying God's commands.

The parallel account in 2 Chronicles 34 – 35, addressed to the post-exilic community with its rebuilt temple, shows more interest in the temple and worship and so presents material differently. It describes how reforms began from the eighth year, with a major thrust from the twelfth. The two accounts are complementary.[9] Neither mention the decline of Assyrian power beginning in the final years of Assurbanipal (died 631 BC, the eighth year of Josiah's reign).[10] In so doing they avoid any suggestion that the reforms had a nationalistic motivation, although the decline did enable Josiah to extend control in the north (23:15–20; 2 Chr. 34:6–7, 33). Focus is on actions exemplifying worship of Yahweh alone, not geopolitical matters.

With discovery of the *Book of the Law, Shaphan the secretary* (v. 8)

---

[8] 'Book of the Law': 22:8, 11 (cf. 23:24); 'Book of the Covenant': 23:2, 21 (cf. 23:3); 'book': 22:10, 13 (2x), 16; 23:3, 24. Although the Pentateuch has come to be known as Torah, 'the Law' (or 'Instruction'), within the Pentateuch itself the phrase 'book of the law' is used of Deuteronomy or part thereof; cf. Deut. 17:18–20; 28:58–61; 29:21; 30:10; 31:9–13, 24–29. As Deuteronomy is preaching concerning the 'covenant' it is appropriately called 'the Book of the Covenant'.

[9] M. A. Sweeney, 'Josiah', *DOTHB*, pp. 575–579.

[10] See further below on 23:29, p. 356.

becomes a key person. The repeated mention of his office (*sōpēr*, NJPSV *scribe*, vv. 3, 8, 9, 10, 12) runs alongside 'book' (*sēper*): his role becomes centred on 'reading' the book to the king (vv. 8, 10). A person with education and training has great responsibility as a transmitter of God's Word.[11] Shaphan and his family also provide an example of faithful leadership through generations: his son *Ahikam* (vv. 12, 14) later was a protector of Jeremiah (Jer. 26:24), and Ahikam's son Gedaliah was appointed by Nebuchadnezzar as governor of Judah after the destruction of Jerusalem and looked after Jeremiah (2 Kgs 25:22; Jer. 39:13 – 41:3); another son, Elasah, was entrusted with Jeremiah's letter to the exiles in Babylon (Jer. 29:3); and yet another, Gemariah, provided the room from which Baruch read Jeremiah's scroll to the people, which was heard by Gemariah's son, Micaiah, who urged the king not to burn the scroll (Jer. 36:10–17, 25).

We do not know Shaphan's thoughts as he came to the king. He had *read* the book himself (v. 8), no doubt recognizing its significance, but he reports that he has fulfilled the king's orders (v. 9; cf. vv. 3–7) before referring to *a book* that *Hilkiah the priest has given me* (v. 10, with no further specification; contrast Hilkiah's *the Book of the Law*, v. 8). Is he remembering the attitude of Josiah's predecessors? It was likely during Manasseh's reign that the book was removed from beside the ark.[12]

Josiah's focus thus far has been temple repair, but now he becomes aware for the first time of Yahweh's requirements and the consequences of failure to worship Yahweh alone. In anguish he *tore his robes* (v. 11), yet grief and remorse without change is inadequate.

2. Humble openness to learning the truth (22:12–20)

His response is swift as he orders a group of top officials to *go and inquire of the LORD for me and for the people and for all Judah* (v. 13). He knows that the Book of the Law with its exhortations and warnings, while crucial for the king, is addressed to all the people of Yahweh. Again it is a prophet, not a king, who knows the course of history, and so they go to a *prophet* in the court, *Huldah ... wife of* the *keeper of the wardrobe* (probably a temple official; compare a similar position in 10:22).[13] She begins by speaking of *the man who sent you to me* (v. 15): when it comes to hearing Yahweh's

---

[11] On the training and role of 'scribes' see D. W. Baker, 'Scribes and Schools'. *DOTHB*, pp. 884–888.

[12] Provan, p. 271.

[13] It is often noted that Jeremiah had begun his ministry five years earlier (Jer. 1:2) and Zephaniah also prophesied during Josiah's reign and was possibly of royal descent (Zeph. 1:1).

word to the people, Josiah the king is 'not better than his brothers' (Deut. 17:20). Her word confirms Josiah's understanding that the book conveyed a prophetic message of *the LORD's anger* (vv. 13, 17) over the people's worship of other gods, and the certainty of destruction of the city and temple (*this place*) is stressed, *my anger . . . will not be quenched.*

There is however a further personal word for *the king* (vv. 18–20). Josiah has *heard* the words of the book (v. 18), and responded appropriately. While NIV's *your heart was responsive* does not convey timidity in the face of threatening circumstances,[14] the associated *humbled yourself before the LORD* is the key. How different was to be the arrogant response around sixteen years later of his son Jehoiakim to Jeremiah's words (Jer. 36). Josiah is given the promise that the coming *disaster* will not be in his lifetime. Of only two people in Kings is it said that they 'humbled themselves': Ahab, the worst king of Israel, and Josiah, the best king of Judah.[15] In both cases promised judgment is deferred till after their death. God's grace is open to all. Hezekiah had also received a word of delay beyond his lifetime (20:16–19), although Josiah's concern for the whole city and people shines through (vv. 13, 19).

So they took her answer back to the king (v. 20). It can be helpful to pause before the scene changes and reflect on responses Josiah may have made, in interaction with our own experiences. Judgment on the city has been affirmed as certain, albeit delayed. What *can* be done that will make any difference? Occasionally it is said, 'The world is doomed, judgment is certain, so what's the point of trying to bring about change? All that is worthwhile is to prepare oneself and others for the future judgment, for eternity.' Sometimes this is a stated reason for stressing evangelism over against matters of social justice. Alternatively, personal situations may lead to hopeless inactivity, perhaps with sorrow, simply waiting for the inevitable. Josiah shows another way forward.

3. The Book and the Covenant (23:1–3)

Josiah acts positively to bring about community change, with a renewal of the covenant (cf. Josh. 8:30–35; 24:1–28). 'Humbling oneself' goes beyond sorrow overcoming punishment. It is not directed inward, but is 'before the LORD' (22:19), a submission to God, with desire to continue the relationship with him. If wrong

---

[14] Elsewhere *rkk* with 'heart' has the sense of being timid, faint-hearted or fearful (Deut. 20:3; Isa. 7:4; Jer. 51:46; Job 23:16).
[15] See on 1 Kgs 21:25–29, p. 199.

against God is admitted, the only valid response is active yearning to do right, to do what pleases God, irrespective of consequences.

Josiah acts to renew the covenantal relationship in the terms Yahweh has given in the book. Has Josiah seen beyond the coming judgment to hope of restoration? This was affirmed in Solomon's prayer at the dedication of the temple three hundred years previously (1 Kgs 8:46–53) and before that in the covenantal book (Deut. 30:1–10). Was he even hopeful that, just as his own response had led to promise of delay, the same may be so if the people respond? What we do know is that he saw no alternative other than for *all the people from the least to the greatest* to renew *the covenant in the presence of the LORD* (vv. 2–3).

> Significantly, however, there is no prayer for deliverance, no call for God to turn back the word of judgment. . . . Josiah's initial desire to turn back God's wrath (22:13) is met by the prophetic word stating the inevitability of destruction for Judah (22:16–17). Still, Josiah proceeds with the reforms. One gathers, then, that we obey God neither for the sake of rewards nor for the aversion of judgment. Rather, obedience to God is simply what faith brings about.[16]

To be in a covenant relationship with Yahweh means listening to his words and following him *with all* one's *heart and all* one's *soul*. The king as leader sets the example, but the people also have to respond (v. 3). Josiah's example and the people's response have ongoing relevance. Here, before the exile, is a modelling of action that can be taken after the exile. Whether the people are facing certain destruction of city and temple, or are away from the city in exile after destruction, the same response is possible, for God continues the covenant relationship.

The book of Job opens with the disturbing and penetrating question, 'Will Job serve God if he gets nothing out of it?' (Job 1:9, my translation). Do people serve God only to avoid judgment or to gain blessing? Josiah's love of God is not to avert judgment; it is the only appropriate action, living in humble relationship with the covenant-keeping God.

Six centuries later a descendant of Josiah was to live a life of perfect obedience. Irrespective of what was ahead he prayed, 'Not as I will, but as you will' (Matt. 26:39). He called others to become his disciples, people learning 'to obey everything I have commanded' (Matt. 28:19–20). Obedient trust is the response to, and the goal of,

---

[16] Seow, p. 286.

God's grace (Rom. 1:5; Eph. 2:8–10). To say with integrity, 'Jesus is Lord', is to be eager to know his will and to do it. Irrespective of what was ahead, Josiah knew that he was called to 'hear' Yahweh alone.

4. Obedience means doing (23:4–20)

At the heart of wedding ceremonies is a mutual promise to love and to honour. Such vows are made in all sincerity, with a genuine desire to keep them. But then come the realities of daily life: now that two have become one, no longer can one please oneself, and the outworking is a lifelong process. The promises of the covenant ceremony, at least for Josiah, are made with 'heart and soul'. Now they are to be put into practice.

Radical changes are needed, beginning with removal and destruction of objects that have been sacred to many. Priority was cleansing of the temple itself, removing objects for worship of *Baal and Asherah and all the starry hosts* that Manasseh had brought in (v. 4; cf. 21:3–5), utterly destroying them by burning, grinding and scattering (vv. 4, 6).[17] There can be 'no other gods before me' (Deut. 5:7). People involved in these cults cannot continue and so *idolatrous priests*[18] who had been brought in are deported and *the quarters of the male shrine prostitutes*[19] destroyed. The bringing to Jerusalem of priests from high places throughout Judah (*from Geba to Beersheba*) and their sharing in priestly provisions, but not in sacrificing (vv. 8–9), accords with Deuteronomy 18:6–8. The *gateway* (NJPSV: 'shrines of the gates') likely brought local revenue. Additional locations and objects of worship alien to Yahweh worship are listed: *Topheth*, mentioned only here in Kings, was 'a notorious cultic site associated with human sacrifice'[20] while *Molek* is mentioned at the time of Solomon (1 Kgs 11:5, 7, 33);[21] sun-worship cult-objects introduced by Manasseh are destroyed and altars erected by Ahaz (cf. 16:11)[22] and Manasseh (21:5) are *removed* and *the rubble* scattered (v. 12).

Turning east, with a play on words the Mount of Olives (*har hammišḥâ*, 'The Mountain of Anointing') is called *Hill of Corruption*

---

[17] Mention of Bethel (v. 5) anticipates vv. 15–16.

[18] *kōmer* is used in MT only for priests of foreign gods; also Hos. 10:5 and Zeph. 1:4.

[19] See on 1 Kgs 14:23–24; 15:12, pp. 152, 155. *Weaving for Asherah* matches a practice known in honouring other gods in ancient Mesopotamia (Cogan and Tadmor, p. 286).

[20] Sweeney, p. 448 and references there. Cf. Jer. 7:31, 32; 19:6, 11–14; Isa. 30:33. For 'causing a son or daughter to pass through fire', see on 16:3, p. 299, n. 43; cf. 21:6.

[21] Also Lev. 18:21; 20:2–5; Isa. 57:9; Jer. 32:35; 49:3; Zeph. 1:5; Acts 7:43.

[22] Rooftop altars are mentioned in Jer. 19:13; 32:29; Zeph. 1:5.

(*har hammašḥît*): the *high places* built by Solomon (all names are in 1 Kings 11:5–8) are destroyed and desecrated forever through the pollution of human bones (cf. Num. 19:18). Then north at Bethel (vv. 15–18) Josiah continues to 'correct the problems introduced by the kings of the past and thereby lay the groundwork for the reunification of Israel and Judah around the worship of YHWH in Jerusalem'.[23] Desecration appropriately copies Moses' destruction of the golden calf (Exod. 32:20). Again the writer notes fulfilment of *the word of the LORD* (v. 16; cf. 1 Kgs 13:1–2), reinforced by stating that people have remembered both *the man of God who came from Judah* and the prophecy and that honour is given in respecting his grave which is shared with the *prophet who had come from Samaria* who had affirmed the prophecy (vv. 17–18; 1 Kgs 13:30–32). The prophecy that Josiah would 'sacrifice the priests of the high places' (1 Kgs 13:2) is fulfilled throughout the region – and *then he went back to Jerusalem* (v. 20). The removal of worship of other gods has been completed, but the culmination was to be positive worship in Jerusalem.

Unstated is the effect of these actions on the life of the people throughout the region of Israel and Judah. One has only to think of feelings aroused by changes in local church structures (even in furniture!) to begin to imagine the upheaval. Habits that are comfortable (even if life-threatening) are not easily changed. Suddenly key religious personnel are 'unemployed' or in their eyes 'demoted' (cf. v. 9), with socio-economic consequences. Probably many choose not to move to Jerusalem. People no longer have access to religious practices that have, in their eyes, given comfort and security. This is a seedbed for future problems (see below). Nevertheless, God's word must be obeyed, rather than maintaining destructive behavioural patterns. Pain is unavoidable if a cancer is to be removed.

5. Communal worship according to the Book (23:21–23)

Josiah as king has taken the reform initiative thus far, but it is the people who are to be involved. The *Book of the Covenant* orders more than removal of all aspects of the worship of other gods – that is the negative side of positive worship and obedience in everyday life. Josiah thus *gave this order to all the people: 'Celebrate the Passover to the LORD your God'.*

The recounting of the celebration has ongoing relevance. The Passover is a family celebration remembering God's acts of delivering the people from slavery in Egypt, the foundation of the covenant

[23] Sweeney, p. 449.

relationship. As such, the Passover and the covenant go back well before the monarchy, a feature highlighted by the comment: *neither in the days of the judges who led Israel nor in the days of the kings of Israel and the kings of Judah had any such Passover been observed* (v. 22). Indeed, in Joshua-Kings the only previous mention of Passover is in celebration at Gilgal under Joshua before beginning the conquest of the land (Josh. 5:10).[24] Passover is a reminder that monarchy is not essential for the covenant relationship and for God's acts of deliverance to continue.

6. Allegiance to Yahweh is complete (23:24–25)

Commitment to Yahweh is to be expressed not only in places and forms of corporate worship, but also in the decision-making of everyday life. Seeking advice or some control over the future through *mediums and spiritists* or *household gods*[25] is prevented by removal (cf. Deut. 18:9–12; Isa. 8:19–22).

The concluding statement embraces all actions taken by Josiah since *Hilkiah the priest . . . discovered* the book *in the temple of the LORD* (v. 24). Wholehearted commitment to God is more than emotions or words, for the commendation of Josiah comes after he has persevered in removing all sources that encourage worship of other gods. It is not enough to say, 'Lord, Lord', or even to 'prophesy' and 'perform many miracles': one must do 'the will of my Father who is in heaven'; that is the only foundation for security when the storm comes (Matt. 7:21–27).

7. Did the reforms have ongoing results? (23:26–30)

a. Judgment is still coming (23:26–27)

Again we are reminded that Josiah's reforms do not avert the coming disaster. Huldah's earlier words (22:15–17) are reinforced in the concluding summary. No longer is Yahweh going to maintain Judah in the land he promised to them, no longer will he remain tied to *the city I chose* and *this temple, about which I said, 'My Name shall be*

---

[24] The statement does not mean the Passover was not celebrated, the key being *such*. With its greater attention to cultic matters, Chronicles gives more details of the celebration under Josiah (2 Chr. 35:1–19) and also describes a celebration under Hezekiah (2 Chr. 30), although that under Josiah was unlike others 'since the days of the prophet Samuel' (2 Chr. 35:18).

[25] 'Household gods' (*tĕrāpîm*) are mentioned in Gen. 31:19–35; Judg. 17:5; 18:14–20; 1 Sam. 19:13, 16; Hos. 3:4. Their use in divination is explicit in Ezek. 21:21 [MT 26] and Zech. 10:2 (NIV 'idols').

there' (v. 27; cf. 1 Kgs 8:29). The reason: *Because of all that Manasseh had done* (v. 26). Manasseh's lasting impact is reaffirmed in the following chapter (24:3–4), and the destruction and exile will be described with little comment (the rest of chapters 24 – 25). Other parts of the OT provide further insight into reasons for the exile and the significance of Manasseh's long reign.

When the exile did take place, people questioned God's justice with the saying, 'The parents eat sour grapes, and the children's teeth are set on edge' (Ezek. 18:2). As previously noted, the only law of Moses to be explicitly quoted in Kings is that rejecting inter-generational liability (2 Kgs 14:6).[26] Ezekiel's response was that 'the children', the generation that experienced the fall of Jerusalem and the beginning of exile, were being punished for their own wrong-doing and failure to do what was right (see the rest of Ezekiel 18). Indeed, in Kings itself 'the four successors of Josiah . . . demonstrate no willingness at all to emulate their predecessor'.[27] Sadly, Jeremiah provides evidence that the reforms may well have been only super-ficial, as often with reforms imposed from above. Josiah's son, Jehoiakim, showed more enthusiasm for making the palace luxurious than for caring about the poor and needy (which is what 'knowing God' implies).[28] Amazingly, when the final destruction took place, some said that everything was all right until they stopped worship-ping the 'Queen of heaven' (Jer. 44:15–19), implying that Josiah's 'reforms' were the reason for the fall of Jerusalem! Ezekiel is yet more scathing (even scatological) in denouncing religious practices and violence in Jerusalem prior to the exile (Ezek. 16; 23).

Traditions are not easily eradicated. Manasseh's reign intensified a pattern endemic for centuries. Josiah might love God with *his* 'heart and soul and strength' and so issue laws for change, but whilst a change of 'heart' (thinking and willing) can be modelled, it cannot be imposed by law or political power. As suggested above, the dramatic cultic changes, with socio-economic consequences, would have been met with varied responses.[29]

The Kings narrative shows how neither the zealous eradication of the wicked by Jehu (chs 9 –10) nor the enforced removal of pagan worship objects by Josiah were able to effect lasting changes amongst the people. Significantly, Jesus neither used nor commended those approaches, although Christian rulers since have sought to bring religious change through political might and warfare. History

---

[26] See exposition there, pp. 288–299.
[27] Hobbs, p. 342.
[28] Jer. 22:15–17.
[29] A comparison is the turmoil with various monarchs of the decades of the English and Scottish Reformations.

provides its examples of times of 'reformation'. When Christians are the majority in a nation issues of political power continue. It is right that leaders and Christian groups set examples, but the use of political means to impose religious change is fraught with failure. Josiah is an example of 'a moral man in an immoral society', showing 'at the same time, (a) the limits of personal impact upon public life and (b) the cruciality of personal engagement that does not grow cynical in its limitation'.[30] While Paul recounted the experienced limitations of external law, foreshadowed by Jeremiah and Ezekiel, through the Spirit life can be lived in simple trust and obedience – that is the goal of our being saved 'by grace'.[31] Josiah continues as an example of living faithfully.

b. Josiah's death (23:29–30)

Josiah's death is told with minimal interpretation, with matter-of-fact statements (vv. 29–30). The description encapsulates a major shift in military and political power in the ancient Near East that was to have great impact in Jerusalem and Judah during the next two decades. Assyrian might was almost at an end. As early as 646 BC Assyrian control had weakened to the north of Jerusalem, with the fortress of Megiddo coming under Egyptian control from 646 BC, but the end was near in 612 BC, with Babylonian forces sacking the capital Nineveh and Assyrian forces retreating west to Harran. In 609 BC Egyptian forces under *Pharaoh Necho* marched to *help*[32] *the king of Assyria* against the Babylonians. In the event, the battle was inconclusive but Judah came under Egyptian control (see below). We are not told why Josiah went to fight against Necho. He may have been trying to expedite the ultimate defeat of the Assyrians, seeing Babylon as removing that threat to Judah – just as Hezekiah welcomed Babylonian aid (20:12–13). All we are told is that he was killed in battle and buried in Jerusalem, 'suffering the same ignominious exit from the stage as his apostate ancestor Ahaziah' (9:27–28).[33] Chronicles is more detailed, with Josiah acting despite warnings which the Egyptian says has come from God (2 Chr. 35:20–24). It is as if the Kings narrator mentions the death circumstances solely to describe his burial *in his own tomb*, while Jerusalem was still enjoying peace, so fulfilling Huldah's prophecy (22:20).

[30] Brueggemann, pp. 563–564.
[31] Jer. 31:31–34; Ezek. 36:24–28; Rom. 8:1–4; Eph. 2:8–10.
[32] The Hebrew *'al* can mean 'against' (so AV/KJV, NJPSV) or 'alongside'. Details have become clearer through publication of *The Babylonian Chronicles* (*ANET*, p. 305); Wiseman, p. 305.
[33] Provan, p. 274.

Once again we meet the paradox evident in the long reigns of Jeroboam II of Israel and, closer at hand, of Manasseh. It is the mystery of the sovereignty of God in human affairs and the calculus of human suffering, along with the complexities of living as individuals within larger society. The Scriptures grapple throughout with the reality of righteous people suffering, including early death, over against a popular view of an individualistic *quid pro quo* God.[34] Examples abound in the book of Job, the questions of Psalms (e.g., Pss. 22, 73) or of people to Jesus concerning the man born blind (John 9:2), and Jesus' own rhetorical questions following news of Galilean martyrs (Luke 13:1–5).

The narrator's silence as to Josiah's motives may be to avoid detracting from Josiah as the model for wholehearted loyalty to Yahweh. The story of his reforms has been given in detail with high commendation. The way forward not only for kings but for people (even when there is no king) is the same: turning to the God who delivers his people and makes a covenant with them (remembered in the Passover), and living in the relationship by serving him alone. Reforms may not have been permanent in the life of pre-exilic Jerusalem and Judah, but their memory continued and are now told as an encouragement to obey in the present. The Book of the Covenant remains as the word of God to be heard.

---

[34] See on 14:23–29, pp. 294–295.

2 Kings 23:31 – 25:26
21. The end comes quickly

1. Jehoahaz's brief reign 23:31–35

Following Josiah's reforms, and decades of freedom from Assyrian hegemony, who could have predicted what followed his death: his successor taken as captive to Egypt; within five years some key officials taken to Babylon; a mere seven years later the king himself taken captive to Babylon, along with large numbers of significant people; and after another decade the city and temple razed and Judah devastated, bringing the end of the kingdom of Judah? Only 'prophets' and the few who heeded their words could have done so (24:2)! They were open to hear Yahweh's word and could see the turmoil and destruction coming, although not specific details and times.

On Josiah's death, 'the people of the land' (v. 30) appointed a younger son, Jehoahaz, as king,[1] probably expecting him to continue Josiah's policies, including resistance of Egypt. Although his reign was brief he is evaluated as being like preceding kings (v. 32; Josiah excluded, cf. 21:2, 20). Necho and the Egyptian forces had hurried north and, although unsuccessful in defeating the Babylonians, Necho spent several months seeking to help his Assyrian allies and established a base at *Riblah*, an Assyrian administrative centre on the Orontes River in north Lebanon.[2] The circumstances leading to Jehoahaz being brought there are unknown, although it is clear evidence of Egyptian control over Judah. He is *put . . . in chains* and

---

[1] Jehoahaz was probably the throne name of Shallum (cf. Jer. 22:10–12). He was two years younger than Jehoiakim (cf. v. 36) and is the fourth son according to 1 Chr. 3:15. For 'the people of the land', see on 11:14, p. 271.

[2] Around 210 miles (330 km) north of Jerusalem; later Nebuchadnezzar's base for the final siege of Jerusalem (25:6).

subsequently taken as prisoner *to Egypt, and there he died* (vv. 33–34), his death being prophesied by Jeremiah (Jer. 22:10–12). Now Pharaoh, not 'the people of the land', determines who will be king. *Jehoiakim* will be his puppet: the name change from *Eliakim* ('my God establishes') to specify the God of Israel, Jehoiakim ('Yah establishes', v. 34), may be ironic, or a claim that Yahweh supported Pharaoh (cf. 2 Chr. 35:21). A tribute was mandated, *a hundred talents of silver and a talent of gold*, not large compared to the 'three hundred talents of silver and thirty talents of gold' paid by Hezekiah to Sennacherib (18:14) or the earlier one thousand talents of silver sent by Menahem of Israel (15:19). Still, it was a sizeable sum to be paid through a form of taxation: *the people of the land* who had supported Jehoahaz pay the price (v. 35).

The vocabulary of verse 35 evocatively shows the reversal of Judah's situation in contrast to the historic deliverance from the 'oppression'[3] of 'Pharaoh' (three times[4]) into freedom in the 'land' (twice), taking with them Egyptian 'silver and gold' (twice).[5] The narrator sees what the people were blind to: refusal to live within the covenantal relationship leads to the undoing of the covenantal deliverance.

2. Jehoiakim and Babylon (23:36 – 24:7)

Other than political decisions (24:1), the narrator tells of Jehoiakim only that *he did evil in the eyes of the LORD, just as his predecessors had done* (23:36). The general evaluation is warranted by the consistently negative oracles and events in Jeremiah, including Jehoiakim's arrogant, dismissive attitude to Jeremiah's prophetic word.[6] At that time Jeremiah spoke of his having been preaching 'for twenty-three years – from the thirteenth year of Josiah', and of messages from Yahweh's 'servants the prophets', but 'you did not listen', so Yahweh said, 'you have aroused my anger' and 'have brought harm to yourselves' (Jer. 25:3–7). As if listing any more sin is pointless, the narrator focuses on the turmoil during his reign, declaring *the LORD sent* various forces; all was *according to the LORD's command* (24:2–3).

Four years into Jehoiakim's reign, around 604 BC, *Nebuchadnezzar king of Babylon invaded the land, and Jehoiakim became his vassal* (24:1). Babylonian forces had decisively defeated Egyptian forces at

---

[3] The verb translated 'exacted' (*nāgaś*) occurs only here in Kings and in Exod. 3:7; 5:6–14 describes the Egyptian 'slave-drivers'.

[4] 'Jehoiakim paid Pharaoh the silver and gold Pharaoh demanded. . . . people of the land to give to Pharaoh . . . '

[5] Exod. 3:22; 11:2; 12:35.

[6] Jer. 19:3–5; 22:13–19; 26:20–23; 36:1–32.

Carchemish in Syria in 605 (Jer. 46:2) and Nebuchadnezzar over successive years increased his control south into Palestine.[7] Somehow Jehoiakim remained as king through switching allegiance, perhaps pleading that he had only supported Egypt because Pharaoh had made him king. At that time, along with temple utensils, a number of the royal household were taken to Babylon, both as hostages and to be trained as future diplomats.[8] It is unclear whether Jehoiakim himself was forced to go to Babylon or merely threatened.[9] In 601 Nebuchadnezzar clashed indecisively with Egyptian forces and due to severe losses retreated to Babylon. This became an occasion for Jehoiakim to rebel, no doubt with some popular support. He may have simply withheld tribute or also looked to Egypt for help. His action was disastrous: Nebuchadnezzar encouraged other vassals, *Aramean, Moabite and Ammonite*, to raid Judah (24:2) before he himself was strong enough in 599/98 to mount a full-scale attack. Egypt was powerless and Nebuchadnezzar soon controlled territory from *the Wadi of Egypt to the Euphrates River* (24:7), the description recalling the extent of Solomon's empire (cf. 1 Kgs 4:21, 24; 8:65).

If this were being reported today one might envisage national leaders and political commentators speaking about Babylonian action being justifiable against a vassal who has broken a treaty – especially if those nations and commentators were themselves worried about upsetting the new superpower. Allowing Judah to rebel with impunity might encourage others, leading to instability – recognized international law is to be upheld! Some might be relieved that Egypt was weak, preventing any escalation of conflict, with its inevitable deaths and destruction. The umbrella of Babylon might seem a guarantee of peace. Would any comment on the justice of one power enforcing its will on another? But what of debate within Jerusalem? The book of Jeremiah shows various parties vying for dominance in Jerusalem through to the final destruction: pro-Egypt, pro-independence and pro-Babylon. Is this any different from the varying views argued in any nation today in times of turmoil and conflict, with the same mixture of vested interests?

The narrator of Kings is not interested in these factors! He penetrates through to see that at core, in all and above all, Yahweh is at work fulfilling his intention *to remove them from his presence because*

---

[7] Babylonian records detail Nebuchadnezzar's battles and advances. P.-A. Beaulieu, 'History of Israel 6: Babylonian Period', *DOTHB*, pp. 478–485, summarizes.

[8] Cf. Dan. 1:1.

[9] Cf. 2 Chr. 36:6; see M. J. Selman, *2 Chronicles*, Tyndale OT Commentaries (Leicester and Downers Grove: Inter-Varsity Press, 1994), p. 546; E. C. Lucas, *Daniel*, Apollos OT Commentaries (Leicester: Apollos; Downers Grove: InterVarsity Press, 2002), pp. 50–52.

of the sins of Manasseh (24:3; cf. 23:26–27). Again Manasseh's *shedding of innocent blood* is specified (24:4; cf. 21:16); international relationships cannot be separated from internal policies. The finality is reinforced: Solomon had prayed that Yahweh would 'forgive' (1 Kgs 8:30, 34, 36, 39, 50), but now the message is *the LORD was not willing to forgive* (24:4).[10] Persistence in rebellion against Yahweh's known will, refusal to live within the covenant relationship, even killing the messengers, leads eventually to certainty of judgment.[11] Yet even that statement is now part of the book which gives hope to exiles, and beyond – beyond judgment, God's purposes for his people as a blessing to the nations will come to pass.

The ability to cut through the complexities of international and internal turmoil and to see the hand of God, remaining faithful to him when all around is chaos, follows from knowing his Word. This does not provide a detailed timetable or roadmap but shows the broad direction and the end to which history is moving. In a similar way early Christians were prepared through the words of Jesus for the later destruction of Jerusalem by the Romans, while the book of Revelation 'revealed' God's sovereignty and ultimate fulfilment of his purposes over against the visible military and economic might of Rome. Through the centuries Christians have turned to such blocks of Scripture and tried to work out timetables, finding coded equivalences in contemporary events. The interpretation of specific events as God's judgment is fraught with danger (Christ's words of Luke 13:2 are relevant here). All too often there is a forgetting of the stated purposes of prophetic material: an encouragement to faithful witness in the midst of conflict and opposition, along with warnings of the consequences of faithlessness. That there will be 'wars and rumours of wars' and 'because of the increase of wickedness, the love of most will grow cold' is followed by, 'but the one who stands firm to the end will be saved. And this gospel of the kingdom will be preached in the whole world as a testimony to all nations, and then the end will come' (Matt. 24:6, 12–14). The bold affirmation by the narrator of Kings, of God's 'command' of the nations, comes with the reminder that continued apostasy and associated injustices have inevitable consequences.

3. Jehoiachin and exile in Babylon (24:8–16)

No details are given here of Jehoiakim's death at a time when Nebuchadnezzar's forces were advancing. In light of the prophecy

---

[10] The only other instance of 'forgive' in Kings is on the lips of Naaman (2 Kgs 5:18).
[11] Cf. Deut. 29:19–20; Matt. 23:33–39; Heb. 6:4–8.

THE END COMES QUICKLY

of Jeremiah 22:19 (cf. Jer. 36:30) that he would have the unceremonial 'burial of a donkey' it is possible a pro-Babylonian group threw his body outside the city, unmourned. Given his age, thirty-six, assassination is a possibility.[12] His eighteen-year-old son *Jehoiachin*[13] was placed on the throne and faced a crisis that was to lead to his reigning *in Jerusalem* only *three months* – although the narrator still refers to him as *king Jehoiachin* thirty-seven years later in exile (25:27). Jerusalem was besieged by Babylonian forces, *Nebuchadnezzar himself* being present (v. 11). Nebuchadnezzar's own account gives 'the precise day of the surrender of Jerusalem – 2 Adar, 16 March, 597 BC – a dating unique in the extra-biblical sources touching upon Israelite history'.[14] Jehoiachin and the whole court *surrendered to him* (v. 12). It is likely that such ready surrender saved lives: king and court were taken prisoner rather than killed.

A rebellious vassal has to pay the cost. Not only does Nebuchadnezzar take *treasures from the temple of the* LORD *and from the royal palace* (v. 13) – as others had done;[15] he also *cut up the gold articles that Solomon king of Israel had made for the temple of the* LORD (v. 13). Centuries before, the Egyptian Shishak had taken away 'the gold shields Solomon had made' (1 Kgs 14:26), but Nebuchadnezzar was thorough, shown in other translations of the strong *qiṣṣēs*, 'stripped off/away' (NJPSV, NLT). Lest it be thought that despoliation of the temple was a sign of Yahweh's impotency, and just another of many similar acts in history by powerful victors, the narrator affirms that all was *as the* LORD *had declared,* fulfilment of words spoken through Isaiah to Hezekiah (20:16–18). In the chaos where the Davidic king is taken prisoner and the temple treated as nothing but a treasure house, Yahweh is in control. What he says comes to pass.

In order to prevent further rebellion Nebuchadnezzar strips the community of all its capable leaders and artisans, sending them to exile in Babylon (v. 14). In a spoken word, emphasis comes through repetition, so the detailing of the number and composition of exiles is given differently: verse 14 is 'concerned mainly with the removal of specifically military personnel from the Jerusalem military establishment [while v]v. 15–16 are more widely based'.[16] In a variety of vocabulary and images the narrator spotlights the tragedy. Just as

[12] Wiseman, p. 309.

[13] His name, 'Yah has established' appears in Jeremiah as Jeconiah (divine name component at the end), although NIV regularly has Jehoiachin (see also Matt. 1:11, 12). A short form 'Coniah' is in Jer. 22:24, 28; 37:1.

[14] A. Malamat, 'The Twilight of Judah in the Egyptian-Babylonian Maelstrom', in *Congress Volume: Edinburgh*, Vetus Testamentum Supplement, 28 (Leiden: Brill, 1974), p. 132.

[15] 1 Kgs 14:26; 15:18; 2 Kgs 12:18; 14:14; 16:8; 18:15.

[16] Hobbs, p. 353.

the gold Solomon had supplied for the temple to honour Yahweh among the nations is now stripped away by a foreign ruler, so too there is human reversal: 'as people used to come from all over the world to Solomon's court so now all the notables of Jerusalem journey on enforced pilgrimage abroad (vv. 14–16; cf. 1 Kgs 10:23–25).'[17] The 'craftsmen', previously mentioned only in connection with temple work, have gone and will prove to enrich the Babylonian economy.[18] Now all that remained, central in the listing of verses 13–16, were 'the poorest people', *dallâ* denoting the unimportant and insignificant, and so powerless.[19] While 'the unimportant of the land' would have been the great majority of the population of Judah, the exiles comprise the leadership structures and skilled personnel.[20] All suffer the consequences of wrongdoing of kings and people. How distant was the time of Solomon when 'the people of Judah and Israel were as numerous as the sand on the seashore; they ate, they drank and they were happy' (1 Kgs 4:20).

4. Zedekiah, the rebellious puppet (24:17–20)

With Jehoiachin a prisoner, Nebuchadnezzar placed *Mattaniah, Jehoiachin's uncle*[21] as puppet king (v. 17). He may be slightly older, but not wiser, nor more obedient to Yahweh. The name given by a foreign power to a vassal king seems ironic, *Zedekiah*, 'Yah is righteous(ness)' (cf. Necho and Eliakim/Jehoiakim, 23:34). Throughout the ancient Near East kings, as divine representatives, had responsibility to do and maintain 'righteousness, what was right' (*ṣĕdāqāh*) and 'justice', often including delivering people from oppressive situations.[22] If Zedekiah was meant to live out his name he failed completely!

---

[17] Provan, p. 278.

[18] Cf. 1 Kgs 7:14; 2 Kgs 12:11; 22:6. The 'artisans' (*masgēr*) are 'metalworkers, smiths' (*HALOT*).

[19] *HALOT;* M. D. Carrol R., '*dll* (#1937)', *NIDOTTE* 1, pp. 951–954.

[20] The various numbers are not immediately reconciled: v. 14, 'ten thousand'; v. 16, 'seven thousand' and 'one thousand'; Jer. 52:28, '3,023'. It would have taken time to organize such a large group and 'ten thousand' may be a total of two groups, around three and then seven thousand. Smaller groups went in 586 and 581 (Jer. 52:29–30). See 'The Scope of the Deportation' in I. Provan, V. P. Long and T. Longman III, *A Biblical History of Israel* (Louisville and London: Westminster John Knox, 2003), pp. 281–285.

[21] Josiah's third son, between Jehoiakim and Jehoahaz (1 Chr. 3:15).

[22] M. Weinfeld, *Social Justice in Ancient Israel and in the Ancient Near East* (Jerusalem: Magnes, 1995). Cf. Ps. 72:1–3; and for all the seed of Abraham, Gen. 18:19. God's acts of deliverance are often described as his deeds of 'righteousness' (e.g., Judg. 5:11; 1 Sam. 12:7; Ps. 103:6; Mic. 6:5). By the time of Christ and since *ṣĕdāqāh* is used for acts of charity and almsgiving (cf. Matt. 6:1).

Other than standard regnal data (v. 18), the narrator tells nothing more of Zedekiah than brief statements: (1) *he did evil in the eyes of the LORD* – the specific comparison with *Jehoiakim* may be because of his rebellion; (2) he *rebelled against the king of Babylon* (v. 19); and (3) later with his army he tried to flee from besieged Jerusalem (25:5–6). The narrative focuses almost entirely on the events of the final fall of Jerusalem and the fate of both temple and people. Much more detail is in Jeremiah, especially chapters 21, 27, 28, 32 – 34, 37 – 39, where we read of Zedekiah's weak vacillating, exacerbated by an incompetent court with strong pro-Egyptian voices. He seems to have tried to be favourable to Jeremiah, but also listened to false prophets who announced 'peace', and failed to put any word from Yahweh into practice (cf. 2 Chr. 36:12). This is also the period of much of the prophecy of Ezekiel, who in exile sees by vision the appalling idolatry and violence in Jerusalem (cf. 2 Chr. 36:14). In a play on the name 'Zedek – Yah', Jeremiah looks forward to a king and city, both of which exemplify in reality the name 'Yahweh is our Righteousness (Zedek)' (Jer. 23:6; 33:16).

The rebellion *against the king of Babylon* is not specified;[23] it is enough that it led to Nebuchadnezzar's return, so that *in the end [the LORD] thrust them from his presence* (v. 20; cf. 17:20). Again God's involvement is asserted: with the eyes of faith, illumined by the long history thus far of the fulfilment of his word, the writer points hearers and readers, then and now, to God's sovereignty as one certainty in a time of turmoil.

5. The fall of Jerusalem (25:1–26)

Kings concludes with 'a composition of six vignettes about the end of the state of Judah . . . First, it destroys decisively any symbol of religious, civil, or military life remaining in Judah. . . . Second, all the symbols that remain intact – the temple vessels and the king, Jehoiachin – are not in Judah, but in Babylon.'[24] Continuity of hope is to be with the exiles in Babylon.

a. Nebuchadnezzar's return and Zedekiah's capture (25:1–7)

The dates are fixed in Judah's memory as the privations and terrors of the siege progress: from the beginning *in the ninth year of*

[23] Troubles Nebuchadnezzar was having in the east, and stirrings in Egypt, are known from around 595 and 589 BC, and Jer. 27 – 28 has its setting in an anti-Babylonian gathering in Jerusalem of representatives from surrounding countries. See Hobbs, pp. 354–355; Wiseman, pp. 310–311; Konkel, p. 664.

[24] Hobbs, pp. 360–361. The text of ch. 25 matches closely Jer. 52:4–34, which has additional information; see also Jer. 39.

Zedekiah's reign, on the tenth day of the tenth month [25] (v. 1), to the breach of the wall in *the eleventh year . . . by the ninth day of the fourth month*[26] (vv. 2–3). The eighteen months covered two harvest periods, so while the Gihon spring provided water *the famine in the city had become so severe there was no food.* The resulting horrors are articulated in the anguish of Lamentations 1:11; 2:11–12; 4:2–10. The language is not poetic hyperbole: the 'unchosen hunger, unchosen necrosis, unchosen obliteration' are features of severe famine in recent times as told by Thomas Keneally, who uses his literary and historical research skills as a novelist to compare 'terrible hungers' in Ireland beginning 1845, Bengal in 1943–1944 and Ethiopia in the 1970s and 1980s. Tragically just as the famine in Jerusalem was brought by the Babylonian siege which would have deepened the divisions already in Jerusalem, so in these recent famines 'mindsets of governments, racial preconceptions and administrative incompetence were more lethal' than the initiating natural causes.[27]

The ignominious escape attempt by Zedekiah and *the whole army* is farcical (vv. 4–5).[28] The escape is seen, and the king is deserted by his soldiers and captured near Jericho, the very place where Joshua began the conquest of the land. 'By portraying the capture of Zedekiah and the end of Davidic rule in this man, the [Deuteronomic Historian] brings Israel's history full circle from beginning to end at the city of Jericho.'[29] Zedekiah's fears during the long journey north to *Riblah*[30] can only be imagined. He has broken an oath of vassalage and so Nebuchadnezzar saw himself as justified in following 'a legalistic procedure, laying charges against Zedekiah in his own court . . . As hierarchical superior, he was entitled to be judge in his own cause and meter out collective punishment upon the culprit and his family.'[31] The writer of Chronicles sees beyond a crime against Nebuchadnezzar to a sin against God: he had broken 'an oath in God's name', referring to the oath of allegiance on his accession (2 Chr. 36:13; cf. Ezek. 17:16–24). Zedekiah's last sight is his own sons being killed before *they put out his eyes* and he is taken *bound . . . with bronze shackles* to Babylon (cf. 20:18). Sadly Zedekiah had rejected the advice he sought from Jeremiah (Jer. 38:14–28) and he

---

[25] 10 Tevet (NLT: 'January 15') 587 BC.

[26] 9 Tammuz (NLT: 'July 18') 586 BC; 'fourth month' is inserted on basis of Jer. 52:6,

[27] T. Keneally, *Three Famines* (North Sydney: Knopf, 2010), quote from dustcover.

[28] See also Jer. 39:4. Ezek. 12:12 describes his attempt to cover his face (cf. vv. 3–11). Analogous to Kings' affirmation of Yahweh's initiative (24:20), to exiles Ezekiel describes Zedekiah's capture and exile with no mention of Nebuchadnezzar: it is God's actions, 'my net . . . my snare; I will bring him to Babylonia' (Ezek. 12:13).

[29] Sweeney, p. 467 (referring to the whole account of Joshua-Kings).

[30] See on 23:33, p. 358.

[31] R. Westbrook, 'Law in Kings', in Lemaire and Halpern , p. 464.

and the city bore the consequences. Zedekiah provides yet another example of the folly of persistent rejection of the word of God.

b. Burning of the temple and city, and more exiles (25:8–12)

Judah had a record of being a rebellious vassal (cf. 24:1) and Jerusalem was a city to be conquered. Hence a month later *Nebuzaradan commander of the imperial guard* came and *set fire to the temple of the* LORD, *the royal palace and all the houses of Jerusalem* – with emphasis the narrator summarises, *every important building he burnt down.* The date is given as 7 Av, 586 BC (NLT: 'August 14'), with Jeremiah 52:12 stating 10 Av. Later rabbinic tradition puts Nebuzaradan entering on the seventh, setting fire on the ninth and fire burning until the tenth.[32] Walls were broken down and people exiled (see also vv. 18–21). Mention of people *who had deserted to the king of Babylon* (v. 11) is a pointer to the diverse views within the city. Again *the poorest people of the land* (cf. 24:14) are left to *work the vineyards and fields,* now with all supporting structures in ruins. The people who remained, along with others who would move in, provide a background to the conflict with returning exiles fifty years later.[33]

The deep grief and questioning, resulting from loss of city, temple and king, burst out in the cries of Lamentations, with a 'complex cluster of emotions – sorrow, anger, guilt, hope, despair, fear, self-loathing, revenge, compassion, forgiveness, uncertainty, disorientation'.[34] The book has given an ongoing language of prayer, as Jewish communities for centuries have sung or read it aloud on the ninth of Ab. That day of fast commemorates the destruction, along with other calamities that occurred on the same date – destruction of the second temple by the Romans (70 AD), start of World War I (1914), and the beginning of the expulsion of the Jews from the Warsaw ghetto en route to the gas chambers of Treblinka (1942) – or are associated, often happening in the same month, such as the declaration of the First Crusade (1095), and expulsion of Jews from England (1290) and Spain (1492).[35]

[32] Talmud *b. Ta'anit* 29a.

[33] E.g., Ezra 3:3; 4:1–4.

[34] F. W. Dobb-Allsopp, 'Lamentations, Book of', in *Eerdmans Dictionary of the Bible*, ed. D. N. Freedman (Grand Rapids: Eerdmans, 2000), p. 785.

[35] 'Tish'ah be-'Av', *The Oxford Dictionary of the Jewish Religion*, edited by R. J. Z. Werblowsky and G. Wigoder (New York and Oxford: Oxford University Press, 1997), pp. 693–694. An early listing (oral tradition written down around 200 AD) is in the Mishnah *Ta'anit* ['Fasts'] 4.6. Readings from Lamentations were also part of the Christian liturgy for 'Tenebrae' ('shadows'), services for the last three days of Holy Week, with musical settings by many composers including two versions by Thomas Tallis (c. 1505–1585), written for Queen Elizabeth I.

c. Break up and removal of temple pillars and utensils (25:13–17)

The description of reversal continues. 1 Kings 7:15–50 detailed bronze items made for the temple (vv. 15–47), followed by a brief list of gold items (vv. 48–50). Now the list is recalled in summary, itemizing material taken to Babylon, broken up if too large. *More than could be weighed* echoes the temple inventory (v. 16; 1 Kgs 7:47).[36] The catalogue is framed by reference to *the bronze pillars* (the first words in Hebrew of v. 13)[37] and longer description of the breakup of the *two pillars* and each *bronze capital* (vv. 16–17). The highly prominent symbols of power, strength and cosmic stability[38] have become mere items of plunder for Nebuchadnezzar – a vivid portrayal of devastation that moves beyond physical buildings to matters of personal and communal stability and meaning, of spiritual, psychological and sociological well-being.

Ezekiel foresaw in a vision Yahweh's glory leaving the temple (Ezek. 9 –10) – he saw and proclaimed that Yahweh and his glory were not tied to the temple. Previously Jeremiah had warned against a trust in 'the temple of the LORD, the temple of the LORD, the temple of the LORD' and called for a 'change' of 'ways' from the current unjust oppression, violence and Baal worship, but the message was rejected by the leadership (Jer. 7:4–15; 26:1–24). In Kings the last time Yahweh is subject of a verb is at the end of chapter 24: 'It was because of the LORD's anger that all this happened to Jerusalem and Judah, and in the end he thrust them from his presence.'[39] Now each time the book is read the writer's word pictures bring to memory 'the end', climaxing in the destruction of the pillars. Their focus of stability and security Yahweh had allowed to become as nothing, mere bronze adding to Babylonian wealth.

Readers today might reflect on other events of destruction and devastation that have become significant in world, national or personal history, often now recalled through photographs and film, freely available for personal viewing.[40] In some cases they are linked with annual remembrance. Without being seen as divine judgment,

---

[36] The only other instance of *mišqāl* in Kings is also Solomonic, the 'weight' of gold he received annually (1 Kgs 10:14).

[37] Distinction between the pillars and other bronze items is seen in MT's repeated 'the house of the LORD' (v. 13): 'The bronze pillars of the house of the LORD, and the stands and the bronze sea that were in the house of the LORD, the Chaldeans broke up, and they carried their bronze to Babylon' (my translation).

[38] See on 1 Kgs 7:15–22, p. 88.

[39] Ch. 25 has only four instances of *Yhwh*, all in the combination 'house of the LORD' (vv. 9, 13 [twice], 16).

[40] A national example is the destruction of the twin towers of the World Trade Center in New York, September 11, 2001.

they may be viewed from the perspective of nostalgia, looking back to some irreplaceable past. Or they become a spur to looking forward, with reassessment of priorities and values, evaluating matters of where one looks for security and meaning.

d. Executing the resistance leaders (25:18–21)

Buildings, especially the temple, have been razed and anything of value removed and now the narrative turns to human leadership. The list of leaders of the national resistance still in the city reads like the accused in war trials: tragically the first two named are the senior priests,[41] to be followed by military and civil leaders and remaining military conscripts. As an example to the people remaining (v. 12) and to remove any focus for future resistance, Nebuzaradan *took them all as prisoners* (v. 18). They were *brought . . . to the king of Babylon at Riblah*, where probably after some trial (cf. v. 6) *the king had them executed* (v. 21).

The concluding summary statement communicates pathos by its simplicity: 'Thus Judah was exiled from its land' (NJPSV). Whereas Solomon's prayer had spoken of being 'captives' (1 Kgs 8:46–50; Hebrew *šābāh*), the verb here is *gālāh* , most commonly used for 'going into exile', highlighting being away from one's homeland, even if a large amount of freedom of activity is evident.[42] Emotions involved in being away 'from one's land' are felt by millions in the world today. The flood of refugees from strife-torn and often ravaged regions bears witness to the anguish, while even migrants who have moved voluntarily still look back to the 'home' country. 'Land' is a focus of identity and tradition, of personal and family memories, of rootedness and belonging – and when buildings have been razed and the land devastated the sense of loss is greater. The first generation of 'exiles' – or refugees or migrants – may have little hope of return, but the place of ancestral land in identity continues in future generations. There can be a sense of a gap in one's life. In a popular TV series in several countries, 'Who Do You Think You Are?', well-known people trace family history.[43] Commonly there is travel to places where one's ancestors once lived, and the emotional responses

---

[41] Zephaniah is mentioned with a key communication role in Jer. 21:1; 29:25, 29; 37:3.

[42] *gālāh*: 2 Kgs 15:29; 16:9; 17:6, 11, 23, 26–28, 33; 18:11; 24:14, 15; 25:11, 21; *šābāh* 1 Kgs 8:46–50; 2 Kgs 5:2; 6:22. On freedom of activity, cf. Jer. 29:4–7. Refer to H.-J. Zobel, '*gālāh*', *TDOT* 2 (1975), pp. 476–488; D. M. Howard, Jr, '*glh* (#1655)', *NIDOTTE* 1, pp. 861–864. The noun 'Golah' continues as a Jewish term for living in the Diaspora, away from the land.

[43] First aired in Britain in 2004 with versions since in Canada, Ireland, Sweden, South Africa, USA, Australia, and elsewhere.

are evident. Such common human experience becomes heightened when life in the homeland has been regarded as under divine guarantee. What will result when one accepts responsibility for failure to serve God alone and sees that exile was because God 'thrust them from his presence' (24:20)? Is there hope for the future?

e. No hope remains in Judah (25:22–26)

Hebrew word order foregrounds *the people who were left in the land of Judah whom Nebuchadnezzar king of Judah left* (literal translation) – is there to be any possibility for them? Nebuchadnezzar astutely puts in charge one of their own, *Gedaliah son of Ahikam, the son of Shaphan* (v. 22), the family known to have been pro-Babylonian.[44] His base is at *Mizpah*, probably 8 miles (13 km) north of Jerusalem in a region that seems to have had little destruction,[45] and there officers from the resistance group come to him. They take *an oath* with Gedaliah and are assured there would be no reprisals. His words echo Jeremiah's earlier message that *it will go well with you* if you *serve the king of Babylon* (vv. 23–24).[46] However just two months later (cf. v. 8), the first named of the group of officers, *Ishmael son of Nethaniah . . . who was of royal blood* came with others and *assassinated Gedaliah* and those with him. This reads like a foolhardy attempt at independence, restoring Davidic rule – were they so caught up in their own clique that they had no idea of reality, including popular support? In the event, *all the people*, irrespective of status, along with *the army officers, fled to Egypt for fear of the Babylonians.* There was to be no future in Judah; this is the end of national existence.[47]

Here is yet another illustration of reversal: the people who had been delivered from Egypt centuries before and brought into the land now flee from the land in fear, returning to Egypt. The biblical narrative of this group ends there; future restoration will come through the exiles in Babylonia. In centuries to come however the Jewish population in Egypt grew and became significant, albeit at times with evidence of syncretism.[48] Their situation under Hellenistic rule three hundred years later led to the translation of the Pentateuch

---

[44] See on *Shaphan* (22:8), p. 349; cf. Jer. 26:24. In Jer. 39:11–14 Jeremiah is released by Nebuzaradan, placed into Gedaliah's care and taken back to his home.

[45] Sweeney, pp. 468–469.

[46] Cf. Jer. 27:8, 17; 38:20; and supporting Gedaliah, Jer. 42:7–17.

[47] Jer. 41 – 43 is a longer account.

[48] Fifth century BC papyri fragments from Elephantine on the Nile, near modern Aswan, refer to a Jewish military colony with a temple dedicated to Yahweh but containing other deities; H. G. M. Williamson, 'Non-Israelite Written Sources: Egyptian Aramaic Papyri', *DOTHB*, pp. 735–739.

into Greek, with other books translated in the following century or so. History – God's working in history – has its unexpected turns: the Greek translation, known popularly as the Septuagint, became the Bible for Greek-speaking Christians. Paul and the early church did not have to worry about Bible translation!

2 Kings 25:27–30
22. A glimmer of hope in Babylon

The previous section ended in Egypt *for fear of the Babylonians* (v. 26), but the conclusion of Kings narrates a favourable action in Babylon by the *king of Babylon* towards *the king of Judah*. Here is an answer to Solomon's prayer that the *captors . . . show . . . mercy* (1 Kgs 8:50). Yahweh has not forgotten his people.

A long period has passed: *the thirty-seventh year of the exile of Jehoiachin king of Judah* (cf. 24:15) is twenty-six years after the fall of Jerusalem, and Jehoiachin is fifty-five years old. Nebuchadnezzar died in 562 BC, and his son *Awel-Marduk . . . released*[1] *Jehoiachin . . . from prison*, probably as an act of amnesty in the accession year. Whereas Nebuchadnezzar had 'pronounced judgment' to Zedekiah (v. 6), now the king 'pronounced good things' (*spoke kindly*) to Jehoiachin (v. 28), giving him a *seat* of relative honour. Like Joseph Jehoiachin can *put aside his prison clothes* and dress appropriately (cf. Gen. 41:14) and he is provided for by the Babylonian king. Unlike his prison provisions,[2] the impression is that his *regular allowance* enables him to live as a king, although still in exile.

That is all that is said. There is no promise of restoration or return and no mention of heirs (1 Chr. 3:17–18 lists seven sons). The final phrase *as long as he lived* suggests that this section was written, and hence the book concluded, while he was still alive. With Jehoiachin's exile as a 'captive' (24:15) and the final mention of Zedekiah with the execution of his sons (vv. 6–7), it had appeared that

---

[1] 'Lifted the head', a bodily symbol of recognition; cf. 3:14 (NIV: 'respect for the presence of'); 5:1 ('highly regarded'); Hobbs, p. 367.

[2] Babylonian cuneiform tablets found in the North Palace name Jehoiachin 'king of Judah' and give details of grain provisions for him and five sons while in captivity under Nebuchadnezzar; *ANET*, p. 308; P.-A. Beaulieu, 'History of Israel 6: Babylonian Period. 5, Judean Exiles in Babylonia', *DOTHB*, p. 483–484.

'the lamp'[3] had gone out, but it was still flickering. Would it return to shine brightly in Jerusalem? While it has been suggested that we see a negative picture of compromise, 'eating defiled food puppetlike at a pagan king's table',[4] the echo of Joseph suggests a positive portrayal, with the possibility of some future honour and return to the land.

There is yet another literary association pointing to hope. In chapters 21 – 23, parallels are drawn with the house of Ahab: Manasseh copies Ahab but just as punishment was delayed with Ahab's response to a word of judgment (1 Kgs 21:20–29), so there was delay with Josiah's reform. After the subsequent 'earlier destruction of the "whole royal family" [all the family of Ahab]' Joash unexpectedly survives through Athaliah's reign. So here after the end of king Zedekiah's heirs (v. 7) Jehoiachin unexpectedly reappears, 'the potential for the continuation of the Davidic line at a later time, when foreign rule has been removed'.[5]

This is the end of the narrative of Kings: the future of Davidic kingship is still in exile, but it is open. In all of Kings only four events have details of 'months': the building and dedication of Solomon's temple (1 Kgs 6:1, 37–38; 8:2); Jeroboam's institution of a new festival, and offering sacrifices in Bethel (1 Kgs 12:32–33); the stages in the end of Jerusalem and the temple (2 Kgs 25:1, 3, 8, 25) – and now the change of circumstances for Jehoiachin, 'king of Judah' (v. 27). The specification here points to an event just as significant as the building of the temple and Jeroboam's 'sin', but associated with a person not a building. Centuries later, surrounded by the awesome might of Rome, there is given to a church facing persecution a vision of the new Jerusalem, where 'the Lamb is its lamp' (Rev. 21:23). God keeps his promises.

How God will show his mercy and compassion, and how and when he will deliver, is unknown but in Babylon, away from the land, there is a change for the better. It is like the smallest cloud that is a portent of rain (1 Kgs 18:44), the flickering of a lamp that had seemed extinguished. 'Neither [Awel-Marduk] nor Jehoiachin know how Yahweh's rule will out. History is cunning and inscrutable . . . Our inability to know is a function of Yahweh's sovereignty that requires listening and waiting.'[6] In these closing verses there is no

[3] God's promise to 'maintain a lamp for David in Jerusalem' is in 1 Kgs 11:36; 15:4; 2 Kgs 8:19.

[4] W. J. Dumbrell, *The Faith of Israel* (Grand Rapids: Baker, 2002), p. 104.

[5] I. W. Provan, 'The Messiah in the Books of Kings', in *The Lord's Anointed: Interpretation of Old Testament Messianic Texts*, edited by P. E. Satterthwaite, R. S. Hess and G. J. Wenham (Carlisle: Paternoster; Grand Rapids: Baker, 1995), p. 75.

[6] W. Brueggemann, *A Commentary on Jeremiah: Exile and Homecoming* (Grand Rapids and Cambridge: Eerdmans, 1998), p. 495, commenting on Jer. 52:31–34 = 2 Kgs 25:27–30.

mention of any spiritual change, of turning to Yahweh (cf. the 'turning' in Solomon's prayer, 1 Kgs 8:47–49). The omission seems significant. As in 2 Kings 13, but not stated here, God may bring about a change in circumstances solely because of his compassion and his promise to the patriarchs.

To be continued

Kings ends with a glimmer of hope; a king without a kingdom is being blessed by the superior nation. The narrative has told of the decline of the nation from the time of David and Solomon, of the failure of God's people, with notable exceptions, to give allegiance to him alone. God's people have lived among the nations, their circumstances affected by the surrounding Egypt, Tyre, Ammon, Moab, Edom, Aram, Assyria and Babylon; there have been reminders of their earlier deliverance from Pharaoh's oppression and entry into the land God had given them, but now they are outside the land. There have been promises concerning a continuing Davidic line, but the last king of that dynasty has no authority or realm, yet is being honoured. Only once has there been specific reference to the promise – 'his covenant with Abraham, Isaac and Jacob' – in a setting of hope (2 Kgs 13:23), but how are all the peoples of the earth to be blessed through God's people? As had Joseph, will the Babylonian exiles through the king be a means of blessing to others (cf. Gen. 45:4–7)?

Kings has told of the Queen of Sheba being drawn by Solomon's glory and wisdom, but there will come 'one greater than Solomon'; there have been accounts of blessing to a widow of Zarephath and an Aramean officer with leprosy, illustrations to be used by Jesus in speaking of his own mission and of people's response. No descendant of Jehoiachin is ever named king,[7] but boldly the NT declares that Jesus is 'the son of David, the son of Abraham', descended through the line of 'Jeconiah and his brothers at the time of the exile to Babylon', continuing 'after the exile' (Matt. 1:1, 11–12). Over against '[the LORD] thrust them from his presence' (24:20), Christ himself is 'God with us' (Matt. 1:23). It was on the cross, where the sign is placed 'KING OF THE JEWS' (Matt. 27:37), that 'God was . . . in Christ' reconciling not only the Jews but 'the world to himself' (2 Cor. 5: 19).

The NT accounts of the early church also end with key leaders whose present and future is apparently determined by Roman authorities – Paul in Acts 28:16, 30–31; John on Patmos in Revelation

[7] Jehoiachin's grandson, Zerubbabel (cf. Matt. 1:12) was appointed governor of the Persian province, Yehud (Hag. 1:1), but is nowhere designated 'king'; W. H. Rose, 'Zerubbabel', *DOTHB*, pp. 1016–1019.

1:9 – but both affirm the unrestricted sovereign rule of God. In a variety of ways as Christians we live 'away from our homeland',[8] subject to laws of our separate nations, with both freedoms and restrictions. Peter described the recipients of his letter as 'exiles' but immediately goes on to write with confidence of God's work in and through us: as God's people we have a 'living hope' which is to shape our lives (1 Peter 1:1–9).

The first readers of Kings do not know how God's purposes are to work out and what will happen to them. The later Chronicles concludes with Cyrus's edict to return and build the temple, but Kings does not know that and so continues to be relevant for people living in darkness and 'exile'. It is like living on Easter Saturday: Sunday may be coming, but how and when? In the light of the rest of the Scriptures, we know the promise of the future, but the actual path through current situations of 'exile' is unknown.

The answer of Kings is to tell the story, to encourage hearers to learn from the past: to look back to God's promises to the patriarchs and the deliverance from Egypt, and to recognize the consequences of rebellion through the generations, including their own; to worship Yahweh alone and to live as his covenant people; but also to know that God has not lost control or failed. They, and we, can turn in repentance and hope to a gracious and compassionate God. Even in exile we can worship him alone and follow his commands, trusting in him for the future. We can see a small change in what has happened to Jehoiachin, still honoured as 'king of Judah', but hope is built on more than this one event. That is simply the open-ended situation where Kings stops: the story is 'to be continued' because God continues through the centuries to fulfil his purposes through his people, bringing blessing to all nations of earth.

---

[8] Phil. 3:20; Heb. 11:16; 1 Pet. 1:1.

The Bible Speaks Today: Old Testament series

The Bible Speaks Today: New Testament series

The Message of the Sermon on the Mount (Matthew 5 – 7)
Christian counter-culture
John Stott

The Message of Matthew
The kingdom of heaven
Michael Green

The Message of Mark
The mystery of faith
Donald English

The Message of Luke
The Saviour of the world
Michael Wilcock

The Message of John
Here is your King
Bruce Milne

The Message of Acts
To the ends of the earth
John Stott

The Message of Romans
God's good news for the world
John Stott

The Message of 1 Corinthians
Life in the local church
David Prior

The Message of 2 Corinthians
Power in weakness
Paul Barnett

The Message of Galatians
Only one way
John Stott

The Message of Ephesians
God's new society
John Stott

The Message of Philippians
Jesus our Joy
Alec Motyer

The Message of Colossians and Philemon
Fullness and freedom
Dick Lucas

The Message of Thessalonians
Preparing for the coming King
John Stott

The Message of 1 Timothy and Titus
The life of the local church
John Stott

The Message of 2 Timothy
Guard the gospel
John Stott

The Message of Hebrews
Christ above all
Raymond Brown

The Message of James
The tests of faith
Alec Motyer

The Message of 1 Peter
The way of the cross
Edmund Clowney

The Message of 2 Peter and Jude
The promise of his coming
Dick Lucas and Christopher Green

The Message of John's Letters
Living in the love of God
David Jackman

The Message of Revelation
I saw heaven opened
Michael Wilcock

The Bible Speaks Today: Bible Themes series

The Message of the Living God
His glory, his people, his world
Peter Lewis

The Message of the Resurrection
Christ is risen!
Paul Beasley-Murray

The Message of the Cross
Wisdom unsearchable, love indestructible
Derek Tidball

The Message of Salvation
By God's grace, for God's glory
Philip Graham Ryken

The Message of Creation
Encountering the Lord of the universe
David Wilkinson

The Message of Heaven and Hell
Grace and destiny
Bruce Milne

The Message of Mission
The glory of Christ in all time and space
Howard Peskett and Vinoth Ramachandra

The Message of Prayer
Approaching the throne of grace
Tim Chester

The Message of the Trinity
Life in God
Brian Edgar

The Message of Evil and Suffering
Light into darkness
Peter Hicks

The Message of the Holy Spirit
The Spirit of encounter
Keith Warrington

The Message of Holiness
Restoring God's masterpiece
Derek Tidball

The Message of Sonship
At home in God's household
Trevor Burke

The Message of the Word of God
The glory of God made known
Tim Meadowcroft